Informants
and
Undercover
Investigations

A Practical Guide to Law, Policy, and Procedure

Informants
and
Undercover
Investigations

A Practical Guide to Law, Policy, and Procedure

Dennis G. Fitzgerald

CRC Press
Taylor & Francis Group
Boca Raton London New York

CRC Press is an imprint of the
Taylor & Francis Group, an informa business

CRC Press
Taylor & Francis Group
6000 Broken Sound Parkway NW, Suite 300
Boca Raton, FL 33487-2742

© 2007 by Taylor & Francis Group, LLC
CRC Press is an imprint of Taylor & Francis Group, an Informa business

International Standard Book Number-10: 0-8493-0412-1 (Hardcover)
International Standard Book Number-13: 978-0-8493-0412-5 (Hardcover)

Library of Congress Cataloging-in-Publication Data

Fitzgerald, Dennis G.
   Informants and undercover investigations : a practical guide for law, policy, and procedure / Dennis G. Fitzgerald.
      p. cm.
   "A CRC Press title."
   Includes bibliographical references and index.
   ISBN-13: 978-0-8493-0412-5 (alk. paper)
      1. Informers--Legal status, laws, etc.--United States. 2. Undercover operations--Law and legislation--United States. 3. Evidence, Criminal--United States.   I. Title.

   KF9665.F584 2006
   345.73'06--dc22

                                                                    2006024883

Visit the Taylor & Francis Web site at
http://www.taylorandfrancis.com

and the CRC Press Web site at
http://www.crcpress.com

The Author

Dennis G. Fitzgerald is a retired U.S. Drug Enforcement Administration (DEA) Special Agent, former City of Miami, Florida, Police Sergeant, and an attorney. Fitzgerald recently completed a 7-year assignment as a legal advisor for the American Bar Association, the U.S. Department of Justice and State Department funded programs in the former Soviet Union. While serving as the Anti-Corruption Strategy Coordinator for the Newly Independent States, he assisted several post-Soviet countries as they revised their laws governing the use of informants and undercover investigations. He is credited with being instrumental in the creation of Lithuania's independent anticorruption agency, the Special Investigation Service, and its witness security program. Both have become models for the post-Soviet and developing countries. In 2005, he was awarded one of Lithuania's highest civilian medals. Fitzgerald also served as a visiting faculty member at the Federal Bureau of Investigation's (FBI) International Training Academy in Budapest, Hungary. He is a graduate of Seattle University School of Law and Florida International University (B.S. Criminal Justice). Fitzgerald has published timely articles on informant-related issues for prosecutors, police, and defense attorneys and is the author of the *Informant Law Deskbook*. He developed the training curriculum for informant handling and undercover investigations that has been presented to thousands of investigators and prosecutors throughout the United States, Central and Eastern Europe, and Central Asia. He has also acted as trial consultant and expert witness in criminal cases that have relied upon informant involvement and testimony.

Foreword

Worse than having no human sources is being seduced by a human source who is telling lies. One of the many conclusions drawn by The Presidential Commission on the Intelligence Capabilities of the United States Regarding Weapons of Mass Destruction dated March 31, 2005.

Informants and Undercover Investigations: A Practical Guide to Law, Policy, and Procedure is the most comprehensive examination of informant-related issues ever to appear in one publication. It was written primarily for prosecutors, judges, law enforcement officials, defense counsel, criminal justice training institutions, and researchers. The book is designed as a sourcebook with clear explanations of the guiding law, policies, and time-tested procedures regarding informant handling. Each chapter addresses a distinct topic, allowing the reader to quickly locate a particular subject area. The material presented applies to all investigations that utilize informants. That includes the most basic search warrant case all the way up to the most complex criminal investigation.

In the last 5 years, informant-related cases have captured international headlines. Whistle-blowers have exposed the most egregious corporate frauds committed in history. An informant in Iraq was paid the largest reward in history by the United States for locating the sons of Saddam Hussein. The FBI's Ten Most Wanted List has Osama bin Laden's picture on it with a $25 million reward offered for his capture, dead or alive. Next to bin Laden's photograph is former FBI informant James J. Bulger, now wanted for 19 murders.

The value of a closely controlled informant to a criminal investigation and the overall mission of law enforcement cannot be overstated. Every day police solve burglaries, robberies, rapes, and murders, thanks in part to information received from their informants. Organized criminal enterprises such as the drug trade have proven to be extremely vulnerable to informants. Terrorist organizations are showing that same vulnerability.

During his law enforcement career the author personally recruited and directed hundreds of informants. He recognizes that without the ability to use informants the mission of law enforcement would be seriously handicapped. The vast amounts of money paid to informants and the increasing number of criminal prosecutions relying upon them reflects their growing importance to law enforcement.

Unfortunately, informants are one of the most unstable and unpredictable component of America's criminal justice system. Many, if not most, informants are felons between prison sentences. Their lives depend upon successfully resisting the rules society imposes upon its members. In the necessarily clandestine world they inhabit, the imposition of institutional control presents unique challenges. That they would present a management challenge to police administrators, prosecutors, and informant handlers should come as no surprise.

Law enforcement, like other professions, should learn from its mistakes. Unfortunately, when it comes to the clandestine nature of informant handling, the same mistakes are repeated time and again, decade after decade, often seeming to occur in a vacuum. It is not until a highly publicized informant-related catastrophe occurs that those mistakes are exposed.

On more than one occasion, Congressional subcommittees investigating informant mismanagement have issued damning reports. The title of a 2003 House of Representatives report speaks for itself, "Everything Secret Degenerates: The FBI's Use of Murderers as Informants." In the executive summary of the report, Committee Chair Tom Davis states, "At a time when the United States is being faced by threats from international terrorism, and a number of law enforcement tools are being justifiably strengthened, it is particularly important to remember that Lord Acton's words are true: 'Everything secret degenerates, even the administration of justice.'"

Failures in the management of informants have captured more than their share of headlines. Informant handlers have been sentenced to lengthy prison sentences. Informant mismanagement has also been the subject of civil litigation. At this writing, $2 billion in lawsuits have been filed in the wake of a massive informant scandal. Multimillion-dollar settlements for injuries sustained by innocent citizens in informant-related cases are not uncommon.

One would hope that corrective measures would be taken; that lessons learned could be shared so that the same mistakes would not be repeated. Informant handling should be a closely supervised investigative technique. Informant handlers should be trained as thoroughly as they are in any other inherently dangerous law enforcement activity.

Unfortunately, that is not the case. That failure could be blamed in part on the lack of an easily accessible guide to informant handling. *Informants and Undercover Investigations: A Practical Guide to Law, Policy, and Procedure* fills that void. The book relies upon controlling or pertinent Supreme Court cases, leading federal and state cases, relevant statutory law, federal, state, and local law enforcement guidelines, and time-tested training materials.

Reported cases, statutes, treatises, and manuals used to establish or fortify the propositions advanced by the author are, to the best of his knowledge, accurate at the time of publication. Over time, all are subject to change and should be verified prior to relying upon them as precedents.

Acknowledgments

Informants and Undercover Investigations would have been a project still waiting to be started were it not for my wife and editor-in-chief, Cathy Chaffin. Her patience, support, and encouragement kept me at my desk when I would attempt to find more important things to do. Its completion is in large part due to her commitment to the success of the project. Cathy's computer research skills yielded a wealth of information found throughout the work. Her patience was tested only by the Freedom of Information Act (FOIA).

Julita Grant Fitzgerald, Miami Metro-Dade Sheriff's Department Corrections Officer (retired), aka my mother, taught me that no task was too great if I really wanted it accomplished. Her tutoring throughout my education on grammar and punctuation was never more appreciated than during the preparation of this work.

My law enforcement career may not have survived the challenges presented by informants were it not for my time in the Miami Police Department's Vice and Narcotics Unit. I owe a great deal to the members of the original "Miami Vice": Mike Mahoney, Bill Riley, Ernie Vivian, Steve Kiraly, Mike Ahearn, Ivo Alvarez, Grady Beall, Mona Polen, Gus Cairo, Don March, Ted Scinski, and Glen O'Daniels.

Special thanks to the late Bernie Schildbach for being my mentor and friend through the police academy and throughout my life. He was the most dedicated, honest police officer I have ever known, and truly one of Miami's finest.

A great deal of the material used to prepare *Informants and Undercover Investigations* was volunteered by law enforcement officers, prosecutors, and other members of the criminal justice system who must go unnamed. Their assistance proved invaluable either when FOIA requests were ignored or when responses were redacted to such an extent that they were worthless. I remain in their debt.

Dennis G. Fitzgerald

Table of Contents

5   Cooperation and Contingency Fee Agreements   87

6   Informant Documentation and Identification   115

10 Controlling the Informant 221

11 The Witness Security Program 261

Informants and Sources Defined

1

1.1 Generally

"Informant" is a generic term often used by police and prosecutors to describe a wide variety of individuals who confidentially provide them with information concerning criminal activity. *Black's Law Dictionary* defines "informer" as "A person who informs or prefers an accusation against another, whom he suspects of the violation of some penal statute."[1] The term generally includes undisclosed persons who volunteer material information of law violations to officers. It does not include persons who supply information only after being interviewed by police officers, or who give information as witnesses during the course of investigation.[2] Neither definition adequately defines or provides a universally accepted term for an individual who occupies the ill-defined role of an informant in today's criminal justice system. For example, the source of information used to provide probable cause for a search warrant might be a concerned citizen, not an informant. He has come forward out of a sense of civic duty and has no ulterior motive underlying his actions. The courts have viewed the citizen and the information he provides the police as more credible than that offered by a criminal informant.[3]

The information and testimony obtained from paid sources or criminal informants is received by the courts with far more caution. A pattern jury instruction illustrates the point:

> The testimony of some witnesses must be considered with more caution than the testimony of other witnesses. For example, a paid informer, or a witness who has been promised that he or she will not be charged or prosecuted, or a witness who hopes to gain

more favorable treatment in his or her own case, may have a reason
to make a false statement because he wants to strike a good bargain
with the government. So, while a witness of that kind may be
entirely truthful when testifying, you should consider that testimony with more caution than the testimony of other witnesses.[4]

Loosely referring to the citizen source of information as an informant in
an investigative report or affidavit can trigger enhanced scrutiny of the information reported by the source. The test applied in *Illinois v. Gates* for evaluating informant information for probable cause purposes is the "totality of
the circumstances" test.[5] The magistrate is required to "simply make a practical, common sense decision whether, given all the circumstances set forth
in the affidavit before him there is a fair probability that contraband or
evidence of a crime will be found in a particular place."[5] The "indicia of
reliability"[6] afforded a citizen source are great, and proper characterization
of the source is essential.

Federal investigative agencies are autonomous in their policies regarding
the utilization of informants (although the Attorney General has oversight
over agencies within the Department of Justice). Each uses different terms
for their sources of information.

State and local law enforcement agencies also promulgate their policies
independently. Terms used to identify informants and methods of utilizing
informants can differ drastically from region to region and agency to agency.
Many have adopted terms from their federal counterparts.

Among the federal agencies with the greatest need and largest budgets
for informants are the Federal Bureau of Investigation (FBI), the Drug
Enforcement Administration (DEA), Immigration and Customs Enforce-
ment (ICE), the Bureau of Alcohol, Tobacco, Firearms, and Explosives
(BATF), the Internal Revenue Service (IRS), and the U.S. Marshals Service
(USMS).[7]

Recognizing the agencies listed above as the leaders in the use of informants, an examination of the varying terms used for their sources of information follows.

1.2 Federal Bureau of Investigation (FBI)

The Federal Bureau of Investigation refers to its sources of information as
either informants or cooperative witnesses. Persons who provide information
to the FBI but do not fall into one of the specific classifications are referred
to generally as sources of information.

The FBI employees who recruit and operate informants and cooperative witnesses are Special Agents. FBI agents have broad investigative responsibilities covering more than 250 federal crimes and are the lead investigative agency for the U.S. Department of Justice. The FBI has concurrent jurisdiction with the Drug Enforcement Administration over drug offenses covered by the Controlled Substances Act.[8]

Scandals and the events of 2001 have been the catalyst for dramatic changes within the Bureau, particularly in the area of antiterrorism law enforcement and intelligence gathering. Informants used in international terrorism, foreign intelligence, or foreign counterintelligence investigations are now referred to as assets. They are operated under the Attorney General's Guidelines for National Security Investigations and Foreign Intelligence Collection, a partially classified document. Since November 2004, all of the FBI's human sources are operated under the newly created Directorate of Intelligence.

Within the FBI, informants and cooperative witnesses are classified according to the type of information they provide.

1.2.1 Informants

The FBI *Manual of Investigative Operations and Guidelines* (*MIOG*) Section 137 governs the Bureau's Criminal Informant (CI) Program. The *MIOG* also includes the Attorney General's Guidelines Regarding the Use of Informants that contains a slightly different definition for "informant" than the *MIOG*.[9] (See Appendix I, Section I.B.6 at B-8.)

The *MIOG* defines an informant as any person or entity who furnishes information to the FBI on a confidential basis.[10] Informants must be classified according to one of the following categories[11]:

1. Organized Crime (OC)
2. General Criminal (C) — Those providing information concerning investigations into matters of a general criminal nature.
3. Domestic Terrorism (DT) — Those providing information concerning investigations into persons or groups involved in terrorist activities within the United States, such as bombings and other criminal terrorist activities.
4. White-Collar Crime (WC) — Those providing information concerning violations falling within the white-collar crime program.
5. Drugs (D) — Those providing information concerning investigations falling within the drug program.
6. International Terrorism (IT)
7. Civil Rights (CR)
8. National Infrastructure Protection/Computer Intrusion Program (NI)

9. Cyber Crime (CC)
10. Major Theft (MT)
11. Violent Gangs (VG)
12. Confidential Sources (CS) — Those providing information to the FBI on a confidential and regular basis as a result of legitimate employment or routine access to records, and not as a result of association with persons of an investigative interest to the FBI. The information provided by a Confidential Source must be relevant to authorized FBI investigations. The operation of a Confidential Source must be consistent with FBI and Attorney General Guidelines. A Confidential Source may be paid reasonable amounts for services and expenses.[11]

The FBI considers the following factors in determining an individual's suitability to be an informant[12]:

1. Whether the person appears to be in a position to provide information concerning violations of law that are within the scope of authorized FBI investigative activity.
2. Whether the individual is willing to voluntarily furnish information to the FBI.
3. Whether the individual appears to be directed by others to obtain information from the FBI.
4. Whether there is anything in the individual's background that would make him/her unfit for use as an informant.
5. Whether the nature of the matter under investigation and the importance of the information being furnished to the FBI outweigh the seriousness of any past or contemporaneous criminal activity of which the informant may be suspected.
6. Whether the motives of the informant in volunteering to assist the FBI appear to be reasonable and proper.
7. Whether the information that the informant can provide could be obtained in a more timely and effective manner through other sources or by a less intrusive means.
8. Whether the informant is sufficiently reliable and trustworthy, and whether there is an adequate means by which to verify his/her truthfulness.
9. Whether the individual appears to be willing to conform to FBI and Attorney General Guidelines regarding his/her operation.
10. Whether the FBI will be able to adequately monitor and control the activities of the informant.

11. Whether his/her use as an investigative technique will intrude upon privileged communications or inhibit the lawful association of individuals or the expression of ideas.
12. Whether the use of the informant could compromise an investigation or subsequent prosecution that may require the government to move for a dismissal of the case. (See Appendix I, The Attorney General Guidelines Regarding the Use of Confidential Informants, Section II.A.1 for additional suitability factors.)

High-profile informant scandals have created the need to further scrutinize an informant's suitability to serve the FBI. Informants who fall into one of the following three categories require approval from the FBI's Confidential Informant Review Committee (CIRC):

- *Long-term confidential informant* — Defined as those who have been registered for more than six consecutive years.
- *High-level confidential informant* — Defined as individuals who are part of the senior leadership of an enterprise that (a) has a national or international sphere of activities, or high significance to the FBI's national objectives, even if the enterprise's sphere of activities is local or regional, and (b) engages in or uses others to commit activity that qualifies as Tier 1 Otherwise Illegal Activity under the Guidelines.
- *Privileged confidential informant* — Defined as individuals who are under the obligation of a legal privilege of confidentiality such as doctors, lawyers, and clergy, or individuals who are affiliated with the news media.

Four other categories of informants require special approval: federal prisoners, parolees, detainees, and supervised releasees; current or former participants in the Witness Security Program; state or local prisoners, probationers, parolees, or supervised releasees; and fugitives.[12]

1.2.2 Cooperative Witness

The *MIOG* defines a cooperative witness (CW) as an individual whose relationship with the government is concealed until testimony is required at trial and who, on a continuing basis and under the direction of an Agent, contributes substantial operational assistance to the resolution or direction of a case through active participation in the investigation.[13]

The FBI applies a narrow interpretation of the definitions for both CWs and informants. The intent is to have individuals who are operational or actively participating in an investigation and who will testify opened only as

CWs. Individuals who only provide intelligence and will not testify are opened as informants.[14]

The need for the distinction was detailed in a "Memorandum to All Special Agents in Charge Re: Cooperative Witness Program Interim Guidelines." Fourteen pages in length, the memorandum provided a historical background for Cooperative Witnesses:

> Historically, individuals who would normally meet the definition of a Cooperative Witness (CW) were "opened" as informants and later testified in court. This resulted in routine disclosure of CW/informant's identity in open court, which has caused continuing erosion of the Criminal Informant Program. By their testimony in court, CWs had the title of "informant" unnecessarily attached to them. When the need arose to protect a true informant, the courts were not as disposed to rule in the FBI's favor because of the number of previous "routine" disclosures of CW/informant identities in connection with testimony at trial. The CW guidelines will now allow Agents to open individuals in the proper category, based upon assistance provided, and to also receive full credit for developing that person. The CW guidelines will also help minimize the need for disclosure of the true informant's identity in open court.
>
> The main reasons for the development of the CW Program are to give Agents credit for the development of CWs when the type of case or investigative situation does not lend itself to the development of traditional informants. It also provides consistent policy and procedures for the operation of CWs throughout the FBI. Many Agents' skills and investigative techniques applicable to informant development are also required in the development of CWs.[14]

The memorandum recognized that informants may one day have to provide testimony and further shielded the program with the following directive:

> In cases where an informant may provide information that is testimonial in nature, and he/she meets the definition of a CW, he/she should be closed as an informant and opened as a CW. This should be done in a timely manner so that testimonial information appears only in the CW file. In the unique case where the informant will testify, and he/she will be productive as an informant after testimony, he/she should remain opened as an

informant. For example, an informant testifies against one person or group, but he/she can still safely provide effective intelligence on another person or group.[14]

Like their informant counterparts, CWs are classified according to the information they provide.

Distinction between a cooperative witness and a witness. The FBI has drawn a distinction between a witness and a CW. The witness is considered to be a citizen or a subject who is willing to testify concerning his or her knowledge of or participation in a crime but will not become operational or actively participate in an investigation. These individuals are not opened as CWs or informants. A witness may be paid one time from case funds, while a CW may be paid multiple times from CW funds for services and expenses.

1.3   Drug Enforcement Administration (DEA)

The U.S. Drug Enforcement Administration is an investigative agency within the U.S. Department of Justice. Its policy and procedures are contained in the *DEA Agents Manual*. In recent years, the DEA has discarded the term "informant" and now uses the term "confidential source" or CS. The DEA employees who are authorized to recruit and to operate sources are referred to as Special Agents. Their job classification within DEA is that of Criminal Investigator.[15]

Guidelines governing the utilization of confidential sources and terms used to identify sources of information are contained in the *DEA Agents Manual*, Chapter 66, Enforcement Procedures, Subchapter 661, Sources of Information. The DEA must also adhere to the requirements of the Attorney General Guidelines Regarding the Use of Confidential Informants. (See Appendix 1.)

Three criteria must be met to establish a person as a DEA confidential source:

1. The person is in a position to measurably assist the DEA in a present or future investigation.
2. To the extent a prudent judgment can be made, the person will not compromise DEA interests and activities.
3. The person will accept the measure of direction necessary to effectively utilize his services.[16]

The term "confidential source" applies to the following individuals.

1.3.1   Confidential Source (CS)

CS is a person who, under the direction of a specific DEA agent, and with or without expectation of compensation, furnishes information on drug trafficking or performs a lawful service for the DEA in its investigation of drug trafficking. According to a July 2005 Office of Inspector General's report, the DEA has approximately 4,000 active confidential sources at any one time.

1.3.2   Defendant/CS

A defendant/CS is as above, but subject to arrest and prosecution for a federal offense; or a defendant in a pending federal or state case who expects compensation for his assistance in either the form of judicial or prosecutive consideration, or compensation of another form.

Only individuals who are believed to be able to furnish reliable enforcement information or lawful services, and who are believed able to maintain the confidentiality of DEA interests and activities may be used as a defendant/CS. The approval of the appropriate U.S. Attorney or other prosecutor shall be obtained prior to seeking the cooperation of or utilizing a defendant/CS.

1.3.3   Restricted-Use CS

A CS who meets any of the following criteria shall be considered a "restricted-use CS," subject to use as authorized below:

1. Persons less than 18 years of age: Only with written consent of parent or legal guardian.[17]
2. Persons on probation or parole (federal or state): Special Agents in Charge (SACs) will establish procedures to obtain permission to use persons on probation (federal and state) and parole (state) within the SAC's area of responsibility.

NOTE: Where the person is currently a federal *prisoner,* and the intended utilization will require temporary furlough or transfer from his detention site, or the use of consensual monitoring devices, it is necessary to obtain prior Department approval.[18]

1.3.4   Source of Information

The DEA applies the term "source of information" to a person or organization, not under the direction of a specific agent, who provides information without becoming a party to the investigation itself (e.g., a business firm furnishing information from its records; an employee of an organization who, through the routine course of his activities, obtains information of value to the DEA; or a concerned citizen who witnesses an event of interest to the DEA). The title "confidential source" does not apply to "sources of information."

Should a person who would otherwise be considered a source of information become a continuing active part of an investigation, then his status should be shifted to that of a CS. A source of information that seeks financial compensation or becomes a recipient of an award from the Assets Forfeiture Fund must be established and assigned a code number for purpose of payment. The source of information is not to be considered a CS in this type of situation.

Generally, a person or organization fitting this definition can be identified by name in investigative reports. However, if there is cause to preserve anonymity, yet the circumstances do not warrant establishing the source as an informant, the term "source of information" may be used. Sources of information will be identified in an administrative memorandum attached to the report.[19]

1.4   U.S. Immigration and Customs Enforcement (ICE)

U.S. Immigration and Customs Enforcement now performs the investigative duties of the former U.S. Customs Service, previously an investigative agency of the U.S. Treasury Department. ICE is the largest investigative arm of the Department of Homeland Security (DHS), responsible for the enforcement of border, economic, infrastructure, and transportation laws. Established on March 1, 2003, it is staffed by approximately 20,000 employees. Prior to the creation of ICE, Customs employed 9,749 officers with arrest and firearms authority. Of this number, 3,540 were criminal investigators with the job description of Special Agent.[20] The majority of those agents were absorbed by ICE and have the authority to operate and pay informants.

The Office of Investigations, home to the majority of former U.S. Customs Special Agents, enforces laws designed to identify, disrupt, and dismantle international drug trafficking and money-laundering operations, the same mission as their predecessor agency. As would be expected, the resources of U.S. Customs moved to ICE along with the former Customs Special Agents. Those resources included the sources of information utilized by the former Customs agents.

Prior to the transformation from U.S. Customs to ICE, Customs Special Agents operated according to the provisions of the U.S. Customs Office of Enforcement's *Criminal Investigator's Handbook*. The discussion that follows is drawn from Chapter 41 of the Handbook, reported to still be in use at this writing. It provides the following definitions for their seven categories of sources of information:

- *Source of information* — A source of information is defined as a person who imparts information or evidence regarding violations of law to an officer without the expectation of their identity being protected.
- *Confidential source of information* — A confidential source of information is defined as a person who imparts information or evidence regarding violations of law, with the expectation that his/her identity will be protected.
- *Participating source of information* — A participating source of information is defined as a source (confidential or otherwise) that can be expected to take an active role in an investigation or interdiction effort. This individual provides information as a result of direct association with persons of an investigative interest.
- *Paid sources of information* — A paid source is one who provides information and/or evidence with the expectation of receiving remuneration or compensation, whether or not they expect anonymity or identity disclosure except those in the Drug Smuggling Awareness (DSA) Program.
- *Anonymous sources of information* — A source who provides original information relating to drug violations with the expectation that their identity will remain anonymous and not subject to possible discovery.
- *Active sources* — Active sources are those whose information and/or evidence is being utilized in an ongoing investigation or interdiction. Further, a source will remain active until all payments due/owed to the source have been made and until all contractual obligations have been met.
- *Inactive sources* — A source is considered inactive when the information or evidence imparted no longer generates investigative interest, the case is closed, and any payments owed the source have been made. A source providing general intelligence information that has not provided information or evidence for six months is considered inactive. When a source becomes active again by providing information, a criminal records check is required to be conducted in order to activate the source.[21]

Although the Handbook appears to avoid the term "informant," agents in the field routinely use the term. The following definition of "undercover operative" demonstrates the flexibility of the term "informant."

- *Undercover operative* — The term "undercover operative" includes the participation of Special Agents, Investigators, or informants who perform short-term or long-term undercover assignments.
- *Undesirable or unreliable source of information* — The final category is the undesirable or unreliable source of information. Agents in the field generally refer to these individuals as "black-balled" informants. To qualify for this distinction the source has either compromised an investigation or failed to follow the direction of his control agent. To alert other agents, the source's name is entered into the agency computer system. Any agent who inquires about the individual will be advised of the unreliable status. The source will be labeled as undesirable and unreliable until proven otherwise.[22]

1.5 Bureau of Alcohol, Tobacco, Firearms, and Explosives (BATF)

The BATF is primarily responsible for investigating the criminal use of firearms and explosives. BATF Special Agents are authorized to recruit and operate informants.[23]

On January 24, 2003, the Bureau of Alcohol, Tobacco, and Firearms (BATF), formerly an investigative agency within the U.S. Treasury Department, had its law enforcement functions transferred to the U.S. Department of Justice. As with Customs, BATF agents took their informants with them when they moved to the Department of Justice.

Prior to being transferred to the Justice Department, the *Investigative Priorities, Procedures, and Techniques Manual* governed the BATF's use of informants. The manual contains the Bureau's informant guidelines in Chapter D, Sections 31 through 48, "Informant Development, Use and Control Guidelines." At this writing, it continues to be followed until a new operations manual is completed. The discussion that follows is drawn from Chapter D of the most current available BATF manual.

The BATF precedes its definition of "informant" with a policy statement that warns the agent of the potential for problems that an informant can present.

Policy on the Use of Informants

It is the policy of the Bureau to use informants to assist in the investigation of criminal activity. Since the use of informants is a sensitive matter and will require the association of our special agents with persons whose motivations may be suspect or ultimately challenged by courts, this investigative technique should be carefully controlled and closely monitored. The proper use of informants requires that individual rights not be infringed and that the Bureau conduct itself within the parameters of ethical and legal law enforcement behavior.

The BATF defines an informant as a person who assists enforcement efforts by providing information or lawful services which otherwise might not be available in return for money or some other specific consideration. The information or services provided must have specific investigative or general intelligence value in enforcing laws and regulations within the Bureau's responsibility.[24]

In addition to providing information, informants may be expected to participate in undercover investigations or testify in open court if required. They may also expect that their identity will not be disclosed, except with their approval.[25]

The BATF has a further category of informant, the undesirable or unreliable informant. According to the manual, an "undesirable/unreliable informant" file is maintained to guard against persons posing as informants to infiltrate the BATF for the purpose of gaining intelligence on current investigations, to steal agent cashier funds, or to commit any other such actions. Failure to follow the directions of a control agent can also result in the classification. When any informant is suspected or known to be undesirable or unreliable, his services are immediately discontinued.[26]

1.6   Internal Revenue Service (IRS)

The Internal Revenue Service is an investigative agency of the U.S. Treasury Department. The IRS Criminal Investigation Division is comprised of 4,500 employees worldwide, approximately 2,900 of whom are Special Agents. Their investigative jurisdiction includes tax, money laundering, bank secrecy act violations, and terrorist financing. It is the only federal agency that can investigate criminal violations of the Internal Revenue Code.[27]

IRS Special Agents assigned to the Criminal Investigative Division (CID) are directed to recruit and manage informants. Informants are utilized by the IRS primarily in the investigation of individuals who are engaged in crimes that produce illegal income.[28] The Internal Revenue Service has five classifications of informants:

- *Anonymous informants* — An anonymous informant is an individual who either refuses to identify himself/herself or uses a fictitious or code name, and his true identity is unknown to the IRS. An anonymous informant can neither be paid nor work at the direction of the IRS.[29]

- *Confidential source of information* — A confidential source of information is an individual who provides information without seeking payment (other than a claim for reward), does not gather information at the direction of the IRS and is not expected to testify.[30]
- *Confidential informant* — A confidential informant is an individual who is not expected to testify but may be paid for the information provided and/or gathers information and evidence at the direction of the IRS.[31]
- *Cooperating witness* — A cooperating witness is an individual who is expected to testify and is a consenting party in consensually monitored conversations and gathers information and evidence at the direction of the IRS. A CW may be paid for the information provided.[32]
- *Cooperating defendant* — A cooperating defendant is an individual who has committed criminal violations and does more to assist the government than testify based on past activity. He/she may be charged or not charged with the criminal violations. A CD is typically not paid as his/her motivation for operation is based upon charging or sentencing consideration rather than money. Further, each CD is expected to testify and gather information at the direction of the IRS, or is a consenting party in consensually monitored conversations.[33]

1.7   U.S. Marshals Service (USMS)

Within the Justice Department is the U.S. Marshals Service that employs approximately 2,650 officers with arrest and firearms authority. The Marshals Service receives all persons arrested by federal agencies and is responsible for their custody and transportation until they are sentenced. It also transfers sentenced federal inmates between facilities with the help of the Bureau of Prisons. Additionally, the Marshals Service has jurisdiction over federal fugitive matters, escaped prisoners, violators of probation, parole, releases on bond, and persons under DEA warrants. Of greatest importance is the USMS' administration of the Witness Security Program.

The U.S. Marshals Service defines "informant" as an individual who furnishes information to the Marshals Service. Such information may be furnished on the informant's own initiative or because of being directed to furnish information by a USMS employee.

The Marshals Service recognizes four categories of informants for the purpose of its reporting system.

- *Anonymous informant* — One who either refuses to identify himself or uses a fictitious name, and whose true identity is unknown to the Marshals Service.
- *Nonconfidential informant* — One who does not request that his name be held in strict confidence.
- *Confidential informant* — One who requests that his name be held in strict confidence.
- *Controlled informant* — One who is paid for the information he has voluntarily provided to the Marshals Service or one who has been developed by USMS personnel as a source of information relating to an area of USMS investigative jurisdiction.[34]

1.8 Central Intelligence Agency (CIA)

The Central Intelligence Agency is charged with the responsibility of collecting intelligence information relating to the security of the United States. It is not a law enforcement agency and reports to the National Security Council (NSC). Since September 11, 2001, the focus of CIA activity is on terrorism.

In recent years its mission had crossed into areas of responsibility thought reserved by the FBI, DEA, and ICE, most notably in the areas of drug trafficking and money laundering. Highly publicized misadventures in Central and South America appeared to confuse the intelligence gathering responsibilities of the CIA with the law enforcement responsibilities of other agencies.[35]

Within the CIA, individuals that law enforcement agencies routinely refer to as informants are known as assets. The assets are often referred to as agents. The information they collect for the CIA is referred to as human intelligence or HUMINT. (HUMINT refers to any information collected from a human source).

The CIA employees who manage assets, collect intelligence, and work in the field are known as case officers.[36] Case officers are taught "tradecraft," or how to collect information and how to recruit and manage assets at the CIA's Camp Peary Training Center. Known as "the farm," the facility is located on a 9,275-acre tract near Williamsburg, VA.

While performing their duties overseas, case officers often operate under diplomatic cover as State Department officials or economic officers assigned to American consulates. Former CIA Director, Admiral Stansfield Turner, provided an insightful job description for case officers. "The clandestine service calls for unusual sacrifice. It is not just the anonymity but the lack of credit for what you do. People know you're Joe Jones. They think you are second secretary or some other position in some government bureau, but

you never get very high, you are never the top person. You are always undercover doing a different job, and to others who don't know what you are really
doing, it appears you're not very successful."[37]

Some case officers do not operate under official cover and are referred
to as NOCs (standing for "No Official Cover"). These officers are the most
covert CIA employees. They work abroad without diplomatic immunity and
often appear to be working for a commercial enterprise.

1.9   State and Local Law Enforcement Agencies

State and local law enforcement agencies are independent government agencies and departments. They do not subscribe to a nationally accepted or
promulgated policy and procedure manual concerning informants. Each
agency is free to develop and follow its own set of rules. As an example, the
New York City Police Department applies the following definition for informant:

A *confidential informant* is a person who has been approved by the department *and registered with the Intelligence Division,* who, through a confidential
relationship with a uniformed member of the service, furnishes the department
with criminal information specifically requested, and such person:

1. Expects monetary consideration for information supplied, or
2. Expects court consideration for information supplied, or
3. Has a prior criminal history or associates with known criminals, or
4. Has demonstrated reliability by providing information of value on
    more than one occasion.

The International Association of Chiefs of Police (IACP), through their
National Law Enforcement Policy Center, produced a "Concepts and Issues
Paper" entitled "Confidential Informants."[38] The work, produced June 1,
1990, was the result of a grant awarded by the Bureau of Justice Assistance,
Office of Justice Programs, the U.S. Department of Justice. It continues to
stand as their policy on confidential informants. The IACP also developed a
"model policy" on confidential informants. The model policy defines four
categories as sources in Section C of the monograph:

•   *General Sources* — Valuable information may be obtained from other
    investigators and officers in one's own or nearby law enforcement
    agencies, other criminal justice officials, the department of motor
    vehicles, utility companies, banks, credit reporting agencies, and

many others. Perhaps one of the best general sources of information and intelligence is the beat officer.

- *Citizen Sources* — Victims, witnesses, and concerned citizens, including Neighborhood Watch members, comprise this category. Generally, these people are credible, and their information is useful. Recognizing that citizens may place themselves at risk of retribution by providing information, caution and anonymity should be encouraged, and their confidentiality should be closely guarded.
- *Street Sources* — In general, these are persons who come into frequent contact with law enforcement officers because of their occupations, activities, or place of residence. They include bar, restaurant, and hotel employees; prostitutes and pimps; cab drivers; and employees of late-night establishments, such as gas stations and convenience stores.
- *Confidential informants (CI)* — To be of value as a CI, a person should have one or more of the following characteristics. A good CI:

    1. Knows, has been associated with, or has intimate knowledge of one or more active criminals.
    2. Is associated with, or has intimate knowledge of, persons practicing a crime specialty such as bank robbery, drug sales, or perpetrating crimes in a specific geographic area.
    3. Has an occupation or residence that lends itself to gathering information about criminals and their plans to commit crimes.
    4. Has status in the criminal justice system, that is, is on pretrial release or bail; probation or parole; convicted pending sentencing; incarcerated; or other status.
    5. Based on these qualifications, a confidential informant could be defined as a private citizen who has entered into a confidential agreement with a law enforcement agency to provide information about criminals or criminal activity in exchange for monetary or other consideration.[38]

State and local police agencies do not have to adhere to the IACP model policy. They are free to develop, as most have, their own guidelines. However, a disclaimer at the conclusion of the paper cautions police agencies when developing a policy on informants:

> Every effort has been made by the IACP National Law Enforcement Policy Center staff and advisory board to ensure that this model policy incorporates the most current information and contemporary professional judgment on this issue. However, law enforcement administrators should be cautioned that no "model"

policy can meet all the needs of any given law enforcement agency. Each law enforcement agency operates in a unique environment of federal court rulings, state laws, local ordinances, regulations, judicial and administrative decisions and collective bargaining agreements that must be considered. In addition, the formulation of specific agency policies must take into account local political and community perspectives and customs, prerogatives and demands, often divergent law enforcement strategies and philosophies, and the impact of varied agency resource capabilities among other factors.

References

1. *Black's Law Dictionary,* 701, 5th ed. (1979).

2. *Gordon v. United States,* 438 F2d 858, 874, 5th Cir. (1971).

3. *See Chambers v. Maroney,* 399 U.S. 42, 46–47 (1970).

4. Pattern Jury Instructions of the District Judges Association of the Eleventh Cir. Crim. Cases, Special Instruction No. 1.1 (1985). *See United States v. Hernandez-Escarsega,* 886 F.2d 1560, 1574–75, 9th Cir. (1989), *cert. denied,* 497 U.S. 1003, 110 S. Ct. 3237, 111 L. Ed. 2d 748 (1990).

5. *Illinois v. Gates,* 462 U.S. 213, 238 (1983).

6. *Illinois v. Gates,* 462 U.S. 213, 233 (1983).

7. Bureau of Justice Statistics Bulletin, NCJ-212750.

8. Bureau of Justice Statistics Bulletin, NCH-164617.

9. *FBI Manual of Investigative Operations and Guidelines (MIOG)* § 137-13 (1998).

10. *FBI Manual of Investigative Operations and Guidelines (MIOG)* § 137.2.1 (1998).

11. *FBI Manual of Investigative Operations and Guidelines (MIOG)* § 137-3 (1998).

12. Attorney General Guidelines Regarding the Use of Confidential Informants, I.B.9, B-9; II.D.3-6, B-20-22.

13. *FBI Manual of Investigative Operations and Guidelines (MIOG),* Part I, § 270-2 (1998).

14. Memorandum to All Special Agents in Charge Re: Cooperative Witness Program Interim Guidelines, from William S. Sessions, April 10, 1990. (Incorporated by reference into *MIOG,* Part I, § 270-1(3)).

15. Bureau of Justice Statistics Bulletin, NCJ-1646 17.

16. *DEA Agents Manual,* Ch. 6612 (C).

17. Blair, J., Ethics of using juvenile informants, *Christian Science Monitor,* April 14, 1998.

18. *DEA Agents Manual,* Ch. 6612.1 (A) (1), (2), (3).

19. *DEA Agents Manual,* Ch. 6612 (B).

20. Bureau of Justice Statistics Bulletin, NCJ-164617.

21. U.S. Customs Service, Office of Enforcement, *Criminal Investigators Handbook.*

22. U.S. Customs Service, *Operations Guidelines* § 41-1 1(F).

23. Bureau of Justice Statistics Bulletin, NCJ-164617.

24. BATF Manual: *Investigative Priorities, Procedures, and Techniques,* Ch. D, § 31.

25. BATF Manual: *Investigative Priorities, Procedures, and Techniques,* Ch. D, § 32(b).

26. BATF Manual: *Investigative Priorities, Procedures, and Techniques,* Ch. D, § 42.

27. Bureau of Justice Statistics Bulletin, NCJ-164617.

28. *Internal Revenue Service Manual,* 9.4.2.5.2.

29. *Internal Revenue Service Manual,* 9.4.2.5.2.1. (12-20-2001).

30. *Internal Revenue Service Manual,* 9.4.2.5.2.2. (12-20-2001).

31. *Internal Revenue Service Manual,* 9.4.2.5.2.3. (08-10-2004).

32. *Internal Revenue Service Manual,* 9.4.2.5.2.4. (08-10-2004).

33. *Internal Revenue Service Manual,* 9.4.2.5.2.5. (08-10-2004).

34. *U.S. Marshals Service Manual,* Ch. 7.12.2(c), (d), (e), (f), 1361.

35. Pincus, W., Crisis at CIA: why are its young officers resigning? *Washington Post* Service.

36. Davis, F., Agent Tells Tale of CIA Defect in Drug War, *Miami Herald,* Sept. 18, 1997.

37. Weiner, T., *New York Times* Service, In latest turncoat scandal, CIA assumes the worst, *International Herald Tribune,* Nov. 21, 1996. *See also,* Gup, T., Nameless Stars of the CIA, *Washington Post,* Oct. 1, 1997.

38. Confidential Informants, Concepts and Issues Paper, June 1, 1990, International Association of Chiefs of Police.

Motivations to Cooperate as an Informant

2

2.1 Generally

Motivations for cooperation will generally fall into one or more of several categories including money, civic duty, fear, revenge, special consideration while incarcerated, repentance, and ego. Very often, an informant may display more than one of the motivators, or his motivation may change during the course of his dealings with the government.

The Drug Enforcement Administration (DEA) recognizes the importance of their agents correctly recognizing an informant's motivation and focuses on the topic during agent training.

> Informants are like anyone else in that they must be motivated to perform. The more strongly motivated they are, the more likely they are to apply themselves to their task and remain committed to achieving success. Motivation is a psychological incentive that moves a person to action, from within. Informants are not motivated by the Agent with whom they work, but rather they are motivated and will work for the Agent who properly identifies their motives and successfully stimulates them into action.

> It is important to remember that no one is motivated solely by one emotion or psychological factor. In spite of the fact that one factor may predominate and even be acknowledged as the reason for cooperation, still there will be other aspects which will underlie

19

this primary motive and therefore modify the resulting actions of the informant. It is common for informants to verbalize one specific motive for giving information but as the case proceeds and the agent/informant relationship develops, some other motive is revealed and ultimately proves to be a much stronger incentive to action. The successful investigator will remain sensitive to these subtle changes in their informant's psychology.[1]

It is absolutely essential that the investigator and his supervisor know the motivation for the informant's cooperation to ensure that his activities are monitored and he is properly controlled.

Intelligence services, police departments and political campaigns rarely spy directly. They depend on traitors willing to sell secrets. Some of these turncoats are brave and virtuous, guided by principle or ideology; some are sleazy or greedy. Some tell the truth, some spin lies. Some like Linda Tripp, the heroine/villainess of this scandal, have a complex mixture of motivations.[2]

Understanding why the informant is working for the government enables the control agent and his supervisor to determine the amount of scrutiny and supervision a particular informant's activity merits.

The prosecutor must also be cognizant of what brought the individual into his relationship with law enforcement. What is at stake, if anything, if he fails to produce for his handler? A prosecutor who does not appreciate the perils of using rewarded criminals as witnesses risks compromising the truth-seeking mission of our criminal justice system.[3]

Many defense attorneys fail to understand the importance of recognizing the motivation of the informant-witnesses as they examine the case against their client. If the informant is going to be a witness in a criminal prosecution, the defense attorney must learn the informant's motivation to properly develop a trial strategy. The more desperate an informant is to stay out of jail or to make money, the more likely that perjury or outrageous government conduct may have occurred, triggering due process concerns.[4]

It is possible that the informant's motivation will go unquestioned. Very often, the confidential informant (CI) or the case is "inherited" by the agent, the prosecutor, or both. Prosecutors retire, transfer, or even more likely, become defense attorneys. Detectives routinely rotate out of an assignment, and federal agents transfer or are promoted. Many retire or resign, and some go to jail. Yet the case and the informant must continue to be dealt with through trial.

2.2 Money

Money is probably the easiest motivation to understand. Informants in this category are often referred to as mercenaries. According to Roger Maier, spokesman for the U.S. Customs Service in El Paso, Texas, "These (informants) can certainly generate cash awards or payments that can go into the five figures or six figures at times depending on the type of information that's provided."[5]

In Christianity, Judas was the first recorded paid informant, receiving 30 pieces of silver for betraying Jesus.[6] He later repented and committed suicide by hanging, illustrating that remorse can be a by-product of cooperation.

In 1692, the English Parliament codified payments and rewards into law with three provisions of the Highwayman's Act.[7] Known as the "Reward Statutes," they provided for:

1. A reward of £40 for the capture and conviction of a thief. If more than one informant was involved, the reward was to be divided.
2. Section 6 provided that the informant could claim the thief's horse, money, weapons, and any other belongings, provided the property was not stolen.
3. Section 7 contained perhaps the most significant incentive. If the informant was wanted for a crime (provided he was not a convicted felon at the time of cooperation), he received not only the £40 reward and the thief's property but also a Royal pardon.

The new incentives to cooperate initially proved fruitful, as there was a marked decline in theft. Unfortunately, the deals offered to criminal informants were so attractive the rewards became known as "blood money certificates." The Acts created an army of professional informers who became skilled in entrapment, blackmail, extortion, and perjury, leading to the execution of many innocent citizens.[8]

In his *Commentaries*, Blackstone discussed a similar practice whereby convicted felons received monetary rewards and in some cases a pardon of all capital offenses for providing information leading to the conviction of another. According to Blackstone, this practice of so-called "approvements" was eventually abandoned: "For the truth was, as Sir Matthew Hale observes, that more mischief hath arisen to good men by these kinds of approvements, upon false and malicious accusations of desperate villains, than benefit to the public by the discovery and conviction of real offenders."[9]

Today informing can be a profitable enterprise.[10] Rewards have been sanctioned on the grounds of public policy interests in bringing crime witnesses forward with their information.[11]

Informants at the federal level can be extremely well paid. Rewards in excess of one million dollars are not unusual.[12] The Internal Revenue Service (IRS), for example, can pay informants up to $10 million per case, up from a ceiling of $100,000 in 1997. In the first 30 years of the IRS informant program, approximately 17,000 informants collectively earned over $35.1 million. The IRS recovered more than $2.1 billion in unpaid taxes because of informant information.[13]

State and local agencies also pay their sources. However, the total amount spent nationally has never been tabulated. Given the sheer numbers of non-federal agencies and criminal investigations involving state and local police informants, the amounts paid can only be the subject of speculation. It may surpass federal spending.

Informants motivated by money view their work as a productivity-based enterprise contingent[14] upon success.[15] The sums paid by federal, state, and local agents following their investigations would suggest that a majority of agents also share that opinion. The bigger case will result in a correspondingly greater award.[16] The informant in the World Trade Center bombing prosecution of 1995 was paid in excess of $1 million by the Federal Bureau of Investigation (FBI) for his efforts in the investigation.[17]

The War on Terrorism and the war in Iraq that followed the September 11, 2001 World Trade Center attack revealed just how much the U.S. Government was willing to spend for informant information. The source that provided the information leading to the location of Saddam Hussein's sons, Uday and Qusay, received $30 million. The reward leading to the capture of Saddam Hussein was $25 million. The Rewards for Justice Program set a $25 million reward for Osama bin Laden. He remains at large, and at this writing, and it is rumored that the reward will be increased to $50 million.[18] To date, the program has paid $57 million for information that has either prevented international terrorist attacks or aided in apprehending those involved in prior acts.

The money-motivated informants are usually the most willing to follow the directions of their handlers.[19] However, problems can arise when information becomes scarce and the informant needs money. He may fabricate accounts of criminal activity or entrap his target. See Chapter 4, "Sources of Compensation for Informants."

2.3 Fear of Punishment

The fear of legal punishment for criminal acts is probably the most frequently encountered motivation for an individual to cooperate with law enforcement agents.[20] Individuals falling into this category are referred to as either criminal informants or defendant informants.[21] They want to have charges dropped or reduced or to have a favorable recommendation made by the prosecutor to the court at sentencing.[22]

"Working off a charge"[23] is a matter of survival for many criminal informants. The concept is not a new one. In 1706, England enacted 5 Anne C.31 in response to the growing problem of what today would be called buying and receiving stolen property. A "receiver," although considered an accessory after the fact, if convicted would be sentenced to death as a capital felon. An informer who provided evidence sufficient to convict his accomplices received both a Royal pardon and a reward of £40.[24]

Today, the criminal or defendant informant is either a defendant in a pending federal[25] or state prosecution or subject to arrest and prosecution for a criminal offense. If he refuses to cooperate with the government, his fate is predictable.[26] Upon conviction, the U.S. Sentencing Guidelines[27] provide a statutory sentencing range for all federal crimes. The Guidelines set predictable minimum and maximum limits of the sentence that can be imposed. In the case of drug crimes, the most common limits are 0 to 20 years, 5 to 40 years, and 10 years to life. Many states have also enacted severe minimum sentences, and three felony convictions can earn a life sentence. Providing information can unlock the trap door in the sentencing floor.[28]

The court in *United States v. Brigham* added that:

> The "mandatory" minimum is mandatory only from the perspective of judges. To the parties, the sentence is negotiable. Did a marginal participant in a conspiracy really understand that a 10-kilo deal lay in store? A prosecutor may charge a lesser crime, if he offers something in return. Let's make a deal. Does the participant have valuable information; can he offer other assistance? Congress authorized prosecutors to pay for aid with sentences below the "floor."[29]

The criminal informant who is "working off a charge" is probably the most dangerous for an investigator to handle. He is from the criminal milieu and should never be trusted.[30] As his trial date draws nearer, he will become more desperate to make a case for his agent handler.[31] There is a significant risk that he will fabricate evidence and entrap his target.[32] He may be on probation or parole and can be in violation of the terms of his release[33] if arrested.[34] He can be sent back to prison if he does not produce.[34] The more desperate his circumstances, the greater the challenges he will present to his handler, as there will be little he will not do to stay out of jail.

Correctional facilities, particularly federal institutions, have become "snitch factories."[35] Prisoners with valuable criminal information compete with each other to win the ear of an interested agent. It is their only hope for a favorable recommendation after sentencing from the arresting officer to the prosecutor.[36]

Many defendants, particularly those charged with a federal violation, are denied bond prior to trial.[37] Federal judicial officers deny bond if it is determined that a release will not reasonably assure the appearance of the person[38] as required or will endanger the safety of any other person or the community.[39] Cooperation with the government will often result in a favorable recommendation by the prosecutor for a bond or recognizance release. The informant in a proactive investigation is of little help to his handler while incarcerated and is usually released prior to trial.

2.4   Fear of Criminal Associates and Revenge

Many are motivated to inform by fear of the threat of physical harm either to themselves, friends, or family.[40] Business associates, fellow members of a criminal organization, or members of rival criminal organizations or gangs can pose the danger.

Ex-paramours can be motivated by either fear, revenge, or a combination of both motivators. The emotional fallout from a divorce can also be a powerful motivator for an ex-spouse to come forward with information.

Business associates may seek revenge by providing law enforcement with damaging evidence against a former partner or competitor. Tips are important to the IRS and are often received from disgruntled employees, unpaid creditors, or angry neighbors. The result can be a protracted civil or criminal investigation of the revenge target.

Threats commonly result from being suspected of informing, jealousy, bad debts, the theft of consigned or "fronted" drugs, or a gang turf war. The target of the threat may be wrongly accused.

The fear- and revenge-motivated informants usually have two goals in mind:

1. Protection.
2. Law enforcement elimination of the source of the threat through incarceration.

The same holds true for the revenge-motivated informant.

The fear- and revenge-motivated informants must be thoroughly debriefed immediately and their information evaluated. The reason for quick action is twofold:

1. The dispute may be resolved, and the burning desire to cooperate is extinguished.
2. The informant may go into hiding or be murdered before a complete debriefing can be completed.

While the informant's value is being evaluated, a threat assessment should be conducted. If there is a substantiated risk of harm present, some measure of protection should be provided to the individual during the evaluation period. See Chapter 11, "The Witness Security Program."

2.5   Citizen Informants

The citizen informant is motivated by a belief that there is a civic duty to report crime and suspicious activity occurring in his community to the police.[41] This type of informant often comes forward with valuable information that may be used to initiate or further an ongoing criminal investigation and is generally treated as reliable.[42]

The citizen informant should neither receive nor be offered any form of compensation by police in return for his information. Unlike informants with ulterior motives for cooperating with police, his "reward" is a sense of personal satisfaction for his contribution.

Their information is often used as probable cause in an affidavit for a search warrant. The affiant must affirmatively set forth circumstances that would allow a neutral magistrate to determine the informant's status as a citizen informer.[43]

The prosecutor is not required to establish either the credibility of the citizen informant or the reliability of his information.[44] The identity of the informant need not be disclosed.

Informant tips vary greatly in their value, credibility, and reliability.[45] If a police officer intends to utilize the citizen informant's information in an affidavit, the details he provides should be corroborated if possible.[46] For example, a report of suspicious activity occurring repeatedly at particular times of the night would merit surveillance to determine if criminal activity was in fact being committed.[47]

However, if an unquestionably honest citizen comes forward with a report of criminal activity, which if fabricated would subject him to criminal liability, rigorous scrutiny of the basis of his knowledge is unnecessary.[48] Conversely, even if there was some measure of uncertainty[49] or suspicion of the citizen informant's motive, the more explicit and detailed description of alleged wrongdoing, along with a statement that the event was observed firsthand, entitle his tip to greater weight than might otherwise be the case.[50]

Many citizen informants occupy positions and occupations that enable them to provide "expert" information to the police. Law enforcement agencies actively encourage individuals in businesses utilized by criminals to report their suspicions.[51]

The U.S. Drug Enforcement Administration, Customs, and local police departments routinely contact employees of hotels near airports to enlist their assistance.[52] They are instructed to be suspicious of the following: guests paying for their rooms with cash, requesting adjoining rooms, refusing maid service for several days, ordering room service and rarely leaving their rooms, heavy telephone activity both incoming and outgoing, and receiving visitors at all hours of the day and night. The described behavior is indicative of drug dealing by hotel guests.

Long before September 11, 2001, airline employees had been taught to regard as suspicious cash purchases of round-trip tickets with open returns by passengers with little or no luggage.[53] Most major airports have a DEA Special Agent or plainclothes police officers assigned to the facility to respond to employee leads.

Real estate sales agents and rental agents in coastal communities are routinely contacted by investigative agencies. It is not uncommon for smugglers to either purchase or rent waterfront property to facilitate an off-loading of drugs or illegal immigrants.

Indoor marijuana-growing operations and clandestine laboratories both rely on goods and services available from legitimate businesses. In the case of growing operations, large amounts of growing medium and fertilizer are needed as well as planting containers, lights, and drip irrigation systems. Commercial outlets offer information to law enforcement agencies that is routinely investigated and developed.

The government's aggressive approach to getting "ordinary citizens" involved in law enforcement[54] can transform an otherwise good citizen informant into a cooperating individual with full informant status. The widely publicized willingness of the government to pay for information or to share in the proceeds of seized property is the leading cause of such transformations. An otherwise well-intentioned citizen may believe he is entitled to a reward for performing his civic duty.

The commercial shipping industry offers an example of the influence rewards have had. By the late 1970s, the movement of narcotics through the U.S. mail reached epidemic proportions. The U.S. Customs Service joined forces with the U.S. Postal Inspection Service and increased its enforcement efforts to stop the trend. Postal employees were instructed in the methods used to package and conceal drugs and the characteristics of postal patrons involved in criminal activity. Controlled deliveries and search warrants resulted from their tips, and well-publicized arrests followed.

Traffickers, also resilient and resourceful, moved to less risky methods of moving their product, particularly for domestic movements of packages.[55] Commercial delivery companies like UPS, Federal Express, and the airlines[56] all began to appear as an attractive option to the traffickers. They were particularly appealing because they were not a governmental entity: No Postal Inspectors = Less Risk.

In the normal course of business, employees of package companies began discovering drug shipments, either when containers were broken or contents were legitimately examined.[57] Lost luggage, for example, is routinely opened and examined by airline employees to identify the owner in furtherance of the legitimate interests of the airline. If contraband is discovered, it is a private search.[58] A wrongful search or seizure by a private party does not violate the Fourth Amendment.[59]

The DEA began responding to the commercial discoveries and began an "awareness program." Agents met with and instructed the carrier employees of what to look for and whom to call when a discovery was made.

Predictably, discoveries of contraband by employees increased as more "legitimate" inspections by employees occurred. The bond between government agents and the employees grew. Had the searches been solely to assist the government agents, they may have been classified as governmental intrusions.[60]

The increasing interaction between government agents and the shippers did not immediately raise Fourth Amendment concerns. The court, in *United States v. Gumerlock*, addressed the issue.

> While a certain degree of governmental participation is necessary before a private citizen is transformed into an agent of the state, de minimis or incidental contacts between the citizen and law enforcement agents prior to or during the course of a search or seizure will not subject the search to Fourth Amendment scrutiny. The government must be involved either directly as a participant or directly as an encourager of the private citizen's actions before we deem the citizen to be an instrument of the state.[61]

The requisite degree of governmental involvement in the inspections would require proof of more direct knowledge and acquiescence in the search. There appeared to develop a "gray area" between the extremes of overt governmental participation in a search and the complete absence of such participation.[62]

The "gray area" became somewhat better defined when an airfreight employee became "suspicious" of a package's contents. He opened the package, inspected its contents, discovered drugs, *but* admitted that he knew a reward was a possibility for his find when he contacted the DEA. There was no legitimate business need or duty present in the employee's actions, and he was found to be acting as an "agent" of the government.

In *United States v. Walther,* the court recommended that resolutions of cases falling within the "gray area" could best be resolved on a case-by-case basis with the consistent application of certain general principles. In determining whether an individual has become an "instrument or agent" of the government, two critical factors in the analysis are: (1) the government's knowledge and acquiescence and (2) the intent of the party performing the search.[63]

The court recognized the value of citizen informants in its decision by concluding:

> We do not by this opinion diminish the duty of any private citizen to report possible criminal activity, nor do we frown upon the use of paid informants. We merely hold that the government cannot knowingly acquiesce in and encourage directly or indirectly a private citizen to engage in activity that it is prohibited from pursuing where that citizen has no motivation other than the expectation of reward for his or her efforts.[64]

The court distinguished the case from *United States v. Valen,*[65] wherein the freight company employee had in the past been paid merely for providing "information."

The Drug Enforcement Administration's internal policy requires agents to refer to citizen informants in their reports as "sources of information."[66] Should a source of information seek financial compensation or become the recipient of an award from the Asset Forfeiture Fund, then he must be established and assigned a code number for purposes of payment. The source of information, however, is not considered by the DEA to be a cooperating source (informant) in this type of situation even though he received payment.[66]

Citizen informants are usually kept confidential to ensure their safety and encourage others to come forward with information. Generally, members of business organizations fitting the definition of source of information in DEA investigations are identified by name in investigative reports. However, if there is a need to preserve anonymity, but circumstances do not merit establishing the source as an informant, the term "source of information" is used. The source is fully identified in an internal memorandum that is attached to the original investigative report.[66]

2.6 Walk-In Informants

The term "walk-in" informant does not describe a motivation to cooperate. Rather, it literally depicts how the informant's relationship with law enforcement began; the individual walked into the police department or federal agency field office to begin work as an informant.

The walk-in may possess one or more of the motivators already discussed. These individuals merit discussion because those outside of law enforcement circles, particularly defense attorneys, doubt the accounts of how such informant–police relationships had their beginning.

Local police narcotics units generally assign a detective to meet with and screen "walk-ins." Often they are unstable individuals imagining criminal activity where none exists. Although the temptation may be great to dismiss "walk-ins" as a waste of time, very often they provide worthwhile information. Once their information is evaluated as being of value, the informant is assigned to a detective or agent for further development.

Federal agencies also delegate the task of screening "walk-ins." The DEA rotates one of its enforcement groups of ten agents on a monthly basis to the role of "Duty Group." These agents receive all telephone tips and screen "walk-in" informants.

"Operation Swordfish," the DEA's first and arguably most successful international money laundering case, owed much of its success to this type of informant. Robert Darias, the lead informant in the case, was a "walk-in," a person unknown to the DEA, who simply arrived at its doorstep offering information and services.[67]

2.7 Jailhouse Informants

The jailhouse informant is motivated by his desire to obtain a release from prison, usually in the form of a favorable recommendation for parole. (See Chapter 11, "The Witness Security Program.") Absent that option, he wants to make his period of incarceration as tolerable an experience as possible. As a member of a jail or prison population, the corrections staff fulfill his immediate needs. They can control nearly all facets of his environment. He can do "easy time" or "hard time." In most cases, he probably views even the best day in jail as "hard time."

Jailhouse informants are not a modern day phenomenon. Perhaps the world's most famous informant of the category was an early nineteenth-century escaped French convict, Eugene-Francois Vidocq. He would later become the head of France's Sûreté.[68]

Police inspectors of that era, the Officers de Paix,[68] had a network of informants who were paid for their information either in cash or with immunity from prosecution.[68] Acting on an informant's tip, Vidocq, a notorious escapee, was arrested by the Head of the Second Division, M. Henry. Vidocq was recruited to become an informant in exchange for incarceration at his prison of preference, La Force, in the Marias district of Paris.[68] There he obtained confessions and informed on inmates for nearly 21 months.[68] Upon release, he was employed as a police agent, establishing a reputation as an effective and controversial law enforcement official.[68]

The jailhouse informant plays an important yet controversial role within the criminal justice system. Many "cold cases," those that have gone unsolved for many years, are solved by jail cell "confessions" given by the perpetrator or an accomplice to a fellow inmate. Recently committed crimes are also solved when a newly incarcerated prisoner confides in his cellmate the details about his latest crime.[69] The jailhouse informant will generally channel his information either by telephone or through a corrections officer to an interested detective in exchange for consideration peculiar to the informant's needs.

The controversy surrounding the jailhouse informant arises when he is instructed by police to obtain information from a targeted prisoner. The problem is compounded when he is strategically placed by the correction staff to be in close proximity to the target as a plant.

The most comprehensive examination of this type of informant was conducted by the Los Angeles County Grand Jury (1989–1990). A 153-page report was released on June 26, 1990.[70] Although the term "jailhouse" informant was used in their report,[70] the California Penal Code[71] refers to this category of cooperating individuals as "in custody informants," defining them as "a person other than a codefendant, percipient witness, accomplice, or coconspirator whose testimony is based upon statements made by the defendant while both the defendant and the informant are held within a correctional institution."[71,72]

Whether or not true, many incarcerated informants believe that law enforcement officials have directly or indirectly solicited them to actively secure incriminating statements from fellow inmates. Some informants in the Los Angeles grand jury investigation claimed that various law enforcement officials supplied them with information about crimes, so they (the informants) could fabricate a defendant's confession.

The Grand Jury determined that inmates were planted by jail authorities with or near criminal defendants in high-profile cases with instructions to obtain information and confessions. If true, the risk of serious Fifth and Sixth Amendment violations should have been apparent to prosecutors and police.[70]

The Fifth Amendment[73] privilege against compulsory self-incrimination draws with it the right to have counsel present during custodial interrogation.[74] The Miranda Court characterized custodial interrogation as questioning initiated by law enforcement officers after a person has been taken into custody "or otherwise deprived of his freedom of action in any significant way."[75]

For Fifth Amendment privilege against compulsory self-incrimination to attach to statements made to an informant, that informant must be acting as the government's agent when the confession or statement is obtained. If an informant is acting on his own initiative when he obtains information, he is not a government agent. Therefore no Fifth Amendment privilege against compulsory self-incrimination is violated whether or not the confessing cellmate was Mirandized before making the incriminating statements.[76]

The Sixth Amendment guarantees that "In all criminal prosecutions, the accused shall enjoy the right ... to have the assistance of counsel for his defense."[77] The guarantee to counsel attaches only "at or after the time that adversary judicial proceedings have been initiated" against the defendant. The five stages at which "adversary proceedings" begin are upon (1) formal charge, (2) preliminary hearing, (3) indictment, (4) information, or (5) arraignment.[78] The Court explained that "the initiation of judicial criminal proceedings begins when the government has committed itself to prosecute, [for it is] only then that the adverse positions have solidified." Once a defendant's right to counsel has attached, law enforcement officials are prohibited from using an informant to deliberately elicit incriminating statements from that defendant.[79]

"[T]he defendant must demonstrate that the police and their informant took some action beyond their merely listening, that was designed deliberately to elicit incriminating remarks."[80] Merely planting an informant next to another inmate is not improper.[80] In *Kuhlmann,* the informant was placed with the defendant in order to find out the identity of the defendant's crime partners. The government already had positive evidence of the defendant's involvement.[80] When it is clear that a defendant's Sixth Amendment rights have attached, a jailhouse informant may gather information about an unrelated crime[81] or merely act as a listening post.[82]

The Grand Jury[70] also learned how the unfettered use of the jail telephones facilitated the gathering of information for use against other inmates. One informant demonstrated his skill for obtaining evidence by telephone, successfully impersonating a bail bondsman, a Deputy District Attorney, and a homicide detective.[70] In the course of his telephone calls, he collected enough details about a criminal case to fabricate a confession that would be believed by detectives.[70]

In exchange for providing evidence for the prosecution, informants expected significant benefits from the government. Based on this expectation, informants supplied information favorable to the prosecution, often irrespective of its truth.[70]

The Grand Jury[70] reported that the benefits to a jailhouse informant could range all the way from as little as added servings of food up to the ultimate reward, release from custody. According to an officer at the central jail, inmates who provided information about problems within the jail might have been rewarded with an extra phone call, visits, food, or access to a movie or television.[70] A former high-ranking official with the California Department of Corrections described:

> [Informants] want something, especially if you are that kind of a person and I don't know anybody that has ever come forward with information inside of a prison or criminal justice system that didn't want something for himself or for some friend of his.[70]

The Grand Jury findings determined that the Los Angeles Sheriff's Department failed to establish adequate procedures to control improper placement of inmates, with the foreseeable result that false claims of confessions or admissions would be made. It also found that the Los Angeles County District Attorney's Office failed to fulfill the ethical responsibilities required of a public prosecutor by its deliberate and informed declination to take the action necessary to curtail the misuse of jailhouse informant testimony.[70]

The prosecution has an affirmative duty to correct misleading testimony of its witness.[83] It also has a duty not to suppress evidence material to guilt or innocence.[84] When the reliability of a given witness may well be determinative of guilt or innocence, nondisclosure of evidence affecting credibility falls within the general rule of *Brady*.[84]

The Grand Jury also cited the American Bar Association (ABA) Disciplinary Rule[85] of the Model Code of Professional Responsibility as determinative of how the prosecutor's office should have proceeded.

> A public prosecutor or other government lawyer in criminal litigation shall make timely disclosure to counsel for the defendant, or to the defendant if he has no counsel, of the existence of evidence, known to the prosecutor or other government lawyer, that tends to negate the guilt of the accused, mitigate the degree of the offense, or reduce punishment.[85]

2.8 Furloughed Prisoners

Even one day away from a correctional institution can be a powerful motivating factor for an inmate. Jailhouse informants can obtain temporary release from prison through an investigative agency's request for an "inmate furlough." The practice occurs when an informant has demonstrated that he is of value in a proactive undercover investigation outside of the prison.

State and local police agencies utilize inmates as informants outside of their correctional facilities primarily on short-term investigations. The most common example is when the inmate is taken out of jail for several hours to make a "controlled buy" for purposes of obtaining a search warrant. Each jurisdiction's requirements for release vary depending upon state prison or local correctional institution policy or custom.

Federal agencies utilize furloughed inmates in complex undercover investigations. The practice is one that presents significant risks depending upon the freedom afforded the inmate upon release. The Bureau of Alcohol, Tobacco and Firearms has addressed that risk:

> In causing a Federal inmate to be furloughed, BATF (Bureau of Alcohol, Tobacco, and Firearms) assumes a great responsibility. Should the inmate or the general public experience personal injury and/or death while the inmate is our responsibility, liability may arise under the Federal Employees' Compensation Act or the Federal Tort Claims Act. There is also a tremendous potential for adverse publicity. Therefore, prudent decisions must be made when considering a request to cause the furlough of a Federal inmate. The end result of the investigation must justify the use of a furloughed inmate.[86]

The DEA requires the agent requesting the release of a prisoner to fulfill relatively little in terms of internal requirements. Its manual[87] closely follows the requirements of the *U.S. Attorney Manual* that requires the following for the utilization of federal prisoners in investigations.

All requests from investigative agencies to utilize federal prisoners (non-Witness Security participants) in investigations, when consensual monitoring devices, furloughs, or extraordinary transfers are necessary must be referred to the Office of Enforcement Operations for review and coordination with the Bureau of Prisons. This also applies to inmates in local halfway houses. The following information must accompany the request:

1. Name of prisoner and identifying data, including Bureau of Prisons register number, if known.

2.   Location of the prisoner.
3.   Necessity of utilizing the prisoner in the investigation.
4.   Name(s) of the target(s) of the investigation.
5.   Nature of the activity requested.
6.   Security measures to be taken to ensure the prisoner's safety, if necessary.
7.   Length of time the prisoner will be needed in the investigation.
8.   Whether the prisoner will be needed as a witness.
9.   Whether the prisoner will have to be moved to another institution upon completion of the activity.
10. Whether the prisoner will remain in the custody of the investigative agency or will be unguarded.

These requests must be endorsed by the appropriate investigative agency headquarters. Upon completion of the review, the Office of Enforcement Operations makes a recommendation to the Director of the Bureau of Prisons. The Office of Enforcement Operations then advises the requestor of the decision of the Bureau of Prisons.

In exigent circumstances, the Office of Enforcement Operations will accept requests and pertinent information by telephone. However, confirmation of the request and appropriate supporting information must be submitted as soon thereafter as possible. The information provided is held in the strictest confidence, and no dissemination of the information can be made without prior approval from the appropriate agency or office.[88]

2.9   Repentance

Repentance can be a motivating factor for cooperation. Informants often claim to cooperate in order to repent for past crimes. However, this is seldom their only motive for cooperating.[89] Fear of going to prison spurs many to claim repentance as their motive for volunteering to cooperate.

Informants and witnesses motivated by a guilty conscience often come forward with information about their own or other's criminal activity to atone for past "sins."[90] The skilled investigator can capitalize on the potential for repentance with individuals who otherwise would refuse to cooperate.[90]

One of the most publicized accounts of a repentant informant is that of former New York City Detective Robert Leuci, the "Prince of the City."[91] Detective Leuci became a valuable witness for the Knapp Commission's investigation into corruption within the New York City Police Department during the 1970s.

Many involved in the case claimed "the Knapp Commission had nothing on Leuci, but he didn't know it,"[91] inferring he came forward out of fear of punishment. Those close to Leuci believe he viewed himself as a good police officer who seemed to genuinely regret the misdeeds he committed while a detective.

The conversion of Detective Leuci from corrupt detective to cooperating government witness is credited to the skills of Nicholas Scoppetta, a Knapp Commission prosecutor and former assistant district attorney. Scoppetta was successful in recruiting the repentant detective. "If Leuci would cooperate, he could wipe his own slate clean."[92]

2.10 Excitement

Individuals motivated by a desire for excitement often view becoming an informant as an outlet for their fantasies. Police officers describe these informants as "007s" or suffering from the "James Bond Syndrome."[93]

The "007" is usually difficult to utilize and control. He may possess valuable information or criminal connections but is often detached from reality. Many of this type see themselves as characters from television, movies, or novels.

The "007" will dress as if in costume, attempting to look like a fictional character, purchase a fake police badge, false or official-appearing identification, and will carry a firearm. He is not beyond telling people that he works for the government. He may impersonate his agent handler by using the agent's business cards.

Obviously, all informant information must be questioned and corroborated. However, the "007's" information deserves even more attention. He may grossly exaggerate[94] his account of criminal activity or completely fabricate his information.

2.11 Police Buffs

The "police buff"[95] is motivated by a strong desire to be a police officer but for a variety of reasons is unable to enter the law enforcement profession. Many "buffs" are disqualified due to physical restrictions or lack of formal education. Some are unable to survive a background investigation due to a bad credit record, poor employment history, or an arrest record.

Many "police buffs" already have a successful civilian career but become bored. "Buffs" will often become the neighborhood crime watch captain or join community police organizations.

Although well intentioned, the "police buff" is generally not a productive informant. He is not involved in criminal activity and has little to offer a handler.

2.12   The Double Agent

The double agent, also known as the perversely motivated informant,[96] begins his relationship with law enforcement to further his own criminal ambitions.[96] In becoming an informant, it is his objective to learn how the agency conducts its investigations[96] and to identify its undercover agents, informants, and targets.

He may be using the police to eliminate his drug competitors. Criminal organizations have directed individuals to infiltrate a police department or agency as an informant to further their own criminal agenda. Bona fide information may be provided by the informant to divert attention away from their operation.[97]

2.13   Unwitting Informants

The unwitting informant is not motivated by a desire either to help the police or to improve his own situation. Instead, he is unwittingly passing along criminal intelligence information to law enforcement.

His involvement generally begins after being befriended by an undercover agent or an informant. This is usually not by accident. The unwitting informant has been identified as possessing information about targeted criminal activity. He may be a member of an ongoing conspiracy and have valuable information about the criminal enterprise.

Once the relationship with the unwitting informant is established, the undercover agent uses his refined skills as an interrogator to extract as much information from the source as possible. Obviously, this must be done without raising suspicion, often an extremely delicate and sometimes dangerous task.

The confidential informant usually capitalizes on a relationship that existed with the "unwitting" prior to his own involvement with the police. Very often, the informant will claim the information he obtains from the "unwitting" as his own, and the true source will remain unknown to the control agent.

Information obtained from an unwitting informant can be extremely reliable. He may be actively involved in the criminal venture he is discussing with the agent or informant and is relaying firsthand information about a crime that is still in the planning stage.

These are also statements that can be viewed as declarations against penal interests. They can carry an indicia of reliability absent in many other informant statements. All information received, however, must be corroborated by the agent to maximize its value to the investigation and ensure its reliability.[98]

2.14 Brokered Informants

Some defendants have nothing of value to offer the government in exchange for favorable consideration. This is usually determined by the government following a debriefing of the prospective informant. Others cannot cooperate with the government because of very real threats against themselves or members of their family. South American trafficking networks are notorious for taking revenge against informants and their families.

Individuals in both predicaments have become extremely resourceful. Some have resorted to recruiting family members, friends, or associates who can produce cases and become informants.

The defendant may also act as a middleman, receiving the information and passing it on to his agent handler for action. Some act as an intermediary and introduce the prospective informant to the agent for evaluation and utilization.

The brokered information or informant, if valuable, will garner the defendant favorable consideration at sentencing. The "proxy" informant, however, may receive nothing in return for his services.

The brokerage scheme, although resourceful, is still dangerous. One defendant in Miami "recruited" eight cooperating witnesses for the government. He and his brother were shot to death in retaliation. Four other people connected to the case were shot.[99]

The high-profile prosecution of General Manuel Noriega apparently relied upon the testimony of a brokered informant. *Newsweek* magazine reported that "a Cali Cartel lawyer offered Noriega's prosecutor a deal: if the Feds would cut the prison sentence of Cali trafficker Luis (Lucho) Santacruz-Echeverri (half brother of a Cali boss), the cartel would produce a witness to nail Noriega."[100] Without asking too many questions, the government agreed, and Lucho's sentence was cut by nine years. All sides understood the need for secrecy. It was later learned that the witness was paid $1.2 million by the cartel for his testimony. It was also learned that his alternative to testifying was not a lengthy prison sentence, it was a threat. In Mexico such an arrangement is referred to as a choice, "*entre la plata el plombo*," that is, "the choice is between silver and lead."[100]

References

1. *Cooperating Individual Management,* Office of Training, U.S. Drug Enforcement Administration.

2. Isikoff, M. and Thomas, E. The secret war, *Newsweek,* Feb. 9, 1998.

3. *United States v. Bernal-Obeso,* 989 F.2d 333 (9th Cir., 1993). *See United States v. Wallach,* 935 F.2d 445 (2nd Cir., 1991).

4. *United States v. Kinkle,* 631 F. Supp. 423. 425 (E.D. Pa., 1986).

5. Hernandez, R., Law officers try to handle informants with care, *El Paso Herald Post,* Aug. 23, 1997.

6. *Matthew* 26:15, 27:3–5.

7. William and Mary C.8.

8. Houston, G., *Thief-Taker General* (St. Martin's Press, 1970).

9. Blackstone, W., *Commentaries on the Laws of England,* Vol. 4, p. 325 (1765). *See* Langbein, J.H., Shaping the eighteenth-century criminal trial: a view from the Ryder Sources, *U. Chi. L. Rev.* 50(1), 106–114 (1983). *See also* Holdsworth, W., *A History of the English Law,* Vol. 13, p. 395 (1952).

10. *United States v. Shearer,* 794 F.2d 1545. 1549 (11th Cir., 1986).

11. *United States v. Murphy,* 41 U.S. (16 Pet.) 203 (1842); *United States v. Walker,* 720 F.2d 1527 (11th Cir., 1983); *United States v. Valle-Ferrer,* 739 F.2d 545 (11th Cir., 1984).

12. See King of the drugbusters, Andrew Murr, *Time* magazine, July 3, 2000, Informant Andrew Chambers paid $2.2 million by DEA. *See* Rampant use of informants in drug cases coming under fire, Mark Smith, *Houston Chronicle,* Aug. 6, 2000, U.S. Customs informant paid $2.2 million in money laundering case. *See also* Arrest may lead to FBI changes, Greg Krikorian, *Los Angeles Times,* April 11, 2003, FBI informant paid $1.7 million.

13. Green, F., Telling on cheats: how to profit by putting the IRS on the tax frauds trail, *San Diego Union-Tribune,* March 29, 1998, p. 11.

14. *United States v. Cervantes-Pacheco,* 826 F.2d 310 (5th Cir., 1987), overruling *Williamson v. United States,* 311 F.2d 441 (5th Cir., 1962). *See also United States v. Edenfield,* 995 F.2d 197 (11th Cir., 1993).

15. Messina, L., Criminals earn cash, beat rap by becoming drug informants, *Charleston Sunday Gazette–Mail,* May 10, 1998.

16. Informants and Undercover Investigations, Contingent-Fee Arrangements, Jan. 1992, p. 19, Department of Justice, Office of Justice Programs, Bureau of Justice Assistance.

17. *Wall Street Journal,* Sept. 22, 1995, p. 1.

18. Kelley, J., Saddam's sons killed in Iraq after raid, fierce firefight, *USA Today,* July 23, 2003.

19. Drug Informants: Motives, Methods and Management, FBI Law Enforcement Bull., Sept. 1993, p. 11.

20. Drug Informants: Motives, Methods and Management, FBI Law Enforcement Bull., Sept. 1993, p. 10.

21. *Cooperating Individual Management,* U.S. Department of Justice, DEA Office of Training, Quantico, VA.

22. U.S. Sentencing Guidelines § 5K1.1.

23. *United States v. Medina-Reyes,* 877 F. Supp. 468, 472 (S.D. Iowa, 1995).

24. 5 Anne C.31.

25. Miller, W., Lobbyist lashes out at Espy trial. Key U.S. witness claims prosecutor bullied him into cooperating, *Washington Post,* Oct. 31, 1998.

26. Shapley, T., Criminal charge will blow lid off FBI's Ruby Ridge cover-up, *Seattle Post Intelligencer,* Oct. 30, 1996.

27. U.S. Sentencing Guidelines.

28. *United States v. Brigham,* 977 F.2d 317, 320 (7th Cir., 1992).

29. *United States v. Brigham,* 977 F.2d 317, 317 (7th Cir., 1992).

30. *United States v. Medina-Reyes,* 877 F. Supp. 468, 473 (S.D. Iowa, 1995).

31. *United States v. Medina-Reyes,* 877 F. Supp. 468, 474 (S.D. Iowa, 1995).

32. *United States v. Kinkle,* 631 F. Supp. 423, 425 (ED. Pa., 1986).

33. *Pennsylvania Board of Probation & Parole v. Scott,* 118 S. Ct. 2014 (1998).

34. *Pennsylvania Board of Probation & Parole v. Scott,* 118 S. Ct. 2014, 475 (1998).

35. Lyons, D., Informant now charged with shakedown, *Miami Herald,* Aug. 19, 1997.

36. Fed. R. Crim. P. 35(b).

37. *United States v. Gebro,* 948 F.2d 1118, 1121 (9th Cir., 1991).

38. 18 USC § 3142(f).

39. 18 USC § 3142(e); *United States v. Medina,* 775 F.2d 1398, 1402 (11th Cir., 1985); *United States v. Fortna,* 769 F.2d 243, 250 (5th Cir., 1985); *United States v. Motamedi,* 767 F.2d 1403, 1406–07 (9th Cir., 1985); *United States v. Chimurenga,* 760 F.2d 400, 405–06 (2d Cir., 1985).

40. *Cooperating Individual Management,* U.S. Department of Justice, DEA Office of Training, Quantico, VA.

41. *Chambers v. Maroney,* 399 U.S. 42, 46–47 (1970); *Jaben v. United States,* 381 U.S. 214, 224 (1965).

42. *United States v. Cova,* 585 F. Supp. 1187 (ED. Mo., 1984).

43. *People v. Hetrick,* 590 N.Y.S.2d 183, 185–86, 604 N.E.2d 732 (N.Y., 1992).

44. *State v. Purser,* 828 P.2d 515, 517 (Utah App., 1992).

45. *Adams v. Williams,* 407 U.S. 143, 147, 92 5. Ct., 1921, 1924, 32 L. Ed 2d 612 (1972).

46. *Illinois v. Gates,* 462 U.S. 213, 241 (1983); *Draper v. United States,* 358 U.S. 307 (1959); *State v. Potter,* 860 P.2d 952 (Utah App., 1993).

47. *United States v. Alexander,* 559 F.2d 1339, 1344 (5th Cir., 1977); *McCray v. Illinois,* 386 U.S. 300, 87 5. Ct. 1056, 18 L. Ed. 2d 62 (1967); *Bourbois v. United States,* 530 F.2d 3 (5th Cir., 1976); *Jones v. United States,* 362 U.S. 257, 271, 80 5. Ct. 725, 735 (1960).

48. *Adams v. Williams,* 407 U.S. 143 (1972).

49. *Davis v. State,* 447 S.E.2d 68, 70 (Ga. Ct. App., 1994); *Rynearson v. State,* 950 P.2d 147, 150–52 (Alaska Ct. App., 1997).

50. *Illinois v. Gates,* 462 U.S. 213, 103 5. Ct. 2317, 2330 (1983).

51. *United States v. Cangiano,* 464 F.2d 320 (2nd Cir., 1972).

52. *United States v. Reed,* 810 F. Supp. 1078, 1080 (9th Cir., 1992).

53. *United States v. Ortiz,* 714 F. Supp. 1569 (C.D. Cal, 1989).

54. Hoffman, L., Be on terror alert, Americans urged, *Seattle Post Intelligencer,* May 20, 2003.

55. *United States v. Pierce,* 893 F.2d 669 (5th Cir., 1990); *United States v. Blackwell,* 127 F.3d 947 (10th Cir., 1997).

56. *United States v. Edwards,* 602 F.2d 458 (1st Cir., 1979).

57. *United States v. Sanders,* 592 F.2d 788 (5th Cir., 1979), *rev'd,* 447 U.S. 649, 100 5. Ct. 2395 (1980); *Burdeau v. McDowell,* 256 U.S. 465, 41 5. Ct. 574, 65 L. Ed. 1048 (1921); *United States v. Lamar,* 545 F.2d 488 (5th Cir., 1977); *United States v. Blanton,* 479 F.2d 327 (5th Cir., 1973); *Barnes v. United States,* 373 F.2d 517 (5th Cir., 1967).

58. *United States v. Gomez,* 614 F.2d 643 (9th Cir., 1979).

59. *Walther v. United States,* 447 U.S. 649, 100 5. Ct. 2395, 65 L. Ed. 2d 410, 417 (1980).

60. *Corngold v. United States,* 367 F.2d 1 (9th Cir., 1966) (en banc).

61. *United States v. Gumerlock,* 590 F.2d 794, 800 (9th Cir.) (en banc), *cert. denied,* 441 U.S. 948, 99 5. Ct. 2173, 60 L. Ed. 2d 1052 (1979).

62. *United States v. Sherwin,* 539 F.2d 1 (9th Cir., 1976) (en banc).

63. *United States v. Walther,* 652 F.2d 788 (9th Cir., 1981).

64. *United States v. Walther,* 652 F.2d 793 (9th Cir., 1981).

65. *United States v. Valen,* 479 F.2d 467 (3rd Cir., 1973), *cert. denied,* 419 U.S. 901 (1974).

66. *DEA Agents Manual,* Ch. 66.

67. McClintick, D., *Swordfish* 7, Random House, New York (1993).

68. Stead, P.J., *The Police of Paris,* Staples Press Ltd., London (1957); Stead, *Vidocq, Picaroon of Crime,* Roy Publishers.

69. *Illinois v. Perkins,* 196 U.S. 292, 110 S. Ct. 2394, 2397 (1990).

70. Investigation of the Involvement of Jail House Informants in the Criminal Justice System in Los Angeles County, Los Angeles County Grand Jury, June 26, 1990.

71. California Penal Code § 1127(a).

72. Barry Tarlow, Silence may not be golden: jailhouse informers and the right to counsel, *Champion Magazine,* May 2005.

73. U.S. Constitution, Amendment V.

74. *Miranda v. Arizona,* 384 U.S. 436, 469, 86 S. Ct. 1602, 1625, 16 L. Ed. 2d 694 (1966).

75. 384 U.S. at 477, 86 S. Ct. at 1629.

76. *United States v. Pace,* 833 F.2d 1307 (9th Cir., 1987), *cert. denied,* 486 U.S.1011, 1988). *Followed* 958 F.2d 268 (9th Cir., 1992).

77. U.S. Constitution, Amendment VI.

78. *Kirby v. Illinois,* 406 U.S. 682, 689, 92 S. Ct. 1877 (1972).

79. *Massiah v. United States,* 377 U.S. 201 (1964); *United States v. Henry,* 447 U.S. 264, 269–270, 100 S. Ct. 2183, 65 L. Ed. 2d 115 (1980); *Maine v. Moulton,* 474 U.S. 159, 106 S. Ct. 477, 88 L. Ed. 2d 481 (1985); *Kuhlmann v. Wilson,* 477 U.S. 436, 106 S. Ct. 2616, 91 L. Ed. 2d 364 (1986).

80. *Kuhlmann,* 477 U.S. at 459, 106 S. Ct. at 2630.

81. *Hoffa v. United States,* 385 U.S. 293 (1966).

82. *Kuhlmann v. Wilson,* 477 U.S. 436, 107 S. Ct. 2616, 91 L. Ed. 2d 364 (1986).

83. *Napue v. Illinois,* 360 U.S. 264, 79 S. Ct. 1173, 3 L. Ed. 2d 1217 (1959); *Giglio v. United States,* 405 U.S. 150, 154, 92 S. Ct. 763, 766, 31 L. Ed. 2d 104 (1972).

84. *Brady v. Maryland,* 373 U.S. 83, 87, 83 S. Ct. 1194, 10 L. Ed. 215 (1963).

85. ABA Disciplinary Rules, Model Code of Professional Responsibility § 7-103.

86. BATF Manual: *Investigative Priorities, Procedures, and Techniques,* Ch. 41, p. 28.

87. *DEA Agents Manual,* Ch. 66.

88. *U.S. Attorneys Manual 9.*

89. Drug Informants: Motives, Methods and Management, FBI Law Enforcement Bull., Sept. 1993, p. 11.

90. Michele Orecklin, Oh, my God! Get Martha on the phone, *Time* magazine, Feb. 16, 2004.

91. Daly, R., *Prince of the City, The True Story of a Cop Who Knew Too Much,* Houghton Mifflin Co., Boston (1978), p. 10.

92. Dershowitz, A.M., *The Best Defense,* Random House, New York (1982), p. 324.

93. Fitzgerald, D.G., Snitches, narcs and making cases, *Champion Magazine,* Dec. 1995, pp. 11, 15.

94. Fitzgerald, D.G., Snitches, narcs and making cases, *Champion Magazine,* Dec. 1995, p. 15.

95. Fitzgerald, D. and Smith, G., Informants: handle with care, *NarcOfficer Magazine,* March/April 1995, p. 49.

96. *Informant Interaction,* U.S. Department of Justice, DEA. *See* Report shows FBI missed Chinese spy, Mark Sherman, *Associated Press,* May 24, 2006.

97. FBI Law Enforcement Bull., Sept. 1993, p. 11.

98. *Henley v. United States,* 406 F.2d 705, 706 (5th Cir., 1969).

99. Slain informant recruited drug-case witnesses, *Miami Herald,* June 25, 1993, p. B1. *See United States v. Nichols,* 606 F.2d 566, 569 (5th Cir., 1979).

100. Katel, P., A deal with the devil: did Feds use the Cali Cartel to get Noriega? *Newsweek,* Oct. 30, 1995, p. 59.

Recruiting Informants

3

3.1 Ruby Ridge

Some readers may not recall the tragic incident that occurred more than a decade ago in rural Ruby Ridge, Idaho. It is recounted here to demonstrate how attempts to recruit unsuitable individuals as informants can yield devastating results.

The chain of events leading to what became known as the "Siege at Ruby Ridge" began as a failed attempt to recruit Randall Weaver as an informant for the Bureau of Alcohol, Tobacco, and Firearms (BATF). Having first come to the attention of the U.S. Secret Service in 1985, Weaver was believed to have ties to the Aryan Nations, a white supremacist group. He also was suspected of having a large cache of illegal weapons and ammunition hidden at his mountaintop home.[1]

In October 1989, at the direction of BATF agents, an informant purchased two "sawed-off" shotguns from Weaver. The sale was secretly recorded by the confidential informant (CI). The BATF now had a chargeable offense to use as leverage in their recruitment of Weaver as an informant.[2]

In June 1990, BATF agents, without having obtained an indictment, arranged for a "chance meeting" with Weaver outside a Sandpoint, Idaho motel. Showing him photographs of the sawed-off shotguns and giving him the opportunity to listen to a tape recording of the sale, he was offered a deal: inform on the Aryan Nations and his cooperation would be brought to the attention of the U.S. Attorney.[3]

Weaver declined their offer, refusing to become an informant. On December 13, 1990, six months after the failed recruitment effort, he was indicted for manufacturing and possessing an unregistered firearm.[3]

Attempts to arrest Weaver in August 1992 resulted in a weeklong siege of his residence that was known as the "Siege at Ruby Ridge." Weaver's son was shot and killed by a deputy U.S. Marshal. Weaver's wife was shot and killed by an FBI (Federal Bureau of Investigation) sniper. Weaver and a visiting friend were seriously wounded by sniper fire.

Weaver was acquitted by a jury of the firearms charges. The government awarded the Weaver family $3.1 million in an out-of-court settlement.

3.2 Factors in Recruiting

Three factors have dramatically affected the methods used to either recruit or induce an individual to become an informant.

1. The amount of money available to pay informants.[4]
2. The U.S. Sentencing Guidelines (U.S.S.G.) and state sentencing initiatives.[5]
3. The Witness Security Program and the ability to protect witnesses and informants from harm.[6]

The amount of money paid to informants has turned informing into a cottage industry. Asset-specific seizures can result in awards to informants of 25% of the amount realized by the government, not to exceed $250,000 per incident.[7] Awards are also available from the Department of Justice Asset Forfeiture Fund for information pertaining to violations of federal law. Federal agencies also have their own budgets for the purchase of information. Drug Enforcement Administration (DEA) agents, for example, can pay informants as much as $25,000 per quarter from their operating funds for participation in investigations.[8] Provisions are in place to grant larger payments, but agency headquarters approval is necessary.

Federal criminal defendants of the 1970s and early 1980s had little reason to become informants. First offenders and those accused of less serious crimes including drug offenses could receive probation or a sentence of several years, depending on the judges' sentencing practices. The U.S. Parole Commission could be expected to reduce that sentence by at least 50%. A defendant could "do his time" and return to the street with his criminal reputation intact, never having become a "snitch." Some defendants did become informants, usually those afraid to do even one day in jail. Others "rolled" only after skillful recruiting efforts by experienced and persevering agents.

The entire landscape of federal law enforcement and informing changed dramatically with the Sentencing Reform Act of 1984.[9] The "Act" created the U.S. Sentencing Commission, a nine-member panel mandated to create uniformity in sentencing applicable to all federal crimes. That goal was achieved through their creation of the Federal Sentencing Guideline System and limiting the sentencing discretion of the sentencing judges.[10]

The U.S. Sentencing Guidelines (U.S.S.G)[11] and 18 USC § 3553[11] provide for sentences below the minimum mandatory in exchange for a defendant's substantial assistance in the investigation and prosecution of another criminal. Together they appear to have provided federal agents with a nearly inexhaustible source of informants to draw upon.

Today a federal defendant knows what his sentence range will be during his first meeting with defense counsel. Indeed, the arresting agent, in an attempt to "recruit" a defendant informant, has probably detailed a vivid account of what a future in prison holds and for how much time the Guidelines' sentencing tables say the defendant will be incarcerated.

The Bureau of Justice Statistics tracked the average sentences in federal drug cases from 1980 to 2003. The dramatic increase serves as an incentive for a defendant to respond positively to an "informant recruitment drive."

Table 3.1

Year	Average Sentence
1980	54.5 months
2003	80.2 months[12]

The Witness Security Program has given federal prosecutors the ability to promise "lifetime protection in exchange for truthful testimony."[13] Those who would otherwise fear coming forward as a witness can be assured of the government's commitment to protecting them from harm.[14]

3.3 Arrested Defendants

Offering an arrested individual the opportunity to cooperate and mitigate his situation is the technique most frequently used to recruit an informant.[15] It offers the potential CI an opportunity to dramatically improve his situation and acts as a powerful motivation for him to provide substantial assistance to police.[16] Severe minimum mandatory sentences imposed for federal crimes have made this recruitment technique even more effective than in the past.

If the arrest of the defendant was designed to recruit the individual as an informant,[17] the incident should have taken place discretely and without fanfare. If not, word of his arrest will have spread quickly "on the street." Once booked into jail, his value to the agents as an informant may rapidly diminish. His criminal associates will quickly learn of the defendant's arrest, usually through bail bondsmen, defense attorneys, or jail personnel. The information is not necessarily spread with a corrupt motive but can be little more than courthouse gossip. The news of the arrest can be extremely damaging to the value of the defendant as an informant.

The first attempt to recruit the individual occurs during the postarrest interview, commonly referred to as an interrogation. The interview occurs shortly after the arrest. The defendant is unnerved, confused, frightened, angry, or experiencing a combination of these emotions. Of greatest importance to the agent, however, is that the individual is probably not yet represented by counsel. This is the period when most defendant informants are recruited.

One informant recruited in this fashion described the method used to persuade him to cooperate. He recounted being told by agents that "There was a red, white, and blue bus coming down the road and there was one seat left on it, and if I didn't get on it, it would run me over."[18]

The decision to offer cooperation as an option during an investigation should never be made without the consent of the prosecutor.[19] At the federal level, law enforcement agencies are encouraged to work closely with the U.S. Attorney Office from the early stages of an investigation.[20]

The DEA, for example, requires the following during the recruiting and development of a defendant or criminal informant:

1. The approval of the appropriate prosecutor (i.e., federal, state, or local) will be obtained *prior* to seeking the cooperation of a defendant.
2. A defendant may be advised that his cooperation will be brought to the attention of the appropriate prosecutor. No further representations or assurances may be given without approval by the SAC (Special Agent in Charge). The prosecuting attorney shall have sole authority to decide whether or not to prosecute a case against a defendant/informant.
3. The appropriate prosecutor shall be advised of the nature and scope of the defendant's cooperation throughout the period of his use. The procedures and frequency of this reporting shall be set by the prosecutor.[21]

Each State Attorney or State Attorney General promulgates their own policy. Although federal courts have recognized that prosecutors have a responsibility to perform investigative as well as courtroom-related duties in criminal matters,[22] the prosecutor should rely heavily upon the experience of the investigator during this period of recruitment. Many prosecutors are poorly prepared to deal with experienced criminals as they negotiate their fate as an informant.

The defendant may or may not be "Mirandized" during the interview. It is a judgment often made solely by the investigator. However, once a suspect invokes his right to have counsel present during a custodial interrogation, all questioning must cease until counsel is present.[23] This right is derived from the Fifth Amendment's privilege against self-incrimination, and may of course be waived.[23] The government bears the burden of proving by a preponderance of the evidence that the defendant knowingly and voluntarily waived this right.[24] The voluntariness of a waiver depends on the absence of police overreaching; that is, the relinquishment of the right must have been the result of a free and deliberate choice rather than intimidation, coercion, or deception.[25] In determining whether a valid waiver is made, a trial court will look at the totality of the circumstances in each case, including the background, experience, and conduct of the accused.[26] Streetwise individuals may refuse to cooperate without the advice of counsel. The demand for an attorney can either derail the recruitment effort or actually facilitate the decision to cooperate.

Many defense attorneys recognize that the U.S. Sentencing Guidelines were designed in part to force criminal defendants to cooperate with law enforcement in exchange for charges being dropped or for lighter sentences. After evaluating the severity of the case against their client, the attorney may encourage cooperation and should participate in drafting the cooperation agreement. Those who refuse to cooperate are dealt with harshly.[27]

Some defense attorneys have firm policies against allowing or encouraging their clients to become informants. They view it as a "dirty business"[28] and have ethical objections to the practice.[29] However, the American Bar Association (ABA) Model Code of Profession Responsibility, EC-7-7 provides that "A defense lawyer in a criminal case has the duty to advise his client fully on whether a particular plea to a charge appears to be desirable." New York's Code of Professional Responsibility has similar provisions regarding plea bargaining.

Once the defendant has an attorney, further attempts to recruit him should be closely examined.[30] Regardless of the competency of the prospective informant's counsel, his involvement in the case triggers the potential for Fifth and Sixth Amendment violations and potential ethical dilemmas for the prosecutor. A distinct set of constitutional safeguards aimed at preserving the sanctity of the attorney–client relationship take effect.[31]

The prevailing view is that, once represented, neither police nor the prosecutor should have contact with the defendant without his attorney present.[32] Courts have been concerned that the Sixth Amendment guarantee of counsel would be rendered meaningless if the prosecutor under the guise of pursuing a criminal investigation circumvented one of its critical components, the attorney–client relationship "characterized by trust and confidence."[33] The federal courts can enforce professional responsibility standards pursuant to their general supervisory authority over members of the bar.[34]

A great deal of confusion had surrounded the issue regarding contact with represented persons by Assistant U.S. Attorneys and federal agents. On March 1, 1994, Attorney General Janet Reno issued a three-page memorandum to all U.S. Attorneys and Division Heads regarding the subject and proposed regulations.[35] The memorandum did not resolve the issue. It was not resolved until Congress passed the McDade Amendment (signed into law on October 21, 1998) that placed new restrictions on the conduct of federal prosecutors and the law enforcement officers who work for them. It requires them to conform to and be subject to state laws and rules and local federal court rules governing attorneys in each state where the prosecutor engages in his duties.

The ABA's Model Rule of Professional Conduct 4.2[36] prohibits communication with a witness about the particular matter on which he is being represented without the consent of his counsel. Many states have similar ethical standards for their attorneys. For example, in the California Bar's Rules for Professional Conduct, Rule 2-100 tracks the language of the ABA Rule 4.2.[36] Thus, beginning upon the moment of indictment at the latest, a prosecuting attorney has a duty under ethical rules such as 2-100 to refrain from communicating with represented defendants.[37]

Criminals who become informants should only be allowed to work up the ladder of a criminal organization. Agreements should only be made with underlings to get bosses, not bosses to get underlings. However, the opposite is often the case.

Sophisticated criminal enterprises operate in a compartmentalized fashion that often insulates decision makers from "soldiers." It is a sound management practice in a business that has historically been attacked from within via informants. This creates a dilemma for the lower-level criminal that is anxious to cooperate. He has no one to "give up." Recruiting an individual occupying such a role serves little purpose.

Those with nothing to exchange for lighter sentences can find themselves receiving more severe sentences than their bosses. In *United States v. Brigham*,[38] the least culpable defendant received a 10-year minimum mandatory sentence, while the more significant violators received less time.

> Bold dealers may turn on their former comrades, setting up phony sales and testifying at ensuing trials. Timorous dealers may provide information about their courses and customers. Drones of the organization — the runners, mules, drivers and lookouts — having nothing comparable to offer. They lack the contacts and trust necessary to set up big deals, and they know little information of

value. Whatever tales they have to tell, their bosses will have related. Defendants, unlucky enough to be innocent have no information at all ... the more serious the defendant's crimes, the lower the sentence — because the greater his wrongs, the more information and assistance he has to offer to a prosecutor.[39]

3.3.1 Deportation and Cooperation

Police and prosecutors seeking the cooperation of an arrested undocumented alien can use the threat of deportation and the reward of an S-visa as leverage in their recruitment effort. On the street, S-visas are referred to as snitch visas.

For an alien, a conviction will result in deportation if it meets the immigration law's definition of "aggravated felony."[40] However, this definition is very broad. While in the past it covered only a few crimes, such as murder and drug trafficking, it now covers dozens of crimes including some that are misdemeanors under state law. The list includes:

- A "crime of violence" with a one-year prison sentence (which has been interpreted broadly to include drunk driving felonies).[41]
- Theft with a one-year prison sentence.
- A drug sale crime, including possession for sale.
- A second conviction for mere possession of drugs.
- Fraud or tax evasion where the loss to the victim or government exceeds $10,000.
- Perjury with a one-year sentence.
- Sexual abuse of a minor.

Intervention on behalf of the alien by the recruiting agent is often the only chance remaining for the prospective informant. Absent that intervention, mandatory deportation for life will result.[42]

In return for cooperation, the government can offer to apply for an S-5 or S-6 visa that will allow the informant to remain in the United States for as long as 3 years. To qualify for an S-5 visa, the requesting law enforcement agency must demonstrate that:

- The alien is in possession of critical reliable information concerning a criminal organization or enterprise.
- The alien is willing to supply information to federal or state law enforcement authorities or a federal or state court.
- And the alien's presence in the United States the Attorney General determines is essential to the success of an authorized criminal investigation or the successful prosecution of an individual involved in the criminal organization or enterprise.[43]

The requesting law enforcement agency directs their request to the Assistant Attorney General for the U.S. Department of Justice's Criminal Division for review. If approved, the request is forwarded using a form I-854.[44]

Upon approval, the alien is classified as an S-5 alien witness or informant.[44,45] If the alien's cooperation proves to be critical to the success of an investigation,[46] the government can also apply for permanent residence for their informant.[47] Both the 3-year admittance and permanent residence status can also be given to the alien's spouse, children, and parents.[48]

To qualify for an S-6 visa, both the Attorney General and the Secretary of State must determine that the person:

- Possesses reliable information regarding an important aspect of a terrorist organization or plot.
- Is willing to share this information with law enforcement officials or to testify in court.
- Has or will be placed in danger for providing that information.
- Is eligible to receive an award from the State Department for providing such information.

At this writing, only 200 people may be admitted under the S-5 status each year, and only 50 may be admitted under S-6 status. From 1995 through 2004, 511 informants and 322 family members were admitted under the S-visa category.

3.4 Old Cases

Federal agencies encourage agents in search of new informants to examine old or closed cases.[49] Interviewing an incarcerated defendant can either yield a new investigation or lead to the indictment of additional defendants in the closed case.

Often referred to as historical cases, the task of examining closed cases is usually left to new agents without informants. Agents who are not producing new cases or have been unsuccessful in recruiting new informants are also directed by their supervisors to review closed cases for new informants. Defendants already serving time for their participation in the conspiracy ordinarily will no longer have a valid privilege to refuse to testify.[50]

Prisoners serving their sentences and wishing to become informants often contact agents. Those defendants who rejected the offer to provide substantial assistance at the time of their arrest or pending trial often have a change of heart after beginning to serve their sentence. In prison, the term "getting on the bus" for a trip to court [to testify] is a frequent topic among inmates hoping for a "Get out of jail free card."[19]

The inmate will generally offer the substantial assistance originally sought by agents at the time of his arrest.[51] He already knows what they want to hear and is only prepared to volunteer that information. Many provide new information concerning criminal activity they hope agents will find valuable.[52]

In exchange, the government will file a motion pursuant to the Federal Rules of Criminal Procedure for Changed Circumstances.[52] The court, on motion of the government made within one year after the imposition of the sentence, may reduce a sentence to reflect a defendant's subsequent substantial assistance in an investigation or prosecution of another person. The motion may be made after one year if the substantial assistance involves information or evidence unknown to the defendant until one year or more after his sentence was imposed.[52]

Inmates who do not come forward but whose cooperation is sought may continue to be the target of recruitment efforts by agents. The agents may believe the prisoner could provide testimony that will lead to the arrests of significant members of his criminal organization. They will pressure him with the threat of further prosecution if he refuses to cooperate.[53] According to one inmate, "They made me an offer I couldn't refuse," the informant wrote in a letter to a friend. "Are you with us or against us? I imagined another indictment for racketeering, or organized crime, with a minimum of life, which means 25 years or more, and me without a lawyer, broke and more cooked than fish in a pan, in other words, fried."[19]

3.5 "Immunity" and Compelled Testimony

The U.S. Attorney can also compel a witness to testify or provide other information regardless of their assertion of the Fifth Amendment[54] privilege against compulsory self-incrimination.[55] The method is reserved for those persons who have either refused or who are likely to refuse to cooperate based upon that privilege.[56] At trial, compelled testimony may provide a tactical advantage to the prosecution. The witness's testimony is forced from him, not bargained for. Defense efforts to portray the witness as a person who has "cut a deal" with the government will have little credibility when presented to a jury.

Prosecutors obtain immunity for witnesses either pursuant to the federal immunity statute[57] or by an agreement. It is helpful to keep this in mind to avoid becoming confused by a number of other terms frequently used to describe immunity, such as formal, informal, use, transactional, letter, desk, pocket, and act-of-production immunity.[58]

Prior to obtaining a compulsion order, the attorney for the government should weigh all relevant considerations including:

- The importance of the investigation or prosecution to effective enforcement of the criminal laws.
- The value of the person's testimony or information to the investigation or prosecution.
- The likelihood of prompt and full compliance with a compulsion order, and the effectiveness of available sanctions if there is no such compliance.
- The person's relative culpability in connection with the offense or offenses being investigated or prosecuted, and his or her criminal history.
- The possibility of successfully prosecuting the person prior to compelling his or her testimony.
- The likelihood of adverse collateral consequences to the person if he or she testifies or provides information under a compulsion order.[59]

The U.S. Attorney must obtain authorization from the Assistant Attorney General for the Criminal Division or the Assistant Attorney General for the division with responsibility for the subject matter of the case.[59]

A witness who refuses to testify or to produce information following the issuance of an order of compulsion[60] may be found in either civil contempt[61] or criminal contempt.[62] The Supreme Court in *United States v. Wilson*[63] advised against resorting to criminal sanctions before attempting to effect compliance to the order through the imposition of civil contempt. "The judge should resort to criminal sanctions only after he determines for good reason, that the civil remedy would be inappropriate."[63,64]

Section 1826 of Title 28, a codification of existing practices, was enacted in 1970 to provide a statutory basis for the application of summary civil contempt powers to recalcitrant witnesses. The purpose of the statute is to secure the testimony or other evidence before a grand jury through the creation of an incentive for compliance, not to punish the witness by imprisonment. When the witness complies with the order, he must be released. Thus, confinement is limited to the life of the court proceeding or the term of the grand jury, but in no event may the confinement exceed 18 months.[65]

The witness is not incarcerated immediately upon his refusal to testify before the grand jury.[66] Following his refusal to testify, he must be brought before a judge and ordered to testify. If he again refuses to comply with the order, he is incarcerated.[67] The swiftness and certainty of the sanction is in recognition of the need to obtain the testimony of the witness.[68]

The Supreme Court in *United States v. Wilson*[69] distinguished the refusal of a witness to testify before a grand jury and a witness's refusal to testify at trial. At a grand jury the proceeding can be interrupted while the witness is afforded notice and a hearing under Rule 42(b).

When a witness refuses to testify at trial there is a need for a swift decision. According to the *Wilson* court, "The face to face refusal to comply with the court's order itself constituted an affront to the Court, and when that kind of refusal disrupts and frustrates an ongoing proceeding summary contempt must be available to provide the recalcitrant witness with some incentive to testify."[70] "Where time is not of the essence, however, the provisions of Rule 42(b) may be more appropriate to deal with contemptuous conduct."[71]

Title 18 USC § 401 and Rule 42 of the Federal Rules of Criminal Procedure provide for criminal contempt punishable by fine *or* imprisonment. Courts may not impose both a fine and imprisonment, nor a fine and probation.[72] Case law limits summary punishment under Rule 42(a)[73]; there is no maximum set for punishing criminal contempt after notice and hearing under Rule 42(b).[74]

Individuals already serving a prison sentence are not immune to the criminal penalties for contempt. If they refuse to testify following a compulsion order their sentence may be interrupted while they serve their intervening sentence for contempt.[75]

3.6 Negotiated Plea Agreements

A negotiated plea agreement can be a powerful tool in the effort to recruit a defendant for cooperation with law enforcement. Used in state and federal prosecutions, the Federal Rules of Criminal Procedure[76] have recognized and codified the concept of plea bargaining in federal cases.

In return for a defendant's plea of guilty or *nolo contendere* to a charged offense or to a lesser or related offense, the Assistant U.S. Attorney can offer one or more of the following options[76,77]:

- Dismissal of charges.
- The prosecutor may make a recommendation or an agreement not to oppose the defendant's request for a particular sentence with the understanding that such recommendation or request is not binding upon the court.
- The prosecutor will agree that a specific sentence is the appropriate disposition of the case.

There are additional options open to the prosecutor and defendant in the plea bargaining process. In exchange for the plea of guilty or *nolo contendere*, the prosecutor can agree to not bring additional charges against the defendant or a third party.[78] The third party receiving consideration is usually a family member,[79] a paramour, or a close associate. Moreover, although not explicitly stating so, Rule 11(e) does contemplate that the plea agreement may require that the defendant further cooperate with the prosecution in another case or in another investigation.[79,80]

To maintain the secrecy of a defendant informant's cooperation resulting from a plea agreement, on a showing of good cause the plea can be taken in camera.[81] Rule 11(e)(2) does not address itself to whether the showing of good cause for an in camera hearing must be made in open court and is left for the courts to address on a case-by-case basis.[82]

Plea bargaining is not mandatory, and the court is free to disallow the plea agreement. If the court rejects the agreement, the rejection must be made on the record or in camera.[83] The court must allow the defendant to withdraw his plea.

Rule 11(e) bars the use in evidence of the following (with exceptions) in any civil or criminal proceeding against the person who made them: (1) a plea of guilty which was later withdrawn; (2) a plea of *nolo contendere*; (3) any statement made in the course of any proceeding under Rule 11 regarding a plea of guilty or *nolo contendere*; and (4) any statement made in the course of plea discussions with an attorney for the government which discussions do not result in a plea of guilty or result in a plea of guilty later withdrawn. Such evidence is admissible, however, in any proceeding wherein another statement made in the course of the same plea or plea discussions has been introduced and the statement ought in fairness to be considered contemporaneously with it, or in a criminal proceeding for perjury or false statement if the statement was made by the defendant under oath, on the record, and in the presence of counsel.[83]

3.7 Nonprosecution Agreements

When all other efforts to recruit a targeted individual as an informant have failed, the prosecution is left with one final option: entering into a nonprosecution agreement in exchange for the individual's cooperation.[84] Although the cooperation or testimony of a person implicated in the criminal case being investigated or prosecuted is extremely valuable, the tactic should be employed when all other recruiting techniques have failed. Nonprosecution agreements are considered only when the individual whose cooperation is sought is subject to prosecution.[84] Factors to be considered are the importance of the case, the expected value of the cooperation sought, and the relative culpability and criminal history of the individual.

Reasons for considering nonprosecution agreements vary, but usually fall into one of four categories:

1. There may be no effective means of obtaining the person's timely cooperation short of entering into a nonprosecution agreement.
2. The person may be unwilling to cooperate fully in return for a reduction of charges.
3. The delay in bringing the person to trial might jeopardize the investigation or prosecution of the case in which his cooperation is sought.
4. It is impossible or impractical to rely on the statutory provisions for compulsion of testimony or the production of evidence.[84]

Two examples illustrate the need for considering a nonprosecution agreement. The cooperation sought from the individual is assistance in an ongoing investigation. Although his testimony may one day be needed, his value to the government is in developing evidence in a proactive manner under the direction of the government.[84] Time-sensitive cases involving the statute of limitations, the Speedy Trial Act, or the need to bring evidence to the grand jury may not permit a timely application for a court order to compel testimony.[84]

In entering into a nonprosecution agreement, the attorney for the government should, if practicable, explicitly limit the scope of the government's commitment to:

- Nonprosecution based directly or indirectly on the testimony or other information provided; or[84]
- Nonprosecution within his or her district with respect to a pending charge or to a specific offense then known to have been committed by the person.[85]

The attorney for the government should exercise extreme caution to ensure that his nonprosecution agreement does not confer "blanket" immunity on the witness. He should attempt to limit his agreement to nonprosecution based on the testimony or information provided. Such an "informal use immunity"[86] agreement has advantages over an agreement not to prosecute on the basis of independently obtained evidence if it later appears that the person's criminal involvement was more serious than it originally appeared to be; second, it encourages the witness to be as forthright as possible, since the more he reveals the more protection he will have against a future prosecution. To further encourage full disclosure by the witness, it should be made clear in the agreement that the government's decision to not prosecute is conditioned upon the witness's testimony or production of information being complete and truthful and that failure to testify truthfully[87] may result in a perjury prosecution.[88]

Even if it is not practicable to obtain the desired cooperation pursuant to an "informal use immunity" agreement, the attorney for the government should attempt to limit the scope of the agreement in terms of the testimony and transactions covered, bearing in mind the possible effect of his agreement on prosecutions in other districts.[88]

3.7.1   Prosecution after the Entry of an Immunity Order

A witness who has provided testimony at a grand jury or trial pursuant to a court ordered grant of immunity, or pursuant to a promise of informal use immunity, or any state investigation pursuant to a state grant of immunity, may nonetheless be prosecuted, even for a crime about which the witness testified. If the prosecution of such a witness is undertaken, the defendant likely will claim that his testimony was used against him. The government will then be required to prove affirmatively that it did not use the witness's immunized testimony against the witness, for example, as direct evidence of the witness's involvement; and that it did not use information directly or indirectly derived from the testimony, for example, as a lead to developing evidence against the witness or in focusing the investigation on the witness.[88]

3.7.2   Use of Immunized Testimony in a Perjury or False Statement Prosecution

The immunity statute does not protect the witness from a prosecution for perjury[89] or false statements to the grand jury or court.[90] The untruthful statements, which form the basis of the indictment, may be used against the witness in the perjury or false statement prosecution.[91] In addition, uncharged statements in the immunized testimony of the witness may be used, for instance, to place the charged statements in context. "Neither the immunity statute nor the Fifth Amendment precludes the use of [the witness's] immunized testimony at a subsequent prosecution for making false statements, so long as that testimony conforms to otherwise applicable rules of evidence."[92] The immunity statute may not protect a witness who "otherwise fails to comply with the order of immunity." As an example, a witness who testified falsely, both to the grand jury and at trial, under a grant of immunity was charged with not only false statements, but a conspiracy to obstruct justice and to give false testimony. The court upheld the conspiracy count, stating that "the sweep of the exception against the use of immunized testimony extends to any conduct aimed at frustrating the purpose of the grant of immunity."[93]

3.8 Other Recruiting Strategies

Investigators often employ creative recruiting strategies for individuals not subject to arrest. The agent usually already knows that the prospective informant is either a member of a criminal organization or is an associate of a criminal targeted for investigation. As a result of intelligence information received from informants or as a judgment based upon experience, the investigator believes that with the correct amount of pressure, the person can be convinced to become an informant.[94] The pressure may take the form of either a hint of a pending arrest or the very direct threat of prosecution for a crime. While it may be either a real or contrived case, the suspect does not know the extent of his exposure to prosecution. Agents may even offer to back off from their investigation into the prospective informant's own criminal operation.[94]

The method selected for exerting the pressure varies and is limited only by the imagination, experience, and skill of the investigator. Generally, it will take the form of a "chance" encounter on the street, an unannounced visit to the target's home or workplace, or by requesting the individual to come to the investigator's office. Occasionally the contact will be an "investigatory stop" of the person, which is designed to appear as escalating into an arrest situation. Regardless, the agent will lead the prospective informant to believe that he has been under surveillance or that others have named him as having committed a crime. The encounter will leave no doubt in the target's mind that his future is dim, that jail is imminent, and his only way out is to cooperate with the agent. His decision to become an informant may take place immediately. Often, however, the subject may choose to contemplate his doom[95] with the agent's office telephone number as his only way out.

A prospective informant may actually be surveilled until he commits a crime or is suspected to be in possession of a controlled substance or other contraband. He is "arrested" following what is usually an illegal search and seizure. The subject, fearful of going to jail, may immediately agree to cooperate (flip) and be "unarrested." He will work as an informant laboring under the impression that charges will be filed unless he cooperates. After the fear factor subsides, informants recruited in this fashion very often become paid informants.

Many agents capitalize on contacts with citizens to recruit informants as they perform the otherwise routine functions of their agency. The Customs Service (Immigration and Customs Enforcement) probably has the highest public profile of any federal investigative agency. Its investigators are trained to capitalize on that visibility in recruiting informants.[96]

Customs Officers develop sources through a variety of means, including official liaison, cultivating acquaintances, canvass-type letters, and through normal contacts while conducting investigations.[96] While all methods are effective, contacts resulting during the course of routine investigations have yielded the greatest number of informants.[97]

The U.S. Customs *Criminal Investigators Handbook* recommends: Valuable information can be obtained by Customs Officers cultivating acquaintances involved in industries who have "special opportunity" to learn of illegal activities (i.e., marine and airport operators; vessel and aircraft dealers and rental agents; employees of Customs brokerage firms, high technology businesses, and financial institutions; security personnel at airports and businesses; and hotel and motel personnel are all potential sources of information).[98]

An occasionally successful method of stimulating sources to come to Customs with information is to encourage those whose motivation is economic gain, revenge, elimination of competition, or simply a concerned citizen. Canvass-type letters from the Special Agent in Charge to people within specific geographic localities, industries, occupations, or other areas of particular interest are also employed. Such letters routinely advise of the Customs Service's presence, activities of concern, possible rewards, and willingness to protect where possible the identity of those who cooperate.[98]

An additional method of cultivating and developing sources of information is through industry liaison programs designed to create a cooperative effort between the U.S. Government and the private sector in disrupting the flow of illegally imported/exported merchandise.[98] The FBI, DEA, and BATF employ similar strategies as do state and local police agencies.

References

1. Department of Justice Report on Internal Review Regarding the Ruby Ridge Hostage Situation and Shootings by Law Enforcement Personnel, § 2 (a), Statement of Facts (Lexis Counsel Connect). *See also* Ruby Ridge: Report of the Subcommittee on Terrorism, Technology and Government Information of the Senate Committee on the Judiciary Hearings, Sept. 6–19, 1995, report published Feb. 1996.

2. Department of Justice Report on Internal Review Regarding the Ruby Ridge Hostage Situation and Shootings by Law Enforcement Personnel, § 2 (c).

3. Department of Justice Report on Internal Review Regarding the Ruby Ridge Hostage Situation and Shootings by Law Enforcement Personnel, § 2 (d).

4. 19 USC §§ 1613, 1619; 21 USC § 886(a)(c); 26 USC § 7623.

5. The Sentencing Reform Act of 1984, Pub. L. No. 98-473, 1987; 18 USC §§ 3551–3559, 3561–3566, 3571–3574, 3581–3586.

6. Witness Security Reform Act of 1984, Pt. F.

7. 28 USC § 524(C)(l)(B)(C).

8. *DEA Agents Manual,* Ch. 61.

9. Title II, Comprehensive Crime Control Act of 1984.

10. 18 USC § 3553(6).

11. U.S.S.G. § 5K1.1.

12. Federal Criminal Case Processing, with preliminary data for 1980, Bureau of Justice Statistics, 2003.

13. The Witness Security Program: Testimony = Lifetime Protection, *The Pentacle,* Feb. 1988, 3. (Publication of the U.S. Marshals Service.)

14. Witness Security Reform Act of 1984, Pt. F.

15. DEA, *Cooperating Individual Management, Informant Development,* Ch. IV, Office of Training, Quantico, VA.

16. U.S. Sentencing Guidelines.

17. Topping, R., Lawsuit takes on use of informants by cops. *Newsday,* Dec. 4, 1996.

18. Lyons, D. and Garcia, M., Felon's testimony may have backfired in Willie, Sal case, *Miami Herald,* Feb. 26, 1996, B1.

19. *United States v. Dailey,* 759 F.2d 192 (1st Cir., 1985);

20. *DEA Agents Manual,* Ch 6612.31(J); *U.S. Attorneys Manual,* 9-27.400, 9-27.600.

21. *DEA Agents Manual,* Ch 6612.1.

22. *Barbera v. Smith,* 836 F.2d 96, 99 (2nd Cir., 1987).

23. *Miranda v. Arizona,* 384 U.S. 436, 474, 86 S. Ct. 1602,1628, 16 L. Ed. 2d 694 (1966).

24. *Colorado v. Connelly,* 479 U.S. 157, 168, 107 S. Ct. 515, 522, 93 L. Ed. 2d 473 (1986); *United States v. Dougherty,* 810 F.2d 763, 773 (8th Cir., 1987).

25. 479 U.S. 170, 107 S. Ct. 523; *Moran v. Burbine,* 475 U.S. 412, 421, 106 S. Ct. 1135, 114.0-41, 89 L. Ed. 2d 410 (1986); *Fare v. C.,* 442 U.S. 707, 726–727, 99 S. Ct. 2560, 2572–2573, 61 L. Ed. 2d 197, *reh'g denied,* 444 U.S. 887, 100 S. Ct. 186, 62 L. Ed. 2d 121 (1979).

26. 810 F.2d 773; *Stumes v. Solem,* 752 F.2d 317, 320 (8th Cir.), *cert. denied,* 471 U.S. 1067, 105 S. Ct. 2145, 85 L. Ed.2d 502 (1985); 442 U.S. 724–725, 99 S. Ct. 2571–2572.

27. *Roberts v. United States,* 445 U.S. 552, 100 S. Ct. 1358, 63 L. Ed. 2d 622 (1980).

28. *United States v. Bernal-Obeso,* 989 F.2d 331, 333 (9th Cir., 1993).

29. Martin, C.R., Apology for a veteran drug lawyer's no-flip policy, *Champion Magazine,* March 1995.

30. *United States v. Shah*, 878 F.2d 272, 273 (9th Cir., 1989).

31. *Patterson v. Illinois*, 487 U.S. 285, 290 n.3, 108 S. Ct. 2389, 2393 n.3, 101 L. Ed. 2d 261 (1988). *See Edwards v. Arizona*, 451 U.S. 477, 101 S. Ct. 1880, 68 L. Ed.2d 378 (1981).

32. *United States v. He*, 94 F.3d 782 (2nd Cir., 1996). *See also United States v. Pinto*, 850 F.2d 927 (2d Cir. 1988).

33. *United States v. Chavez*, 902 F.2d 259, 266 (4th Cir., 1990) (quoting *Morris v. Slappy*, 461 U.S. 1, 21, 103 S. Ct. 1610, 1621, 75 L. Ed. 2d 610 (1983).

34. *In re Snyder*, 472 U.S. 634, 645 n.6, 105 S. Ct. 2874, 86 L. Ed. 504 (1985).

35. Memorandum from Attorney General Janet Reno to all U.S. Attorneys and Division Heads regarding contacts with represented persons. *See also* 59 Fed. Reg. No. 42, March 3, 1994; Proposed Rules and Legal Times, March 14, 1994, 21, Fixing the Rules on Contact with Represented Parties, by Nathan, I.B., Principal Associate Deputy Attorney General, U.S. Department of Justice.

36. Model Rules of Professional Conduct 4.2.

37. *United States v. Lopez*, 4 F.3d 1455, 1461 (9th Cir., 1993); *United States ex rel. O'Keefe v. McDonnell Douglas Corp.*, 961 F. Supp. 1288 (E.D. Mo. 1997).

38. *United States v. Brigham*, 977 F.2d 317 (7th Cir., 1992).

39. *United States v. Brigham*, 977 F.2d 318 (7th Cir., 1992).

40. 8 USC § 1101(a).

41. 18 USC § 16.

42. 8 USC § 1101(a). *See also* The Illegal Immigration Reform and Immigrant Responsibility Act, April 1, 1997. Pub. L. No. 104-208, 110 Stat. 3009.

43. 8 USC § 1255.

44. Title 8 CFR § 214(t), 1-1-97 edition.

45. 8 USC § 1255 (j)(2).

46. Barry, J., Tortured au pair celebrates new way of life, *Miami Herald*, Aug. 1, 1998.

47. 8 USC § 1255(j)(2).

48. Lomangino, A., Representing the criminal alien: forms of relief available, in *1997–1998 Immigration and Nationality Law Handbook, Vol. II, Advanced Practice*, pp. 317–335, American Lawyers Association, 1997.

49. DEA, Cooperating Individual Management, Informant Development.

50. *U.S. Attorneys Manual*, 9-27.610(B)(1)(a).

51. U.S.S.G. § 5K1.1.

52. Fed. R. Crim. P. 35(b).

53. 18 USC § 1001 False Statements and 18 USC § 1621 and 18 USC § 1623 Perjury.

54. U.S. Constitution, Amendment V.

55. 18 USC § 884.

56. *U.S. Attorneys Manual,* 9-23.110. *See also United States v. Balsys,* 118 S. Ct. 2218 (1998).

57. 18 USC § 6001, enacted in 1970 and upheld by the Supreme Court in *Kastigar v. United States,* 406 U.S. 441, 453, 92 S. Ct. 1653, 32 L. Ed. 2d 212 (1972).

58. *United States v. Doe,* 465 U.S. 605, 612–614 (1984) for Doe immunity.

59. *U.S. Attorneys Manual,* 9-23.210.

60. 18 USC § 6002. *See Kastigar v. United States,* 406 U.S. 441, 460–461, 92 S. Ct. 1653, 32 L. Ed. 2d 212 (1972).

61. 28 USC § 1826.

62. 18 USC § 401, and Fed. R. Crim. P. 42.

63. *United States v. Wilson,* 421 U.S. 309, 317 n.9 (1975).

64. *United States v. Wilson,* 421 U.S. 309, 317 n.9 (1975), quoting *Shillitani v. United States,* 384 U.S. 364, 371 n.9 (1966).

65. *U.S. Attorneys Manual,* 9-23.000; 28 USC § 1826.

66. 28 USC § 1826(a).

67. Jefferson, J., McDougal jailed for not testifying, The Associated Press, Sept. 10, 1996.

68. *United States v. Coplon,* 339 F.2d 192 (6th Cir. 1964).

69. *United States v. Wilson,* 421 U.S. 309, 316 (1975).

70. 421 U.S. 316.

71. 421 U.S. 316, 319. *See also Harris v. United States,* 382 U.S. 162 (1965).

72. *MacNeil v. United States,* 236 F.2d 149 (1st Cir.), *cert. denied,* 352 U.S. 912 (1956).

73. Fed. R. Crim. P. 42(a).

74. Fed. R. Crim. P. 42(b). *See, e.g., United States v. Sternman,* 415 F.2d 1165 (6th Cir., 1969), *cert. denied,* 397 U.S. 907 (1970).

75. *United States v. Liddy,* 510 F.2d 669, 672–673 (D.C. 1974), *cert. denied,* 420 U.S. 980 (1975); *See also In re Liberatore,* 574 F.2d 78 (2nd Cir., 1978).

76. Fed. R. Crim. P. 11(e)

77. Fed. R. Crim. P. 11(e) R. 11(e)(l)(A) to (C).

78. *U.S. Attorneys Manual,* 9-27-600.

79. *State of Florida v. Crystal Frazier and Christopher Frazier,* Case Nos. 97-866 & 97-847 (3rd District, 1997); *United States v. Nickols,* 606 F.2d 566, 569 (5th Cir. 1979). *See also Santobello v. New York,* 404 U.S. 257, 92 S. Ct. 495, 30 L. Ed. 2d 427 (1971).

80. H.R. Rep. No. 247, 94th Cong., 1st Sess., 6 (1975).

81. Fed. R. Crim. P. 11(e)(2).

82. *U.S. Attorneys Manual,* 9-27.400.

83. Fed. R. Crim. P. 11(e)(4).

84. *U.S. Attorneys Manual*, 9-27.600.

85. *U.S. Attorneys Manual*, 9-27.630.

86. Nonstatutory immunity is often referred to as letter immunity or pocket immunity. *Federal Grand Jury Practice*, U.S. Department of Justice, Criminal Division, Jan. 1993.

87. *United States v. Apfelbaum*, 445 U.S. 115, 131 (1980).

88. *Kastigar v. United States*, 406 U.S. 458–459. *Federal Grand Jury Practice*, Chapter Eight, Immunity Procedures and Practice, U.S. Department of Justice, Criminal Division.

89. 18 USC § 1621.

90. 18 USC § 1623.

91. *United States v. Martinez-Navarro*, 604 F.2d 1184, 1186–1187 (9th Cir., 1979), *cert. denied*, 444 U.S. 1084 (1980); *United States v. Glover*, 608 F. Supp. 861, 863 (S.D.N.Y. 1985), *aff'd*, 779 F.2d 39 (2nd Cir.), *cert. denied*, 475 U.S. 1026 (1986).

92. *United States v. Apfelbaum*, 445 U.S. 115, 131 (1980).

93. *United States v. Gregory*, 611 F. Supp. 1033, 1037 (S.D.N.Y. 1985).

94. *United States v. Simpson*, 813 F.2d 1462, 1469 (9th Cir., 1987).

95. *United States v. Ryan*, 548 F.2d 782,788–789 (9th Cir., 1976).

96. U.S. Customs Service, Office of Enforcement, *Criminal Investigators Handbook*, Ch. 41.

97. Whitacre, M., as told to Henfoff, R., My life as a corporate mole for the FBI, *Fortune*, Sept. 4, 1995, 1, 52. *See* Jones, D. and Eldridge, E., Archer Daniels informant faces charges, Jan. 16, 1997.

98. U.S. Customs Service, Office of Enforcement, *Criminal Investigators Handbook*, Ch. 41.

Sources of Compensation for Informants

4

4.1 Generally

The U.S. Government's response following the events of September 11, 2001 left no doubt that an unprecedented price tag had been put on information regarding terrorism. Never before in history had a government launched such an aggressive worldwide attempt to enlist the aid of paid informants.

As an example, the U.S. Treasury and State Departments jointly sponsor the "Rewards for Justice" program. The program offers up to $25 million for information about individuals or organizations that finance terrorism and that leads to an arrest or conviction or the dismantling of a terrorist financing system. According to former Secretary of State Colin L. Powell, the program "gives us millions of additional pairs of eyes and ears to be on the lookout. It puts informants in every place a terrorist might try to operate or hide." As of September 2005, the United States has paid more than $50 million from the fund.

Leaving the subject of terrorism behind, the traditional work of law enforcement has historically relied upon paid sources of information. The court in *United States v. Cervantes-Pacheco*[1] recognized that it is sometimes necessary to compensate an informant before he will agree to undertake the often dangerous task of an undercover investigation.[2] "Few would engage in a dangerous enterprise of this nature without assurance of substantial remuneration."[3] It is simply unreasonable to expect the government "to depend exclusively upon the virtuous in enforcing the law."[4]

The Drug Enforcement Administration (DEA), Immigration and Customs Enforcement (ICE), the Bureau of Alcohol, Tobacco, and Firearms (BATF), and the Federal Bureau of Investigation (FBI) have each adopted their own philosophy and methods for compensating their informants. (See Appendix 4B, "FBI Statistical Accomplishment Form.") All allot funds from their annual appropriation for their informant payments. Each agency also uses funds derived from criminal and civil forfeiture to reward their informants.

State and local agencies also pay informants from monies allotted from their departments' operating funds. In addition, many state and local agencies pay their informants from funds derived from forfeitures arising under state law. Since 1984, many agencies participate in a "sharing" of federal forfeiture proceeds obtained from cooperative investigative efforts.

It is not unusual for a law enforcement official to pay their informants significant sums, often more than the agent's annual salary. At the federal level, reports of kickbacks being paid to control agents prompted legislation that criminalizes the practice. Federal law provides that employees or officers of the United States receiving any portion of informant compensation are subject to prosecution. State and local agencies are free to promulgate their own policies regarding kickbacks.

4.2 DEA Awards and Compensation to Cooperating Individuals

Special Agents of the Drug Enforcement Administration are authorized to expend official advanced funds for payments to informants and to purchase evidence.[5] The funds are a portion of the DEA's annual funding appropriation from Congress.

Each DEA Field Division (domestic and foreign offices) receives an annual allowance for the purchase of evidence (PE) and payments for information (PI) for the active participation of an informant. Special Agents in Charge (SAC) of a DEA Field Division are authorized to pay up to $25,000 per informant per quarterly accounting period. DEA Headquarters must approve expenditures above $25,000 from the PI budget.[6] Payment to a confidential source that exceeds an aggregate of $100,000 within a one-year period are made only with the authorization of a senior field manager and the express approval of a designated senior headquarters official. In addition, regardless of the time frame, any payments to a confidential source that exceed an aggregate to $200,000 should be made only with the authorization of a senior field manager and the express approval of a designated senior headquarters official. Factors used to determine the amount to be paid include the significance of the investigation, whether the expenditure will further the investigation, and the anticipated expenditures that other investigations may demand.

Payments to informants for seizures of contraband without arrests are generally held to a minimum amount. To be eligible for PE/PI payments, an informant must be fully documented, established, and given a code number.

Undercover expenses necessary to further an investigation are often incurred. They can include the rental of vehicles, hotel rooms, meals, and beverages. Depending upon the length and complexity of the case, the expenditures can prove costly. Although they may directly benefit the informant, they are not necessarily reflected in the overall amount an informant has been paid. If vouchered by the control agent as an investigative expense, it is not chargeable as either PE or PI. The sums will not be reported in a manner that will reduce the informant's PI potential. Those sums might not be reflected in informant payment disclosures made at trial. The nondisclosure of the payments to the defense can give rise to allegations of *Brady* violations. On more than one occasion, agents have disguised awards as an investigative expense paid directly to the informant.[6]

PE and PI payments are documented on a carbon copy DEA form 103.[7] The informant is required to sign his true name on the last page of the multicopy form. All other forms for distribution will only reflect the informant's code number. The payment can only be made by a DEA Special Agent and must be witnessed by another agent.

In addition to the DEA 103, an entry reflecting the payment must be made on the Informant Payment Record.[8] The DEA 356 is the first form seen when opening the informant's internal file and reflects all payments made to the confidential informant (CI).

The DEA often participates in investigations with other agencies where non-DEA informants are utilized. These CIs must also be documented and receive a code number if they are to be paid. They do not have to be fingerprinted and photographed in the same manner as a DEA confidential source and are deactivated upon payment.

The DEA has earned a reputation in law enforcement circles for "stealing" informants from police agencies. The abbreviated documentation process in joint investigations helps to alleviate police fears of informant theft.

4.2.1 Department of Justice Asset Forfeiture Fund

The Drug Enforcement Administration and the Federal Bureau of Investigation are also authorized to pay cooperating individuals awards from the Department of Justice (DOJ) Asset Forfeiture Fund (AFF). There are two types of forfeiture available to the government: civil forfeiture and criminal forfeiture. In civil forfeiture, property used or acquired in violation of law is confiscated; criminal forfeiture is imposed as part of the defendant's punishment following conviction. While the procedures followed in the two types of forfeiture are very different, the result is the same. If the government prevails, which is usually the case, the rights, title, and interest in the property reverts to the United States. The proceeds from the sale of the forfeited assets such as real property, vehicles, businesses, financial instruments, vessels, aircraft, and jewelry are deposited into the AFF and are used to further law enforcement initiatives including the payment to informants. Under the AFF's Equitable Sharing Program, proceeds from sales are shared with the state and local law enforcement agencies that participated in the investigation that led to the forfeiture of the assets. State and local agencies also use the funds for payment to informants.

The U.S. Marshals Service administers the AFF by managing and disposing of the property seized and forfeited. In 2005, $614.5 million in receipts from forfeiture activities and interest earned was deposited into the DOJ's AFF.

Awards paid from the AFF to CIs are not charged against either agency's operating budget but reimbursed from the AFF.[9] Other contributors to the fund include the U.S. Marshals Service, the U.S. Attorneys Offices, the Department of State's Diplomatic Security Service, and the Bureau of Alcohol, Tobacco, Firearms, and Explosives.

There are two types of awards paid from the AFF:

4.2.2   Award Type I: 28 USC § 524(c)(1)(B)

An award payment of up to $250,000 may be paid to a cooperating individual for either assistance or information which relates directly to violations of:

- The criminal drug laws of the United States.
- Money laundering offenses covered by 18 USC §§ 1956 and 1957.[10]
- Reports on domestic coins and currency transactions covered by 31 USC §§ 5313 and 5324.[11]
- Section 60501 of the Internal Revenue Code of 1986.

Awards under 28 USC § 524(c)(l)(B) can be made regardless of a successful criminal or civil forfeiture. The award is program related and is paid in connection with one or more of a series of related criminal activities. Internally, the DEA recommends that asset seizure should be a factor taken into consideration when recommending the amount of reward.[12] 28 USC § 524(C)(1)(B) awards disqualify the CI from additional awards for subsequent forfeitures based upon the original information.

4.2.3   Award Type II: 28 USC § 524(c)(1)(C)

Awards for information or assistance leading to a civil or criminal forfeiture are available under 28 USC § 524(c)(1)(C). Awards are asset specific. To qualify, a cooperating individual must provide original information that results in the seizure and forfeiture of one or more assets. The award may not exceed the lesser of $250,000 or one-fourth of the amount realized by the United States from the forfeited property.

Cooperating individuals are eligible for more than one award if their information results in several seizures under the same investigative case number. The information pertaining to each seizure must be separate and distinct. The application for separate awards under the same case number has to clearly explain the unique character of the information.[12]

The amount of the award is determined by the amount realized by the government. That amount is defined as the gross receipts of the forfeiture, either cash or proceeds of sale, less management expenses attributable to the seizure and forfeiture of the property. In the event the property is retained for official use, for example an aircraft put into service by the FBI, the amount realized for award purposes is the amount realized by the United States from the property forfeited and is the value of the property at the time of the seizure less any management expenses paid from the Fund. The net figure is used as the basis for calculating the award.

An award granted under 524(c)(1)(B) precludes the CI from receiving an additional award based on a forfeiture that results from the same information or assistance. Conversely, an award granted under 524(c)(1)(C) precludes an additional award based upon the same information or assistance.[12]

Awards under 524(c)(1)(B) and (C) are discretionary in nature.[13] The DEA requires that the application for the award originate in a memorandum from the Special Agent in Charge to the Assistant Administrator for Operations. The memorandum must address ten items:

- The type of award, either 524(c)(1)(B) or 524(c)(1)(C).
- Amount requested by the award applicant, if an amount is claimed.
- Recommended amount or percentage proposed by the Special Agent in Charge.
- Cooperating individual code number.
- Seizure number for the asset claimed against.
- Amounts received by the CI in the same investigation.
- Whether the CI will receive funds from any other agency as a result of the investigation under consideration.
- Whether the individual desires to be paid by check or cash.

- The significance of the CI's information or assistance in the investigation and the resulting asset seizure.
- Whether the CI is requesting more than one award under the same case number; a complete explanation must describe how seizures are separate and distinct from each other.[12]

4.3 Tax Responsibilities

On April 22, 1992, the DEA issued the following notice to all of its Special Agents regarding instructions that must be given to cooperating sources concerning federal income tax and rewards, awards, and payments for information.

The controlling Special Agent will advise all cooperating individuals that they must file federal income tax returns to include all payments, awards, and rewards paid to them by the DEA. In addition, the controlling Special Agent will advise the cooperating sources that all payments must be reported as "other income" on their federal income tax returns, and it will be their responsibility to obtain receipts and other supporting documentation to offset the legitimate expenses from income for possible audit by the Internal Revenue Service. Special Agents will advise all cooperating sources that their tax liability is a matter strictly between them and the Internal Revenue Service. A statement attesting to this policy will be documented on the back of the DEA-202. Special Agents will remind cooperating individuals of this policy when any payment is made.[14]

However, there is no requirement for the paying agency (payor) to notify the Internal Revenue Service (IRS) of the payment.[15] The Code of Federal Regulations governs the area of payments for which no return of information is required to be made by the payor. 26 CFR l.604l-3(2)(n)[16] does not require IRS notification for:

> A payment to an informer as an award, fee, or reward for information relating to criminal activity but only if such payment is made by the United States, a State, a Territory, or political subdivision thereof, or the District of Columbia, or any agency or instrumentality of any one or more of the foregoing ... [16]

Recognizing that a large percent of the informant population is from the criminal milieu, their failure to report rewards on an income tax return would not be surprising. If the informant does not report an award, the IRS will be none the wiser in the routine processing of the informant's tax return.

4.4   Immigration and Customs Enforcement Awards and Compensation to Sources

Immigration and Customs Enforcement employs four different methods to either reward or reimburse individuals who supply information or evidence concerning criminal violations or provide services utilized in the course of an investigation. Their payments, like their predecessor agency, the U.S. Customs Service, are referred to as awards of compensation or moiety, purchase of information or evidence, confidential fund payments, and per diem. With the exception of moiety, their methods mirror those of the DEA.

Moiety, meaning "half share," is a term that is as old as Customs itself, and today it is used almost exclusively by that agency. The "Moiety Acts" of the eighteenth century were statutes designed to encourage citizens to report crime by authorizing payment of half the fines collected by the government. Customs no longer awards 50%. The amount awarded to any individual for a particular case cannot exceed $250,000. There is no prohibition against paying an informant more than $250,000, provided the payments involve more than one case.[17]

Immigration and Customs Enforcement (ICE) contributes to the Treasury Forfeiture Fund (TFF), very similar to the Justice Department's AFF. The TFF was established in 1992 as the successor to the Customs Forfeiture Fund. In 2004, it collected $335 million from its participating agencies. Those agencies include:

- Internal Revenue Service Criminal Investigative Division (IRS-CID)
- U.S. Department of the Treasury
- U.S. Customs and Border Protection (U.S. CBP)
- Immigration and Customs Enforcement (ICE)
- Department of Homeland Security
- U.S. Secret Service, Department of Homeland Security
- U.S. Coast Guard, Department of Homeland Security

The fund receives all nontax forfeitures made by participating agencies. Awards to informants are made in the same manner as the Justice Department's AFF.

The Department of Justice Asset Forfeiture Fund[18] also replenishes the Treasury Forfeiture Fund. For example, ICE often participates with either the DEA or FBI in joint enforcement operations that result in forfeitures. Those funds are deposited to the DOJ Asset Forfeiture Fund. An amount appropriate to reflect the degree of participation of ICE in the forfeiture[19] is transferred to the Treasury Forfeiture Fund.[20]

4.5   Federal Bureau of Investigation

The FBI compensates its confidential sources, cooperative witnesses, and informants in accordance with their *Manual of Investigative Operations and Guidelines (MIOG)*. Informant funds are part of the FBI's annual appropriation from Congress.

An FBI Memorandum entitled "Citizen Cooperation" listed the factors that determine whether and how much a source will be paid for information.

4.5.1   Citizen Cooperation

The FBI considers citizen cooperation to be an important and invaluable investigative tool in fulfilling its investigative responsibilities. Due to the myriad of criminal matters investigated by the FBI and the increasing sophistication of some individuals in the criminal element, it has become imperative, over the years, for the FBI to rely upon the information provided by citizens to resolve many of the complex cases under investigation. The FBI has enjoyed success in the resolution of numerous complicated cases due, in no small part, to citizen cooperation. Employment of some investigative techniques such as electronic surveillances is dependent upon information provided by knowledgeable citizens.

Virtually every major case investigated by the FBI involved citizen cooperation in some capacity, and the information provided by them results in substantial numbers of arrests and convictions each year. Citizens provide information of intelligence value leading not only to the solution of crimes, but also to the recovery of stolen property, the locating of wanted persons, and the detection of some crimes in the planning stages.

Citizens often furnish information regarding criminal acts that are in violation of state laws or of federal laws over which the FBI has no jurisdiction. This information is disseminated to the appropriate law enforcement agencies to assist in their investigations.

Citizens are not used by the FBI to circumvent legal or ethical restrictions. Citizens are given specific instructions not to participate in acts of violence, use unlawful techniques to obtain information, or initiate a plan to commit criminal acts. Citizens are sometimes authorized to participate in criminal activities with persons under investigation if it is determined that such activities are necessary to obtain information needed for purposes of federal prosecution. If this participation in otherwise criminal acts involves significant risk of violence, corrupt actions by high public officials, or severe economic loss to a victim, the concurrence of an appropriate U.S. Attorney or higher is obtained prior to the authorization being given.

Citizens are paid for services and expenses on a cash-on-delivery basis for information provided in authorized investigative activities. The amount paid to a citizen is determined by the FBI based on the value of the information provided by the citizen.

These items are always specifically considered when determining payments to citizens who help the FBI:

- Significance of the investigation.
- Degree of assistance rendered by the citizen.
- Was the citizen responsible for initiation of the case?
- Did the citizen provide general or specific information?
- Was the information available from other citizens?
- What length of time was spent by the citizen in assisting in the investigation?
- Did the citizen participate in consensual monitoring activities?
- Were undercover Agents introduced by the citizen?
- What was the potential risk of violence toward the citizen?
- Was the citizen able to continue his or her normal job while working for the FBI?
- Did the citizen suffer any financial losses as a result of the citizen's cooperation?
- What was the value of seized and forfeited property obtained as a result of the citizen's cooperation?
- What other substantial accomplishments are attributable to data supplied by the citizen, i.e., arrests, convictions, violent acts prevented, Title Ills (wiretaps) generated, search warrants executed, etc.?
- In how many consensually monitored and recorded conversations did the citizen participate?
- Will the citizen testify if deemed appropriate, and what is the potential for future investigative contributions?

4.6   Compensation for FBI Informants and Confidential Sources

The FBI may pay informants and confidential sources a reasonable amount of money or provide other lawful consideration for information furnished, services rendered, or expenses incurred in authorized investigative activity. No payment of money or other consideration, other than a published reward, shall be conditioned on the conviction of any particular individual.[21]

In investigations involving serious crimes or the expenditure of extensive investigative resources, the FBI may compensate informants or confidential sources with an extraordinary payment in excess of $25,000. The Attorney General shall be informed of any such extraordinary payment as deemed necessary.[21] Where practicable, compensation agreements with informants or confidential sources in connection with a significant FBI undercover operation shall provide that compensation will depend on compliance with the obligation of confidentiality for investigative information, and shall further provide that any profits derived from a violation of the obligation shall be forfeited to the United States.[21]

The FBI is also able to pay its confidential sources and informants from the Department of Justice Asset Forfeiture Fund.[22] With the exception of Agency specific restrictions, the FBI is entitled to pay the same amounts to sources as the DEA and be reimbursed from the Fund. The Bureau follows the same procedures as the DEA in making applications to the Fund.

Amounts paid to individual informants outside of "Fund" awards have received recent attention in high profile investigations. The key FBI informant in the first World Trade Center terrorist bombing was paid more than $1 million and was reported to have entered the Witness Security Program.[23] Rewards offered for information regarding the September 11, 2001, attack dwarf that amount.

Obviously, not all information commands million-dollar awards. The informant who exposed the alleged plot to murder a Black Muslim leader resulting in the arrest of Malcolm X's daughter was reported to have only been paid $45,000. The FBI also paid for his living quarters, food, and transportation during the investigation.[24] The informant in that case was also placed in the Witness Security Program.[25] However, in 1998 the brother of the Unabomber received a $1 million reward for his information.

Informants are also paid for work in cases that do not result in arrests or prosecution. An FBI agent in 1991 was quoted as saying, "Many informants working on a long-term case will get a weekly allowance of $1,000 and a large reward at the end, as much as $100,000. Actually, some of the bigger informants are downright bargains." The agent supervised 257 active CIs used by the FBI's Atlanta office.[26]

4.7 Informant Lawsuits

Lawsuits have been filed by informants against federal agencies over disputes concerning the amount of reward or award payments. The claims generally relate to issues of breach of contract, negligent misrepresentation, and fraud. Although not officially reported, counsel for several informants claim to have settled out of court with agencies over contested amounts claimed due by the CIs.

The essence of many of the disputed claims seems to be centered upon the language in the Department of Justice Asset Forfeiture Fund provisions. The informants generally argue that their control agent promised them one-fourth of the amount of money seized or one-fourth of the value of the property forfeited.[27]

"Fund" language on amounts available may be responsible for the heightened expectations of compensation by the informant: Any award paid from the Fund for information, as provided in paragraph (1)(B) or (C), shall be paid at the *discretion* of the Attorney General or his delegate, under existing departmental delegation policies for the payment of awards, except that the authority to pay an award of $250,000 or more *shall not be delegated* to any person other than the Deputy Attorney General, the Associate Attorney General, the Director of the Federal Bureau of Investigation, or the Administrator of the Drug Enforcement Administration. Any award for information pursuant to paragraph (1)(B) shall not exceed $250,000. Any award for information pursuant to paragraph (1)(C) shall not exceed the lesser of $250,000 or *one-fourth* of the amount realized by the United States from the property forfeited.

Agents in the field may either mistakenly or deliberately communicate a "flat rate of 25%" to their informants. They may also give the impression that they are the decision maker as to how much is paid. In reality it is the Special Agent in Charge (in DEA cases) who makes a recommendation concerning the amount to DEA Headquarters.[28]

Treasury and Homeland Security agents are not immune from similar misunderstandings. 19 USC § 1619(2) states the Secretary may award and pay such person (informant) an amount that does not exceed 25% of the net amount so recovered.[29]

4.8 Trafficker Directed Funds

Informants are also paid by the criminals they are targeting. The monies are described as "trafficker directed funds."[12] The practice is officially sanctioned by some federal agencies including the Drug Enforcement Administration.

The increasing sophistication of criminal organizations has made it necessary for law enforcement agencies to reassess traditional approaches of investigation methods and methodology. One of the most notable tactics being employed is generally referred to as a "sting."

The term of art used by the agency that has employed the "sting" most frequently is "Reverse Undercover." The DEA views the term as generic in its description of any variation of the traditional role of undercover personnel (agents or informants) as the "buyer" of an illegal product or service. Instead the role of the undercover agent or informant is reversed to one of seller of illegal products or services.[12]

The undercover agent or informant is often called upon by the criminal target to provide or purchase a "difficult to obtain" item or service.[30] Such items or services are described as "an item necessary to the commission of an offense other than a controlled substance" or a "service in furtherance of illegal trafficking which is difficult to obtain."[31] The items or services are provided by the government agent or informant and paid for by the trafficker.

The standard for the term "difficult to obtain" is subjective and depends upon the circumstances of a specific situation.[32] In so-called "transportation cases," informants or agents will often be given significant sums of money known as "trafficker directed funds" to secure aircraft or boats to smuggle loads of drugs into the United States. Particularly in the case of informants, their daily needs and luxuries may be paid for by the trafficker. Informants have been permitted to retain ownership of aircraft, boats, and cars that were provided for by criminals or paid for with trafficker directed funds. Retention is generally permitted at the discretion of the control agent and his supervisor.

Money launderers have proven to be extremely vulnerable to the "reverse undercover" tactic. The year 1986 marked a new beginning in federal law enforcement's efforts to immobilize criminal organizations. Targeting the proceeds of crime, new money laundering laws[33] made it increasingly more difficult to move the immense profits of illegal gambling, narcotics trafficking, and other cash-intense crimes through financial institutions. Since September 11, 2001, the government's search for financiers, fundraisers, or donors who provide financial support to terrorists has increased the risk of detection for all money launderers.

Concealing the nature, source, location, or ownership of the proceeds of specified unlawful activity[34] has become increasingly more difficult. The movement of monetary instruments[35] or funds from inside the United States to foreign countries has also presented new challenges to criminal and terrorist organizations alike.

Both activities have caused criminal organizations to suffer tremendous losses of funds to the "reverse undercover" or "sting" method of investigation.[36] Traffickers routinely turn over millions of dollars to informants and undercover agents in the belief the money will be moved without detection. In protracted investigations, funds are actually moved for the target. In return the informant is paid "points" or a percentage of the money moved to a safe haven. Monies are often retained by the informant through agreements with their agent handler.[37]

4.9 Whistle-Blowers

Not traditionally viewed as informants per se, "whistle-blowers" have reaped significant rewards through *qui tam* lawsuits. *Qui tam* is an abbreviation of "*qui tam pro domino rege quam pro seipse*," meaning "he who sues for the king as for himself." One whistle-blower received $126 million for his efforts in cases against several pharmaceutical companies.[38]

Originally known as the Lincoln Law, the federal Civil False Claims Act was passed to punish profiteers defrauding the Union Army during the Civil War. The *qui tam* provision of the Act provided the inducement for individuals to come forward by giving half of any money recovered by the government to the whistle-blower who disclosed the fraud. The whistle-blowers or informants are known as "relators."[39]

The Civil False Claims Act was substantially amended by the False Claims Amendments Act of 1986.[40] Congress enacted the new amendments to enhance the government's ability to recover losses sustained as a result of fraud against the United States. Congress acted after finding that such fraud in federal programs, procurement, and in the payment of obligations owed to the government is pervasive, and that the False Claims Act, which is characterized as the primary tool for combating fraud against the government, was in need of modernization. The amendments were intended by Congress to create incentives for individuals who are aware of fraud against the government to disclose that information without fear of reprisals or government inaction.

As amended, the False Claims Act (FCA) provides that any person who with actual knowledge, in reckless disregard, or in deliberate ignorance of the truth, submits a false or fraudulent claim to the U.S. Government for payment or approval, or who makes or uses a false record or statement to avoid an obligation to pay money to the government, is liable to the government for a civil penalty of not less than $5,000 and not more than $10,000 for each claim, *plus three times* the amount of the damages sustained by the government because of the false claim. The Act allows any person having knowledge of a false or fraudulent claim against the government to bring an action in federal district court for himself and for the U.S. Government and to share in any recovery.

The law's *qui tam* provision encourages individuals to pursue their own suits when the government, after investigating, declines to intervene.[41] If the government does not proceed with an action under the Act, the "relator" is entitled to not less than and not more than 30% of the proceeds of the action or settlement. The reward is paid out of the proceeds.

The "relator" is also entitled to recover reasonable expenses that the court finds to have been necessarily incurred, plus reasonable attorney's fees and costs. All such expenses, fees, and costs are rewarded against the defendant.[42] The whistle-blower can receive 15 to 25% of the proceeds of the action or settlement of the claim,[43] if the government takes over the prosecution of the action.[44] Litigation risks associated with FCA allegations include penalties, *treble damages,* and suspension or debarment from further contracting.

The threat of either penalty creates intense pressure to resolve matters by settlement and not by litigation. An FCA allegation has been called the civil law equivalent of the death penalty for a contractor.

In 1988, only 60 *qui tam* cases were filed, and $390,431,000 was recovered in settlements and judgments. In 2003, the number rose to 334 cases with $1.5 billion in recoveries.[39,45] The largest sum collected by a relator was $150 million following a government settlement with United Technologies Corporation. A former vice president of the company who claimed that payments were overstated in a Defense Department aircraft contract initiated the action.[46]

4.10 Sharing of Federally Forfeited Property with State and Local Agencies

State and local law enforcement agencies rely heavily upon confidential informant participation in criminal investigations. Like their federal counterparts they also pay their sources rewards for information leading to arrests and seizures. Many of the forfeitures generating significant sums of money for law enforcement are the direct result of informant-generated investigations. In the extensive list of permissible uses of equitably shared funds, payments to informants are in the first category of allowable expenses.[47] Arguably informants generate a significant percentage, if not the majority, of investigations resulting in forfeited property.

Prior to 1984, police agencies relied upon their individual budget appropriations to establish a source for informant payments. Consequently, the sums paid to informants were far less than those paid by federal law enforcement agencies.

Passage of the Comprehensive Crime Control Act of 1984 authorized the sharing of federal forfeiture proceeds with cooperating state and local law enforcement agencies. By March 1994, the Department of Justice Asset Forfeiture Fund shared over $1.4 billion in forfeited assets with more than 3,000 state and local law enforcement agencies. From 1999 through September 30, 2004, equitable sharing allocation levels averaged $232,017,000. In 2005 that number grew to $270 million.[48] As evidence of the program's growth, in 2001 the Monroe County, Florida Sheriff's Office (in the Florida Keys) received a check for $25 million as their share of forfeitures resulting from a money laundering investigation. The county law enforcement agency had been a member of a joint federal, state, and local task force responsible for the investigation.

The Department of the Treasury Forfeiture Fund also has equitable sharing provisions for state and local agencies participating in investigations or for local agencies referring seizures. In 2004, the TFF received $335 million from all sources. $93 million went to state and local law enforcement agencies as equitably shared funds.[49]

Many states have their own forfeiture laws. Some require that the forfeited assets go into the state's general fund, not directly to the law enforcement agency responsible for the forfeiture. Some local law enforcement agencies, in an effort to circumvent the general fund requirement, refer their forfeiture investigations to a federal agency. If the forfeiture action is successful, the recovery is equitably shared, with the proceeds handed over directly to the referring local law enforcement agency.

4.10.1 Statutes Enforced by Federal Investigative Agencies That Permit Equitable Sharing with State and Local Agencies

The guidelines for participating in the sharing process[49] grant the Attorney General authority to share federally forfeited property seized pursuant to federal statutes with participating state and local law enforcement agencies.[50] The exercise of that authority is *discretionary*. The Attorney General is not required to share property in any case. Those statutes include:

8 USC § 1324(b)
> Civil forfeiture of conveyances that have been used in the attempted or accomplished smuggling of aliens into the United States or transportation of illegal aliens within the United States.

17 USC § 509
> Civil forfeiture of specific property that has been used to illegally manufacture, reproduce or distribute phonograph records or copies of copyrighted materials.

18 USC § 512
> Civil forfeiture of automobiles and parts involved in specific prohibited conduct.

18 USC § 545
> Civil forfeiture applicable to merchandise imported contrary to law.

18 USC § 1955
> Civil forfeiture of property used in an illegal interstate gambling business.

18 USC §§ 1956/1957
> Money laundering offenses.

18 USC § 981
> Civil and criminal forfeiture provisions — property representing gross receipts of money laundering section is subject to seizure and forfeiture.

18 USC § 1961

Racketeer Influenced and Corrupt Organizations ("RICO") — upon conviction, property constituting or derived from proceeds of racketeering shall be forfeited.

18 USC § 2253, 18 USC § 2254, 18 USC § 1467

Child Protection Act of 1984, Sexual Exploitation of Children — visual depictions, equipment used to manufacture or reproduce child pornography, and property derived from a violation of this Act may be seized and forfeited under the Customs laws.

18 USC § 2513

Civil forfeiture of certain property used to illegally intercept wire, oral, or electronic communications.

19 USC § 1436

Seizure and forfeiture of merchandise not properly reported (including monetary instruments per amendment to 19 USC § 1401. Definition of "merchandise" or any conveyance used in connection with a violation of this section. 19 USC § 1462 Civil forfeiture is authorized for any article, the importation of which is prohibited, the container or vehicle.

19 USC § 1497

Penalties for failure to declare include seizure and forfeiture of undeclared articles as well as controlled substances and civil penalty equal to the value of the article or 200% of street value of a controlled substance.

19 USC § 1584

Penalties for falsity or lack of manifest includes provision permitting forfeiture if penalty is unpaid.

19 USC § 1586

Any vessel, merchandise, or cargo associated with the unlawful unloading or transshipment is subject to seizure and forfeiture.

19 USC § 1587

Vessel and cargo aboard may be subject to seizure and forfeiture.

19 USC § 1588

Merchandise transported between U.S. ports via foreign ports is subject to seizure and forfeiture.

19 USC § 1590

Aviation Smuggling — authorizes seizures and forfeitures of vessels and/or aircraft used in connection with or aiding or facilitating a violation of this section.

19 USC § 1592

Merchandise entered, introduced or attempted to be entered or introduced by false or fraudulent means may be seized in limited circumstances and forfeited if the monetary penalty is not paid.

19 USC § 1594

>Seizure of conveyance — conveyances subject to seizure and forfeiture to secure payment of Customs penalties. Common carriers are subject to seizure and forfeiture in limited situations.

19 USC § 1595

>Searches and seizures through civil warrant expanded to cover any article subject to seizure (not just imported merchandise), e.g., to seize conveyances, monetary instruments, and other evidence of Customs violations.

19 USC § 1595

>Forfeitures — authorizes forfeiture of conveyances aiding or facilitating importation, introduction, or transportation of articles contrary to law.

19 USC § 1703

>Vessels and aircraft built or fitted out for smuggling and their cargo shall be seized and forfeited.

21 USC § 333(e)(3)

>A conviction under this section of the Food Drug and Cosmetic Act for distribution of Human Growth Hormones, or for possession with intent to distribute Human Growth Hormones, shall be considered a felony violation of the Controlled Substances Act for the purposes of forfeiture under 21 USC § 848 Continuing Criminal Enterprise (CCE) — upon conviction, profits, interest in and everything affording a source of influence over the enterprise shall be forfeited.

21 USC § 853

>Criminal forfeiture.

21 USC § 857

>Civil forfeiture of drug paraphernalia.

22 USC § 401

>Arms, munitions, or other articles exported in violation of law and conveyances used in exporting or attempting to export shall be seized and forfeited.

31 USC § 5317(b)

>Authorizes forfeiture of monetary instruments being transported in situations where reports required by 31 USC § 5316 are not filed or contain material omissions or misstatements. Provision as amended by the Anti-Drug Abuse Act of 1986 includes a "tracing" provision, e.g., seizure and forfeiture of any property traceable to unreported or misreported instruments.

50 USC App. § 16

> Trading with the Enemy Act — any property or conveyance concerned in a violation of this Act shall be forfeited.

50 USC App. § 2410

> Export Administration Act — upon conviction, any property associated with the violation shall be forfeited.

Appendix 4A: Voucher for Purchase of Evidence/Payment for Information/Services

U.S. Department of Justice

Drug Enforcement Administration

   I. GENERAL (complete for all submissions)
     1. Claimant
     2. Group No.
     3. Office
     4. Case No.
     5. G-DEP Code
     6. Purpose of Submission (check one)
        __Purchase of evidence
        __Payment for Information/Services Evidence
  II. PURCHASE OF EVIDENCE complete as appropriate)
     7. Exhibit No.
     8. Amount Expended $_____
     9. Description of Exhibit (same as DEA Form *7/7a):
        *Drug & Non-Drug Evidence Forms
 III. PAYMENT FOR INFORMATION/SERVICES (complete as appropriate)
    10. Purpose (check one)
        __Information/ Services
        __Security
        __Reimbursement of Expenses
    11. Source of Funds (check one)
        __PE/PI (Purchase of Evidence/Information)
        __AFF (Asset Forfeiture Fund)_____
        __Trafficker Directed/Generated Proceeds
    12. Basis for Payment (Brief narrative of reason for payment)
    13. I certify that I received payment in the amount of $____ in U.S. currency or the equivalent amount in another currency. (Sign last copy only) Code Number____ Date_____
  IV. CERTIFICATION (complete for all submissions)
    14. PURCHASER/PAYOR (Signature) _____
        Type or Print Name _____ Date_____
    15. WITNESS (Signature, only for III above) _____
        Type or Print Name _____ Date_____
    16. CLAIMANT (Signature, if different from 14 above)_____
        Type or Print Name_____ Date_____
    17. SUPERVISOR (Signature) _____
        Type or Print Name_____ Date_____
   V. ACCOUNTING CLASSIFICATION (see instructions)
  FUND CITATION AMOUNT $_____

Fiscal Officer (Signature)_____
Type or Print Name_____Date_____

Appendix 4B: FBI Statistical Accomplishments Form

Criminal Informant/Cooperative Witness (CI/CW)

1. Number of Subjects Arrested:
    a. FBI ____
    b. Other Federal Agencies ____
    c. State and Local Agencies ____
2. Number of Subjects/Victims Identified and/or Located:
    a. FBI ____
    b. Other Federal Agencies ____
    c. State and Local Agencies____
3. Number of Investigative Matters Initiated:
    a. FBI____
    b. Other Federal Agencies____
    c. State and Local Agencies____
4. Number of Disseminations Based Upon CI/CW Information:____
5. Number of Violent Acts Prevented:____
6. Number of Times CI/CW Information Used in Title III Affidavits:
    a. FBI____
    b. Other Federal Agencies ____
    c. State and Local Agencies____
7. Number of Times CI/CW Information Used in Search Warrant Affidavits:
    a. FBI____
    b. Other Federal Agencies____
    c. State and Local Agencies____
8. Number of Times CI/CW Information Used in Obtaining Complaint/Information/ Indictment:
    a. FBI____
    b. Other Federal Agencies____
    c. State and Local Agencies____
9. Merchandise Recovered (Value)
    a. FBI____
    b. Other Federal Agencies____
    c. State and Local Agencies____
10. Asset/Property Seized (Value at Time of Seizure):
    a. FBI____
    b. Other Federal Agencies ____
    c. State and Local Agencies____
11. Monetary Value of Asset/Property Actually Forfeited to Government: $____
12. Number of Convictions Obtained as a Result of Information Furnished by CI/CW or as a Result of other Significant Operational Assistance Furnished:
    a. FBI____
    b. Other Federal Agencies ____
    c. State and Local Agencies____
13. Number of Times Undercover Agent or Other Law Enforcement Officer Introduced into an Investigative Matter by CI/CW:
    a. FBI____
    b. Other Federal Agencies____
    c. State and Local Agencies____

14. Drugs Recovered (Wholesale Value):
    a. FBI____
    b. Other Federal Agencies____
    c. State and Local Agencies____
15. Number of Consensually Monitored Conversations CI/CW participated in:
    a. FBI____
    b. Other Federal Agencies____
    c. State and Local Agencies____

References

1. *United States v. Cervantes-Pacheco,* 826 F.2d 310, 315 (5th Cir., 1987).

2. *Associated Press,* D.C. cops to pay $98 million for informant's death, man killed during drug buy in Starbuck's homicide probe. Jan. 21, 1999.

3. *United States v. Cervantes-Pacheco,* 826 F.2d 310, 315, quoting *United States v. Reynoso-Ulloa,* 548 F.2d 1329, 1338 n.19 (9th Cir., 1977).

4. *United States v. Cervantes-Pacheco,* 826 F.2d 315, citing *United States v. Richardson,* 764 F.2d 1514, 1521 (11th Cir., 1985).

5. 21 USC § 886(a), (b), and (c).

6. *DEA Agents Manual,* Ch. 61. *See* The Drug Enforcement Administration's Payments for Confidential Sources, Audit Report, Office of the Inspector General, July 2005.

7. DEA Form 103.

8. DEA Form 356.

9. 28 USC § 524.

10. 18 USC § 1956; 18 USC § 1957.

11. 31 USC § 5324.

12. *DEA Agents Manual,* Ch. 66.

13. 28 USC § 524(c)(1)(b).

14. *DEA Agents Manual,* Ch. 6612.3.

15. *Reuters* News Service, Item to waive tax on Unabomber reward in U.S. bill, Oct. 19, 1998.

16. 26 CFR 1.6041-3(2)(l).

17. 19 USC § 1619(c).

18. 28 USC § 524(c)(l).

19. 31 USC § 9703(p).

20. 28 USC § 524(11).

21. *FBI Manual of Investigative Operations and Guidelines (MIOG),* Vol. II, Pt. 1, § 137.

22. 28 USC §§ 524(c)(l)(B), (c)(l)(C).

23. Waldman, P. and McMorris, F.A., *Wall Street Journal,* Sept. 22, 1995, 1.

24. Pesce, C., *USA Today,* March 24, 1995.

25. *Miami Herald,* March 24, 1995, 3A.

26. Curriden, M., Making crime pay, *ABA L.J.,* June 1991, 43.

27. *DEA Agents Manual,* Ch. 6612.44(A)(2). *See Perri v. United States,* 53 Fed.Cl. 381 (2002).

28. *DEA Agents Manual,* Ch. 6612.

29. 19 USC § 1619(2).

30. *DEA Agents Manual,* Ch. 6626.2.

31. *DEA Agents Manual,* Ch. 6626.2(A).

32. *DEA Agents Manual,* Ch. 6626.2(B).

33. 18 USC §§ 1956, 1957.

34. 18 USC § 1956(a)(1)(B)(1).

35. 18 USC § 1956(a)(2)

36. McClintick, D., *Swordfish,* Phantom Books (1993).

37. FBI Proprietary Agreement.

38. Weinberg, N., The dark side of whistle-blowing, *Forbes,* March 14, 2005.

39. Berkman, H., Spoils to bounty hunters, federal contractors gripe, *Nat. L.J.,* March 4, 1996, 1.

40. 31 USC §§ 3729–3732, as amended, Pub. L. 99-562, 100 Stat. 3153(1986).

41. 31 USC § 3730(4)(6).

42. 31 USC § 3730.

43. Shaw, D., Whistle-blower's case serves as cautionary tale, *Seattle Times,* Feb. 8, 1998.

44. 31 USC § 3730(C).

45. Fraud Statistics — Overview, Oct. 1, 1986–Sept. 30, 2004, Civil Division, U.S. Department of Justice.

46. Ferziger, M.J. and Currell, D.G., Snitching for dollars: the economics and public policy of federal civil bounty programs (1999), *University Of Illinois Law Review,* 1999, 1141. *See also* Jackson, J.A. and Fulk, A., A Law Gone Rogue: Time to Return Fairness to the False Claims Act, Washington Legal Foundation, Vol. 20, No. 64, Dec. 16, 2005.

47. *A Guide to Equitable Sharing of Federally Forfeited Property for State and Local Law Enforcement Agencies,* U.S. Department of Justice, 10.

48. *A Guide to Equitable Sharing of Federally Forfeited Property for State and Local Law Enforcement Agencies,* U.S. Department of Justice, March 1994. *See* Asset Forfeiture Fund and Seized Asset Deposit Fund Annual Financial Statement Fiscal Year 2004, U.S. Department of Justice, Office of the Inspector General Audit Division, Audit Report March 2005.

49. 31 USC §9703(1)(a)(G).

50. 21 USC § 881(e)(l)(A) and (e)(3); 18 USC § 981(e)(2).

Cooperation and Contingency Fee Agreements

5

5.1 Generally

In what has been called a textbook example of how cooperating with prosecutors can pay, former WorldCom CFO Scott Sullivan received a five-year sentence vs. the 27 years in prison he faced. He was alleged to have been the chief architect of one of the biggest U.S. frauds in history. The lenient sentence was in return for information and testimony that resulted in the conviction of WorldCom CEO Bernie Ebbers for an $11 billion fraud. Ebbers received a term of 25 years in prison, one of the most severe sentences ever given in a white collar criminal case.

Federal Judge Stephen Trott had this to say about making deals with criminal defendants while he was Assistant Attorney General:

> Make agreements only with "little fish" to get "big fish." A jury will understand this approach, but they will reject out of hand anything that smacks of giving a deal to a "big fish" to get a "little fish." It will offend their notion of basic fairness and play into the hands of the defense. In a well known east coast legal disaster, a police chief was let off the hook relatively easily in order to prosecute subordinates. Angered at this inverted set of priorities, juries acquitted all of the subordinates. It is also the case that sometimes, even though you have a bigger fish in mind, the one you already have in the net is simply too big to give anything substantial in return for his cooperation. Don't keep going when the stakes are

no longer favorable. You must be prepared in compelling terms to defend and justify the deal you have made to the jury in your final argument, after it has been attacked by the defense. Why did you give this witness immunity? Because it is unacceptable to get just the bag man and let the crooked senator get away, that's why. The integrity of government — indeed our very way of life — demands it![1]

The U.S. Supreme Court has held that a traditional agreement that promises prosecutorial leniency in return for the testimony of an accomplice does not violate the due process rights of the defendant.[2] Like most courts, however, the Supreme Court has recognized that accomplice agreements may encourage perjured testimony.[3] Many courts have held that the terms of accomplice plea agreements merely affect the weight of the testimony, not its admissibility.[4]

Recognizing that the terms of the plea agreement will be disclosed[5] in court, it is essential that the document be carefully drafted. The agreements are usually either as simple or as complex as the facts of the case that caused the arrest of the cooperating defendant. They contain one or more promises designed to ensure that the witness will testify favorably for the government. (See Appendix 5C, "Informant Letter Agreement.")

Most prosecutors insist that the defendant plead guilty to some offense. Many agreements offer the reduction of an offense to a lesser included one with a promise to recommend either probation or a reduced sentence. Depending upon how important the sought-after cooperation is to the government, many prosecutors offer dismissal of the most serious charge, immunity from prosecution, rewards, or the promise to forego forfeiture of property or return property already forfeited. It is not unusual for the prosecution to promise not to prosecute a defendant's family member or associate in return for cooperation. (See Chapter 3, "Recruiting Informants.")

Whether the document is referred to as a plea agreement, informant contract, or an informant agreement, the writing should serve to clarify from the beginning of the relationship what performance the government expects from the informant. It should also incorporate what the informant can expect from law enforcement in return for his cooperation and truthful testimony.

Informant agreements are a two-edged sword for the prosecutor. While the existence of a plea agreement may support the witness's credibility by showing his or her interest in testifying truthfully, the plea agreement may also impeach the witness's credibility by showing his or her interest in testifying as the government wishes regardless of the truth.[6] Introduction of the entire plea agreement permits the jury to consider fully the possible conflicting motivations underlying the witness's testimony and thus enables the jury to more accurately assess the witness's credibility.[7]

Offering too attractive a deal or too many deals to an informant can backfire on the prosecutor.[8] In the 1996 high-profile drug trafficking trial of two reputed drug kingpins, the government presented 27 eager witnesses from the U.S. prison system to testify against the defendants. That testimony failed to persuade the jury, and the defendants were found not guilty.[9] The fact that the foreman and one other juror in the case were found guilty in 2003 of accepting cash bribes certainly did not help the government's case.

Some agreements cover one-time statements by informants, while others contemplate continuing active cooperation. Instances in which the informant is to make a one-time statement can have one of two focuses: (1) the informant wants to share information, but asks for immunity before sharing it, or (2) the informant wants a benefit — promise of nonprosecution, a reduced charge, or sentence reduction — and is willing to make a statement to get it.[10] Judge Stephen Trott made the following observation:

> The first problem that usually arises is the "catch 22" situation where you want to know exactly what the witness has to offer before committing yourself to a "deal." But the witness — even though desirous of cooperating — is afraid to talk for fear of incriminating himself unless he is promised something first. When you get into such a situation, never buy a pig in a poke! If you first give a criminal absolute immunity from prosecution or commit to a generous deal and then ask him what he knows, the probability is that you will get nothing but hot air. *Remove the witness' incentive to cooperate and you will lose all the fish, both big and little.* Never forget that almost always they are cooperating because you have them in a trap. Open the door too early and their willingness to cooperate will evaporate.
>
> The answer to this seeming dilemma is very simple. Promise the witness in writing that you will not use what he tells you at this stage of the proceedings against him, but make it equally clear that your decision whether or not to make a deal will not be made until *after* you have had the opportunity to assess both the value and the credibility of the information. I tell them "It's an opportunity to help yourself; take it or leave it." If they don't trust *you* enough to go first, how in the world are you going to trust them? You can talk possibilities, but that is all! And remember, once you have committed to something, your word must be as good as gold,

both with respect to what you will do if he delivers and what you will do if he doesn't.[1]

A similar approach to the stalemate is the "no-deals deal."[11] The no-deals agreement immunizes the informant's statement, but the immunity does not include the fruits of the statement including leads, evidence, and witnesses identified in the statement. Nor does it preclude use of the statement for impeachment purposes. No promises are made about future charges, plea negotiations, or sentencing recommendations.[11] The no-deals deal serves the needs of both the investigator and the informant: The informant receives adequate assurances, and the investigator can assess the value of the informant's information without having made unconditional promises to the informant.

If the informant is expected to work with law enforcement officers on a continuing basis, the written agreement may be quite different. A benefit may be specified, though most likely it would exclude immunity for violent crimes (as is the policy in Arizona). The agreement also should specify how compliance will be measured, requiring, for example, daily check-in with a specific individual.[11]

At a minimum, the plea agreement should include:

- That the defendant agrees to cooperate with the prosecutor and the law enforcement agency investigating the case.
- That the defendant will be forthcoming with all information known to him during debriefings by investigators.
- That the defendant will provide all physical evidence requested by investigators and all evidence known by him to exist including, but not limited to books, records, documents, or computer generated files.
- That the defendant agrees to waive the venue both for trial and sentencing. That the defendant agrees to submit to a polygraph examination.

All informant agreements should include a provision allowing the law enforcement agency to withdraw from the agreement if the informant fails to comply with the agreed upon terms. As an example:

> Defendant will give her full cooperation and a truthful statement regarding [certain transactions] and will testify truthfully at any grand jury proceedings and/or trials which may result as a consequence of her cooperation ... . The Government, in exchange for the above, will move to dismiss Count Two of the indictment filed herein at the time of sentencing. *Additionally, the Government*

will, in its sole and absolute discretion, determine whether or not the defendant's subsequent cooperation and testimony, if any, is, in fact, substantial assistance. If the Government, in its sole and absolute discretion, so determines that such cooperation is in fact substantial assistance, the Government will move for departure pursuant to § 5K1.1.

The defendant understands, agrees and acknowledges that the Government has made no promise express or implied, to make any such motion at this time, is under no obligation to make such motion, and will not make any such motion unless the Government decides that the defendant has provided substantial assistance. The defendant further understands, agrees, and acknowledges that, if any such motion is made by the Government, any departure or reduction to the defendant's sentence shall be determined by the court.[12] (Emphasis added.)

When a plea agreement leaves discretion to the prosecutor, the court's role is limited to deciding whether the prosecutor has made its decision to withdraw from the agreement in good faith.[13] The agreement must include all promises made to the informant.

In *United States v. Boyd*,[14] one of the "El Rukn Gang" proceedings alleging serious prosecutorial misconduct, numerous "side deals"[15] outside of the written plea agreement were alleged by the defense. They were not disclosed at trial or when guilty pleas were taken by the court.[15] At the defendant's sentencing, his attorney stated "the reality of [Clay's] plea agreement was an understanding among everybody, not discussed by anybody, that if this prosecution was successful there could and would be renegotiation of the plea agreement." The Assistant U.S. Attorney representing the government at the defendant informant's sentencing did not dispute the assertion. Coupled with other acts of prosecutorial misconduct the defendant's motion for a new trial was granted.[15]

In a case involving a contract dispute between an informant and the Federal Bureau of Investigation (FBI), *Doe v. United States*,[16] the source was recruited to work in an undercover capacity assisting in a money laundering operation. The informant agreement, referred to as a contract, anticipated some of the future needs of the informant and the FBI. It included provisions that:

The FBI would request payment of an award to Doe from assets obtained through forfeiture but that the agreement "in no way constitute[d] a guarantee that such an award [would] be made or the amount of any such award."

The FBI, at a time which it "deem[ed] appropriate" would request the Department of Justice to "provide witness protection, relocation, and related security service in accordance with applicable Federal laws and regulations."

"When directed by the FBI," [the informant would] "testify and furnish all information in his possession" related to the investigation.

Under the heading "Confidentiality," the informant agreed that he would "in no way reveal the confidentiality and sensitive nature of [the] investigation or identify any undercover FBI agents."[16]

The contract further provided:

This document constitutes the full and complete agreement between Doe and the FBI. Modifications to this agreement will have no force and effect unless and until such modifications are reduced to writing and signed by all parties thereto.[16]

Conspicuously omitted was any clause requiring the FBI to maintain the confidentiality of the source. The informant in this instance submitted claims to the FBI under both the Federal Torts Claim Act[17] and the Contracts Disputes Act for $39,980,000[17] for the FBI's disclosure of his identity to infamous members of a Colombian drug cartel arrested due to his cooperation.[18]

Informant agreements also serve as a yardstick against which to measure an informant's cooperation.[19] While drafting the agreement care should be taken to guard against placing undue pressure[19] on a defendant informant to produce cases. (See Appendix 5B, "Contract.")

The agreement should contain a time frame for the promised cooperation to occur. If an unreasonably short amount of time is granted for the informant's performance, perjury or entrapment of an investigative target may result. Failing to include when performance by the informant must occur may impede an investigation. Informants seem inclined to postpone their cooperation until the latest possible time, usually shortly before trial or sentencing.

A defendant informant should not be required to, in "an allegorical sense … deliver the head" of a specific individual "to the prosecutor on a silver platter."[20] The cooperation agreement in *Medina-Reyes*[20] described by the court as "a remarkable document, the likes of which neither [the judge] nor the prosecutor nor the three defense lawyers" had ever seen, required in part that:

> The prosecutable cases contemplated by this agreement include purchases of narcotics from the above named persons. These purchases must be corroborated to the satisfaction of the office of the county attorney. ... the discretion of the investigating officers, the defendant may make introductions of undercover narcotics officers for the purpose of making above said purchases. Corroboration will be sufficient if such introductions result in successful purchases of controlled narcotics. The defendant must, within 30 days of the signing of this agreement, accomplish 2 purchases each from the California connections (specified target's name) and the Texas connection (unnamed), a total of 4 purchases.[20]

> A prosecutable case may also include providing information which results in a seizure by search warrant which results in evidence sufficient, in the opinion of the office of the county attorney, to charge one or more of the above listed persons with charges relating to possession of controlled substances with the intent to distribute.[20]

The risk of perjury or entrapment by the informant is too great when his only hope to stay out of jail is to seal the fate of another individual with a prosecutable case. The *Medina-Reyes* agreement clearly provided an incentive for the informant to frame his designated targets.

Informants who are being used to further routine investigations also are required to sign informant agreements. Many law enforcement agencies utilize a fill-in-the-blank standard form for all of their informants. The agreement is often a list of acts the informant *must not commit* while working with police. In effect it is a standard of conduct for the informant to adhere to. The agreement is generally not case specific and can be appended to more detailed contracts. (See Appendix 5C, "Informant Letter Agreement.")

The Drug Enforcement Administration's (DEA) form 473[21] is that agency's Confidential Source Agreement. It requires that informants be advised at the outset that:

1. They shall not violate criminal law in furtherance of gathering information or providing services to the DEA, and that any evidence of such a violation will be reported to the appropriate law enforcement agency.
2. They have no official status, implied or otherwise, as agents or employees of the DEA.

3. The information they provide may be used in a criminal proceeding, and that, although the DEA will use all lawful means to protect their confidentiality, this cannot be guaranteed.
4. It is a federal offense to threaten, harass, or mislead anyone who provides information about a federal crime to a federal law enforcement agency. Should they experience anything of this nature, as a result of their cooperation with the DEA, they should contact their controlling agent immediately.[21]

The confidential source (CS) is required to sign the form acknowledging that he has read and agrees to its conditions. The document is witnessed by two agents and placed in the informant's file. Informants who refuse to sign the agreement are not precluded from working. A statement by the recruiting agent is entered on the form that the CS was advised of and agreed to the conditions set forth on the form but refused to sign.

The Bureau of Alcohol, Tobacco, and Firearms (BATF) employs a similar agreement, but it is more comprehensive in its terms. It prohibits the informant from inducing others to commit crimes, warns the informant to respect the attorney–client privilege of his target, and reminds the informant that he is not a law enforcement officer or an employee of the BATF.

5.2 Proprietary Agreements

Many agencies conduct protracted covert investigations that employ "store-front"[22] operations including but not limited to precursor chemical supply houses, import–export businesses, pawn shops, and investment firms. Informants can either be placed in the "front" company or allow the law enforcement agency to use their business to further an investigation.

Business enterprises used in reverse undercover operations or "stings" can generate millions of dollars in revenue. Sources can expect to earn generous commissions during an investigation.

Customs has its agents execute a comprehensive informant agreement. Known as a proprietary agreement, it enumerates the responsibilities of the source and the benefits he can expect to reap if he complies with the document's terms. (See Appendix 5D for an example of the U.S. Customs Proprietary Agreement.)

5.3 Contingent Fee Agreements

Paid informants and defendant informants are clear in what motivates them to assist law enforcement. Although money[23] or leniency at sentencing[24] is what is being sought by the informant in exchange for cooperation, either reward is to some extent dependent upon the success of the investigative mission or the prosecution of the defendant.[25] In practically all instances, the informant is in reality working on a contingency basis.[26]

The prosecutor may offer one or a combination of several different inducements to a criminal in order to encourage testimony. These may include promises to dismiss one or more charges, immunity from prosecution, payment of money, an agreement not to forfeit property, or even the return of forfeited property.[27] Other inducements include reduction of offenses to lesser included charges, recommendation of probation or a reduced sentence, or an agreement by the prosecutor to forego prosecuting a witness's loved ones.[27] Most importantly, however, is that whichever inducement the witness agrees to can be made dependent upon that witness's testimony or the outcome of the trial.[28]

The use of criminal contingent agreements has been used in one form or another for more than 500 years.[29] However, early courts also recognized the great potential for perjury and, as a result, modified the use of criminal contingency agreements.[30] In current practice, prosecutors are restricted very little in their use of contingency agreements. Such agreements are entered into on the premise that the testimonial evidence would otherwise be unobtainable.[31] Some take comfort in the presumed and traditional safeguards of testimony such as swearing to an oath or affirmation, or reliance upon perjury, contempt, and false statement statutes.[31]

5.4   Contingent Fee Agreements and the Courts

At least one law review article has commented that most courts are not willing to examine contingency fee agreements closely to determine the witness's perception of performance required under the contract.[32] Generally, criminal contingent fee agreements are not objectionable if the witness is made to understand that his only requirement to fulfill his end of the bargain is to testify to all he knows regarding the specific crimes and defendants and to testify truthfully.[33] Courts hesitate to find that a witness has perjured him- or herself because of a criminal contingency agreement when there has been no direct testimony or specific language to that effect.[34]

As early as 1966, the Sixth Circuit Court of Appeals stated that, "the fact that a witness hopes or expects that he will secure a mitigation of his own punishment by testifying on behalf of the prosecution does not disqualify him."[35] Both the Fifth and Eighth Circuits have promulgated a relatively extensive amount of decisions regarding the use of criminal contingent arrangements.

5.5 Fifth Circuit

In 1962, the Fifth Circuit refused to sanction such an agreement.[36] The court would not allow a criminal contingent arrangement where a witness was to receive a stated amount for each defendant he provided evidence against. It was not until 25 years later that the Fifth Circuit overruled itself and subsequently approved the use of criminal contingent agreements.[37] In doing so, the Fifth Circuit held that it should be left up to the jury to determine the credibility of the compensated witness just as the jury determines the credibility of all the other witnesses.[38] Originally, the Fifth Circuit had determined that the agreement was "unacceptably coercive."[39] In a 1986 case, the court reasoned that the agreement in question was contra to the truth-seeking function of the judiciary because:

> [O]ne of the basics of our jurisprudence is the search for truth, and by this is meant *not the purchased truth, the bartered for truth,* but the unvarnished truth that comes from the lips of a man [sic] who is known for his integrity … . It may be that we must live with informers. It may be that we must live with bargained-for pleas of guilty. *But we do not have to give a receipt stamped "paid in full for your damaging testimony" or "you will be paid according to how well you can convince the jury even though it be in the face of lies."*[40]

Cervantes-Pacheco was later heard *en banc* by the Fifth Circuit, and the court watered down this language by determining that contingency fee agreements are *not per se* unconstitutional.[27]

In 1984, the District Court for the Southern District of Texas disallowed the testimony of an alleged coconspirator.[41] The court found the influence of the witness's contingency agreement coupled with other factors made the witness's testimony questionable. The essence of the agreement was that the witness was to testify against the defendants regarding past and future acts in a manner that would suffice for arrest and indictment. In exchange, the witness was to receive dismissal of pending charges, immunity, exemption from fines or forfeitures, reduction of bond, use of his property without threat of seizure, and release of a prior lien on his property. However, if the witness testified truthfully but insufficiently, he would get none of the above benefits. The court found that due process had been violated because the government agents were so obsessed with indicting specific defendants that they "created a situation which was indeed an invitation to Quiroga [the witness] to commit perjury.[42]

5.6 Eighth Circuit

The 1980s and the war on drugs produced an onslaught of criminal contingent arrangement cases, particularly in the Eighth Circuit. However, the Eighth Circuit began its approval of such arrangements as early as 1976.[43] In that year, the Eighth Circuit upheld the admission of testimony from an accomplice who was receiving monetary support from the government and determined that the support payments and the witness's immunity from prosecution were not problematic.[44] Five years later, the Eighth Circuit reinforced its previous decision, even though it believed that the witness committed perjury by laying the decision in the hands of the jury.[45] The witness had received such benefits as immunity from prosecution, recommended lenient sentence in state court, relocation, and federal subsidy payments.[46] The court declined to reverse convictions based on the witness's testimony, instead determining that "despite the apparent holes in his testimony, the jury chose to believe Anthony Ciulla. This was their prerogative, and the case was properly submitted to them."[47] The Eighth Circuit continued to uphold the use of criminal contingency agreements throughout the 1980s.[48]

However, in 1984, the Eighth Circuit determined that it is not "fair procedure" to "reward those who testify for the government contingent upon the content and the results of their testimony."[49] In *Waterman,* the government had agreed to recommend a two-year reduction of sentence for a witness's testimony, provided that the testimony resulted in more indictments.[50] No indictments, no recommendation. The court concluded that the government cannot offer favorable treatment to a prosecution witness contingent upon the success of the prosecution. Such an agreement is an invitation to perjury since the premium set by the government relates not to complete and truthful testimony but rather to result-oriented testimony.[51] One year later, however, the Eighth Circuit analyzed another contingent fee arrangement, distinguished it from *Waterman,* and found that the agreement withstood scrutiny.[52]

Appendix 5A: U.S. Attorney's Proffer to Informant's Attorney

U.S. Department of Justice
United States Attorney
Southern District of Florida
United States Courthouse
Miami, Florida

Defense Attorney
000 Flagler Street
Miami, Fla.

Re: [Client's Name]

Dear Mr. Defense Attorney:

As we have discussed, the government is conducting a grand jury investigation regarding allegations that [_____]. Of course, the government welcomes any information that may aid it in reaching a proper determination of this matter. Accordingly, the government seeks a proffer of the testimony of your client, [_____], regarding his knowledge of the facts underlying the investigation.

The government requires a completely truthful statement of your client in this proffer. Anything related to the government by you or your client during the proffer cannot and will not be used against your client, [_____], in the government's case-in-chief. However, the government is completely free to pursue any and all investigative leads derived in any way from the proffer, which could result in the acquisition of evidence admissible against your client in subsequent proceedings. Likewise, nothing shall prevent the government from using the substance of the proffer for impeachment or in rebuttal testimony should your client subsequently testify contrary to the substance of the proffer.

This letter embodies the entirety of the agreement to make a proffer of your client's testimony. No other promise or agreement exists between your client or this office regarding the proffer. Please have your client read this letter, sign the acknowledgement copy and return it to me.

Very truly yours,

_____

United States Attorney
or

_____

Division Chief

Appendix 5B: Contract

IT IS HEREBY AGREED between the State of _____ and _____, that in return for pleading guilty to Possession of a Narcotic Drug, a class four felony, *with* probation available, which is currently pending in cause number _____, before the Superior Court of _____ County, that _____ will perform all of the conditions listed in this agreement:

1. That he will execute a standard _____ County Informant's agreement and abide by the conditions set forth therein.
2. That he will provide control agents with introductions to drug dealers and/or information that will enable the control agent to obtain search warrants resulting in a total of 15 cases. A case shall be defined as involving at least 100 pounds of marijuana or 6 ounces of cocaine or heroin.
3. That he has 180 days from the first of _____ in which to complete these 15 introductions.
4. That he understands that, if possible, he shall not be required to testify unless he has become a material witness in a case.
5. That he agrees that if the State determines that he is a material witness, he shall testify truthfully at all proceedings required by the prosecutor including, but not limited to, interviews, pretrial motions, trials, retrials, or any other proceeding that the State deems necessary. He further agrees that all such testimony shall be truthful and that failure to testify truthfully will, at the prosecutor's discretion, result in felony charges of perjury being filed and/or this agreement being revoked and the original charges being reinstated and prosecuted to the fullest extent of the law. He further understands and agrees that the State has this right even though he may have been found guilty and sentenced. The prosecutor shall have sole right to determine whether the terms and conditions set forth have been breached.
6. He understands that if the full terms of this agreement are not completed, the attorney for the State shall determine what credit will be given for the parts that were completed.

Failure to abide by any of the conditions set forth in this agreement will result, at the discretion of the State, in revocation of the agreement and resumption of prosecution on the original charges.

I have read and understand the terms of the agreement set forth above and agree to the conditions set forth. Signed this _____ day of _____, 2_____.

_____

DEFENDANT

I have discussed the terms set forth in the agreement with _____ and believe that he understands the terms and conditions contained in the agreement. Signed this _____ day of _____, 2____.

_____

ATTORNEY FOR DEFENDANT

I hereby bind the State of _____ to the terms and conditions set forth in the above agreement. Signed this _____ day of _____, 2____.

_____

DEPUTY COUNTY ATTORNEY

Appendix 5C: Informant Letter Agreement*

RE: Investigation of (on-going) (nature of investigation)

Dear _____ :

    This letter is the written assurance and understanding of the State of _____ through the _____ County Attorney regarding your cooperation with law enforcement in the investigation of the structure and potential or actual criminal activity being done on the part of (insert target).

    The State is interested in obtaining accurate and complete information about the above matters, and is willing to consider cooperation in these investigations as a factor in its future decisions regarding possible criminal charges against you. You are advised of your Constitutional rights to remain silent and to an attorney, including, but not limited to, the following rights:

1. That you have a right to remain silent;
2. That anything you say can and will be used against you in criminal prosecution, pursuant to and limited by the terms of this Agreement;
3. That you have a right to the presence of an attorney to assist you prior to questioning and to be with you during questioning if you so desire;
4. That if you cannot afford an attorney you have a right to have an attorney appointed for you prior to questioning at no cost to yourself.

    You further acknowledge by signing this that no one has used any sort of violence or threats or any promise of immunity or benefit whatsoever to encourage you to answer questions, and that no representations have been made to you other than the representations set forth in this Agreement.

    You nevertheless agree that the State may use any information, leads, evidence or witnesses supplied by you, that is, any "fruits" of your cooperation, in any way.

    Within the limitations above, I assure you and agree with you that if your complete and truthful cooperation implicates you in past crimes, your statements themselves will not be used in evidence against you in any State criminal prosecution so long as the following conditions are met:

1. Your statements are complete and truthful to the best of your knowledge.
2. For your information to be useful, law enforcement will need time to follow up on it before possible defendants are aware you have given statements. So, as an additional condition of our Agreement, I will need your assurance that you will not disclose to anyone (except your attorney if you retain one and then only within attorney–client confidence) the fact that you have given statements or the contents of the statements or questions asked of you unless and until ordered to do so by a court. In consideration of this, and because of danger to yourself, any law enforcement people, including myself, involved in the follow-up will treat you as a "confidential" source, and will not disclose the fact of your statements or their contents unless and until ordered to do so.
3. You commit no criminal act except as specifically requested *in advance* by one of the Interviewers signing this Agreement, who will request such activity only to further the investigation and later prosecution of crime. If you commit any criminal act outside the condition set forth above, you are subject to prosecution for such act, and this Agreement is null and void.

4. The State is opposed for reasons of principle to entering into Agreements with people who have directly caused a person's death or serious physical injury, so, although we have no reason to believe you have done so, we specifically exclude liability for directly causing death or serious physical injury from this Agreement. Offenses within these two excluded areas, if any, will have to be dealt with on an individual basis on their individual facts.

I emphasize that the protection against State criminal prosecution granted to you under this Agreement is in no way dependent or conditioned upon the substance of the testimony or other information you may hereafter provide to the State, except for the requirements of complete honesty and truthfulness, nor is it in any way dependent or conditioned upon the return of any indictment(s) or the obtaining of any criminal convictions against any individuals or entities. In short, your obligation hereunder is to tell the truth, the whole truth and only the truth. If you fail to live up to or abide by any of the conditions, these assurances are no longer effective and the State will proceed accordingly, including, if it is determined that you have lied, in a prosecution for perjury or false swearing. Since your fulfillment of your part of this Agreement will constitute a waiver of your Fifth Amendment privilege against self-incrimination, if you violate any provision of this Agreement, you will become subject to prosecution for having violated it, and any statements or information you provide to the State would be admissible in evidence against you, in addition to leads or witnesses gained pursuant to this Agreement.

In return for your cooperation, the State agrees that it (insert benefits). To gain information on (insert target) it is agreed that your cooperation includes infiltration of that group by becoming a full-fledged member and that you continue to give information for a minimum of six (6) months from the date you become a member. As stated previously in this Agreement, you are not to commit any crime during this investigation. Furthermore, if you become aware of activity that places another in jeopardy of death or serious physical injury, you are to report that immediately to one of the Interviewers signing this Agreement. It is also required under the terms of this Agreement that you shall have daily contact with one of the Interviewers signing this Agreement. I fully understand and agree that the State will not file charges on the condition that the terms of this Agreement are fulfilled.

It is also understood that this Agreement binds the ____ County Attorney's Office, but that other jurisdictions are not bound by this Agreement as they are not parties to the Agreement and the _____ County Attorney's Office has no authority to bind other jurisdictions.

Your signature in the space provided below will confirm that the foregoing accurately sets forth the terms of our understanding. Except as set forth above, there are no understandings or agreements of any kind between the State and you in this matter.

This agreement and waiver is to cover all statements made by you and/or actions taken by you at the request of the undersigned Interviewers commencing at the time this Agreement is signed by the Interviewers and continuing until rescinded in writing by you or until superseded by another written agreement, or until the commencement of your trial on charges arising out of the above-mentioned investigation, whichever occurs first. Any modification of this Agreement must be in writing. No oral modification has any force or effect.

_____

County Attorney

by._____

Deputy County Attorney

ACCEPTED AND AGREED

_____   _____
Signature of Witness   Date and Time

INTERVIEWERS

_____   _____
                              Date and Time

_____   _____
                              Date and Time

Appendix 5D: U.S. Customs Proprietary Agreement

Paragraphs marked by asterisk should be included in all agreements.

AGREEMENT

* This agreement made this ____ day of _____, 200_ between _____ hereinafter called Source, and the United States Customs Service, hereinafter called USCS, specifies various terms and conditions as follows:

1. Source will assist the USCS in the operation of an export business to include arranging for the purchase of items for export and the exporting of said items. Source agrees to assist in any manner deemed in furtherance of said exporting business by the USCS.

* 2. Source understands that this assistance will be for an unspecified period of time not to exceed ____ weeks from the date of this agreement; commencement of assistance has already begun.

* 3. Source understands that he is entitled to reimbursement for expenses incurred in furtherance of this exporting business only when such expenses have previously been approved by an appropriate official of the USCS.

* 4. Source understands and agrees not to discuss or in any manner disclose this agreement and details of his activities without prior written authorization and approval by the USCS.

* 5. Source understands that he will keep such records of his time and activities as required by the USCS. Source agrees that unless authorized by the USCS, he will not record in any manner any conversations with USCS agents or employees.

* 6. Source understands and agrees to submit promptly to such polygraph examinations as may be requested by the USCS, limited to the case with which this agreement is concerned.

* 7. Source understands that his assistance may be terminated at any time, upon notice of such termination, at the sole discretion of the USCS.

* 8. Source understands that he will take no action in furtherance of the operation of the export business to be conducted by USCS without the prior approval of the USCS.

* 9. Source understands that any action taken by him without prior approval of the USCS places him outside the terms of this agreement and subjects him to any civil or criminal penalties which may be pertinent to the action he has taken. Further, any such independent action absolves the USCS from any liability incurred as a result of any such actions.

* 10. Source understands that the USCS, by entering into this agreement, makes no promises or agreement with regard to any court action now pending or which may be pending in the future concerning Source, and he acknowledges that his entering into this agreement with the USCS is fully and completely voluntary, and that he is under no coercion or pressure from the USCS to participate in this USCS operation of the export business.

* 11. Source understands that if requested he will fully and truthfully testify in any judicial proceeding.

* 12. Source understands that he is not an employee of the USCS.

13. Source is to retain ___% of amounts received and deposited into Account No. ___, at the ____ Bank of ____, ___, from respective purchasers, approved by USCS, as

his normal brokerage commission, not to exceed ____ million during the course of this agreement. Such commission is to be paid solely out of the receipts to Account No. ___ and not out of any funds appropriated to the USCS by Congress. If it is ultimately determined by an appropriate court that the purchaser's money must be returned, Source agrees to return all of the brokerage commission referred to above.

14. USCS in no way obligates itself to pay Source any monies for compensation for services or for expenses relative to this agreement except as explicitly provided herein. Furthermore, the USCS may, *without liability to Source,* at any time and for any reason decide not to engage in any transaction or sale, or to terminate any transaction or sale in progress under this agreement.

15. Retention by Source of the brokerage commission referred to above does not preclude Source from applying for Payment for Information and/or Payment for Information that may be provided in accordance with USCS guidelines, considering the magnitude and importance of the case at conclusion.

16. Retention by Source of the brokerage commission referred to above does not preclude Source from filing for or receiving an Award of Compensation to Informers in accordance with 19 USC 1619 or other applicable statutory or regulatory provisions.

17. USCS agrees it will not delay or otherwise encumber Source's commission referred to in paragraph 13. Source agrees that acceptance by him of any compensation from prospective purchasers in any manner other than that in this agreement (or otherwise approved by the USCS) authorizes the USCS to immediately rescind any payments due to Source under this agreement, and Source further agrees to return any brokerage commissions received by him under paragraph 13.

* 18. Source agrees that the terms of this agreement may be changed at any time, in writing, upon the mutual agreement of Source and the USCS.

* 19. This agreement contains the entire understanding among the parties hereto and supersedes all prior written or oral agreements among them respecting the within subject matter unless otherwise provided herein. There are no representations, agreements, arrangements, or understandings, oral or written, among the parties hereto relating to the subject matter of this agreement which are not fully expressed herein.

---------------------------------   ---------------------------

SOURCE   DATE

---------------------------------   ---------------------------

SAC   WITNESS
Special Agent in Charge

Appendix 5E: U.S. Attorney's Ground Rules Letter to Informant's Attorney

United States Attorney
Southern District of Florida
155 South Miami Avenue,
Suite 700
Miami, Florida 33130
Date

John Smith, Attorney
P.O. Box 89
Miami, Florida 33155

RE: United States v. (client)

Dear Mr._____,

Through you, your client has informed the government that he would like to plead guilty and cooperate with the government in the subject case and in the investigation of future cases, with a view toward obtaining a favorable sentence in the subject case. Let me outline the ground rules of your client's cooperation.

The government requires from your client a completely truthful written statement of his involvement in this case and the involvement of the other participants therein, including his codefendant. He also must provide complete and truthful information regarding any other criminal activity of which he has personal knowledge. This office agrees that no statements made by (client) in any written proffer or debriefing pursuant to this letter will be offered into evidence against him as part of the government's direct case in any criminal proceeding.

However, the government remains free to make derivative use of the information derived from your client directly or indirectly for the purpose of obtaining leads to other evidence. Such information may be used against (client) in any subsequent prosecution. Your client expressly waives any right to claim that such evidence should not be introduced because it was obtained as a result of his statements. This provision is specifically imposed to preclude the necessity of a *Kastigar* hearing in any proceeding in which such evidence is to be used against your client.

Further, the government may use statements made by your client in any written proffer or debriefing and all evidence, derived directly or indirectly for the purpose of impeachment of cross-examination, if (client) testifies at any trial or hearing, and/or in any rebuttal case against him in a criminal trial in which he is a defendant or a witness.

No additional promises, agreements, or conditions have been entered into other than as set forth in this letter, and none will be entered into unless in writing and signed by all parties. This letter does not confer any derivative use immunity or transactional immunity upon your client.

If the foregoing accurately reflects the understanding and agreement between this office and your client, it is requested that (client) and yourself execute this letter as provided below.

Very truly yours,

UNITED STATES ATTORNEY

BY:_____
ASSISTANT UNITED STATES ATTORNEY

ACKNOWLEDGEMENT

I have received this letter from my attorney, John Smith, have read it and discussed it with him, and I hereby acknowledge that it fully sets forth my understanding and agreement with the office of the United States Attorney for the Southern District of Florida. I state that there have been no additional promises or representations made to me by any official of the United States Government or by my attorney in connection with this matter.

Dated: _____
DEFENDANT

Witnessed by: _____
COUNSEL FOR DEFENDANT

Appendix 5F: Informant Agreement and Waiver

["No-Deals Deal"][1]

I, _____, acknowledge that I have been advised of and fully understand my Constitutional rights to remain silent and to an attorney, including, but not limited to, the following rights:

1. That I have a right to remain silent.
2. That anything I say can and will be used against me in a criminal prosecution, pursuant to and limited by the terms of this Agreement.
3. That I have a right to the presence of an attorney to assist me prior to questioning and to be with me during questioning if I so desire.
4. That if I cannot afford an attorney I have a right to have an attorney appointed for me prior to questioning at no cost to myself.

I further acknowledge that no one has used any sort of violence or threats or any promise of immunity or benefit whatsoever to encourage me to answer questions, and that no representations have been made to me other than the representations set forth in this Agreement.

My consent to cooperate with the investigation of _____ is limited to consent to derivative use of my statements, and to the direct use of my statements for impeachment and to the direct use of my statements in actions against myself for violations of any of the terms of this Agreement. I do not consent to any other direct use of my statements made pursuant to this Agreement against myself. I agree that the State may use any information, leads, evidence, or witnesses supplied by me, i.e., any "fruits" of my cooperation, in any way.

This interview is being conducted so that the State is made aware of all information I have in the matter of_____. At this point, I understand that the State makes no promises or benefits regarding any future plea negotiations or sentencing recommendations in [pending case].

I enter into this Agreement in the hope that my cooperation will be considered as a mitigating circumstance by the State in any future plea negotiations in [pending case]. However, I acknowledge that the State retains complete discretion in plea negotiations and sentencing recommendations and that the State has no power to assure that the Court will even consider any particular mitigating circumstances or sentencing recommendations. I agree that any favorable action by the State as a result of my cooperation is contingent on the State's evaluation of the truthfulness, completeness, and usefulness of my cooperation and that the State's judgment in all respects is final and binding upon me. In particular, I agree that any untruthfulness on my part will disqualify me from any benefit due to my cooperation whatsoever.

This Agreement and Waiver is to cover all statements made by me and/or actions taken by me at the request of the undersigned Interviewer(s) commencing at the time this Agreement and Waiver is signed by the Interviewer(s) and continuing until rescinded in writing by me or until superseded by another written Agreement or until the commencement of the trial in [pending case], whichever occurs first.

_____   _____
Date and Time   Signature of Witness

_____   _____
Date and Time   Witness's Attorney, if any

_____   _____
Date and Time   Interviewer

_____   _____
Date and Time   Interviewer

Appendix 5G: Plea and Cooperation Agreement

IN THE UNITED STATES DISTRICT COURT FOR THE NORTHERN DISTRICT OF FLORIDA, TALLAHASSEE DIVISION

UNITED STATES OF AMERICA
      vs.   TCR 96-00000
GEORGE SMITH
_____ /

PLEA AND COOPERATION AGREEMENT

1.   Parties to Agreement

This agreement is entered into by and between GEORGE SMITH, GREGG OLSON, attorney for GEORGE SMITH,
    and
the United States Attorneys Office for the Northern District of Florida. This agreement specifically excludes and does not bind any other state or federal agency, including other United States Attorneys Office, from asserting any civil, criminal or administrative claim it may have against GEORGE SMITH.

2.   Conditions Precedent

This agreement is conditioned on a proffer being made by GEORGE SMITH of the anticipated and expected testimony and cooperation of GEORGE SMITH. This proffer will be made to the United States Attorney's Office or its authorized representative. Upon proffer, the United States Attorney's Office, in its sole discretion, will accept or reject the proffer. If the United States Attorneys Office rejects the proffer, this agreement shall be null and void, and the parties shall have no further obligations pursuant to this agreement other than as provided by Fed. R. Crim. P. 11. If the United States Attorneys Office accepts the proffer, the parties will further agree as set forth below.

3.   Terms

If the proffer of GEORGE SMITH is accepted and GEORGE SMITH provides complete and truthful testimony and cooperation, the parties agree to the following terms:

    A.   GEORGE SMITH will plead guilty to Count I of the Indictment and faces a maximum possible penalty of ten years to life imprisonment and a $4,000,000 fine, a five-year term of supervised release, and a $50 special monetary assessment. Defendant will also plead guilty to Counts IV and V of the Indictment and faces on each count a maximum possible penalty of ten years imprisonment, a $250,000 fine, a three-year term of supervised release, and a $50 special monetary assessment. GEORGE SMITH agrees to pay the $150 special monetary assessments on or before the date of sentencing.

    B.   The parties stipulate and agree that the relevant weight of cocaine involved is 100–150 kilograms.

    C.   The defendant acknowledges that the Sentencing Guidelines apply.

D. GEORGE SMITH agrees to cooperate with the United States Attorneys Office and its designated representatives or any agency which the United States Attorneys Office directs, including truthful testimony at grand jury, trial, or as otherwise requested involving any matters under investigation.

E. GEORGE SMITH hereby specifically waives any Fifth Amendment privilege or any other privilege inconsistent with the cooperation required by this agreement.

F. If all terms and conditions of this agreement are satisfied and there exists no cause for revocation as outlined in section 4, any statements made by GEORGE SMITH pursuant to this agreement, except as provided by sentencing guideline §1B1.8, will be treated by the United States as given under Rule 11(e), Federal Rules of Criminal Procedure.

G. Upon the district court's adjudication of guilt of GEORGE SMITH for violation of Title 21, United States Code, Section 846 and Title 18, United States Code, Section 922(g), the United States Attorney, Northern District of Florida, will dismiss the remaining counts of the Indictment against GEORGE SMITH and agrees not to file any further criminal charges against GEORGE SMITH arising out of the same transactions or occurrences to which GEORGE SMITH has pleaded. Further, the United States Attorney will not file an Information pursuant to Title 21, United States Code, Section 851.

H. Upon request of GEORGE SMITH, the United States Attorney agrees to make known its opinion as to the nature and extent of defendant's cooperation.

I. The parties agree that the sentence to be imposed is left solely to the discretion of the district court.

J. The United States Attorney further agrees that it will make no specific recommendation as to any length of incarceration or any amount of fine, but reserves the opportunity to advise the district court and any other authorities of its version of the circumstances surrounding the commission of the offense by GEORGE SMITH, including correcting any misstatements by defendant or defendant's attorney.

K. Nothing in this agreement shall protect the defendant in any way from prosecution for any offense committed after the date of this agreement, including perjury, false declaration, or false statement, in violation of Title 18, United States Code, Sections 1611, 1623, or 1001, or obstruction of justice, in violation of Title 18, United States Code, Sections 1503, 1505, or 1510, should the defendant commit any of these offenses during the cooperation phase of this agreement. Should the defendant be charged with any offense alleged to have occurred after the date of this agreement, the information and documents disclosed to the government during the course of the cooperation can be used against the defendant in any such prosecution.

L. GEORGE SMITH waives and relinquishes any right or entitlement to all transportation, housing, per diem, and witness fees relative to all grand jury and court appearances which may be required as part of his cooperation.

4. Revocation

A. The parties agree that the United States Attorney's Office may revoke this agreement due to any of the following:
   1. The defendant's refusal to cooperate as provided by this agreement
   2. Defendant's statements or testimony are incomplete or untruthful
   3. Failure of the defendant to comply with all terms of this agreement

       4.   Upon a showing that the defendant has any criminal liability for homicide

B.   If this agreement is revoked,

       1.   Any plea of guilty entered by GEORGE SMITH pursuant to this agreement and any judgment entered thereon shall remain in full force and effect and will not be the subject of legal challenge by defendant.

       2.   The United States may reinstate charges previously dismissed pursuant to this agreement or to otherwise file charges without limitation by this agreement.

       3.   All statements made by GEORGE SMITH pursuant to this agreement may be used against him in any subsequent prosecution.

5.   *Sentencing Guidelines*

A.   The defendant understands and agrees that the sentencing court will make the final determination of facts as to any sentence and as to any mitigating or aggravating factors concerning the proper sentence to be imposed. Adverse rulings shall not be grounds for withdrawal of defendant's plea. The Court is not limited to the facts and events contained in the factual statement provided by the United States Attorney.

B.   If, in the sole discretion of the United States Attorney's Office, GEORGE SMITH is deemed to have provided substantial assistance in the investigation or prosecution of other persons who have committed offenses, the United States Attorney's Office will file a §5K1.1 certification, Rule 35 or other appropriate motion with the district court. The determination of whether the defendant provides substantial assistance will not depend upon any charges being filed or convictions obtained as a result of defendant's cooperation. The defendant understands that should a motion be filed, any departure from the sentencing guidelines or reduction of sentence is left solely to the discretion of the district court.

C.   The government reserves the right to appeal any sentence imposed.

6.   *Conclusion*

There are no other agreements between the United States Attorney, Northern District of Florida, and GEORGE SMITH, and GEORGE SMITH enters this agreement knowingly, voluntarily, and upon advice of counsel.

                                 _____

                                 United States Attorney

_____   _____

GEORGE SMITH   Assistant U.S. Attorney

Defendant   315 S. Calhoun, Suite 510

                                   Tallahassee, Florida 32301

                                   (904) 942-8430

_____   _____

GREGG OLSON   Date

Attorney for Defendant

_____

Date

IN THE UNITED STATES DISTRICT COURT FOR THE NORTHERN DISTRICT OF FLORIDA, TALLAHASSEE DIVISION

UNITED STATES OF AMERICA
    vs.   TCR 96-00000 WS
GEORGE SMITH

_____ /

GOVERNMENT'S CERTIFICATION OF SUBSTANTIAL ASSISTANCE PURSUANT TO SECTION 5K1.1 OF THE UNITED STATES SENTENCING GUIDELINES

COMES NOW the United States of America, by and through the undersigned Assistant U.S. Attorney, and files this Section 5K1.1 certification and states:

1. GEORGE SMITH pleaded guilty to conspiracy to possess between 100–150 kilograms of cocaine with intent to distribute and three firearms charges.
2. GEORGE SMITH has provided the following assistance to the Government:
   A. SMITH has been debriefed by law enforcement and has candidly admitted the facts underlying the indictment with which he is charged.
   B. SMITH is willing to testify against codefendant CATHERINE CHAFFIN.
   C. SMITH provided key information leading to the indictment of *United States v. Steve Chaffin and Charles Pilchard*, Case No. TCR 96-00000 WS. Defendant Chaffin is a fugitive. Defendant Pilchard is scheduled to be tried by a jury in November 1996. SMITH is expected to be a key Government witness against both defendants.

For the above reasons, the Government certifies that GEORGE SMITH has provided substantial assistance to the Government pursuant to Section 5K1.1 of the United States Sentencing Guidelines.

Respectfully submitted,

_____

UNITED STATES ATTORNEY

_____

Assistant United States Attorney
315 S. Calhoun, Suite 510
Tallahassee, Florida 32301
(904) 942-8430

References

1. Trott, S.S., Assistant Attorney General, Crim. Div., The successful use of snitches, informants, co-conspirators, and accomplices as witnesses for the prosecution in a criminal case, Jan. 1984 Revision FOIA request #CRM-960224F. *See* Farrell, G., Sullivan gets 5-year prison sentence, *USA Today,* Aug. 12, 2005, B1.

2. *Lisenba v. California,* 314 U.S. 219, 227 (1941).

3. *Washington v. Texas.* 388 U.S. 14, 22–23 (1967).

4. *United States v. Gomez,* 810 F.2d 947, 956 (10th Cir.), *cert. denied,* 482 U.S. 908 (1987); *United States v. Kimble,* 719 F.2d 1253, 1257 (5th Cir., 1983), *cert. denied,* 464 U.S. 1073 (1984); *United States v. Evans,* 697 F.2d 240, 245 (8th Cir.), *cert. denied,* 460 U.S. 1086 (1983); *United States v. McCallie,* 554 F.2d 770, 772 (6th Cir., 1977).

5. *United States v. Koyjayan,* 8 F.3d 1315 (9th Cir., 1993).

6. *United States v. Arroyo-Angulo,* 580F.2d 1137, 1146 (2nd Cir.), *cert. denied,* 439 U.S. 913, 99 S. Ct. 285, 58 L. Ed. 2d 260 (1978). *See also United States v. Borello,* 766 F.2d 46, 56 (2nd Cir., 1985); *United States v. McNeill,* 728 F.2d 5, 14 (1st Cir., 1984); *United States v. Barnes,* 604 R2d 121, 151 (2nd Cir., 1979), *cert. denied,* 446 U.S. 907, 100 S. Ct. 1833, 64 L. Ed. 2d 260 (1980).

7. *McNeill,* 728 F.2d, 14; *United States v. Winter,* 663 F.2d 1120, 1134 (1st Cir., 1981); *United States v. Craig,* 573 F.2d 955 (7th Cir., 1977); *United States v. Townsend,* 796 F.2d 158, 163 (6th Cir., 1986).

8. Keneally, K., White collar crime, at a loss for an explanation, *Champion Magazine,* Nov. 1998. *See also* Glaberson, W., Ruling against testimony-for-leniency jolts court system, *New York Times,* Oct. 27, 1998. *Cf. United States v. Singleton,* 165 F.3d 1297, 1301 (10th Cir., 1999).

9. *United States v. Falcon,* 91-6060-CR. *See* Felon's testimony may have backfired in Willie, Sal case, *Miami Herald,* Feb. 26, 1996, 1, 6B.

10. *Informants and Undercover Investigations,* 16, U.S. Department of Justice, Bureau of Justice Assistance, Police Executive Research Forum, Nov. 1990.

11. *Informants and Undercover Investigations,* U.S. Department of Justice, Bureau of Justice Assistance, Police Executive Research Forum.

12. *United States v. Vargas,* 925 F.2d 1260, 1266 (10th Cir., 1991).

13. *United States v. Rexach,* 896 F.2d 710 (2nd Cir.), *cert. denied,* 498 U.S. 969, 111 S. Ct. 433, 112 L. Ed. 2d 417 (1990).

14. *United States v. Boyd,* 874 F. Supp. 179, 180 (N.D. Ill., 1994).

15 *United States v. Boyd,* 874 F. Supp. 180 (N.D. Ill., 1994).

16. *Doe v. United States,* 58 F.3d 494, 495 (1995).

17. 28 USC §§ 1346(b) and 2680(a).

18. *United States Department of Justice v. Landano,* 113 S. Ct. 2014 (1993); *Keltner v. Washington County,* 800 P.2d 752 (1990).

19. *Informants and Undercover Investigations*, U.S. Department of Justice, Bureau of Justice Assistance Police Executive Research Forum, 16, 1992.

20. *United States v. Medina-Reyes*, 877 F. Supp. 468, 475 (S.D. Iowa 1995).

21. *DEA Agents Manual*, Ch. 6612.

22. *DEA Agents Manual*, Ch. 66, Reverse Undercover Operations.

23. *United States v. Reynoso-Ulloa*, 548 F.2d 1329, 1338 n.19 (9th Cir., 1977).

24. *United States v. Kimble*, 719 F.2d 1253 (5th Cir., 1983). *See also United States v. Insana*, 423 F.2d 1165, 1169 (2nd Cir., 1970).

25. *United States v. Bernal-Obeso*, 989 F.2d 331 (9th Cir., 1993).

26. *Williamson v. United States*, 311 F.2d441, 446 (5th Cir., 1962) Cameron, Cir. J., dissenting opinion.

27. Perroni, S.A. and McNutt, M.J., Contingency fee agreements: how fair are they? 16 *U. Ark. Little Rock L.J.*, 211 (1994).

28. *United States v. Baresh*, 595 F. Supp. 1132, 1137 (S.D. Tex. 1984), a case described by the court as an invitation for the informant to commit perjury.

29. Hughes, G., Agreements for cooperation in criminal cases, 45 *Vand. L. Rev.* 1, 7 (1992).

30. Eisenstadt, N.B., Let's make a deal: a look at *United States v. Dailey* and prosecutor–witness cooperation agreements, 67 *B.U. L. Rev.* 749, 761 (1987).

31. Perroni, S.A. and McNutt, M.J., Contingency fee agreements: how fair are they? 16 *U. Ark. Little Rock L.J.*, 212 (1994).

32. Accomplice testimony under conditional promise of immunity, 52 *Colum. L. Rev.* 138, 139–140 (1952).

33. Perroni, S.A. and McNutt, M.J., Contingency fee agreements: how fair are they? 16 *U. Ark. Little Rock L.J.*, 213 (1994).

34. *United States v. Vida*, 370 F.2d 759 (6th Cir., 1966), *cert. denied*, 387 U.S. 910 (1967).

35. 370 F.2d, 767–768.

36. *Williamson v. United States*, 311 F.2d 441 (5th Cir., 1962).

37. *United States v. Cervantes-Pacheco*, 826 F.2d 310 (5th Cir., 1987). *See also United States v. Lane*, 693 F.2d 385 (5th Cir., 1982); *United States v. Fallon*, 776 F.2d 727, 734 (7th Cir., 1985).

38. *Cervantes-Pacheco*, 826 F.2d, 315.

39. *United States v. Cervantes-Pacheco*, 800 F.2d 452 (5th Cir., 1986), *reconsidered*. *United States v. Cervantes-Pacheco*, 826 F.2d 310 (5th Cir., 1987).

40. *Cervantes-Pacheco*, 800 F.2d, 460.

41. *United States v. Baresh*, 595 F. Supp. 1132 (S.D. Tex. 1984).

42. *United States v. Baresh*, 595 F. Supp. 1137 (S.D. Tex. 1984).

43. *United States v. Librach*, 536 F.2d 1228 (8th Cir., 1976).

44. *United States v. Librach*, 536 F.2d 1230 (8th Cir., 1976).

45. *United States v. Winter*, 663 F.2d 1120 (1st Cir., 1981), *cert. denied*, 460 U.S. 1011 (1983).

46. *United States v. Winter*, 663 F.2d 1133 (1st Cir., 1981), *cert. denied*, 460 U.S. 1011 (1983).

47. *United States v. Winter*, 663 F.2d 1132 (1st Cir., 1981), *cert. denied*, 460 U.S. 1011 (1983).

48. *United States v. McCaghren*, 666 F.2d 1227 (8th Cir., 1981); *United States v. Janis*, 831 F.2d 773 (8th Cir., 1987), *cert. denied.* 484 U.S. 1073 (1988); *United States v. Spector*, 793 F.2d 932 (8th Cir., 1986), *cert. denied*, 470 U.S. 1031 (1987); *United States v. Risken*, 788 F.2d 1361 (8th Cir.), *cert. denied*, 479 U.S. 923 (1986).

49. *United States v. Waterman*, 732 F.2d 1527, 1532–1533 (8th Cir., 1984), *cert. denied*, 471 U.S. 1065 (1985); *see also United States v. Payne*, 940 F.2d 286 (8th Cir., 1991).

50. 732 F.2d at 1530.

51. 732 F.2d at 1531–1532.

52. *United States v. Bonadonna*, 775 F.2d 949 (8th Cir., 1985).

Informant Documentation and Identification

6

6.1 Generally

The proper documentation of an informant is essential. Failures at this critical stage can result in defense claims of prosecutorial misconduct and allegations of *Brady*[1] violations for failure to disclose evidence that would erode an informant's credibility at trial.

In extending the *Brady*[1] duty to searches for evidence, the Fifth Circuit framed the matter as one of incentives for the government, arguing that, without the extension, "we would be inviting and placing a premium on conduct unworthy of a representative of the United States government."[2]

The Seventh Circuit warned that a prosecutor's office cannot get around *Brady*[2] by keeping itself in ignorance, or compartmentalizing information about different aspects of a case.[3] The prosecutor must insist that his case agents fully explore the backgrounds of their informants to avoid the potential for *Brady* errors.

The defendant and the truth-seeking mission of an investigation and prosecution can also suffer damage if the agents fail to develop and disclose all that is known about an informant.

> In *Barbee v. Warden, Maryland Penitentiary,*[4] the court held that the prosecution is liable for the nondisclosure of exculpatory evidence in the hands of the police. "Failure of the police to reveal such material evidence in their possession is equally harmful to a defendant whether the information is purposely or negligently

115

withheld. And it makes no difference if the withholding is by officials other than the prosecutor. The police are also part of the prosecution, and the taint on the trial is no less if they, rather than the State's Attorney, were guilty of the nondisclosure. If the police allow the State's Attorney to produce evidence pointing to guilt without informing him of other evidence in their possession which contradicts this inference, state officers are practicing deception not only on the State's Attorney but on the court and the defendant. 'The crudest lies are often told in silence.'"[4]

Agent safety can also be compromised if the documentary process is not strictly followed. The Bureau of Alcohol, Tobacco, and Firearms (BATF) trains its agents that:

> A special agent increases his/her personal hazard when working with an informant whose identity is known only to him/her. In the event the special agent is injured, killed, held hostage, etc., while working in connection with the informant, the Bureau would find it extremely difficult to undertake an investigation if the informant's identity and background information were not available. To ensure that this does not occur, all informants will be identified and documented in accordance with the provisions of this chapter. Only after identification, documentation, and approval by the Special Agent in Charge will an agent use an informant.[5]

Needlessly placing an undercover officer in the company of an unstable or dangerous informant can be avoided. A comprehensive background investigation may determine that the informant was "black-balled" by another agency for misconduct and deactivated.[6] The informant may have a criminal history unknown to the agent that could nullify his testimony in court.[7]

Once recruited, the informant must be fully identified and documented by the agent handler. An effective informant today is often tomorrow's target of investigation. Most informants were from the criminal element when they began working for a law enforcement agency. During the course of their relationship with an agency, the confidential informant (CI) often becomes schooled in the latest investigative tactics and technology used by law enforcement. Many leave their work as a CI to become a more effective criminal. Some utilize their newly acquired talents to further their own criminal enterprise while simultaneously working for the police, attempting to "work both sides." (See Chapter 10, "Controlling the Informant.")

Informants have been known to "set up" their agent handler for "rip-offs" (robbery) during high-stakes drug transactions. Fully documenting the informant assists the agency in arresting and prosecuting informants who violate the law or in enforcing the terms of their agreement.

The documenting process also provides for internal controls of agent conduct. Failures in the management of cooperating individuals constitute the most obvious single cause of serious integrity problems in the Drug Enforcement Administration (DEA) and other law enforcement agencies.[8]

Comprehensive documentation and informant file systems[9] also serve to verify the existence of the source to prosecutors and police managers. Creating informants rather than recruiting informants has been an allegation made by defense attorneys for decades. Prosecutors and police alike have routinely dismissed these claims as a defense smoke screen designed to mandate an evidentiary hearing.[10]

The unfortunate truth is that some police officers do "invent" their informants. Agents are able to obtain search warrants by attributing fictitious accounts of criminal activity in affidavits to a nonexistent "reliable informant." Police officers who lie under oath privately refer to the practice as "testilying."[11]

Graphically illustrating the practice was a Boston Police Department search warrant executed on February 17, 1988. A "reliable informant's" account of drug dealing was used to support an affidavit for a search warrant filed by a Boston Police detective. During the execution of the warrant, the affiant's partner was shot and killed by the occupant of the residence.

The gunman was arrested shortly after the shooting and charged with the murder of the officer. The defendant's attorney began a diligent investigation of the case and discovered discrepancies in the affidavit and search warrant regarding the informant.

Attempts by police to locate the informant failed. At one point in the investigation, the detectives claimed the informant had been killed in a drug dispute. "The detectives said they could not find the informant, nor did they have any idea of where to locate him or anything about his background, even though the affidavits showed the detective and the informant had met more than 120 times."[12] The defense team traced the informant to 38 other affidavits. An independent investigation conducted by the Suffolk County District Attorney found 50 warrants using that same informant in a one-year period.[12]

In January 1990, the lead detective testified in a preliminary hearing that the informant never existed. He also testified that his superiors had told him to "use this form affidavit because it contains everything we need to get over constitutional hurdles to have a good search warrant."[13]

The court wrote:

> This case shows that some police officers will lie and will lie further in an effort to cover up the initial lie. This is a case, in which defense counsel ... has uncovered contemptible and disgusting misconduct by police officers in blatant violation of their sworn duties.[13]

Illustrating that the Boston case was not an aberration, the *National Law Journal*[12] reported the following instances of fabricated informants:

> In 1993, in Waltham, outside Boston, seven drug convictions were thrown out when two investigators admitted they had fabricated the existence of informants to obtain warrants. "The detectives had gone into an apartment without a warrant, searched the house carefully and found drugs and money," says Peter A. Bella, a former Waltham, MA, prosecutor who represented one of the defendants. "The detectives then created an imaginary informant and attributed all the information to him, (then) went to a judge to get their search warrant."[12]

> In 1991, a Los Angeles Sheriff's Sergeant testified in the trial of six drug cops he supervised that in the mid-1980s the squad made up informants for search warrants and, in one case, fed a CI information and paid him to appear before a judge to repeat the details.[12]

> In 1991, a former Metro-Dade County police officer in Miami, Florida cooperated with federal prosecutors and testified in a racketeering trial of four other cops that he had stated falsely on search warrant affidavits that his information came from CIs "known for previous reliability." In fact, they did not exist. The former officer testified that he needed warrants to break into drug dens, where he stole thousands of dollars. He was placed on five years probation in June 1991.[12]

Inventing an informant and attributing accounts to a nonexistent source in a sworn affidavit would merit a *Franks* hearing.[14] Any evidence seized in a warrant issued by a magistrate so grossly misled as in the nonexistent informant cases would almost certainly be suppressed.[15]

The U.S. Supreme Court has described the requirements that the defense attorney must meet before an evidentiary hearing (*Franks* hearing) will occur:

To mandate an evidentiary hearing, the challenger's attack must be more than conclusory and must be supported by more than a mere desire to cross-examine (the affiant). There must be allegations of deliberate falsehood or of reckless disregard for the truth, and those allegations must be accompanied by an offer of proof. They should point out specifically the portion of the warrant affidavit that is claimed to be false; and they should be accompanied by a statement of supporting reasons. Affidavits or sworn or otherwise reliable statements of witnesses should be furnished, or their absence satisfactorily explained. Allegations of negligence or innocent mistake are insufficient. The deliberate falsity or reckless disregard whose impeachment is permitted ... is only that of the affiant, not of any nongovernmental informant.[16]

The documenting of sources makes the fabrication of an informant difficult if not impossible to accomplish. In the *Lewin* case, investigators determined that the "informant handler" had intentionally failed to follow police procedure concerning identification, supervision, and payment of informants. The incident has led the Boston Police Department to revise their informant guidelines.[12]

The process employed in documenting an informant can vary drastically between agencies. (See Appendix 6B, "Confidential Source Establishment Report DEA Form 512" and Appendix 6C, "FBI Request to Open Cooperative Witness File.") Depending upon a department's size and sophistication in handling informants, the questionnaire used for documentation can be the size of an index card, or it may be several pages in length, similar to a complete background investigation. (See Appendices 6A and 6B.) Most agencies employ a form of their own design that is completed by the recruiting agent and witnessed by a second agent. It is forwarded to a supervisor for review and approval. (See Appendix 6D, "FBI Informant Review Sheet" and Appendix 6E, "FBI Supervisor's 60 Day Informant File Review Log.")

Information obtained through the documentation process and later incorporated in the informant's file may be discoverable by the defense, depending upon the circumstances surrounding the demand and jurisdiction. Federal prosecutors have an obligation[17] under *Brady v. Maryland*[18] and *Giglio v. United States*[19] to provide the defense with material exculpatory evidence in its possession. Information that may be used to impeach an informant's credibility is generally found in the informant file.[20] Defense attorneys should carefully draft their requests for documents and records to encompass all that should be contained in the informant's file.

The same may also hold true for information about the case agent held in his personnel file. In 1991, the Ninth Circuit Court of Appeals held that law enforcement agencies must disclose to criminal defendants any and all impeachment materials contained in a testifying officer's personnel file. The government has a duty to examine "personnel files" upon a defendant's request for their production, even though the defendant makes no initial showing of materiality. No apparent distinction was made by the Ninth Circuit between official personnel files and unofficial files kept by supervisors concerning affected agents.[21]

Federal agents failing to conscientiously document an informant's true identity and criminal history could be responsible for a serious *Brady* violation. However, adverse actions are rarely taken by an agency against one of its agents for errors in documenting an informant. Sanctions could be sought through the U.S. Department of Justice, Office of Professional Responsibility. It is empowered to take actions against Justice Department agents for *Brady* violations.[22]

6.2   Documentation Data Format

The format followed for documentation will include some or all of the following data and may require additional information. (Italicized items 1–15 are required by the Bureau of Alcohol, Tobacco and Firearms, Investigative Priorities, Procedures, and Techniques.)

1. *Informant's true name and all known aliases.*

   The informant's true name must be obtained for purposes of completing a criminal background check. Some agencies, including Customs, allow CIs to adopt assumed names both for future identification and payment purposes.[23] The informant's true name is maintained in an agencies' primary CI file.

   Aliases are often as valuable as true names for identification purposes. Many CIs have been arrested, prosecuted, and incarcerated under an alias. Hyphenated names are often used interchangeably. Nicknames should also be included in the informant file. Many informants are known to their associates only by their nicknames. Having their nicknames can be a valuable piece of information when attempting to locate an informant who is avoiding contact with his handler or is wanted for a crime.

2. *Residence/business address or addresses and telephone numbers.*

   All residences used by the informant should be recorded, including the CI's parents, siblings, and paramour's home addresses. The information is extremely helpful in locating the informant during periods when he wishes to conceal his location, usually prior to trial. Recording business addresses accomplishes the same purpose.

Obtaining *all* telephone numbers serves a purpose other than communication. They also provide intelligence information concerning the criminal contacts the informant has outside of his dealings with his control agent. The CI's number(s) may appear on subpoenaed toll records of criminal targets other than those he is working on with police. His number may also appear on pen registers or touch tone decoders or be dialed during a wiretap investigation.

3. *Personal description, including date and place of birth.*

Biographical data are necessary to secure a complete criminal background check of the informant. The informant's place of birth can also provide investigative leads in determining the informant's whereabouts. Tattoos are also an indelible indication of present or past gang affiliations.

4. *Fingerprints and current photograph of the informant.*

Many informants object to having their fingerprints and photographs taken. Unless the informant has a verified Federal Bureau of Investigation (FBI) number (because of a previous arrest or fingerprint submission), there can be no excuse for not fingerprinting the informant. Fingerprinting informants serves several administrative purposes, although its primary goal is to fully identify the individual and learn the full extent of his criminal record.

The process employed in submitting an informant's fingerprints to the FBI is similar to those followed with an arrestee, but with one exception. When completing the FBI fingerprint card[24] the space designating "charge" is listed as "criminal inquiry." The box asking "reply desired"[25] is always checked "yes." The FBI will forward a copy of the informant's criminal record ("rap sheet") to the requesting office. The processing of fingerprints and receipt of a "rap sheet" does not occur quickly. Many agencies, including the DEA, allow utilization of informants on a "provisional basis" while awaiting an FBI response.[26] It is a dangerous practice and can expose an agent handler and an investigation to compromising situations. It is also an unnecessary risk. The FBI has installed DATALOG terminals throughout the United States allowing fingerprints to be electronically transmitted to the Bureau. Although generally reserved for use with defendants, it can also be employed for informants. State and local law enforcement agencies also maintain fingerprints and arrest and conviction records. Queries by other law enforcement agencies are respected, and the requesting agent will be provided with a state version of a "rap sheet" and fingerprint information.

Informants who object to being photographed resent the idea of having a "mug shot" taken. They also fear that the photo will be circulated, and their involvement as a CI will be exposed to others. As with fingerprints, there is no excuse for not photographing the CI. Law enforcement agencies routinely request driver's license photographs from state driver's license bureaus. They are in color and generally of good quality. Photos can also be obtained surreptitiously with a digital camera.

Photos, as with fingerprints, serve a valid law enforcement purpose. Informants routinely commit crimes while working as informants. They often "turn" on their agent handler, setting him up for armed robbery during a drug deal or exposing him to other danger. Both photographs and fingerprints assist in identifying the CI and can aid in his apprehension. They can also help in identifying the CI's remains in the event of death.

5. *Employment history; if unemployed, current source of income.*

A current target of investigation may have employed the informant. His existing relationship with the target could further an ongoing investigation or assist in the initiation of a new case. The informant may possess special skills that could increase his value to the agency. Informants with boat captain and pilot licenses are routinely employed.

Unexplained income can be an indicator that the informant is involved in illegal activity while working as an informant. Although this routinely occurs, most agencies have policies that prohibit the practice. Such a policy is difficult, if not impossible, to enforce. The reality is that most informants are criminals, and the money paid to them by law enforcement is usually not enough to sustain their lifestyle or drug habit.

6. *Social Security number.*

Social Security numbers are contained in numerous computer indexes outside of the government. They are a valuable investigative tool in tracking the activities of the informant and are available to law enforcement.

New Social Security numbers are issued to informants who enter the Witness Security Program. The U.S. Marshals Service in cooperation with the Social Security Administration facilitates the account transition. (See Chapter 11, "The Witness Security Program.")

7. *Past activities (criminal or criminally associated).*

Each informant must be fully debriefed by the recruiting agent. The nature and extent of the debriefing varies with the individual informant's background, whether he is a long-time associate of criminals or has information pertaining to one criminal event.

Agencies whose focus is restricted to particular crimes such as the DEA and BATF are encouraged to explore all areas of criminal activity in the debriefing of informants. Information developed outside their area of responsibility should be disseminated to the appropriate agency "unless there is a valid reason not to do so."[27]

8. *FBI number, state and local criminal I.D. numbers.*

Informants routinely conceal their criminal histories from their agent handlers. Lies by an informant about his felony criminal record can be relevant evidence at later trials concerning the informant's credibility.[28] A serious felony record could cause a jury to completely disregard the informant's testimony and possibly to conclude that the government's entire case is suspect.[29]

The informant may not have understood the questions asked regarding his record or did not realize the significance of a false answer. Fully querying all criminal information systems available to the agent can resolve any confusion surrounding the informant's record.

9. *Criminal reputation and known associates.*

Information regarding a prospective informant's criminal reputation and known associates could be found in the intelligence files of the department. There is a great deal of criminal intelligence information collected by federal, state and local police agencies. Much of the information is stored in computer databases and is readily accessible to agents within their own agency (see Chapter 8, "Corroboration of Informant Information"). Interagency sharing of information does occur to a certain extent, but there is no "central clearinghouse" of criminal intelligence files.

Some of the systems available to agents include:

A. *The National Crime Information Center (NCIC).* The NCIC is a telecommunications system operated by the FBI. The system is accessible to various federal, state and local law enforcement agencies throughout the country. An NCIC query will provide a criminal history and determine whether the informant is a fugitive.

B. *The Treasury Enforcement Communications Systems (TECS).* TECS is a telecommunications system with terminals located in Department of Treasury facilities throughout the world. If the informant's name appeared in any report written by a Treasury agent, it would appear in TECS.

C. *Narcotics and Dangerous Drugs Information System (NADDIS).* NADDIS is the DEA's computerized information system. All intelligence and criminal related information collected by the agency and memorialized in an investigative report (DEA 6) finds its way into the NADDIS system. If the informant's name, telephone number, addresses, or vehicle license plate number appeared in a report prepared by the DEA, it would be found in NADDIS.

10. *Military, citizenship, parole/probation status.*

Military records for personnel discharged from all branches are maintained at the National Personnel Records Center, Military Personnel Records, 9700 Page Boulevard, St. Louis, Missouri.

Citizenship. Immigration and Customs Enforcement maintains records pertaining to noncitizens. The records are maintained up until the time the alien becomes a naturalized citizen.

Parole and probation. Each agency has its own guidelines pertaining to the use of informants on parole or probation.[30] Conversely, each state's parole and probation commission has its own policy on probationers or parolees working as informants. An investigative agency ignoring the requirements of a parole or probation department risks violating the terms of the informant's release. Probation files may hold information bearing upon the credibility of an informant and be discoverable.[31]

11. *Brief résumé of information furnished in the past, including:*

A. *Reliability of information provided.* Many agencies maintain a log of all instances in which the informant has provided reliable information. In jurisdictions applying the *Aguilar-Spinelli*[32] two-prong test, the basis of knowledge or "underlying circumstances" is the first prong, and reliability or veracity is the second prong of the test. Logging reliability is essential in those jurisdictions. In 1983, the Supreme Court abandoned the two-prong test in *Illinois v. Gates,*[33] adopting a totality-of-the-circumstances analysis.

B. *Date and value of information furnished.* Many agencies log all official reports generated because of informant information. The number of arrests, amount of contraband seized, money or property forfeited, and monies paid to the source are conspicuously noted.

C. *Whether the informant will testify in open court.* Agencies differ on their policies concerning the testimony of informants. Many local agencies have clauses in their informant agreements stating that they will recommend dismissal of a prosecution if the CI must testify. It should be noted that a majority of CI cases are "search warrant" cases whose affidavits contain accounts of unidentified informants. The Supreme Court has long sanctioned the use of these unnamed CIs.[34] Therefore, testimony by an informant in these cases is rarely an issue.

Federal agencies attempt to keep informants off the witness stand[35] but warn prospective CIs that they may have to testify. There is no fixed rule on the government's privilege to withhold the identity of the informant.[36]

D. *Identity of other agencies to which the informant is currently supplying information.* Agencies should not utilize informants who are simultaneously working with another agency. It is difficult if not impossible for the CI to effectively and loyally serve two agencies at the same time. Federal and state agencies routinely use informants in joint investigations, but the CI is controlled by the recruiting agency.

12. *Reason for becoming an informant (if known).*

The informant's true motive for cooperating must be determined. (See Chapter 2, "Motivations to Cooperate as an Informant.")

13. *A statement as to whether the informant has shown any indication of emotional instability, unreliability, or of furnishing false information.*

An informant who has previously committed perjury in court should not be utilized. False testimony is the strongest form of impeachment.[37]

If the informant has a reputation as a liar, there is little sense in expending time, effort, and money in his utilization. In *Mesarosh v. United States,*[38] the court reversed convictions when it was learned that the informant had told numerous lies about his background in subsequent trials. The court said that the informant's reputation as a liar "tainted" any conviction obtained with his testimony:

The question of whether his truthfulness in these other proceedings constituted perjury or was caused by a psychiatric condition can make no material difference here. Whichever explanation might be found to be correct in this regard, Mazzei's credibility has been wholly discredited by the disclosures of the Solicitor General. No other conclusion is possible. The dignity of the United States Government will not permit the conviction of any person on tainted testimony. This conviction is tainted, and there can be no other just result than to accord petitioner a new trial.

> The untainted administration of justice is certainly one of the most cherished aspects of our institutions ... the government of a strong and free nation does not need convictions based upon such testimony.

14. *The nature of the information or service to be supplied.* (See Chapter 5, "Cooperation and Contingency Fee Agreements.")
15. *Financial or other arrangements agreed to or expected by the informant in return for providing information or services.* (See Chapter 5, "Cooperation and Contingency Fee Agreements.")

6.3 Informant Code Numbers and Assumed Names

For security and confidentiality purposes, agencies either assign their informants a code number or a fictitious name. Some agencies issue both, utilizing the number in their investigative reports and the fictitious name for payment purposes.

The Drug Enforcement Administration has adopted a code number system. The code assigned to an informant appears in all investigative reports in lieu of the informant's true name.

The code will have nine characters, each designated as follows:

- The first character is always the letter "S."
- The next two characters are the designator of the establishing office (i.e., Miami is G1).
- The next two characters will be the last two digits of the fiscal year the informant was recruited.
- The last four characters will be a four-digit number indicating the order in which the informant was recruited during the fiscal year.
  For example: SG4-94-0001
  - G = Miami Field Division
  - 4 = Jacksonville Resident Office
  - 94 = Year
  - 0001 = The CI was the first informant recruited in 1994.

If a joint task force (staffed by federal, state, and local agents) recruits the informant, a letter X replaces the first of the four sequential numbers. G1-94-X001 indicates the CI is a task force informant, probably recruited by a police officer assigned to the task force.

Once the code number is assigned, it remains with the CI regardless of his geographic location. He can move from office to office without being issued a new number.

The Bureau of Alcohol, Tobacco and Firearms also employs an eight-digit code numbering system specifically for use in their investigative reports. The first five digits identify the district office responsible for recruiting the CI. The last three digits are the sequential number for the informant. For example: 93110-002: 93110 indicates the Los Angeles Strike Force, and 002 is the sequential number for the individual CI. In those instances where the CI is being paid or subpoenaed as a witness, a true name or "alias" can be utilized.[39]

Illustrating the autonomy of the respective agencies, the Customs Service uses a completely different approach to identifying their informants. It utilizes a five-character designator and an assumed name system.

All Customs informants are identified on a "source card" and numbered as follows:

S: preprinted on the source card.

001: a sequential number indicating the order of recruitment and assigned by the office of the agent handler.

NY: two letters indicating the office of origin (New York).

(IA: Some informants will have an additional two letters indicating that the CI belongs to Internal Affairs.)

The source is also given an assumed name. The practice is a mandatory requirement in the source documentation process. The source may use either his true or assumed name when signing for rewards. (See Appendix 6A, "Source Identification Card.")

The Drug Enforcement Administration maintains all reports relating to a particular cooperating individual in a CS file.[40] The DEA CS file contents are representative of what most agencies require, although different form numbers are utilized by each agency.

The file is maintained by the Confidential Source Coordinator who is responsible for issuing the informant code number. The file contains the following information:

- Confidential Source (CS) Establishment Report (see Appendix 6B, "DEA Form 512").
- CS Payment Record (see Chapter 4, "Sources of Compensation for Informants").
- CS Agreement. Must be signed and witnessed. Prohibits CS from violating laws; defines his status as a nonemployee; and states

confidentiality cannot be guaranteed (see Chapter 5, "Cooperation and Contingency Fee Agreements").

- Voucher for Payment of Information and Purchase of Evidence (see Chapter 4, "Sources of Compensation for Informants").
- Report of Investigation for Debriefing reports; Case Initiation reports; Deactivation reports.
- Criminal Inquiry Request for Date-of-Births (DOBs) after 1955.
- FBI Form FD-249 (Fingerprint Card).
- Current Photograph.
- Rap Sheets (State and FBI).
- Administrative Correspondence or Asset requests.
- Original CS Statements.

Local police agencies use similar methods for identifying their sources. A combination of numbering systems and assumed names seem to be the preference of those agencies.

6.4   Once Documented, Who "Owns" the Informant?

Many agents become extremely protective and secretive about their sources. It must be recognized that the informant should not be the "property" of one agent. Such a policy reduces the potential for agent misconduct or compromise. The International Association of Chiefs of Police (IACP) and the Bureau of Justice Assistance (BJA) described the difficulties a proprietary approach to informants by agents can create in the documentation process.

> Investigators may be reluctant to maintain department files on informants they use. They may fear that potential informants will not participate if they know records of their activities will be on file. They may not believe departmental security procedures will be effective in protecting their informant's identity — and may fear that incompetent or corrupt law enforcement personnel will gain access to their informant's name. Some may fear that a supervisor or another investigator will destroy a trust relationship built with a considerable investment of effort and time or "steal" the informant for his own use.[41]

The IACP/BJA model policy is based on the view that the department, rather than the individual investigator, must ultimately control the use of informants. It is a practical recommendation from a management standpoint but routinely resisted by state and local investigators.

Informants working for federal agencies routinely move throughout the United States and other nations. By necessity, there should be instances where agents other than the one responsible for recruitment control them. DEA policy clearly states that informants are assets of the agency, not of a specific agent.[42]

However, a federal agent who recruits an informant will rarely give up control of his CI without resistance. Federal agents are rated annually based upon the cases they have initiated or have brought to a conclusion. Informants are the fuel used to generate a significant percentage of those investigations and are one of the vital keys to the investigator's performance evaluation. As a result, an agent will jealously guard his cadre of informants.

Appendix 6A: Source Identification Card

```
NAME (Last, First, Middle)                    SOURCE NO.
SA-
_____
_____

A/K/A*:
 1)_____2)_____
ADDRESS:_____
_____
                    (Street-P.O. Box-Apt., etc.)
_____
_____

(City)                  (State)                  (Country)
(ZIP)
DOB: /    /    /  POB:
_____

_____
SSN:  /    /        D/L:
_____

_____
DESCRIPTION:   RACE/SEX: _____/_____ _____
HGT: _____'_____ __WGT: _____
EYES: _____ HAIR: _____ _____
SCARS / MARKS: _____
_____

NCIC: _____ TECS: _____
OTHER _____
MOTIVATION: _____EXPERTISE: _____
_____

Reporting Officer / Alternate Officer - Date Documented
*Form utilized by U.S. Customs Service to identify sources and assign
  assumed name. A/K/A — Also Known As.
```

Appendix 6B: Confidential Source Establishment Report* DEA Form 512

U.S. Department of Justice
Drug Enforcement Administration

Privacy Act Information

The following Privacy Act Statement must be read or shown to the confidential source beforehand. Collection of personal history information is authorized under Title 21, U.S. Code. Your supplying of identifying personal information is voluntary. This information is an element used to create a record of your cooperation. However, failure to provide the information requested may disqualify you from becoming a confidential source.

1. Name (Last, First, Middle)
2. No.
3. Source Date of Birth (MM/DD/YY)
4. Alias Name
5. Alternate Date of Birth
6. NADDIS No.
7. FBI No.
8. Social Security No.
9. Misc. Numbers (e.g., TECS; DRUG-X; Registrant, CSS No., etc.)
10. Place of Birth (City, State/County)
11. Citizenship (Country)
12. Alien Status
    Illegal
    Legal (Alien Registration No.)
13. Race
    Black
    White
    Native American
    Unknown
    Asian-Pacific Islander
14. Ethnicity
    Hispanic
    Non-Hispanic
    Unknown
15. Sex
    Male
    Female
16. Color Hair
17. Height
18. Occupation
19. Color Eyes
20. Weight
21. Address (No., Street, Unit, City, State/Country, Zip Code)

22. Identifying Characteristics (Scars, tattoos, marks, physical defects, etc.)
23. Telephone Number (including Area Code)
24. Employer Name and Address
25. Employer Telephone Number (including Area Code)
26. Passport No.
27. Issue Date
28. Issuing Country
29. Expiration Date
30. Name on Passport
31. Driver's License No.
32. Issuing State/Country
33. Expiration Date
34. Name on License
35. FAMILY INFORMATION
    a. (Last, First, Middle Name)
    b. Age
    c. Address (No., Street, Unit, City, State/Country)
    d. Phone Number
        Father
        Mother
        Spouse
        Companion
        Paramour
        Children
        Other Relatives (Name) (Relationship)
36. Confidential Source Type (Check one)
    Regular
    Defendant
    Restricted Use
    Other (Nonhuman) *Author's note: Wiretaps often produce information that must be acted upon. To preserve the secrecy of the wiretap's existence they are assigned an informant number.*
37. Confidential Source Action (Check one)
    Original
    Supplemental
    Reactivation
38. Source Type Qualification
    (Brief statement of situation qualifying the Source Type — 6612.29)
39. Confidential Source System (CSS) Check Coordinator
    (Name and Date Checked)
    CSS Results
        Negative
        System Hit
        CS Number(s)
40. Type of Cooperation (Brief statement on proposed cooperation: Include case number and NADDIS number if any)
41. Source Declared Unsatisfactory (8812.63)
    Yes
        CS Number
        Date

No
42. Unsatisfactory CS Reestablished
Yes
No
Date
OC Approval Date
43. Is (has) Source (been) Enrolled in U.S. Marshals WITSEC?
Yes
    CS Number
    Date
No
44. CS Status *(Check one)*
Probationer or Prisoner   Name of Approving Supervised Official:
Release   Title of Approving Official:
Parolee   Agency Approving:
          Date Approved:
(Check one) Fed. State
45. Criminal History Check — NADDIS: NCIC, Computerized Criminal History (CCH).
Interstate Identification Index (III); and INTERPOL (6612.26)
(Submit copies of positive & negative results along with DEA-202)
Date inquiry Performed
Criminal History
Yes No Active Warrant(s) No Yes
    (Do not proceed with approval process without discharging warrant.)
    Agency Name
    Agency Willing to Extradite No Yes
46. Interpol Check (6612.26) Name & Telephone No. of Interpol Contact, Date Performed, Results (i.e., negative)
47. Prosecutor Approval If Defendant Source
Prosecutor Name:
Area Code and Telephone Number:
Judicial District:
Date of Approval:
48. DEA - 473, Cooperation
Agreement, included Yes
49. Two (2) Photographs included Yes
50. DEA-105, Criminal Inquiry
Request for FD - 249, Fingerprint Cards *(3 cards)*
Yes N/A   Yes N/A Exempt
Waiver (only for 6612/26)
51. DEA - 6. Initial Debriefing
Report Included Yes
52. Telephonic Approval *(Date)*
GS/RAC received telephonic approval for CS establishment by SAC/CA
        (Name) Via ASAC/ACA *(Name)*
53. Remarks
54a. HQS, Command Center System Coordinator Issuing Number:
54b. Coordinator's Name

54c. Date
55a. Agent/Officer Name *(Print or Type)*
55b. Signature   Date
56a. Coagent/Officer Name *(Print or Type)*
56b. Signature 56c.   Date
57a. Supervisor Name *(Print or Type)*
57b. Signature 57c.   Date
58a. ASAC Name *(Print or Type)* 58b. Signature
58c. Date Concur   Yes   No
59a. Assoc. SAC Name *(Print or Type)*
59b. Signature
59c. Date   Concur   Yes   No
60a. SAC Name *(Print or Type)*
60b. Signature
60c. Date   Approved Yes   No

Appendix 6C: FBI Request to Open Cooperative Witness File

UNITED STATES GOVERNMENT MEMORANDUM

TO: SPECIAL AGENT IN CHARGE
FROM: <u>SPECIAL AGENT JOHN JONES</u>
SUBJECT: COOPERATIVE WITNESS

It is requested that the individual described below be opened and maintained by the Confidential File Room as a Cooperative Witness:

1. True Name and Aliases: _____
2. DOB: _____ POB: _____
3. Physical Description: Race: _____ Sex: _____
   Height: _____ Weight: _____ Hair: _____
   Eyes: _____
4. FBI/SSN or other identifying numbers: _____
5. Code Name:
6. Residence: City:
   State: _____
   Telephone: _____
7. Occupation: _____
   Employer: _____
8. Arrest Record: _____
9. Areas in which CW will furnish assistance (List primary coverage first by classification number): _____
10. (Field Office) indices checks:
    a. Indices: _____
    b. ELSUR_____
    c. REDACTED_____
    d. Results of NCIC Check: _____
11. Give a brief synopsis regarding the recruitment of CW and the operational role the CW will have in the investigation scenario (i.e., wear body recorder, purchase narcotics/evidence, etc.): (attach memo if necessary).
12. Is CW subject of Bureau or DEA case: _____
13. Is CW:
    YES   NO

    a. A member of News Media ____   ____
    b. Now or ever admitted to Witness Security Program ____   ____
    c. Privileged Occupation, i.e.: Attorney, Physician, Clergyman ____   ____
    d. On Federal Parole ____   ____
    e. On Federal Probation ____   ____
    f. On State Probation or Parole ____   ____
    g. Police Officer ____   ____

If any of the above responses are positive, an ASAC or above has to certify that the individual is suitable for use as a Cooperative Witness. Please contact the Informant Coordinator on extension ____.

14. Is a Plea Agreement in effect or being negotiated?
    Yes _____ No _____: if yes, provide name of AUSA: _____
    Alternate Agent: _____

Supervisor Certification:

I have reviewed this request and approve the use of the above named individual as a Cooperative Witness as defined in the *MIOG*, Part I, Section 270-2.

_____

Supervisory Special Agent

```
INFORMANT COORDINATOR'S
USE ONLY:
FILE:  270-      -CW-
WSP CHECK: _____
```

Appendix 6D: FBI Informant Review Sheet

Informant Review Sheet FD-237 (Rev. 4-28-81)

Mark opposite each item the number of the serial or serials in which the information appears. Although these items are regarded as nonvariable, changes may be noted by adding the new serial number and crossing out the old. When the form is complete as to all applicable items, the Agent and Field Supervisor should initial the form at the end. Items 1 through 18 are to be completed no later than the second meeting with the informant after the informant has been certified "suitable" by the supervisor. All remaining items should be completed as information is developed.

Symbol Number _____   Office File_____
                          Bureau File_____
                                                    Serial No.

1. Description and background information
2. Photograph
3. Local Criminal Check _____
4. Bureau Identification Record _____
5. Code Name _____
6. Advised of FBI Jurisdiction _____
7. Advised of Confidential Relationship_____
8. Advised Not Employee of Bureau _____
9. Advised to Furnish Information Only to the Bureau _____
10. Advised Payments Are Income, If Paid_____
11. When Designated for Suitability _____
12. When Designated Approved Informant and/or Bureau Authority Obtained Pursuant to *MIOG* 137-3.2 and 1373.3_____
13. Indices Search Slip (FD-160) Summarized_____
14. Service Record Checked, If Appropriate _____
15. Alternate Agent _____
16. NCIC Test Inquiry_____
17. Advised of Policy re: Defense Strategy_____
18. Supervisor's Certification of Suitability_____
19A. Supervisor Meeting with Informant _____
  B. Supervisor Observing Informant _____
20. Principal Legal Advisor's Review of Informant's File when required by *MIOG* 137-3.3_____
21. Statistical Accomplishments _____
22. Characterization of Informant Used in Legal Documents_____
23. Informant Advised of Attorney General Guidelines _____
24. Confidential Source Advised of Attorney General Guidelines_____
25. Authorizations for Participation in Criminal Activities _____

Completed: _____ Approved:_____

NO SERIAL NUMBER   ____

KEEP ON TOP OF OTHER SERIALS IN FILE

Appendix 6E: FBI Supervisor's 60-Day Informant File Review Log

Date:	Initials:	Date:	Initials:
Remarks:		Remarks:	
Date:	Initials:	Date:	Initials:
Remarks:		Remarks:	
Date:	Initials:	Date:	Initials:
Remarks:		Remarks:	
Date:	Initials:	Date:	Initials:
Remarks:		Remarks:	
Date:	Initials:	Date:	Initials:
Remarks:		Remarks:	
Date:	Initials:	Date:	Initials:
Remarks:		Remarks:	
Date:	Initials:	Date:	Initials:
Remarks:		Remarks:	
Date:	Initials:	Date:	Initials:
Remarks:		Remarks:	
Date:	Initials:	Date:	Initials:
Remarks:		Remarks:	
Date:	Initials:	Date:	Initials:
Remarks:		Remarks:	
Date:	Initials:	Date:	Initials:
Remarks:		Remarks:	
Date:	Initials:	Date:	Initials:
Remarks:		Remarks:	
Date:	Initials:	Date:	Initials:
Remarks:		Remarks:	

References

1. *Brady v. Maryland,* 373 U.S. 83, 87, 83 S. Ct. 1194, 10 L. Ed. 215 (1963).

2. *United States v. Brooks,* 966 F.2d 1500, 1502–1505 (DC Cir., 1992). *See United States v. Joseph,* 996 F.2d 36, 39 (3rd Cir., 1993); *United States v. Bertoli,* 854 F. Supp. 975, 1041 (D.N.J, 1994).

3. *Carey v. Duckworth,* 738 F.2d 875, 878 (7th Cir., 1984).

4. *Barbee v. Warden, Md. Penitentiary,* 331 F.2d 842 (4th Cir., 1964).

5. BATF Manual: *Investigative Priorities, Procedures, and Techniques,* Ch. D, § 34(6).

6. *DEA Agents Manual,* 6612.51.

7. *United States v. Bernal-Obeso,* 989 F.2d 331, 333 (9th Cir., 1993).

8. DEA Integrity Assurance Notes, Vol. I, No. 1, Aug. 1991, published by the Planning and Inspection Div., DEA.

9. IACP, Confidential Informant Concepts and Issues Paper, June 1, 1990, 6.

10. *Franks v. Delaware,* 438 U.S. 154, 171 (1978).

11. Zuckoff, M. and O'Neill, G., "Testilying" reporting plan set up, *Boston Globe,* Dec. 27, 1997.

12. Curriden, M., Secret threat to justice, *Natl. L. J.,* 1, 29 (Feb. 20, 1995) *quoting* Defense Attorney Max Stern.

13. *Commonwealth v. Lewin,* 405 Mass. 566, 542 N.E.2d 275 Mass. (1989).

14. *Franks v. Delaware,* 438 U.S. 154(1978). *See State v. Olson,* 726 P.2d 1347, 1351–1353 (Ran. App. 1986).

15. *United States v. Leon,* 468 U.S. 897 (1984).

16. *Franks v. Delaware,* 438 U.S. 154, 171 n.9 (1978).

17. *United States v. Kojayan,* 8 F.3d 1315 (9th Cir., 1993).

18. *Brady v. Maryland,* 373 U.S. 83, 83 S. Ct. 1194 (1963).

19. *Giglio v. United States,* 405 U.S. 150, 92 S. Ct. 763 (1972).

20. *United States v. Bernal-Obeso,* 989 F.2d 331 (9th Cir., 1993).

21. *United States v. Henthorn,* 931 F.2d 29 (9th Cir., 1991).

22. 28 C.F.R. § 0.39e.

23. *U.S. Customs Service Manual,* 41.20.

24. FBI Form FD 249.

25. Item L on FBI Form FD 249.

26. *DEA Agents Manual,* 6612.24.

27. *DEA Agents Manual,* 6612.32(C).

28. Fed. R. Evid. 608(b).

29. *United States v. Bernal-Obeso,* 989 F.2d 331, 336 (9th Cir., 1993).

30. *United States v. Trevino,* 89 F.3d 187 (4th Cir., 1996); *Pennsylvania v. Ritchie,* 480 U.S. 39 (1987); *United States v. Figurski,* 545 F.2d 389 (4th Cir., 1975).

31. *United States v. Strifler,* 851 F.2d 1197 (9th Cir., 1988). *See also Moore v. Kemp,* 809 F.2d 702 (Hth Cir. 1987).

32. *Aguilar v. Texas,* 378 U.S. 108 (1964); *Spinelli v. United States,* 393 U.S. 410 (1969).

33. *Illinois v. Gates,* 462 U.S. 213 (1983).

34. *United States v. Ventresca,* 380 U.S. 102, 108 (1965).

35. *United States v. Kojayan,* 8 F.3d 1315 (1993).

36. *See Roviaro v. United States,* 353 U.S. 53 (1957).

37. *Bagley v. Lumpkin,* 798 F.2d 1297 (9th Cir., 1986). *See also United States v. Cohen,* 888 F.2d 770, 776–777 (11th Cir., 1989).

38. *Mesarosh v. United States,* 352 U.S. 1, 9, 14. (1956).

39. BATF Manual: *Investigative Priorities, Procedures, and Techniques,* 35j.

40. *DEA Agents Manual,* 6612.24(E).

41. Confidential Informants, Concepts and Issues Paper, p. 2, IACP National Law Enforcement Policy Center.

42. *DEA Agents Manual,* 6612.31A.

Undercover Purchases of Evidence by Informants and Probable Cause

7

7.1 Generally

Issuing magistrates, prosecutors, police managers, and defense counsel are very often left in the dark when it comes to how informants must be managed in controlled purchase investigations. Yet employing informants for use in obtaining a search warrant is usually one of the first lessons taught to new detectives and agents.

A search warrant is issued upon a showing of probable cause[1] to believe that the legitimate object of a search is located in a particular place.[2] The controlled buy[3] allows the detective to send his informant into the premises, purchase an exhibit of evidence from the target, make observations[4] of other items of evidentiary value while at the location, and return to his handler with the evidence and his information.

The method available to an agent to reasonably ensure that the informant does not supply the evidence himself is to follow a set of prescribed procedures for the controlled buy.[5]

1. Thoroughly debrief the confidential informant (CI).[6]
2. CI must sign for the buy money.[5]
3. Thoroughly search the CI and his vehicle, if used to travel to the targeted location.[5]

4. Observe the CI enter and exit the location.[5,6]
5. Have a prearranged meeting immediately after the buy.[5]
6. Collect evidence and electronic equipment from CI.[5]
7. Search the CI again for all contraband and money.[5]
8. Debrief the informant and obtain a written and signed statement.[5]

The procedure corroborates the informant's account of the events occurring before, during, and after the controlled purchase of evidence.[7] It allows the trial judge to determine how the informant came by his information and evidence.[8] Each step must be followed. There should be no shortcuts.

This is not a treatise on the law governing search warrants or the Fourth Amendment. It is an examination of the tactical role the informant and his agent handler play in undercover purchases of evidence and developing probable cause for search warrants.[9]

Historically, "search warrant cases" have been at the heart of a large percentage of drug prosecutions. They have been the staple of police departments conducting investigations with limited manpower or financial resources. Informants have depended upon purchasing evidence for financial support or reduction of charges. The number of federal search warrants relying exclusively on an unidentified informant has increased dramatically in the last decade.[10]

Search warrants have also yielded devastating results in violent deaths and injuries to agents and occupants of targeted residences. Raiding the wrong address has tarnished the image of federal, state, and local agencies alike. James Otis believed that search warrants placed "the liberty of every man in the hands of a petty officer."[11] Heavily publicized police search warrant misadventures of the 1990s validated his beliefs.

7.2   The Controlled Undercover Purchase of Evidence

Agents routinely receive information from informants regarding the location of contraband and criminal activity.[12] The illegally possessed items are usually narcotics, stolen property, counterfeit money, or illegal weapons. The investigation will generally develop information intended to establish probable cause to support the issuance of a search warrant.[13] When established procedures are not followed, the results can be devastating to innocent citizens.

After the kind of investigation that is supposed to come before a search, embarrassed federal officials paid $2.75 million to homeowner Donald Carlson, 44. He came out of the 1992 raid with one quarter of his lung capacity destroyed by federal bullets.

Despite warnings from another cop, the agents had swallowed an entirely fictitious tale concocted by an informant.[14]

The controlled buy[15] is an investigative technique used to corroborate[16] the informant's original information that contraband is located at a particular location with the investigative objective of obtaining a search warrant.[17] The CI is usually a trusted acquaintance or customer of the individual in possession of the contraband. Crimes involving the illegal items are usually economically driven, making the items available for sale to the informant while under the supervision of a control agent.

The informant's handler should orchestrate the controlled purchase in a prescribed manner. It will ensure that the informant is being truthful in his account of where the illegal items he obtained during the controlled buy are located. The technique has been utilized in both untaxed liquor cases and drug investigations since the 1930s. It involves a series of steps that ensure that the events related in the affidavit are truthful and minimize the opportunity for an informant's misconduct. Following established procedures also reduces acts of omission by the control agent during the operation.

Controlled buys are also a method of reviving "stale" information.[18] The U.S. Supreme Court requires that for probable cause information to support the issuance of a search warrant "the proof must be of facts so closely related to the time of the issue of the warrant as to justify a finding of probable cause at that time."[19] The controlled buy is also referred to as an undercover buy,[5] a controlled informant buy,[20] and simply as an informant buy.[21]

7.3 Initial Informant Debriefing

Initial accounts related to the police by informants are often confused and sketchy. The confusion usually concerns the exact location of where contraband items are located and the identity of the violator in possession of the illegal item. The control agent should conduct a complete debriefing of the informant. It must include all information known by the source about the targeted premises and its occupants.

The Fourth Amendment requires that "no Warrants shall issue, but upon probable cause, supported by Oath or affirmation, and particularly describing the place to be searched."[22] The uniformly applied rule is that a search conducted pursuant to a warrant that fails to conform to the particularity requirement of the Fourth Amendment is unconstitutional.[23] However, police raiding the wrong address occurs frequently.

A Colorado woman was hospitalized after eight Drug Enforcement Administration (DEA) agents forced open her door, cursed
her, and beat her to the ground — before realizing they were at
the wrong house. The man they were really after was later charged
with amphetamine manufacture. The Jefferson County DA has
not commented on whether charges will be brought against the
agents. In a letter to the District Attorney (DA), the Wheat Ridge
Mayor wrote, "drug manufacturers must be controlled but not by
people who cannot even get the address for the raid correct."[24]

It is enough if the description is such that the officer with a search warrant
can with reasonable effort ascertain and identify the place intended.[25] Yet the
Colorado incident illustrates the obvious — verifying the exact location is
critical. The debriefing begins the process of fully identifying the location
where contraband is believed to be possessed. The interview also begins the
task of evaluating the veracity[26] of the informant.

Following a preliminary review by the investigator, the potential value
of the information must be assessed. If the criminal conduct described by
the informant meets the agency's criteria for initiating an investigation, the
case will move forward.

Often the obvious is overlooked. At some point, the informant must be
physically taken into the field to point out to agents the exact physical location
where the offense is being committed. The process need not expose the CI
as cooperating with the police. He can be driven to the location in a surveillance vehicle with darkened windows. The investigator will then be able to
obtain both a physical address[27] and a physical description[28] of the premises
for the search warrant.

This is not a time for the investigator to take short cuts. While on site
with the informant, he should ask questions regarding which door the CI
enters when visiting the premises. The agent should already anticipate that
a controlled buy will be attempted and that a search warrant will be executed
at the location. In the case of residences such as duplexes with multiple
entries, knowing the exact point of entry the CI will use assists the surveilling
agents during the controlled purchase in monitoring the informant's movements. That information will also prevent the raid team executing a search
warrant from entering the wrong side of the duplex.

Once the exact address is known, the agent can begin the process of fully
identifying the violator. Utility companies can be contacted to determine the
name of the individual receiving services. A subpoena may be required to
obtain a copy of the original credit application. The named applicant is not
necessarily the suspect, but the information may supply leads that will assist
in the investigation.

A thorough debriefing[5] also serves to fully identify the violator. The informant may not know the individual's full name but only refer to him by a "nickname" or an alias. The "nickname" may be recognized by the interviewer,[29] allowing for full identification of the subject. Other officers may recognize both the nickname and the address as having a reputation for criminal activity. Their knowledge can serve to corroborate the informant's account in assessing whether probable cause exists.[30] Many agencies maintain "nickname files" which can be queried by computer. (See Chapter 8, "Corroboration of Informant Information").

The informant may also have a residential telephone number or cell phone number for the subject. Subscriber information[31] can be obtained through "criss-cross" directories. Nonpublished telephone numbers can be obtained from the service provider with a subpoena.

Companies providing cell phone service can also provide subscriber information. However, two problems often arise following official inquiries. The provider may compromise the secrecy of the investigation and reveal the request to the customer. The second problem is that the phones are often freely passed around to members of an organization with no exclusive use by one person.

Once a verifiable name and date of birth of the subject is obtained, photographs[31] also often become available. Law enforcement agencies can request copies of the color photograph taken for a driver's license. Targets of investigation without licenses may have arrest photographs or mug shots on file with a local police agency. Many violators have state identification cards issued which also require a photograph to be maintained. Once a photograph is secured, the informant can be given the opportunity to identify the subject from a group of photos to verify the subject's identity.[32]

The informant should also be questioned about vehicles that the subject has been seen driving or that are routinely located at the target location. Agents can perform "drive by" surveillance and obtain license numbers of vehicles frequenting the residence or business. Regular customers of the target and possibly a source of supply may be identified in this manner. If present at the time a search warrant is executed, their "presence plus"[33] the intelligence obtained by prior surveillance may be enough to justify a search of their persons and vehicle.[34] The information can also serve to isolate details that further corroborate the source's accounts of criminal activity.[35] The Supreme Court has recognized the value of corroborating the informant's tip by independent investigation.[35,36]

To maximize the effectiveness of a search warrant the informant must be effectively questioned regarding what he has observed while inside the premises. The Fourth Amendment requires that "no Warrant shall issue, but upon probable cause, supported by Oath or affirmation, and particularly describing the ... " persons or things to be seized.[5]

Obviously, in a drug search warrant the objects to be searched for are drugs.[37] Because drugs are easily concealed, agents are allowed wider latitude in the extent of their search. An agent lawfully searching for drugs may inadvertently discover evidence of another crime (for example, a pistol with silencer). Although weapons were not listed as an item to be searched for in the warrant, seizure of the gun is constitutionally allowed under the plain view doctrine.[38]

Agents often get "tunnel vision" in their debriefing approach. A detective assigned to develop probable cause for the search of a warehouse for stolen Harley Davidson motorcycles may debrief his informant only about the location of the stolen vehicles. The informant should also be questioned about other contraband items used or possessed within the premises to be searched.[39] A warrant directing agents to search only for motorcycles would not allow for agents opening desk drawers and discovering a vial containing narcotics. If the informant reports having observed narcotics[40] on the premises in addition to the stolen motorcycles, "drugs or narcotics"[41] must be listed as an item to be seized if the seizure and warrant are to stand a challenge by the defense.[42]

A full debriefing can often elicit information that will ensure that items that might ordinarily be overlooked will be included as items to be seized. Many individuals involved in any of the full range of criminal enterprises utilize traditional paper files or personal computers to track their business activity. Such items need to be identified as objects of the search.

The full inquiry of what was observed inside the premises by the informant also satisfies valid officer safety issues. Many residences used for drug dealing are heavily fortified. Steel doors, bars across ordinary doors and windows, and booby traps are common. The entry team needs to be aware of any impediments to a fast and effective entry.[43] (See Appendix 7A, "The DEA Raid Execution Process.")

A thorough debriefing of an informant does not occur accidentally. Many agencies have predesigned forms that cover a full range of questions for the interviewing detective to ask the informant. Such formats combined with the detective's experience can elicit far more detailed information regarding the targeted location than a rambling interview. (See Appendix 8A, "DEA Source Debriefing Guide.")

It must be determined what the informant's relationship with the occupant of the targeted location is and for how long they have been associated. The length of the relationship and type of relationship will have a bearing upon the credibility of the CI's information. A live-in paramour will obviously know more about a criminal operation than an occasional visitor.

The investigator must also attempt to determine the exact motivation[44] for the informant's coming forward with information.[45] (See Chapter 2, "Motivations to Cooperate as an Informant.") Revenge as a motive should be explored when a spouse or paramour comes forward with information about their partner.[46] The CI could be using the police as a lever in a lover's quarrel or a custody dispute by attempting to have the ex-spouse arrested. The informant could "plant" drugs in such a scenario.

The informant must be questioned regarding firearms he has either seen at the location or heard about existing on the premises. Weapons are not only used for protection from police but also for protection against home invasions by other criminals.

7.4   Search of Informant and Vehicle

Thoroughly searching the informant prior to the controlled buy is the only method that ensures the informant does not supply the contraband himself. The item the informant is instructed to purchase dictates the extent of the search. If the informant is purchasing a concealable amount of drugs or other small item, he must be strip-searched.[47] All body cavities should be checked, as should any clothing to be worn during the buy.

Many agents do not like the practice of strip-searching informants. Some agents resist the process because it is time consuming. Others find the procedure embarrassing or distasteful.

Informants generally do not like to be searched. Informants with a "police buff" mentality find the procedure degrading. Some informants do not like the search process because it makes it either difficult or impossible to orchestrate a contrived purchase.

Probable cause requires the affiant to provide enough information so there exists "a fair probability"[48] of the existence of criminal activity at the location to be searched. The strip search serves to further that probability. It allows the magistrate "to make a practical, common-sense decision whether, given all the circumstances set forth in the affidavit ... there is a fair probability that contraband or evidence of a crime will be found in a particular place."[49]

If the informant is purchasing stolen automobile parts from a "chop shop," he does not necessarily need to be strip-searched. Some agencies require it regardless of the type of evidence being purchased. At a minimum, the informant should be thoroughly searched. He should also surrender the contents of pockets or purse to the control agent until after the controlled buy is completed. The informant should not be allowed to carry a firearm during a controlled buy or any police-supervised activity. The informant's vehicle,[50] if used to drive to the buy location, should also be thoroughly searched.

The *Gates* "totality of the circumstances test" remains the benchmark for Fourth Amendment purposes when determining whether probable cause exists based upon an informant's information. However, the constitutional law of some states is stricter. Those states require application of the *Aguilar-Spinelli* two-prong test of an informant's knowledge and veracity when determining whether sufficient probable cause exists for the issuance of a search warrant.[51]

7.5   Funds Provided for the Purchase of Evidence

The case agent provides the informant with the funds for the purchase of evidence. The informant must sign for the money.[52] The term "marked money" is often mistakenly used to describe the funds. The money is not marked for later retrieval purposes; instead the serial numbers are recorded on a piece of paper or memorialized in a report. Some agencies simply Xerox the notes. "Buy money" or official advanced funds (O.A.F.)[53] are serialized for two purposes. During a search warrant, all funds discovered in the premises or on the person of the target are seized. The serial numbers on the seized funds can be compared with the prerecorded funds used during the previous controlled buy. The recovery of official advanced funds during the search is extremely damaging evidence.

Money is also serialized to assist in its recovery in the event of theft by either the informant or the target of the investigation. Robbery is a common occurrence during a buy operation.

7.6   Observation of the CI Entering and Exiting the Location[54]

Once the informant and his vehicle have been searched, both must be surveilled until the operation is completed. This eliminates the possibility that the informant obtained evidence from any place other than the targeted location.

During the debriefing process, the location of the "buy" was predetermined. The informant should be directed to make no stops while enroute to the location. Members of the control agent's team should establish prebuy surveillance. The agent following the CI to the buy location maintains radio communication with the surveillance team to alert them of the CI's impending arrival. The surveillance team must make every effort to observe the informant enter the targeted location.

The surveillance team should have personally observed the informant prior to the buy or have been provided with a photograph of the informant. Often, surveillance agents are given little more than a clothing and physical description of the CI, a mistake that can undermine the investigation.

Surveilling agents must maintain surveillance of the targeted premises until the informant exits. The informant should be followed from the buy location to a predetermined meeting place. The surveillance team must establish that the informant meets with nobody other than the control agent or a member of the surveillance team. One agent should maintain surveillance of the premises after the informant's departure. Accomplices and sources of supply are often identified through postbuy surveillance.

7.7 Postbuy Informant Search

Following the buy, the informant should go directly to a predetermined location. Here the informant will give the control agent the purchased evidence. Evidence or original containers containing evidence should be submitted to the agencies' laboratory for latent fingerprint examination. Once again, the informant should be thoroughly searched. The process ensures that he did not retain any evidence or keep any buy money.[55] Similarly, his vehicle, if used, should also be thoroughly searched. It is not unusual for informants to attempt to keep some of the buy money or evidence for themselves.

7.8 Follow-Up Informant Debriefing

Once again, the informant must be debriefed. The subjects covered in the initial debriefing must be reviewed. The amount and location of contraband observed during the controlled buy must be determined. The information will assist in assessing the immediacy of obtaining a search warrant. Undue delay may cause the information to become stale.[56]

Informants are rarely called upon to testify in controlled buy search warrant cases.[57] Affidavits containing hearsay from confidential informants are permitted by the Supreme Court,[58] and magistrates routinely allow the prosecution to withhold the informant's identity.[59]

7.9 Informant's Statement

Many departments and agencies require that the informant provide a written statement. The practice memorializes in the informant's own words the events that occurred during the undercover purchase. The statement also makes it more difficult for the recalcitrant informant to deny his role in the investigation.[60]

Agents routinely prepare a statement for informants who are unable to write the account of what occurred. The statement should mirror the CI's description of the events that occurred during the controlled buy. Any mistakes or pen changes must be initialed by the informant on the original copy. The original statement must be signed by the CI and witnessed by two agents. The DEA uses the following format[61]:

- *Heading*: The heading should contain the informant's code number or code name; the date, time, and location of the statement; the names of the agents taking the statement; and a brief description of the events covered.[61]
- *Body*: The body of the statement should be in the informant's own words. If prepared by the agents for the informant, it should be reported in the body of the statement.[61]
- *Conclusion*: The conclusion should state that the informant has read the foregoing statement consisting of __ pages, that he has initialed each page and all corrections, that it is true and correct to the best of his knowledge and belief, and that he gave the statement freely and voluntarily, without threats, coercion, or promises.[61]
- *Signatures*: The agents sign all copies; the informant will sign only the original that remains in the informant file.[61]

Agencies at the federal level each have their own policies on informant statements. The DEA requires a statement when the informant has provided information or has participated in an activity that may require his testimony. That policy may be waived if taking a statement will adversely affect the outcome of the investigation. All relevant information must be reported in the investigative report. Both the supervisor and prosecutor must concur in the decision to not take a statement.[62]

The Bureau of Alcohol, Tobacco, and Firearms (BATF) requires an informant statement only if the infomant is present during the commission of a crime or accompanies a special agent working in an undercover capacity during the commission of a violation. If the agent is unable to obtain a signed statement from the informant, he is required to submit a memorandum of testimony for the informant with his case report.[63]

Customs only requires source debriefings in instances where payments to the informant exceed $3,000 or an aggregate total of $3,000 or more per investigation. The debriefing is documented in a memorandum to the source's file. His identity does not appear in the debriefing, only the source's number.[64]

State and local agencies have promulgated their own policies regarding informant statements. The practice appears more prevalent among departments that have grown dependent upon informants and experienced difficulties in their use.[65]

7.10 Informant Purchases

Controlled buys from individuals by informants are made anticipating that the informant will be called upon to testify as a material witness. These buys are not necessarily designed to obtain a search warrant but to charge the defendant with the sale. Regardless, the procedures remain the same as the search warrant controlled buy. The procedure assists in corroborating the informant's testimony and to collect damaging evidence.

Prior to the controlled buy, the informant should be directed by his control agent to place a telephone call to the target. The call is consensually tape recorded[66] by the agent who is present while the call is made. The consent of the informant must be voluntarily obtained. The tape recording must be retained as evidence, initialed by both the agent and informant. (See Chapter 9, "Informants and Electronic Surveillance.")

The informant may also be asked to wear either a concealed tape recorder or transmitter[67] during the controlled buy. The recording of the conversation in the absence of the agent is permissible since the informant is acting "under color of law."[68] The tape recording produced during the purchase is maintained as evidence. When properly utilized, concealed recorders produce a far superior tape recording than that produced via a concealed transmitter. Generally, transmitters are used for the security of the individual wearing the device. Transmitters allow monitoring agents to hear what occurs during the undercover meeting and to react accordingly.

Upon return to the prearranged secure location following the purchase, some investigators have the CI telephone the target. This call is also tape recorded and used to elicit conversation about the transaction that had just transpired. The postbuy telephone call is generally used if the CI had not consensually tape recorded the earlier transaction. It also is used to arrange subsequent purchases.[69] The tape recording of the conversation is also retained as evidence.

7.11 Informant Introduction of Undercover Agent

Informants are also used to perform what are known as "agent introductions."[70] One of the primary values of an informant is his ability to aid agents in beginning their investigation at the level of criminal involvement the CI occupies. Without an informant, an agent would have to begin at the bottom rung of an organization *if* he were able to penetrate the security of the group.

In drug investigations, the purpose of the introduction is to enable the undercover agent to make the purchase of evidence directly from the targeted individual. That includes the agent physically handing the advanced funds to the target and receiving the contraband directly from the target. The informant should serve no other purpose than to introduce the agent buyer to the seller.[71] The investigative strategy should be to "cut out" the informant so he is not present or needed at subsequent transactions. If present or a key witness or participant in the crime charged, he may have to testify.[72] He must be material or essential to the defense.[73]

To avoid revealing the informant's identity and requiring the CI to testify, the prosecutor may decide to not prosecute any of the transactions that the informant was involved in. "Charging around" the buy involving the CI only avoids the often unpleasant experience of having the informant testify. It does little to actually conceal the informant's involvement from the defendant.[74]

Mere presence during a criminal transaction is not a guarantee that the informant will either be disclosed or be called upon to testify.[75] The common law "informer's privilege" generally shields an informant's identity, but countervailing constitutional or policy considerations may result in court-ordered disclosure. The defendant may be able to establish a right of disclosure "where the informant is a key witness or participant in the crime charged, someone whose testimony would be significant in determining guilt or innocence."[76]

In *United States v. Roberts*,[77] the informant introduced an undercover agent to the defendant and was present when the defendant and the agent negotiated two sales of heroin. The court, noting that the informant was "present during all the significant events,"[78] found that he was "obviously a crucial witness to the alleged narcotics transaction," and therefore his whereabouts should have been revealed to the defense if properly requested.[79] However, disclosures of the identity or address of a confidential informant is not required unless the informant's testimony is shown to be material to the defense.[80]

In *United States v. Jimenez*,[81] the court made clear it is not sufficient to show that the informant was a participant in and witness to the crime charged. In *Jimenez*, the informant was both participant and witness, but the district court's refusal to order disclosure of the CI's identity was upheld on the ground that the defendant had failed to show that the testimony of the informant "would have been of even marginal value to the defendant's case."[82]

In *Roviaro v. United States*, the U.S. Supreme Court articulated the following balancing test to dictate when the government must disclose the identity of the confidential informant:

We believe that no fixed rule with respect to disclosure is justifiable. The problem is one that calls for balancing the public interest in protecting the flow of information against the individual's right to prepare one's defense. Whether a proper balance renders non-disclosure erroneous must depend on the particular circumstances of each case, taking into consideration the crime charged, the possible defenses, the possible significance of the informer's testimony, and other relevant factors.[83]

The Supreme Court further emphasized that protecting an informant's identity serves an important public interest in that it encourages citizens to supply the government with information concerning criminal activity.[84] A defendant may satisfy his burden and overcome the privilege by demonstrating that the informant is a material witness or that his or her testimony is crucial to his case.[85] "That the government has this privilege is well established, and its soundness cannot be questioned."[86]

The Supreme Court allows the government in certain circumstances to avoid disclosing the identity of a confidential informant participating in an investigation.[87] In *United States v. Mendoza-Burciaga*,[88] the court developed a three-part balancing test, under which the trial court must consider (1) the level of the informant's involvement in the alleged criminal activity, (2) the helpfulness of disclosure to the asserted defense, and (3) the government's interest in nondisclosure.[89]

Defense challenges to the credibility of a detective's account of an informant's information or the informant's existence are routine. Direct attacks upon the credibility of the investigator "if regularly countenanced, would erode the [informant's] privilege, for an argument could always be made that disclosure is needed to challenge the credibility of the witness who reports an informant's declarations."[90]

For years, criminal defense attorneys have voiced suspicions that police sometimes fabricate informants to obtain search warrants, but they had little or no evidence.[10] A properly conducted control buy leaves behind both witnesses and a "paper trail" that provides either exculpatory or incriminatory evidence when allegations of fabricated informants are made.

Nothing in the Due Process Clause of the Fourteenth Amendment requires a state court judge in every such hearing to assume the arresting officers are committing perjury. "To take such a step would be quite beyond the pale of this Court's proper function in our federal system. It would be a wholly unjustifiable encroachment by the Court upon the constitutional power of States to promulgate their own rules of evidence . . . in their own state courts."[91]

Informant statements and prescribed undercover purchase procedures serve to inhibit if not prevent the rare police practice of inventing a confidential informant for probable cause purposes. One such "informant" was "used" by the Boston Police Department in at least 31 search warrants during a three-year period. Their last search warrant resulted in the shooting death of a Boston detective during the execution of the warrant. The officer responsible for inventing the informant was convicted on 25 counts of perjury.[92]

The fictitious informant is usually the product of an overzealous detective's frustration with a legal system he neither respects nor understands. Greed may also be a contributing factor. "It is tempting to agents to take their suspicions, put them down on paper and attribute them to some made-up snitch that they know they will never have to produce."[10] The practice usually brings with it more than the crime of perjury. Theft of narcotics and official funds are usually a companion crime.

To bolster the accounts of his "informant," fabricated controlled buys often take place. The detective withdraws funds from his department for the purchase of evidence (PE), keeping the money for personal use. The evidence "purchased" by the fictitious CI is usually drugs taken by the officer from other arrests or searches that were not logged into evidence. It may be evidence from other cases that was to be destroyed following disposition of the case.

The invented informant may also become a paid informant. To further his ruse the detective can withdraw funds for the payment of information (PI) to his source. The money is pocketed by the detective for his own use.

The fictitious informant can serve more than the misplaced energies of an idealistic detective. The same method is used to gain "legal" entry into homes and businesses to commit theft. Nothing more than "home invasions with a warrant," the practice allows officers to gain entry into the targeted premises with the armed support of other unwitting officers. Once inside they are free to steal drug money, narcotics, and other valuables.

> In 1991, a former Metro-Dade County police officer in Miami cooperated with federal prosecutors and testified in a racketeering trial of four other cops that he had stated falsely on search warrant affidavits his information came from CIs "known for previous reliability." In fact, they didn't exist. The ex-officer testified that he needed warrants to break into drug dens, where he stole thousands of dollars. He was placed on five years' probation in June 1991.[10]

Two officers not involved in the Miami scheme but assigned to assist in the execution of one of the search warrants were shot and wounded by occupants of the residence.

The detective who fabricates an informant recruits an unwitting participant into his crime — the judge issuing the search warrant. The veracity of the assertions supporting probable cause is integral to the criminal justice system.[93] The court in the Boston police informant scandal said:

> Perjurious police conduct is reprehensible. [The detective's] knowingly false application for the search warrant completely discredits a fundamental safeguard on which constitutional protection against unreasonable searches and seizures is based. Our system tests the existence of probable cause to conduct a search based on information from an unnamed informant by considering the information that a police officer gave under oath to the magistrate who issued the search warrant. The validity of the process depends on belief in the integrity of affiant police officers. For a defendant to be entitled to go behind the police officer's application to show that in fact there was no probable cause to justify issuance of the warrant, the defendant must make "a substantial preliminary showing that a false statement knowingly and intentionally, or with reckless disregard for the truth, was included by the affiant in the warrant affidavit. A substantial showing of such a false statement is not easily made. Lies about the existence of an undisclosed informant and his reliability are easy to tell yet most difficult to uncover."[94]

The task of the issuing magistrate is simply to make a practical, common sense decision whether, given all the circumstances set forth in the affidavit before him, "there is a fair probability that contraband or evidence of a crime will be found in a particular place."[95] Most magistrates, although required to be neutral, detached, and capable of determining whether probable cause exists for the requested search warrant,[96] are also eager to issue the warrant.

A Chief Magistrate in Georgia recalled:

> I know for sure that neither myself nor any of the magistrates under me have ever required to know the identity of the informer, and I've never heard of that happening, but maybe we should.[97]

The informant fabrication scheme relies upon the reality that many search warrant cases never go to trial. Most result in negotiated pleas and demand for the informant's identity are never made.

The magistrate is also permitted to exercise discretion in allowing the prosecution to keep the informant's identity confidential. Asserting the "informer's privilege" usually occurs during attacks by the defense in suppression hearings.[98] In reality, it is the prosecution's privilege in maintaining confidentiality that is being asserted, not the informant's.

In 1993, in Waltham, outside Boston, seven drug convictions were thrown out when two investigators admitted they had fabricated the existence of informants to obtain warrants. "The detectives had gone into an apartment without a warrant, searched the house carefully and found drugs and money," says Peter A. Bella, a former Waltham, Massachusetts prosecutor who represented one of the defendants. "The detectives then created an imaginary informant and attributed all the information to him, [then] went to a judge to get their search warrant."[99]

The Massachusetts Supreme Judicial Court has held "the public interest in deterring police misconduct requires the trial judge to exercise his or her own discretion to order an in camera hearing[100] where the defendant by affidavit asserts facts which cast a reasonable doubt on the veracity of material representations made by the affiant concerning a confidential informant."[101] The Court added: "The purpose of the in camera hearing would be to enable the judge through interrogating the affiant, and, if necessary, the informant to determine whether there is a substantial preliminary showing that the affiant has made false statements intentionally or recklessly. . . . The judge may conduct an in camera hearing without counsel or he may, in his discretion, permit the prosecutor, but not defense counsel, to attend."[102] The Colorado Supreme Court has noted that "in proper cases, such a hearing can avoid an otherwise irreconcilable conflict between the legitimate need for informant anonymity and the right of the defendant to be free of unfounded infringements of his privacy and liberty.[103]

In 1978, the U.S. Supreme Court held in *Franks v. Delaware* that defendants could challenge the veracity of affidavits for search warrants.[104] Prior to that time a defendant's ability to challenge the affiant's veracity in the affidavit in support of a search warrant varied from jurisdiction to jurisdiction.

Under *Franks,* there is a two-step process. First, the defendant must provide enough evidence to convince the court that a hearing is necessary. Once the defendant gets over this initial burden, a hearing is held. If the defendant shows intentional or reckless falsehoods that, if stricken from the affidavit, remove probable cause, then the search warrant must be voided and the fruits of the search excluded. The Supreme Court in *Franks* put the standard this way:

> In the event that at that hearing the allegation of perjury or reckless disregard is established by the defendant by a preponderance of the evidence, and, with the affidavit's false material set to one side, the affidavit's remaining content is insufficient to establish probable cause, the search warrant must be voided and the fruits

of the search excluded to the same extent as if probable cause was lacking on the face of the affidavit.[105]

In *Franks,* the Court limited the attack on false affidavits, stating, "The deliberate falsity or reckless disregard whose impeachment is permitted today is only that of the affiant, not of any nongovernmental informant."[106] When a defendant seeks a *Franks* hearing, the issue is the good faith of the affiant.

When a police officer is furnished false information by a confidential informant and that information is later discovered to be false, there is no violation of *Franks.*[107] As long as the affiant is not aware of the falsity of the informant's statement, nor has any reason to doubt the accuracy of the information, there is no recklessness or intentional deceit on the part of the affiant. Thus, the "substantial preliminary showing" required for a *Franks* hearing is not established.[108]

However, police cannot insulate themselves from falsehoods. For example, in a pre-*Franks* case the Supreme Court held that "the police could not insulate one officer's deliberate misstatement merely by relaying it through an officer affiant personally ignorant of its falsity."[109]

The court in *United States v. Cortina*[110] was confronted with a search that occurred only because an FBI agent lied to the magistrate.[110] The district court had determined that the agent's testimony was "incredible" and that "J. Edgar Hoover would be rolling over in his mausoleum if he heard that man in this courtroom."[111]

The court found that:

> When he lied to the magistrate, he committed two offenses: one against the constitutional guarantee against unreasonable searches, and a second against the judicial system. In addition to the consequences flowing from the lack of probable cause, this second injury to the judiciary itself requires this court to guarantee that none of the tainted evidence reaches the courtroom. Our responsibility to uphold the integrity of the judicial system therefore requires the suppression of all the evidence resulting from the search as to all defendants.[111]

Seemingly even more troublesome to the court was that the agent's offense was committed within the sanctity of the court itself.[112] "The violation here is particularly insidious because it is difficult to uncover misrepresentations in an affidavit underlying a search warrant. The information needed to prove such assertions false is peculiarly within the hands of the government."[113]

In 1986, the court held in *United States v. Reivich*[114] that, based upon *Franks*, an individual might challenge a facially insufficient affidavit on the ground that it contains deliberate or reckless falsehoods or deliberate omissions. To prevail, however, the challenger must show:

1. That the police omitted facts with the intent to make, or in reckless disregard of whether they thereby made, the affidavit misleading.
2. That the affidavit if supplemented by the omitted information would not have been sufficient to support a finding of probable cause.[115]

Omissions of facts are not misrepresentations unless they cast doubt on the existence of probable cause.[116]

Appendix 7A: The DEA Raid Execution Process

The DEA Tactical Training Unit currently teaches a raid execution technique that is referred to as the "snake" method, and that generally involves a six-person entry team (not including the perimeter team). This technique — or similar variations of it — has been adopted by many law enforcement agencies for use in drug raids because of its simplicity, safety, and effectiveness. For most raid situations, the DEA Tactical Training Unit advocates the use of speed, surprise, and "violence of action" in order to secure as much of a structure as possible within approximately six to ten seconds after gaining entry. After about ten seconds have elapsed — or at any earlier point in time that the entry team knows or believes that they have lost the element of surprise (thereby affording occupants time to gather weapons or to hide) — we suggest that the raid process *slow down* and that the remainder of the structure be cleared methodically by moving from one area to another using all available cover/concealment and applying fundamental room clearing tactics (e.g., "slicing the pie," "quick peeks," "limited penetration," and the use of portable mirrors and ballistic shields if necessary). The success of this technique is dependent upon a greater degree of teamwork and "raid discipline" than has historically been applied in many raids conducted by drug law enforcement agents. Simply stated, raid execution tactics *must* improve in order to overcome the challenge of drug traffickers who are becoming increasingly willing to resist and/or to kill law enforcement personnel.

The "snake" technique is based upon a very fundamental principle: each entry team member covers the person in front of himself/herself and team members never work alone. The following is a synopsis of each member's role in the "snake" formation:

The #1 person on the entry team primarily dictates the team's pace and direction of travel throughout the structure and, therefore, can be thought of as the "head" of the snake. #1 is the first person to enter each area/room and must aim his/her weapon at "danger areas" upon approaching and entering them (which includes the approach to the initial entry point). Note: If team members 2 through 6 cannot safely aim their weapons at danger areas (e.g., when moving along a narrow hallway behind #1), they should carry weapons in the "low ready" position (pointed *downward*). All entry team members *must* keep their fingers off the triggers of their weapons until they *intend* to fire at a threat.

The #2 person follows #1 into *all* areas/rooms to be cleared. #2 simply keys off of #1 and covers in the direction that #1 does *not* cover. For example, if #1 dynamically (rapidly) enters a bedroom and turns towards the right, then #2 follows immediately and turns/covers towards the left. This procedure eliminates the need to "predetermine" which direction #1 and #2 will turn/cover upon entering rooms.) Unless silence is required, #2 should loudly announce, "clear ... coming out!" prior to exiting rooms that other team members have not accessed.

The #3 person covers #2. #3 must decide, based upon the configuration of the structure, where to position himself/herself to assist #2 and to cover other uncleared areas. For example, #3 might choose to enter a bedroom with #1 and #2 and then cover the exterior hallway from within that room. Note: *All* entry team members should avoid positioning themselves in hallways and stairways without sufficient cover and must *never* stop or hesitate when moving through doorways.

The #4 person in the formation is the agent in charge of the entry team ("team leader"). #4 covers #3, is primarily responsible for announcing the raid team's identity and purpose (e.g., "DEA ... search warrant!") as they enter and move throughout the structure, and insures that the team clears all potential danger areas. After the entire structure has been secured, the team leader is responsible for notifying the perimeter team (by portable radio or some other means) that the location is secure and/or that the entry team is exiting the structure. (No perimeter team member shall enter prior to this notification; the use of multiple entry points is strongly discouraged.)

The #5 person may be a breacher at the entry point (if #6 needs assistance in gaining entry), may be called upon for handcuffing, searching, or controlling occupants, and covers #4. Note: Agents should apply the "contact/cover" principle when arresting occupants. (One agent should cover an arrestee with a weapon, while one or more agents holster their weapons and physically control, handcuff, and search an arrestee.)

The #6 person is the primary breacher at the entry point, may also be called upon for the handcuffing, etc., of occupants, covers #5, and may be responsible for rear security. Note: After #6 has breached the initial entry point, he/she should step aside (moving the entry tool, if any, out of the doorway) and allow #1 through #5 to enter the structure ahead of himself/herself. Note: If feasible, agents should consider attempting ruses to gain entry. (For example, by simply knocking on the door and awaiting a response, an occupant may open the door. This will allow the entry team to immediately detain/arrest one occupant and also gain entry more easily.)

The six-person entry team moves (whether it be quickly or slowly) only in the direction that #1 dictates, generally clearing all danger areas along the way. If, for example, a potential danger area is bypassed, the agent in charge may stop the team and direct them to clear that area. This procedure prevents the separation of the entry team within a structure, thereby eliminating the possibility of team members unexpectedly confronting fellow agents and potentially discharging weapons at each other. As with any technique or tactic, the "snake" method can be adapted depending upon varying factors such as the number of agents available to conduct the raid, the nature of the situation, the size or characteristics of the structure to be raided, or the number of occupants inside the location. (For example, it may be necessary to increase/decrease the number of agents assigned to the entry team or to "target" a specific room within a structure to quickly secure it prior to clearing the remaining areas.)

The entry team should ideally consist of personnel who are familiar with each other and who have received similar raid execution training. All entry team members must follow the raid plan, be able to think and react quickly and appropriately under stress, be able to apply safe and effective raid tactics, and be highly proficient in the use of firearms and the application of defensive tactics. The group supervisor or agent in charge of conducting a raid should, as time permits, hold a postraid meeting so that entry and perimeter team members can discuss and constructively analyze the performance of the entire raid team.

Appendix 7B: Operational Plan Format

Date_____

I.   SITUATION
    A. Type of operation (check appropriate area)
        1. Buy–Bust_____
        2. Search–Arrest Warrant_____
            a. Court/Judge_____
            b. Warrant #_____
        3. Surveillance_____
        4. Other_____
    B. Address of location(s)
        1. _____
        2. _____
        3. _____
        4. _____
    C. Description of location(s) (attached diagram)
        1. _____
        2. _____
        3. _____
        4. _____
    D. Suspect(s) (name, description, prior criminal background)
        1. _____
        2. _____
        3. _____
    E. Possible weapons (possessed or available to suspects)
        1. _____
        2. _____
    F. Countersurveillance (possible description of vehicles, etc.)
        1. _____
        2. _____
II. MISSION
    A. Background Information (obtained from informant, surveillances, investigation, etc.)

        _____
        _____
        _____

    B. Brief overview of plan

        _____
        _____
        _____

III. PERSONNEL INVOLVED
    A. Undercover personnel
        Name   Vehicle

        _____
        _____
        _____

    B. Assisting personnel
        Name   Vehicle   Call Letters

_____

_____

_____

IV. PERSONNEL ASSIGNMENTS AND INSTRUCTIONS
   A. Assignments
      1. Containment Personnel (list name, specific locations, i.e., rear door, side, etc.)
         Names   Location

_____

_____

_____

      2. Entry personnel
         Names   Location

_____

_____

_____

      3. Surveillance personnel
         Names   Location

_____

_____

_____

   B. Instructions (describe entire plan — duties of U/C, search team, entry team, money man, surveillance, etc.)

_____

_____

_____

V. COMMUNICATION AND LOGISTICS
   A. Communication
      1. Radio frequency_____
      2. Code designations (i.e., primary and secondary locations, etc.)

_____

_____

      3. Emergency signals (arrest signal, etc.)

_____

   B. Logistics
      1. Equipment required (raid jackets, protective vests, binoculars, etc.)

_____

      2. Equipment issued (list items and to whom issued)

_____

_____

VI. ARREST PROCEDURES
   A. Location of booking

_____

_____

   B. Prisoner transportation (indicate who will transport)

_____

_____

Note: For security reasons, plans should be collected at the end of each operation and destroyed. File copies should be retained for inclusion in the case folder.

Appendix 7C: Evidence Fund Accounting Receipt

INFORMANT PRODUCTIVITY INFORMATION*

14845

ON (DATE): _____ THIS INFORMANT WAS: effective _____ not effective _____
THIS INFORMANT'S INFORMATION WAS: Totally accurate _____ Partially accurate

Not accurate _____ OTHER: _____
A SEARCH WARRANT WAS: Issued _____ Not issued _____ Served_____
Not Served _____
COMMENTS: (Include a brief, concise explanation of this expenditure)
_____
_____
_____

SEIZURE INFORMATION

PRIMARY PROPERTY/DRUGS SEIZED WAS: _____
_____
OTHER PROPERTY SEIZED (cash, guns, etc.) WAS:
_____
PROPERTY RECEIPT #s: _____
VEHICLES SEIZED (year, make, model, lic. #) WERE: _____
_____
TOTAL AMOUNT OF DRUGS SEIZED WERE: _____
TOTAL APPROX. $ VALUE OF PROPERTY/DRUGS SEIZED IS:_____

AMOUNT AND TYPE OF EXPENSE

$ _____ BUY MONEY (explain in comments and seizure section above)
$ _____ PAID INFORMANT FOR INFORMATION
$ _____ PAID INFORMANT FOR SEARCH WARRANT INFORMATION
$ _____ PAID INFORMANT FOR OTHER (explain in comments section   above)
$ _____ TOTAL AMOUNT OF THIS EXPENSE

EXPENSE INFORMATION

DATE OF EXPENSE: _____ PPB CASE #: _____ OTHER #: _____
INFORMANT CODE #: _____
INFORMANT CODE NAME (print): _____
"I (INFORMANT'S SIGNATURE) _____ ACKNOWLEDGE THE
RECEIPT OF THE TOTAL AMOUNT OF MONEY LISTED ABOVE."
INVESTIGATOR'S SIGNATURE: _____BPST: _____
WITNESSING OFFICER'S SIGNATURE: _____ BPST: _____
SPECIFIC LOCATION OF EXPENSE: _____
NOTE: 50% of expense transactions must be witnessed   REVIEW:
     (35% by another officer, 15% by a supervisor)

DISTRIBUTION: WHITE ORIGINAL TO SUPERVISOR IMMEDIATELY

SGT. __

PINK COPY ATTACHED TO MONTHLY VOUCHER   LT. ___

YELLOW COPY IS OFFICER'S COPY

*Similar Form Utilized by Portland, OR Police Bureau

References

1. *Johnson v. United States,* 333 U.S. 10, 14, 68 S. Ct. 367, 92 L. Ed. 436 (1948).

2. *Steagald v. United States,* 451 U.S. 204, 212–213 (1981).

3. Burkoff, *Search Warrant Law Deskbook* § 5.2 (West Group).

4. *State v. Wiley,* 366 N.W.2d 265, 269 (Minn., 1985).

5. DEA Office of Training, Informant Interaction, VIIIA, Use of a CI to Make an Undercover Buy.

6. *United States v. Tirinkian,* 502 F. Supp. 620, 630 (D.N.D., 1980).

7. *United States v. Sanchez,* 689 F.2d 508, 513 (5th Cir., 1982).

8. *Stanley v. State,* 19 Md. App. 507, 313 A.2d 847, 851 (1974).

9. *Ripley v. State,* 23 FLW D649, 1st DCA, March 13, 1998.

10. Curriden, M., Secret threat to justice, *Natl. L.J.* (Feb. 20, 1995), p. 29; Federal magistrate judges issued 31,571 search warrants in 2001, Bureau of Justice Statistics, Table 5.26 (2001).

11. *Boyd v. United States,* 116 U.S. 616, 625 (1986).

12. *Ortega v. United States,* 897 F. Supp. 771, 780 (S.D.N.Y., 1995).

13. U.S. Constitution, Amendment IV.

14. Katel, "The trouble with informants," *Newsweek,* Jan. 30, 1995, pp. 1, 48.

15. Burkoff, *Search Warrant Law Deskbook* § 5.2 (West Group).

16. *United States v. Khownsavanh,* 113 F.3d 279, 285 (1st Cir., 1997), quoting *Terry v. Ohio,* 392 U.S. 1, 21–22 (1968).

17. *Commonwealth v. Miley,* 460 A.2d 778 (Pa. Super., 1983).

18. *People v. David,* 326 N. W.2d 485, 487–488 (Mich. Ct. App., 1982); *United States v. Guitterez,* 983 F. Supp. 905, 919 (N.D. Cat., 1998); *State v. Newton,* 489 S.E.2d 147, 151 (Ga. Ct. App., 1997); *United States v. Wagner,* 989 F.2d 69, 75 (2nd Cir., 1993); *People v. Broilo,* 228 N.W.2d 456, 458 (Mich. Ct. App., 1975); *State v. Gillespie,* 503 N.W.2d 612, 616 (Iowa Ct. App., 1993); *People v. Acevedo,* 572 N.Y.S.2d 101, 102 (App. Div., 1991); *State v. Spallino,* 556 So. 2d 953, 955 n.l (La. Ct. App., 1990).

19. *Sgro v. United States,* 287 U.S. 206, 210 (1932).

20. *Narcotics Investigators Manual,* U.S. Drug Enforcement Administration and International Association of Chiefs of Police, 1974.

21. Street Level Narcotics Enforcement, Bureau of Justice Assistance, April 1990, p. 11.

22. U.S. Constitution, Amendment IV.

23. *Massachusetts v. Sheppard,* 468 U.S. 981, 988 n.5 (1984).

24. *Denver Post,* July 16, 1993.

25. *Steel v. United States,* 267 U.S. 498, 503 (1925).

26. *United States v. Harris,* 403 U.S. 573 (1971); *People v. Cooks,* 141 Cal. App. 3d 224, 190 Cal. Rptr. 211, 261, *cert. denied,* 464 U.S. 1046 (1983); *State v. Burton,* 416 So. 2d. 73, 74–75 (La., 1982) *(disapproved by Illinois v. Gates,* 462 U.S. 213 *reh'g denied* (1983); *United States v. Bush,* 647 F.2d 357, 363 (3rd Cir., 1981); *People v. Cooks,* 141 Cal. App. 3d 224, 190 Cal. Rptr. 211, 261, *cert. denied,* 464 U.S. 1046 (1983); *Showmaker v. State,* 52 Md. App. 463,451 A.2d 127,134–135 (1982); *Commonwealth v. Salvaggio,* 307 Pa. Super. 385, 453 A.2d 637, 641 (1982); *People v. Kilmer,* 87 App. Div. 2d 949, 451 N.Y.S.2d 244, 245 (1982).

27. *United States v. Dancy,* 947 F.2d 1232 (5th Cir., 1991).

28. *United States v. Barnes,* 909 F.2d 1059, 1068 n.ll (7th Cir., 1990).

29. *United States v. Harris,* 403 U.S. 573 (1971).

30. *United States v. Ventresca,* 380 U.S. 102, 110 (1965); *Illinois v. Andreas,* 463 U.S. 765, 771 n.5 (1983). *See also United States v. Tirinkian,* 502 F. Supp. 620, 627 (D.N.D., 1980).

31. *United States v. Ordonez,* 737 F.2d 793, 807 (9th Or., 1984).

32. *People v. Simmons,* 569 N.E.2d 591 (111. App. 2nd Dist., 1991); *State v. Taylor,* 889 S.W.2d 124 (Mo. Ct. App., 1994); *Mayfield v. State,* 800 S.W.2d 932 (Tex. App., 1990).

33. *State v. Carrasco,* 147 Ariz. 558, 711 P.2d 1231, 1233–1234 (App., 1985). *See also State v. Broadnax,* 98 Wash. 2d 289, 654 P.2d 96,103–104 (1982).

34. *United States v. Ross,* 456 U.S. 798, 809 (1982). *See also Carroll v. United States,* 267 U.S. 132, 156 (1925).

35. *Illinois v. Gates,* 462 U.S. 213, 241 (1983).

36. *Jones v. United States,* 362 U.S. 257 (1960); *Draper v. United States,* 358 U.S. 307 (1959). *See State v. Amerman,* 581 A.2d 19, 33–36 (Md. Ct. Spec. App., 1990). *But see People v. Paquin,* 811 P.2d 394, 398 (Colo., 1991).

37. *United States v. Klein,* 565 F.2d 183 (1st Cir., 1977); *United States v. Rome,* 809 F.2d 665 (10th Cir., 1987).

38. *Horton v. California,* 496 U.S. 128, 141 (1990); *Maryland v. Buie,* 494 U.S. 325, 330 (1990); *Arizona v. Hicks,* 480 U.S. 321 (1987); *Texas v. Brown,* 460 U.S. 730, 741–744 (1983); *Coolidge v. New Hampshire,* 403 U.S. 443, 466–471 (1971).

39. *Stanford v. Texas,* 379 U.S. 476, 486 (1965); *Steel v. United States,* 267 U.S. 498, 504 (1925).

40. *United States v. Lunt,* 732 F. Supp. 599, 603 (W.D. Pa., 1990).

41. *Morris v. United States,* 507 U.S. 988, 977 F.2d 677, 680–682 (1st Cir., 1992), *cert. denied,* 113 S. Ct. 1588 (1993).

42. *State v. Herbst,* 395 N.W.2d 399 (Minn. App., 1986); *Massachusetts v. Sheppard,* 468 U.S. 981 (1984).

43. *United States v. Ramirez,* 118 S. Ct. 992 (1998).

44. *Thompson v. State,* 16 Md. App. 560, 298 A.2d 458 (1973); *United States v. Harris,* 403 U.S. 573 (1971); *People v. Rodriguez,* 52 N.Y.2d 483, 438 N.Y.S.2d 754, 420 N.E.2d 946 (1981); *State v. Lair,* 95 Wash. 2d 706, 630 P.2d 427 (1981).

45. *Thompson v. State,* 16 Md. App. 560, 298 A.2d 458, 461–462.

46. *Wesley v. State,* 162 Ga. App. 737, 293 S.E.2d 27, 28 (1982).

47. *Narcotics Investigator's Manual,* Undercover Operations, Ch. 10, p. 100. U.S. Drug Enforcement Administration and Bureau of Operations and Research, International Association of Chiefs of Police (1974).

48. *Illinois v. Gates,* 462 U.S. 213, 238, 246 (1983), rejecting *Aguilar v. Texas,* 378 U.S. 108 (1964), and *Spinelli v. United States,* 393 U.S. 410 (1969). *See also Massachusetts v. Upton,* 466 U.S. 727, 733 (1984). *See, however, Texas v. Brown,* 460 U.S. 730, 742 (1983) (plurality opinion of Rehnquist, J.); *United States v. Wayne,* 903 F.2d 1188, 1196 (8th Cir., 1990).

49. *Illinois v. Gates,* 462 U.S. 213, 238 (1983).

50. *United States v. Cuomo,* 479 F.2d 688 (2nd Cir., 1973).

51. *State v. Jones,* 706 P.2d 317, 322 (Alaska, 1985); *State v. Sherlock,* 768 P.2d 1290, 1292 (Haw., 1989); *Commonwealth v. Alvarez,* 661 N.E.2d 1293, 1298 (Mass., 1996); *Commonwealth v. Upton,* 476 N.E.2d 548 (Mass., 1985); *People v. Sherbine,* 364 N.W.2d 658 (Mich., 1984); *State v. Cordova,* 784 P.2d 30, 31–36 (N.M., 1989); *People v. P.J. Video, Inc.,* 501 N.E.2d 556, 562, 508 N.Y.S.2d 907 (N.Y., 1986), *cert. denied,* 479 U.S. 1091 (1987); *People v. Maldonado,* 546 N.Y.S.2d 50, 51 (App. Div., 1989); *State v. Coffey,* 788 P.2d 424 (Or., 1990); *State v. Alvarez,* 776 P.2d 1283, 1284–1285 (Or., 1989); *State v. Valentine,* 911 S.W.2d 328, 330 (Tenn., 1995); *State v. Jacumin,* 778 S.W.2d 430, 436 (Tenn., 1989); *State v. Emmi,* 628 A.2d 939, 941–42 (Vt., 1993); *State v. Alger,* 559 A.2d 1087, 1090 (Vt., 1989); *State v. Jackson,* 688 P.2d 136 (Wash., 1984); *State v. Mejia,* 766 P.2d 454, 457 (Wash., 1989); *State v. Dobyns,* 779 P.2d 746, 750 (Wash. Ct. App., 1989). *See also State v. Iowa Dist. Court,* 472 N.W.2d 621, 623, 624 (Iowa, 1991); *State v. Swaim,* 412 N.W. 2d 568, 571–572 (Iowa, 1987). *See* Burkoff, *Search Warrant Law Deskbook* § 4.3 (West).

52. *Use of CI to Make an Undercover Buy,* VIII (A) (2), Cooperating Individual Management, U.S. Drug Enforcement Administration Office of Training, Quantico, VA.

53. *DEA Agents Manual,* Ch. 61.

54. *Use of a CI to Make a Undercover Buy,* VIII (A) (4), Cooperating Individual Management, U.S. Drug Enforcement Administration Office of Training, Quantico, VA.

55. *United States v. McMillan,* 508 F.2d 101, 106 (1974).

56. *United States v. Miles,* 772 F.2d 613, 616 (10th Cir., 1985), *cert. denied,* 476 U.S. 1158 *reh'g denied,* 478 U.S. 1032 (1986); *Gerdes v. State,* 319 N.W.2d 710, 713 (Minn., 1982); *Evans v. State,* 161 Ga. App. 468, 288 S.E.2d 726, 729, *appeal after remand,* 166 Ga. App. 602, 305 S.E.2d 121 (1982); *United States v. McCall,* 740 F.2d 1331, 1336–1337 (4th Cir., 1984); *United States v. Shomo,* 786 F.2d 981, 984 (10th Cir., 1986); *United States v. Batchelder,* 824 F.2d 563 (7th Cir., 1987).

57. *United States v. Scafe,* 822 F.2d 428, 928 (10th Cir., 1987). *See also United States v. Freeman,* 816 F.2d 558, 562 (10th Cir., 1987); *United States v. Wilson,* 107 F.3d 774 (10th Cir., 1997).

58. *United States v. Ventresca,* 380 U.S. 102 (1965).

59. *McCray v. Illinois,* 386 U.S. 300 (1967). *See also Roviaro v. United States,* 353 U.S. 53, 1 L. Ed.2d 639, 77 S. Ct. 623 (1957).

60. *United States v. Di Caro,* 772 F.2d 1314 (7th Cir., 1985).

61. *DEA Agents Manual,* Ch. 66.

62. *DEA Agents Manual,* Ch. 6612.

63. BATF Manual: *Investigative Priorities, Procedures, and Techniques,* 43(b)(1)(2).

64. U.S. Customs Service, Office of Enforcement, *Criminal Investigators Handbook,* Ch. 41.

65. *People v. Lucente,* 506 N.E.2d 1269 (Hi., 1987).

66. 18 USC § 2511(2)(c).

67. *On Lee v. United Stales,* 343 U.S. 747 (1952).

68. *United States v. Haimowitz,* 725 F.2d 1561(11th Cir., 1984).

69. *Narcotics Investigators Manual,* Undercover Operations, Ch. 10, U.S. Drug Enforcement Administration and International Association of Chiefs of Police (1974).

70. *United States v. Mendoza-Salgado,* 964 F.2d 993 (10th Cir., 1992).

71. *United States v. Ortiz,* 804 F.2d 1161, 1166 (10th Cir., 1986).

72. *United States v. Russotti,* 746 F.2d 945, 950 (2nd Cir., 1984).

73. *United States v. Saa,* 859 F.2d 1067, 1073 (2nd Cir., 1988), *cert. denied,* 489 U.S. 1089 (1989). *See also Scher v. United States,* 305 U.S. 251, 254 (1938).

74. *Davenport v. State,* 464 NE2d 1302, (Ind.) *cert. denied,* 469 U.S. 1045 (1984).

75. *State v. Carnegie,* 472 So. 2d 1329 (Ha. App., 1985) (informant present for two "buys," detective was also present and it could not be said that CI was sole material witness, disclosure not ordered).

76. *United States v. Russotti,* 746 F.2d 945, 950 (2nd Cir., 1984); *United States v. Roberts,* 388 F.2d 646, 648–649 (2nd Cir., 1968). *See United States v. Price,* 783 F.2d 1132 (4th Cir., 1986); *United States v. Barnes,* 486 F.2d 776 (8th Cir., 1973).

77. *United States v. Roberts,* 388 F.2d 646 (2nd Cir., 1968).

78. *United States v. Roberts,* 388 F.2d 649 (2nd Cir., 1968).

79. *State v. Riccio,* 551 A.2d 1183, 1186 (R.1.1988), quoting *State v. Lanigan,* 528 A.2d 310, 316 (R.I., 1987). *See also People v. Gates,* 618 N.E.2d 847, 861 (111. Dist. App. Ct., 1993).

80. *United States v. Valenzuela-Bernal,* 458 U.S. 858, 870–871, 102 S. Ct. 3440, 3448, 73 L. Ed 2d 1193 (1982); *United States v. Lilla,* 699 F.2d 99, 105 (2nd Cir., 1983). *See also State v. Fisher,* 942 P.2d 49, 53 (Kan. Ct. App., 1997).

81. *United States v. Jimenez,* 789 F.2d 167, 170 (2nd Cir., 1986).

82. Quoting *United States v. Saa,* 859 F.2d 1067 (2nd Cir., 1988). *See also People v. Friend,* 533 N.E.2d 409 (111. App., 1988).

83. *Roviaro v. United States,* 353 U.S., 62, 77 S. Ct., 628–629 (1957).

84. *Roviaro v. United States,* 353 U.S., 59, 77 S. Ct., 627 (1957); *United States v. Brown,* 3 F.3d 673, 679 (3rd Cir.), *cert. denied,* 510 U.S. 1017, 114 S. Ct. 615, 126 L, Ed. 2d 579 (1993).

85. *Roviaro,* 353 U.S., 64–65; *Monroe v. United States,* 943 F.2d 1007, 1012–1013 (9th Cir., 1991), *cert. denied,* 503 U.S. 971 (1992). *See United States v. Mathis,* 357 F. 3d 1200, 1208 (10th Cir., 2004).

86. *Wigmore, Evidence* § 2374 (McNaughton rev., 1961), quoted in *McCray v. Illinois,* 386 U.S. 300 (1967).

87. *Roviaro v. United States,* 353 U.S. 53, 57 (1957).

88. *United States v. Mendaza-Burciaga,* 981 F.2d 192 (5th Cir., 1992).

89. *United States v. Singh,* 922 F.2d 1169. 1172 (5th Cir., 1981); *United States v. Diaz,* 655 F.2d 580, 586 (5th Cir., 1981), *cert. denied,* 455 U.S. 910 (1982); *United States v. Vizcarra-Porras,* 889 F.2d 1435, 1438 (5th Cir., 1989), *cert. denied,* 495 U.S. 940 (1990); *United States v. Ramirez-Rangel,* 103 F.3d 1501 (9th Cir., 1997).

90. *United States v. Russotti,* 746 F.2d 945, 948 (2nd Cir., 1984). *See also United States v. Soles,* 482 F.2d 105, 109 (2nd Cir.), *cert. denied,* 414 U.S. 1027 (1973).

91. *Spencer v. Texas,* 385 U.S. 554, 568–569 (1967), quoted *in McCray v. Illinois,* 386 U.S. 300 (1967).

92. *Commonwealth v. Lewin,* 542 N.E.2d 275 (Mass., 1989).

93. *United States v. Corting,* 630 F.2d 1207, 1213 (7th Cir., 1980).

94. *Commonwealth v. Lewin,* 542 N.E.2d 275, 286 (Mass., 1989). *See also Franks v. Delaware.* 438 U.S. 154, 155 (1978); *Commonwealth v. Nine Hundred & Ninety-Two Dollars,* 383 Mass. 764 767, 422 N.E.2d 767 (1981).

95. *Illinois v. Gates,* 462 U.S. 213, 238 (1983). *See also Alabama v. White.* 496 U.S. 325 (1990); *United States v. Sokolow,* 490 U.S. 1, 7 (1989); *New York v. P.J. Video. Inc.,* 475 U.S. 868 (1986).

96. *Shadwick v. Tampa,* 407 U.S. 345, 349 (1972). *See also United States v. Leon,* 468 U.S. 897, 914 (1984); *Connally v. Georgia,* 429 U.S. 245, 246 (1977).

97. Chief Magistrate, Cobb County, GA, quoted in Curriden, M., Secret threat to justice, *Nat. L.J.* (Feb. 20, 1995), p. 29.

98. *McCray v. Illinois,* 386 U.S. 300 (1967).

99. *Natl. L.J.* (Feb. 20, 1995).

100. *State v. Moore,* 438 N.W.2d 101, 106 (Minn., 1989). *See also United States v. Leaky,* 47 F.3d 396, 398 (10th Or., 1995).

101. *Commonwealth v. Amral,* 554 N.E.2d 1189, 1196 (Mass., 1990).

102. *Commonwealth v. Amral,* 554 N.E.2d 1197, 1198 (Mass., 1990).

103. *Dailey,* 639 P.2d 1068, 1077 n.ll (Colo., 1981). *See also United States v. Mendosa-Burciaga,* 981 F.2d 192, 195–196 (5th Cir., 1992), *cert. denied,* 510 U.S. 936 (1993); *United States v. Johns,* 948 F.2d 599, 606 (9th Cir., 1991), *cert. denied,* 505 U.S. 1226 (1992).

104. *Franks v. Delaware,* 438 U.S. 154 (1978).

105. *Franks v. Delaware,* 438 U.S. 156 (1978); 2 *Drug L. Rep.* 24, Suppressing searches when the police officer misleads the magistrate (Clark Boardman Callaghan, 1991). *See also United States v. Carlson,* 697 F.2d 231, 238 (8th Cir., 1983); *United States v. Hole,* 564 F.2d 298, 302 (9th Cir., 1977); *United States v. Botero,* 589 F.2d 430, 433 (9th Cir., 1978).

106. *Franks,* 438 U.S., 171. *See also Mosher Steel-Virginia v. Tieg,* 327 S.E.2d 87, 92 Va., 1985).

107. *United States v. Fawole,* 785 F.2d 1141 (4th Cir., 1986).

108. *United States v. McDonald,* 723 F.2d 1288,1293 (7th Cir., 1983); *United States v. Southard,* 700 F.2d 1 (1st Cir., 1983).

109. *Rugendorf v. United States,* 376 U.S. 528 (1964); 2 *Drug L. Rep.* 24 (Clark Boardman Callaghan, 1991).

110. *United Stales v. Cortina,* 630 F.2d 1207, 1213 (1980).

111. *United Stales v. Cortina,* 630 F.2d 1207, 1214 n. 4 (1980).

112. *Rea v. United States,* 350 U.S. 214 (1956).

113. *Cortina,* 630 F.2d, 1216.

114. *United States v. Reivich,* 793 F.2d 957, 960 (8th Cir., 1986).

115. *United States v. Reivich,* 793 F.2d, 961; *United States v. Walker,* 919 F.2d 501 (8th Cir., 1990).

116. *United States v. Parker,* 836 F.2d 1080, 1083 (8th Cir., 1987).

Corroboration of Informant Information

8

8.1 Generally

The value of corroborating an informant's tip cannot be overstated. The Supreme Court in *Illinois v. Gates* emphasized "the value of corroboration of details of an informant's tip by independent police work."

The 1983 lesson of *Gates* was apparently lost on the U.S. intelligence community between September 11, 2001 and the Iraq war. According to a commission established by President Bush, prewar claims that Iraq was producing weapons of mass destruction were based almost entirely on an informant described as "crazy" by his handlers and a "congenital liar" by his friends. Code-named "Curveball," the source was developed by Germany's intelligence service. They passed along his information to the Defense Intelligence Agency (DIA). The commission reported that the DIA "did not even attempt to determine Curveball's veracity." The commission went on to say that "worse than having no human sources is being seduced by a human source who is telling lies."[1]

On a less grand scale than a war, failure to corroborate an informant's information can have devastating consequences on an innocent citizen's life, as demonstrated in *Carlson v. United States.*[2] In August 1992, homeowner Donald Carlson was shot and seriously wounded during the execution of a search warrant on his Poway, California, home.

The probable cause for the search warrant was the result of information provided by an informant who was considered unreliable by at least two law enforcement officers involved in the case. Customs agents failed to recognize warning signals that indicated that the informant's accounts were either seriously flawed or false.[3] Corroboration through investigation did not occur. The government settled the case for $2.75 million.

Accounting for the failure to adequately investigate the informant's claims, an unidentified Customs agent told a reporter,

> I'm not saying we willfully violate people's rights. It's just that you get caught up in the whirlwind, where the only thing that's important is to make seizures and you end up cutting corners.[4]

Corroboration is a corner that cannot afford to be cut.[5] The amount of investigation is case specific.[6] Some of the investigative avenues open to investigators range from the simple to the complex.[7]

8.2 Surveillance

The reliability of an untested informant's tip can be verified or corroborated through independent investigation by law enforcement officers.[8] Surveillance is perhaps the most valuable of the traditional investigative methods.

A tip concerning a Florida drug smuggling conspiracy received from an undisclosed and previously untested informant demonstrated the value of surveillance in *United States v. Alexander.*[9] Following the initial tip, agents began the time-consuming task of verifying the informant's account and developing investigative leads.

The case consumed nearly two weeks of investigation. Surveillance enabled agents to observe an off-loading of drugs unfold before them.[10] Several arrests and a significant seizure of drugs followed.

In ruling favorably for the government in a motion to disclose the identity of the informant, the court noted "the information furnished by the informant had to be corroborated by substantial information gathered by extensive surveillance in order to provide probable cause. The suspicious activity observed during this surveillance that suggested criminal conduct was necessary to provide probable cause. Under these circumstances, appellants had no right to compel disclosure of the informant's identity."[11]

The objectives of surveillance include:

- Determine whether a violation exists
- Identify coconspirators
- Obtain evidence
- Determine an informant's reliability
- Corroborate an informant or undercover agent's testimony

- Protect agents and informants while acting in an undercover capacity
- Develop probable cause

Types of surveillance employed:

- Foot surveillance teams (employed in urban settings)
- Vehicle
- Aerial
- Fixed observation point
- Still photographs
- Audio
- Video
- Electronic (including global positioning systems [GPS])[12]

8.3 Mail Covers

A mail cover is the process by which a nonconsensual record is made of any data appearing on the outside cover of any sealed or unsealed class of mail.[13] Mail covers are routinely used by law enforcement and are permitted by law to obtain information to:

- Protect national security
- Locate a fugitive
- Obtain evidence of commission or attempted commission of a crime
- Obtain evidence of a violation of a postal statute
- Assist in the identification of property, proceed, or assets forfeitable under law[13]

The Office of the Postal Inspection Service regularly reports the recorded information to the requesting agent.

Except for mail covers ordered to locate fugitives or subjects engaged in activities involving national security, mail covers remain in effect for 30 days. At the expiration of 30 days the requesting authority must provide a statement of the investigative benefit of the mail cover and the anticipated benefits expected to be derived from its extension.[13]

8.4 "Trash Runs"

Many investigators employ an investigative technique known as a "trash run."[14] Agents retrieve garbage prior to its normal collection. Suspects who have successfully avoided detection by other investigative methods often throw valuable evidence into their garbage.

Trash searches routinely yield receipts, bills containing credit card numbers, and bank account information providing investigative leads. Narcotics wholesalers discard packaging material containing traces of controlled substances. Clandestine laboratory operators also dispose of original containers of precursors or chemicals used to process illicit drugs.

Whether the Fourth Amendment protects a trash can[15] is governed by the Katz Test,[16] also referred to as "The Reasonable Expectation of Privacy Test." That expectation of privacy exists only if:

- An individual actually expects privacy, and
- His expectation is reasonable.[16]

Trash cannot be collected from the suspect's curtilage.[17] The investigator must collect trash after it has been discarded or deposited for routine pickup. Jurisdictions vary in their treatment and acceptance of trash runs.

8.5 Telephone Toll Records

Telephone toll records and subscriber information are valuable investigative tools and can be utilized to corroborate information received from an informant. It has been held that no constitutional prohibition is violated by their disclosure to law enforcement. The subscriber information reveals who has applied for and receives telephone service for a particular telephone number. The credit application for service yields numerous investigative leads including the history of service (previous telephone numbers) and prior addresses. Personal references listed may reveal criminal associates.

The toll information is a record of a subscriber's outgoing long distance telephone calls. The material supplied to law enforcement contains the same information included in a subscriber's telephone bill.

Law enforcement access to the transactional records and information from the service provider is regulated by law.[18] The procedures followed by federal agencies to obtain the information include:

1. An administrative subpoena or grand jury subpoena.
2. A warrant issued under the Federal Rules of Criminal Procedure.
3. A court order for such disclosure as long as the government entry shows that there is reason to believe the records or other information sought are relevant to a legitimate law enforcement inquiry.
4. Consent of the subscriber or customer to such disclosure.

The requesting agency is not required to notify the subscriber that his telephone records have been subpoenaed. Telephone companies have their own policies on notifying their customers of the record request. A subpoena can request, but not require, that a company delay notification. The request generally contains the following language:

> Pursuant to an official criminal investigation being conducted by the requesting agency of a suspected felon, we request that your company furnish on *(date)* toll record information pertaining to *(name)* for the period *(month, day, year)* through *(month, day, year)* inclusive, and that you not disclose the existence of such request for a period of 90 days from the date of its receipt. Any such disclosure could impede the investigation being conducted and thereby interfere with enforcement of the law.

A court order can prevent the service provider from notifying the customer.

Telephone toll data are analyzed either by the agent making the request or an intelligence analyst. Tolls have proven valuable in conspiracy investigations assisting in corroborating evidence of an overt act.

Toll data can be organized in association matrixes and link association charts. Toll analysis is often a preliminary step prior to wiretap investigations.

Investigators with the Treasury Department use a computerized telephone toll analysis system known as TELAN. During an investigation, telephone numbers acquired by special agents from various sources, such as the telephone company, toll data reports, informers, and arrested persons, are used to determine patterns of activity and to identify other possible conspirators in the crime being investigated.[19] The information is entered into the TELAN system. The historical master file retains submitted information for a minimum of five years. The computerized system retrieves, sorts, compares, and matches telephone numbers for use in criminal investigations.

The telephone numbers called from a target telephone can also be collected through the use of a dialed number recorder referred to as a DNR (earlier versions of the DNR were known as pen registers). The DNR records the date, time, and duration of outgoing calls. Law enforcement agencies employ a variety of computer programs that are compatible with the DNR. The numbers recorded by the DNR are arranged in order of frequency of calls to telephone numbers, possibly indicating the criminal significance of the subscriber called. Incoming calls to a target telephone are identified through the use of a trap and trace device. Trap and trace technology is routinely used in tandem with DNRs.

8.6 Credit Card and Financial Records

Informants often provide accounts of the travels of a criminal target. Credit card charges recorded on billing statements can often corroborate that information. Although cash transactions have been the criminal's preferred method of doing business, an increasingly cashless society has encouraged credit card use. Airline travel, hotel stays, and restaurant visits are all memorialized once a credit card is used. The evidence can be invaluable in a conspiracy investigation.

A variety of methods are employed to obtain credit card numbers. Informants may be in a position of trust that enables them to report the account numbers. Mail covers reveal bills arriving at the target home or business. Although their contents may not be examined, a request to the billing company may reveal account information. Trash runs are also a successful method of obtaining discarded invoices or bills.

Informants also may have information regarding financial institutions utilized by the target. The Right to Financial Privacy Act governs obtaining financial records and credit card records from a financial institution.[20]

Access to financial records on a customer may be gained from a financial institution by any of six methods:

1. Pursuant to the prior written consent of the customer.
2. Pursuant to a search warrant.
3. Pursuant to an administrative subpoena.
4. Pursuant to a formal written request.
5. Pursuant to a judicial subpoena.
6. Pursuant to a grand jury subpoena.

In federal investigations requests for financial records are generally conducted with the assistance of the U.S. Attorneys Office.

8.7 Criminal History Record Systems

The essential task of corroborating an informant's information often begins at the keyboard of a computer. Today's law enforcement officers have at their disposal a vast network of computer databases to assist in their investigations. Many of those systems have been integrated since the events of September 11, 2001.

Federal, state, and local law enforcement agencies have developed criminal intelligence networks that collect and analyze information collected in the field. Although an informant may report "new information," it would be extremely unlikely that there would be no method available to corroborate, at least in part, his account by querying available systems.

Technological advances have not eliminated the need for "traditional" investigative means of corroborating an informant's account of criminal activity. Ready access to data or criminal intelligence already collected allows the investigator to more effectively act on informant information. It also makes it more difficult for the informant to lie or attempt to mislead his handler without detection.

The same databases used to corroborate information obtained from the informant can also be used in evaluating whether to use the informant. Fully checking the background of the confidential informant (CI) is more effectively accomplished when all available information systems are queried.

In *United States v. Bernal-Obeso*,[21] the Drug Enforcement Administration (DEA) utilized an informant apparently without realizing that the CI had been charged with two counts of murder. The CI had pleaded guilty to the reduced charge of voluntary manslaughter with a firearm enhancement.[22] The defense discovered the conviction on their own initiative and claimed that the government had failed to discharge its obligation under *Brady v. Maryland*[23] and *Giglio v. United States*[24] to provide the defense with material exculpatory evidence that could have been used to impeach the informant's credibility.[25] The entire issue would not have arisen if the agents had queried all systems available to them.

8.7.1   Federal Systems

The National Crime Information Center (NCIC) is an automated database of criminal justice and justice-related records maintained by the FBI and utilized by both state and federal law enforcement agencies. The database includes the "hot files" of wanted and missing persons, stolen vehicles, and identifiable stolen property, including firearms. Information regarding known terrorists is also available through NCIC.

Access to NCIC files is through central control terminal operators in each state that are connected to NCIC via dedicated telecommunications lines maintained by the FBI. Local agencies and officers on the beat can access the state control terminal via the state law enforcement network. Inquiries are based on name and other nonfingerprint identification. Most criminal history inquiries of the system are made via the NCIC telecommunications system. NCIC data may be provided only for criminal justice and other specifically authorized purposes. For criminal history searches, this includes criminal justice employment, employment by federally chartered or insured banking institutions or securities firms, and use by state and local governments for purposes of employment and licensing pursuant to a state statute approved by the U.S. Attorney General. Inquiries regarding presale firearm checks are included as criminal justice uses.

The Federal Bureau of Investigation (FBI) also maintains criminal history record files on federal offenders, as well as files on state offenders to the extent that such information is voluntarily submitted by states. The FBI has accepted and recorded state offender information for several decades and has compiled a criminal history database that, to a great extent, duplicates the files of the state repositories.[26]

The FBI also maintains a nationwide telecommunications system that enables federal, state, and local criminal justice agencies to conduct national record searches and to obtain information about individuals who are arrested and prosecuted in other states. In addition, the FBI provides criminal record services to federal and nonfederal criminal justice agencies that are authorized by federal law to obtain such records.[26]

Currently, the FBI operates a centralized criminal history file that serves as the primary source for national record searches and interstate record exchanges. By the end of the 20th century, however, the FBI began serving as the "51st State repository" with respect to federal offenders. The FBI also maintains the following systems:

- The Interstate Identification Index, which permits authorized requestors to determine whether any state or federal repository maintains a criminal history record about a particular subject.
- The National Fingerprint File, which provides positive identification of all offenders, is indexed in the national system.[26]

Other federal law enforcement agencies maintain their own independent computer databases. As an example, the Narcotics and Dangerous Drug Information System (NADDIS) is the DEA's computerized information system. All intelligence and criminal-related information collected by the agency and memorialized in an investigative report (DEA 6) finds its way into the NADDIS system.

The method employed to enter data is an agency-wide indexing system. At the end of the text of each DEA 6 is a section utilized to index information contained in the report. As an example, a report describing the execution of a search warrant and the arrest of several individuals will fully identify all arrestees. Their biographical data will be entered into NADDIS. The ensuing search may reveal telephone numbers belonging to suppliers or customers. Subscriber and toll information is ordered and reported in subsequent DEA 6s. The data are also indexed and entered into NADDIS. The same holds true for license plate numbers of vehicles located at the scene. In later investigations a telephone number or name entered into a DEA report will be routinely queried through NADDIS by agents or intelligence analysts. Any mention of the individual or any number match found in NADDIS will refer the agent to a case number for further investigation.

The Treasury Department uses the Treasury Enforcement Communications System. Known as TECS, it is similar to NADDIS with the exception that it provides lookout information on individuals, businesses, vehicles, aircraft, and vessels.

8.7.2   State Systems

Each state operates a central criminal history record repository that receives case processing information contributed by law enforcement agencies, prosecutors, courts, and corrections agencies throughout the state. These repositories compile the information into comprehensive criminal history records or "rap sheets," as they are often called. Rap sheets are made available to criminal justice personnel, for authorized purposes, by means of statewide telecommunications systems.[27]

Maintenance of such central repositories relieves local and state criminal justice agencies of the need to maintain expensive and duplicate information systems that attempt to compile comprehensive offender records. They need only maintain systems that support their own case processing needs and can rely upon the state central repositories for information about the processing of cases in other agencies.[28]

The State repositories also make criminal history records available to some noncriminal justice agencies, such as state agencies that are authorized by law to obtain the records for such purposes as employment screening and occupational licensing.[27] Customarily, the repositories are charged under state law with the following:

- Establishing comprehensive files of criminal history records.
- Establishing an efficient and timely system for retrieving the records.
- Ensuring that the records are accurate and up-to-date.
- Establishing rules and regulations governing the dissemination of criminal history records to criminal justice and noncriminal justice users.

Today, all 50 states, Puerto Rico, and the District of Columbia have established central repositories for criminal history records.[30]

Criminal history record information is increasingly becoming available outside of the criminal justice system. Even nonconviction information is now being made more available to noncriminal justice agencies. Twenty-nine states have adopted open record or freedom of information statutes that cover some types of criminal history record information. This does not mean that criminal history record information is publicly available in these states in all circumstances, but it does mean that some types of information are more available than before.[29]

As a part of this trend, a majority of the states now permit access to some criminal history records by at least some types of noncriminal justice agencies and private entities. For example, special access rights are increasingly accorded to governmental agencies with national security missions and to licensing boards and some governmental and private employers screening applicants for sensitive positions, such as those involving public safety, supervision of children, or custody of valuable property.[29]

8.8   Information Obtained from Public Record Sources

Information obtained from an informant about a subject of an investigation can be verified and expanded upon through sources available from outside of the law enforcement community. Public records are invaluable tools that can both corroborate an informant's account and provide leads for expanding an investigation.

Skilled investigators routinely examine information from the following public record sources (contributed by William Riley and Steven Kiraly, Private Investigators, of Riley and Kiraly, Miami, Florida). Much of the information is available online:

ASSESSOR'S OFFICE:
Owner(s) of property
Address of property
Parcel number
Legal description
Recorder's docket/page number
Full cash value of property and land
Purchase price
Last purchase date
Type of land
Personal property records

BANKRUPTCY COURT:
Name of person or business filing bankruptcy
Bankruptcy filing type
Date filed
Case number
Creditors
Detail of claims, motions, and judgments

CITY BUSINESS LICENSE:
   Name of business
   Type of business (corporation, sole proprietor, etc.)
   Business classification
   Owners/officers
   Date started
   Reported monthly sales revenue
   Current status

CORPORATION COMMISSION:
   Name of business
   Name(s) of officers/directors
   Addresses of officers/directors
   Date officers/directors took office
   Statutory agent
   Articles of incorporation
   Annual reports with balance sheets
   Shareholders' names
   Business description
   Address of business

CRISS-CROSS DIRECTORY:
   Cross-reference phone numbers with addresses and names

LIBRARY:
   Business statistics (Dunn & Bradstreet, etc.)
   Newspaper articles
   Out-of-state phone books
   Professional directories (attorneys, etc.)
   Maps

MOTOR VEHICLE DEPARTMENT:
   Driver's license information
   Vehicle data by VIN, title, person, registration, plate number, make/model/year, lien holder, status of registration

RECORDER'S OFFICE:
   Recorded documents by name
   Affidavit of Value (contains owner/seller, sales price, date of purchase, etc.)

SECRETARY OF STATE:
   Trade names
   Application for trade names
   UCC statements
   Business information

STATE EMPLOYMENT:
   Quarterly wage reports by social security number
   Employer information
   Business information

SUPERIOR COURT:
   Civil and criminal case history by name or date filed
   Divorce decrees
   Calendar listing

TREASURER'S OFFICE:
   Party(s) responsible for paying taxes on property, delinquent taxes,
      amount of taxes

UTILITIES:
   Person(s) responsible for payment of utilities
   Employer information
   Social security number
   Previous address
   References

VOTER REGISTRATION:
   Name, address and phone number of registered voter
   Birth date and place of birth
   Occupation
   Date of registration
   Party affiliation

8.9   Polygraph Examination of Informants

Successfully directing and monitoring a confidential informant requires that
officers never put their full trust or safety in an informant. Agents are trained
to "NEVER TRUST AN INFORMANT."[30] The CI may exaggerate or fabricate
the criminal acts of a target. He can make deals with targets as easily as he
can with the police using both sides to his advantage. The CI is also in a

position to arrange for rip-offs of large flash rolls. They have been known to sell government property used in investigations or to pledge it as collateral for loans.[31]

An informant's activity can rarely be monitored 24 hours a day. His information cannot always be corroborated by traditional investigative means. The polygraph can offer the investigator an opportunity to verify and confirm[32] an informant's information, particularly when efforts to corroborate his information prove unsuccessful. The instrument should not be used as a substitute for investigation.

The polygraph is a widely accepted law enforcement tool utilized by all federal and many state and local law enforcement agencies. In addition to its application in criminal investigations, it is also employed in screening police applicants in preemployment examinations and in the internal investigations of employees.[33]

Appendix 8A: DEA Source Debriefing Guide

Prepared by the Drug Enforcement Administration, Intelligence Division, with the advice and assistance of the Intelligence Community.

Preface

The DEA Intelligence Division has updated this *Source Debriefing Guide* to assist debriefers in formulating questions concerning international and domestic drug trafficking.

The *Source Debriefing Guide* is a source document used to supplement the skills and knowledge of debriefers in the technical areas of drug production, smuggling, and distribution. Information gained from responses to the questions in this *Guide* can provide tactical, operational, and strategic intelligence for drug law enforcement activities.

It is not expected that every person interviewed, whether defendant, suspect, or witness, will supply information about all aspects of the drug traffic. A series of general questions provided in Part One of this *Guide* is designed to identify the areas of knowledge of the person being debriefed. It is recommended that all of the general questions be posed first.

Part Two of the *Guide* consists of eight subject sections, each with specific questions that may be asked to develop information on relevant subjects. Using the general questions in Part One, the debriefer can then identify specific areas of knowledge and refer to the relevant set of questions in Part Two.

Should the interviewee's answers to the general and specific questions indicate extensive technical or area knowledge on his or her part, it is recommended that technical debriefing assistance be requested from DEA elements or other Federal agencies with in-depth knowledge of the subject.

Drug traffickers often are aware of other criminal activity, such as burglary, robbery, homicide, etc. You should make note of any knowledge of these activities for later referral to other agencies.

This publication was revised to include additional guidance on precursor and essential chemicals, evolving financial practices, and the increasing use of computers among drug traffickers.

Part One: Drug Trafficking (General)

1. Which illegal drugs have you used, sold, transported, or have knowledge of? When? Are there "brands" or trade names on the drugs?
    Specify and explain:
    *   Heroin
    *   "Black Tar"
    *   Morphine Base
    *   Opium
    *   Cocaine hydrochloride
    *   "Crack"
    *   Hashish
    *   Hashish Oil
    *   Marijuana
    *   Amphetamines
    *   Barbiturates
    *   LSD

- PCP
- Other Drugs (specify)

2. Who is the source of supply? Where is this person located? Where did this person obtain the drugs? Who are the U.S. distributors? Who are the foreign distributors?
3. Who else is involved in the trafficking of these drugs?
4. Do you know of any locations where drugs are cultivated, manufactured, processed, or stored? (See Part Two: Section I, A and B; and Section II, A and B).
5. Do you have any knowledge of the smuggling of drugs across the U.S. Border? If so, where are the entry points? (See Part Two: Section I, C.) Do you know about smuggling across other international borders? Is this for end use or for transit purposes?
6. Do you have any knowledge of methods used to transport drugs? (See Part Two: Section IV.)
7. Describe the method of concealment, type of conveyance, and persons involved in drug smuggling. (See Part Two: Section IV.)
8. Are false documents used to conceal the identity of smugglers or couriers? How are these documents obtained? How are they falsified, and by whom? What type of documents are used?
9. What are the prices and purities of the drugs when they enter the United States? Do you know the prices and purities at other stages of the trafficking?
10. Have you ever seen or been told of opium poppy, coca, cannabis, or mescal cultivation either in or outside the United States? (See Part Two: Section I.)
11. Do you have any knowledge of heroin, cocaine, hashish, "crack," or dangerous drugs laboratories within or outside the United States? (See Part Two: Section II or III.)
12. Who finances the drug trafficking operations?
13. How are drugs paid for? Is the money paid up front, or are the drugs sold on consignment or exchanged for other goods? If payment is in currency, identify which country's currency. If payment is by exchange, identify the exchange goods.
14. How are funds used to pay for the drugs being moved? By cash? Letter of credit? Bank deposits? Bank wire transfer? International checks? Or, traditional "underground" banking systems? (See Part Two: Section VI.)
15. Do you know how or where the proceeds of any drug transactions have been hidden or invested? Who controls laundered drug funds?
16. Do you know the associates or businesses of any drug trafficker?
17. Do you have knowledge of any drug transactions?
18. What types of ledgers, journals, classified ads, computers, bulletin boards, or other documents or mechanisms are used to manage drug transactions? Are codes used?
19. Are you familiar with any areas of the United States or of the world? Describe those areas. Have you ever lived in those areas? When? For how long?
20. Do you know of any other smuggling activity into or out of the United States? Are drugs exchanged for other goods? Do you know of any non-U.S. international smuggling activity?
21. Is there any exchange of one drug for another? For example, cocaine for heroin? Are weapons being traded for narcotics? Identify the sources and recipients of the weapons and the drugs. (See Part Two: Section VII.)
22. Is there any official corruption involved? By whom? Paid by whom? How much? For how long? With which major traffickers are they associated? (See Part Two: Section VII.)

23. Have you been involved in or do you have any knowledge of any non-drug criminal activity? Give dates of involvement. Identify the crime category, the type of operation, and the level of operation.
    Crime Categories:
    • Contraband smuggling, sexual assault, prostitution, pornography, weapons or explosives violations, stolen property or vehicle, forgery, fraud, or other.

    Types of Operation:
    • Smuggling, financing, wholesaling, or other.

    Levels of Operation:
    • Syndicate, international foreign based, international domestic based, national, local, other.
24. What is the principal ethnic group involved in the drug activity? What syndicates or organizations, multi-national or national, are involved? Will the traffickers deal outside their own group or organization?
25. What language(s) do you speak?
26. What special skills do you have? Are you a pilot? Radio operator? Chemist? Photographer? Money launderer? Other?
27. Have you ever worked as a confidential informant? For whom? Give dates and current status.
28. Have you ever been confined in prison or any other institution? Give names, dates, locations, and reasons for confinement.

Part Two: Drug Trafficking (Specific)

Section I. Opium–Heroin–Morphine Base, Coca–Cocaine–"Crack," and Marijuana–Hashish–Hashish Oil

A. Sources
    1. Where are the opium poppy, cannabis, or coca cultivation fields? Give geographic coordinates, names of roads, and local name for the area. Identify landmarks.
    2. Identify the owners and cultivators of the fields, their residences, telephone numbers, and associates.
    3. When are the fields planted and harvested?
    4. How many harvests are there per year?
    5. What yield is expected and obtained from the fields? How many opium poppy bulbs per plant? Does this yield vary with the harvest season if there is more than one?
    6. What is the size of the field? How many plants per square meter or hectare? (1 hectare = 2.47 acres)?
    7. What are the arrangements between owners and cultivators?
    8. Specify and explain the support for growing areas including:
        • Water sources and irrigation methods used,
        • Chemicals and fertilizers used, and
        • How seeds and other supplies are obtained and paid for.
    9. Is the opium gum, coca leaf or paste, or cannabis stored at the field or moved? If moved, how? Where? When? By whom? And to whom?
    10. Are the fields protected? If so, by police? Military? Government officials? Guerrillas? Or, others? Are the protectors armed? Do the fields have electronic

surveillance devices? Are the fields booby-trapped? Are attempts made to hide or disguise fields? If so, how?

11. Do the local authorities know of the fields? Have they previously destroyed them? When? If not, why not? Identify the local authorities.

B. Laboratories
   1. What are the geographic coordinates and locations of laboratories?
   2. Are the laboratories at or near the fields? How are the labs built, and how is equipment brought in?
   3. What equipment is used at the lab? Are the labs mobile? How large are they?
   4. What chemicals are used? Where do they come from? What else do you know about the chemicals?
   5. Describe and name the chemist(s). How is he trained? By whom? Does the chemist have any other interests in the operation?
   6. Who finances the laboratory? How?
   7. What security measures are used?
   8. Is the heroin or cocaine dyed, diluted, or adulterated?
   9. Does the laboratory operate continually? If not, does it operate only when an order is received? Only at harvest time? Or, on some other schedule?
   10. How are orders and instructions received or passed? Is there a telephone? Two-way radio? Electronic teletype? Computer? Or, contact point? Identify telephone number, radio call sign, teletype address, computer password, codes, or contact point.
   11. What conveyances are used? Describe the type, ownership, drivers, and transportation routes.
   12. How many people are involved in the operation of the lab? What are their names and identities? How often is the lab moved? Who decides when to move the lab?
   13. What are the hours of operation of the lab? How many days a week is it in operation?
   14. Are records maintained regarding drug production and distribution?
   15. What else do you know about the lab and its operations?

C. Transportation and Storage
   1. How is the product moved? Does the buyer pick up the product at the lab? At the growing field? Or, at some other point?
   2. Who are the backers, financiers, and protectors? Identify the principals' family members and relationships.
   3. Are any other persons or groups involved? What routes and contact points do they utilize?
   4. What nationalities, ethnic groups, religious organizations, criminal syndicates, or other groups do the couriers belong to? Are they males or females, adults, or children?

D. Obtaining or Moving Drugs
   1. How is contact made for the order, delivery, pickup, security, and transfer of drugs, etc.?
   2. What communications methods are used? If telephones, faxes, or beepers, what are the numbers? If radios are used, what call signs and frequencies are used? If written messages or cables, what addresses? If signals or couriers, what are the details? If computers, what are the passwords? What kind of computers are used? What software or computer programs are used?
   3. Do the traffickers employ any communications security? Do they utilize communications centers? Who controls them?

4. What counterintelligence methods are used by the traffickers?
5. Are controllers used to monitor drug movements? How do they get their instructions?
6. How are couriers recruited and by whom?
7. Are periodic reports made on the progress of the shipment? If so, to whom and by what means?
8. What ports or places of entry are used for these shipments? Why?
9. What methods are used to conceal shipments? Describe and explain. Are the shipments transferred within a country to other means of movement or concealment? Describe.
10. Are false documents involved in the shipments? Describe these documents and identify the supplier.
11. Who knows when the shipments are en route and the methods being used? Identify fully.
12. When is payment made? In advance or upon delivery to intended recipient? or at some other time? Are the same people involved in payment and movement of the drugs? Are payments made in cash or by wire transfer, bank draft, in products, or in some other form? Are drugs exchanged one for another? Are drugs exchanged for weapons?
13. Identify any business (wittingly or unwittingly) involved in the traffic. Describe the extent of this involvement.
14. Are there any package markings used to identify recipients? Are the markings related to the seller as well as to the recipient or buyer? Describe the packaging and the markings.
15. Who packages the drugs and where are they packaged? Are they ever repackaged at any point?

Section II. Dangerous Drugs

A. Sources
1. What drugs are involved? Which chemicals are used?
2. What is the finished form of the drug, e.g., powder? Crystal? Liquid? Capsule? Tablet? Blotter? Or, other?
3. Were you a courier? How are arrangements made to pick up the drug? Are children being used as couriers?
4. How do you get the drugs, e.g., from street sellers? From a minor or major distributor? Or, directly from the lab?
5. From whom and how are they obtained? By direct or indirect contact through a second or third party? Is the supplier associated directly with the manufacturer?
6. How much do the drugs cost? How much can they be sold for? How much for greater or lesser quantities? Who is buying and using the drugs?
7. How are the drugs distributed, e.g., personal pickup or delivery? U.S. Mail? UPS? Or, other kinds of shipment? What are the names of distributors and sellers?
8. Can you obtain samples? Make purchases? Introduce someone?
9. Give names of people financing the operation. Do they take part in the actual physical transactions? Is anyone else involved in any way?
10. Do you know the location or address of the lab? Who owns and operates the lab? Who are the chemists? Who is financing the lab?

11. Are the drugs intended for U.S. consumption? What proportion goes where?
12. In the case of mescaline or peyote and similar drugs, where are the plants located or grown? Who is "harvesting" the crop? Where do they bring the raw material?
13. How are the drugs or chemicals smuggled? Describe in detail.
14. Do you have any other knowledge concerning drugs, diluents, or chemicals used to make drugs?

B. Illicit Laboratories
1. How many people are involved in the operation of the lab? What are their identities? Where is the lab located? How often is the lab moved? Who decides when the lab is to be moved?
2. What are the lab's hours of operation? How many days a week does it operate? What quantity of the drug is produced?
3. What type of equipment is used? Describe the type, capacity, and quantity of equipment in use at the lab, for example, pill press, mixing equipment, etc.
4. Who supplies the equipment? Who installs the equipment? How is it powered?
5. What manufacturing process is used? Is more than one process used? What formulas are used? Do you have or can you get the formula?
6. What chemicals are used? Where did they come from? How were they obtained? Where are the chemicals stored? What method is used to divert the chemicals from any legitimate source? Give the name of firms, country of origin, and method of operation, e.g., the use of brokers, false invoices, and transshipments to other countries.
7. How are the drugs packaged, e.g., in plastic bags? Bundles? Jars? Bottles? Or, packages? How many dosage units or hits in a package? Describe them. Where does the packaging come from? (Follow same questions as for chemicals, #6.)
8. What payment, paperwork, equipment dealers, brokers, and company names are used? Describe. (Follow same questions as for chemicals, #6.)
9. What diluents are used? Are the same ones always used? (Follow same questions as for chemicals, # 6.)
10. Do you have or can you obtain samples?
11. To whom is the drug distributed after sale? In what form? What do they do with it?
12. Are any of the suppliers or laboratories involved in manufacturing illicit drugs? Are any of these drugs being diverted?
13. Do these labs have security systems? What methods or weapons are available to defend the labs?
14. How are the equipment and chemicals disposed of?

C. Diversion of Legitimate Drugs
1. How are the drugs obtained? By prescription from physicians? Dispensed without a prescription? Excessive quantities of over-the-counter medications dispensed by pharmacists? Or, directly from physicians? Identify the physicians and pharmacists involved.
2. Are any records falsified by legitimate handlers to cover illicit distribution? How? Are fraudulent names used on dispensing records?
3. Are the drugs stolen? Give details: By whom? From whom? How? Where? When?
4. How is payment made for the prescription? Does it differ according to the controlled substance obtained?
5. How often can you get a prescription and for which drugs? How many dosage units are prescribed per prescription?
6. Is the physician part of a conspiracy?

7. Are the drugs sold by a pharmacist without a prescription? What volume? What price? What form?
8. Will the pharmacist sell one or many prescriptions at a time? How large a volume will he or she prescribe or sell?
9. Does the pharmacist prepare a phony prescription to cover the transaction?
10. Does he provide illegal refills for a legitimate prescription?
11. Are real or fictitious names used? If fictitious, how are these names obtained?
12. Does the physician perform an examination? If an examination is performed, what is the procedure?
13. Does the physician know that the controlled substances he dispenses or prescribes are not for legitimate use?
14. Will the physician sell one or numerous prescriptions at a time? How large a volume will he or she prescribe or sell?
15. Does the physician identify the pharmacist who will fill the prescriptions?
16. Is the transaction documented in a record and, if so, how is it recorded and maintained?
17. If the physician sells directly, where are the drugs obtained and in what quantities? Are drug samples involved in the diversion?
18. Does the physician require a person to take or administer the drug in his presence?
19. What other drugs are available from the source?
20. If the drugs are obtained from a wholesaler or manufacturer, at what point are they diverted? If in finished form, are the lot numbers available?
21. Are the employees or the owners involved?
22. Is the diversion by employee theft? If so, how was security breached?
23. Is the diversion covered by falsification of records?

Section III. Detailed Laboratory Questions

A. Chemicals and Equipment
    1. What kinds of drugs are being produced? What is the main drug? What other kinds of drugs can be made in the lab? What is the production capacity?
    2. List all the chemicals being used in the lab. For each chemical, list the following:
        • Chemical name
        • Amount of chemical
        • Size and type of container
        • Company or manufacturer name on the label
        • Where was each chemical purchased or otherwise obtained?
        • Was it a local company or source?
        • Ordered from out of town?
        • Imported from another country?
        • What was the unit cost?
        • What was the total cost?
    3. List all the equipment used at the lab, e.g., glassware, tubing, heating mantles, vacuum pumps, hydrogenators, pill presses, and other equipment. List the brand names or manufacturer names. Where was the equipment purchased or obtained? What did it cost?
    4. What else do you know about the chemicals and equipment?
    5. What are the sources of the laboratory equipment, chemicals, labor, etc.?

B. Production
    1. During what hours and how often is the lab operated?
    2. What processes are used to make the drugs? Are there formulas? Directions? Or, a cookbook? How long does it take to make a batch? What does the finished product look like? What is done with it? How are old chemicals and equipment disposed of, e.g., thrown out in the trash? Poured down the drain? Poured into a lake or stream? Or, buried?
    3. What chemicals are used? Where do the chemicals come from? How are the chemicals obtained? Where are the chemicals stored? What method is used to divert the chemicals from any legitimate source? Give the name of firms, country of origin, and method of operation, such as the use of brokers, false invoices, transshipment to other countries, etc. What else do you know about the chemicals?
    4. What safety equipment is in the lab, e.g., fire extinguishers? Fire alarms? Or, oxygen masks?
    5. Is the laboratory protected from or by the police? Military? Or, Guerrillas? If so, by whom? Are there armed guards? Are there electronic surveillance devices or booby traps installed? Are there locks? Bars? Alarms? Guard dogs? Radio scanners? Guards? Lookouts? Or, weapons?
    6. Is the lab also used for any legitimate purpose, e.g., commercial production? Student teaching? Research? Experiments?
    7. What else do you know about the laboratory and the production of drugs? How much is the chemist paid?
C. Marketing
    1. What records are kept? Can you obtain copies? Are the records coded? Do you know the codes used?
    2. How is the product packaged? Shipped? Or, stored? Is the product marked? What is the meaning of the marking?
    3. To what extent do local marketing conditions influence the use or modifications of operating procedures? For example:
        Heroin produced in Southeast Asia is deliberately made fluffy in consistency because operators are paid off in volume of product, rather than weight. (Knowledge of such local customs would enable more accurate estimates to be made of the country or region of origin of subsequent seizures or purchases.)
    4. What else do you know about the marketing of these drugs?

Section IV. Detailed Smuggling and Transportation Questions

A. Smuggling
    1. Do you have direct knowledge of any drug smuggling? If so, how did you acquire this knowledge?
    2. What kind of drug is being smuggled?
    3. Where is the drug smuggling occurring? Give detailed locations, Identify transshipment points, if any. Does ownership of drugs change after transshipment or staging points?
    4. Who is involved? Is this person a runner for someone else? If so, for whom? Who are the lieutenants of the drug smuggling group?
    5. How is the drug smuggling done? Give details of any special devices or procedures used by the drug smuggler.

6. How are the smuggling means acquired and from whom?
7. How often does the drug smuggling occur? Is there a pattern?
8. Is any border official involved? Who? How is he paid off? How much? By whom?
9. Who else knows about this drug smuggling?
10. When did you first learn about it? How long has it been going on?
11. Is there a fixed fee for couriers? Is payment made in cash? Merchandise? Drugs? Or, stolen goods?
12. Are any of these shipments co-op ventures? Are "insurance" schemes involved to reduce risk or loss?
13. Do you know of special instructions concerning crossing points? Times to cross? Cover stories? Backup arrangements for delivery, etc.?
14. Have you knowledge of any seizures which have taken place? Can you attribute these seizures to a specific organization?

B. Transportation
Cars, Trucks, Campers
1. Are you aware of any pattern of transportation of drugs by car? Truck? Or, camper? Describe.
2. Which drugs are being moved?
3. Who is involved? Identify with names, addresses, or locations, aliases, and associates.
4. What routes are used? Identify pickup points, transshipment points, stash points, and delivery points. Are the same routes used each time?
5. Has any vehicle been modified in any way to carry drugs? Describe in detail.
6. Where and by whom was the modification made?
7. How much is earned per shipment? How often?
8. How long has this system been active?

Air — Private Planes
9. Which drugs are being transported by private aircraft?
10. Who is the pilot? Does he own the plane? If not, who owns the plane? Is he a contract pilot? For whom? Who was the broker for the purchase of the plane?
11. Is the plane rented? From whom?
12. What is the make of the plane? If unknown, how many engines does it have? What color is the aircraft? What is the tail number? Has the tail number been altered?
13. How much is carried per shipment? How are the drugs packaged? Are drug shipments owned by only one person or more than one?
14. How often are the drugs transported? Is there a pattern?
15. Does the plane or ground crew have any special equipment?
16. Where is the pickup point? Identify by name of field, city, farm, or other location. Give directions to that point.
17. Where is the shipment delivered? To whom?
18. Are pilots or ground crews armed? With what type of weapons?
19. Is the organization involved in airdrop activities? Where do the airdrops occur: over land or at sea? What are the names or numbers of pickup vessels?
20. Has the aircraft been modified for airdrop activities? How does the crew contact vessels or ground crews?
21. What happens to the shipment once it leaves the plane? Identify and give the license numbers of any ground vehicles used. Identify ground crews or drivers.
22. Where is the ultimate destination of the shipment? Who are the recipients?

23. What are the air smuggling routes? Are there drug transshipment points? Where are the staging areas for the aircraft?

24. Are any special techniques used to avoid detection? Specify. Do the smugglers know the locations of drug enforcement radars?

25. Who owns or operates the landing fields?

Air — Commercial Aircraft

26. Which couriers or runners are using commercial planes to transport drugs? Identify by name and give description. Do the couriers travel alone or in groups?

27. Are aliases or false passports used? Give details. Who provides the false passports? Is there any nationality which is preferred?

28. Identify airport and city at both departure and arrival point. Why are these airports used? Have others been used? Why?

29. What drugs are transported? In what quantities? And how often?

30. How are they concealed? By body carry? In cargo? Or, in the aircraft? Where in the aircraft?

31. How frequent are the shipments? Is there a pattern?

32. Identify the airline and the person or group responsible for shipment of the drugs. For whom are they intended? Which flights do couriers prefer, e.g., red-eye or nonstop?

33. Describe any methods known for shipping drugs concealed in cargo. Are there particular times during which couriers fly, e.g., rush hours or weekends?

34. Identify any airport or airline personnel involved.

35. How are airline tickets purchased? How are they paid for? By cash? Credit card? Or, other?

36. Describe any special techniques used to avoid customs or other airport security.

37. Are false documents used for shipping? Explain. Who provides them?

38. How are the drug shipments delivered to the intended receiver by the courier(s)?

Boats and Ships — General

39. How are on-loads, transits, and off-loads coordinated?

40. With whom does the vessel communicate? When? Which radio frequencies are used? Does the vessel communicate with aircraft? What are the alternate plans in the event of communications breakdown?

41. Where does the vessel obtain fuel and provisions?

42. What do you think the risk of interception is?

43. What intelligence and guidance do you receive prior to sailing?

44. What do you know of maritime law enforcement operations and methods?

45. How many smuggling trips have you made?

46. Do you transit directly or travel near the coasts of foreign countries en route? Which countries?

47. If a rendezvous is missed, what are the alternate plans?

48. Which ports or anchorages are considered to be safe havens?

49. Do smuggling vessels transit the Panama Canal?

50. What is the destination of a courier after a drop off?

51. Do you ever see any aircraft overflying you? Do you report it? To whom? How?

Boats and Ships — Private

52. Describe and identify any private boats used to transport drugs. Are there established procedures for breakdown? Repair? Rescue? Or, replenishment? How common are breakdowns?

53. Who owns the boat or ship? Where is it kept? Identify the crew members. Who is the major dealer involved?

54. What drugs are transported onboard? In what quantities? What are the source countries?

55. Are the drugs concealed aboard the boat? Where?

56. What ports, harbors, marinas, or coastal areas are used to load and off-load the drugs? What sort of vessels do you off-load to?

57. What specific routes are used by maritime smugglers?

58. What techniques are used to avoid detection? Does the boat have special equipment or hidden compartments? Describe.

59. How often is the boat used for drug smuggling? Is there any pattern? How close do smuggling vessels travel to each other? Are there vessel holding areas en route?

Boats and Ships — Commercial

60. What commercial ships are being used to transport drugs? Identify vessel names, voyage numbers and direction, routing, and the shipping line involved. Are the officers of the shipping company involved?

61. Are any ship's officers or crew members involved? Identify them.

62. Where are the drugs loaded and off-loaded? Are freight forwarders or consolidators used? Who and where?

63. Are false shipping documents used? Who provides them? Were shipping charges prepared? How and by whom?

64. What special procedures and techniques are used to avoid detection? drop-offs? or pickups? Are the drugs shipped directly or transshipped through other countries?

65. How frequently are shipments made? Is there a pattern?

66. Are any port officials or workers involved? Identify them.

67. Is the shipping agent involved? Identify the shipping agent.

68. Who hires the crew?

69. In what country is the ship registered?

70. What is the name of the ship? Is the name of the ship altered at sea?

71. What is the radio frequency of the ship? Call sign? Code used?

72. Are cargo containers used to conceal the drugs? Are they rented or owned? What are the container numbers?

73. Provide information from the bill of lading to include number, shipper, consignee, description of cargo, and persons to be notified when shipment arrives.

74. How are the drugs transported to the ship? If transported in advance of the ship's arrival, where are the drugs stored?

Section V. Persons Apprehended at a Border While Smuggling Drugs

A. Drugs

1. How many times have you crossed the border with drugs? Where did you cross the border? When (times, dates)? Are these preferred times and places? Was anyone with you?

2. What routes did you follow?

3. How are drugs supposed to get through the border checkpoints? Are there any advance or following vehicles escorting the drugs? Were the escorts armed? Did

you encounter any law enforcement activity en route? Did you use countersurveillance?

4. What was the drug involved? What is the average amount of drugs you have carried across the border?
5. How much did it cost? How much were you paid to smuggle it? How much have you been paid in the past? From whom did you get the money? Where and when did you get the money?
6. How many accomplices do you have?
7. Do you make drug smuggling trips alone or in groups? Describe any acts of complicity on the part of officials or authorities.
8. Where are the drugs going?
9. How much will the drugs sell for?
10. Do you know anyone else smuggling drugs across the border? Tell what you know about times, locations, vehicles or trains, compartments, involvement of officials, etc.
11. Describe any techniques of concealing drugs known to you. What modifications such as false compartments are made to the vehicles?
12. Are you selling drugs? How much are you being paid for it? How much have you received in the past?
13. Do you know of any staging areas or stash sites on either side of the border?

B. Drug Traffickers
1. From whom did you obtain the drug? For whom are you moving or selling the drug? Describe the trafficking organization and the members you are involved with. Are you related by blood or class to these members?
2. Where, when, and in what place did you obtain the drug?
3. To whom would you sell the drug?
4. Do you have more than one source-of-supply? Who is your current source-of-supply? How many times have you been supplied by this person?
5. What quantity are you moving per week? Identify the location of the source of supply. Name and describe him or her.
6. Do you know any other customers of your source of supply?
7. To whom do they sell? Where do they make their sales? Who is involved in the sale? Describe them.
8. How were you recruited to smuggle or sell drugs?

Section VI. Financial

A. Transportation of Funds
1. How are drug payments made? Are the drugs paid for in advance or are they shipped on consignment?
2. How are drug payments and proceeds moved?
3. What are the domestic or international routes used to move money?
4. What methods of concealment are used?
5. Is there any particular pattern to the movement of funds? A particular day of the week, airline, etc.?
6. In what currency are drug payments made? What denominations?

B. Money Laundering Activities
1. What countries are drug monies laundered to or through? Why are these countries preferred?
2. Which U.S. cities are drug monies laundered to or through?

3. What laundering techniques are employed?
4. What banks are used to secure drug monies? Are bank officials witting?
5. Who are the major money launderers?
6. How many people are involved with your group in laundering monies? What type of people or businesses are involved?
7. What is the rate charged by the money launderer?
8. What financial instruments are used to launder monies?
    - _____ Cash
    - _____ Wire Transfer
    - _____ Checks
    - _____ Money Orders
    - _____ Letters of Credit
    - _____ Traditional underground instruments
    - _____ Others?

C. Asset Identification
1. What assets are held by members of the organization and where are they located?
2. Do members of the organization hold assets in their names or in nominee names? Explain.
3. What types of business investments do members of the organization make and where are they located?
4. Are computers used to record activities? What kind of computers are used? What software or computer programs are used?
5. Are money counting machines used? What type and model?
6. What type of financial records and books are retained by the organization?
7. Have you knowledge of any asset seizures? Can you attribute these seizures to a specific organization?

Section VII. Corruption and Terrorism

The primary use of this *Source Debriefing Guide* is to collect information which will lead to the prosecution of major drug traffickers and their organizations as well as to the forfeiture of assets. Information pertaining to drug smuggling methods, routes, and trends as well as to growing areas, refining techniques, and so on, is of significant interest to all federal drug enforcement agencies and can help them to better allocate or deploy their resources.

On occasion, a cooperating individual will claim to have knowledge of an activity of significant interest to the security interests of the U.S. Government, which may or may not relate directly to a drug violation. The following questions will assist the debriefer in some of these situations.

A. Official Corruption
1. What is the nature of the official involvement? Are government officials taking advantage of their positions to profit from the drug trade?
2. Is cooperation with U.S. law enforcement efforts used as a cover for drug-related activities?
3. What firsthand knowledge does the informant have concerning this issue?
B. Foreign Government Involvement in Drug Trafficking
1. What is the nature of the involvement? Is it a government official or is it part of a government policy?

   2. How does the informant know? Who told him? How reliable was his source
      of information?
   3. What services are provided to drug traffickers? Are traffickers of all national-
      ities treated the same? How much do the services cost? What is done with the
      proceeds?
C. Exchange of Drugs for Weapons
   1. Who supplies the drugs?
   2. Who furnishes the weapons? What type of weapons?
   3. How do you know that this has occurred?
   4. What were the weapons to be used for? What was the destination of the
      weapons?
D. Involvement of Terrorist and Insurgent Groups in the Drug Trade
   1. What is the extent of involvement by terrorist or insurgent groups? Direct?
      Indirect? Or, through extortion?
   2. What evidence, other than allegations, do you have to support this informa-
      tion?
   3. Is there a direct exchange of drugs for weapons?

Conclusion.   The above topics are not areas in which all sources of information need to be
questioned. The debriefer should, however, be sensitive to the need to fully explore areas of
drug-related activity that go beyond the primary investigative goal. These are sensitive issues
which, while they may not affect prosecutions, may shed new insights into areas of concern
for policymakers.

   The DEA Intelligence Division should be contacted immediately for assistance whenever
it appears that a cooperating individual has information which falls into these general
categories. If appropriate, other federal agencies shall be consulted.

References

1. *Illinois v. Gates*, 462 U.S. 213, 241 (1983). *See Draper v. United States*, 358 U.S. 307 (1959); *United States v. Garcia*, 528 F.2d 580, 587 (5th Cir., 1976). *See also* Miller, G. and Drogin, B., Intelligence analysts whiffed on a 'curveball,' report says one Iraqi defector single-handedly corrupted pre-war weapons estimates, *Los Angeles Times*, April 1, 2005. *See also* Commission on Intelligence Capabilities of the United States Regarding Weapons of Mass Destruction Report, March 31, 2005.

2. *Carlson v. United States*, 93-953G. *See State v. Shaw*, 37 S.W. 3d 900, 903 (Tenn., 2001).

3. Jones, D. and Eldridge, E., Archer Daniels informant faces charges, *USA Today*, Jan. 16, 1997.

4. Alvord, J., Snitches, licensed to lie? *San Diego Union Tribune*, May 30, 1995, A-7.

5. Tulsky, F.N., Evidence casts doubt on Camarena case trials; probe suggests perjury helped convict three in DEA agent's murder, *Los Angeles Times*, Oct. 26, 1997. *See* Kassin, S.M., Human judges of truth, deception and credibility: confident but erroneous, 23 Cardozo L. Rev. 800 (2002).

6. Kessler, R.E., Ex-informant sentenced for perjury in Pan Am Flight 103 hoax, *Miami Herald*, May 17, 1998.

7. Leen, J., Castro drug probe collapses in heap of dead ends, lies, *Miami Herald*, Nov. 24, 1996.

8. *United States v. Mendoza*, 547 F.2d 952 (5th Cir.) *cert. denied*, 431 U.S. 956 (1977); *United States v. Tuley*, 546 F.2d 1264 (5th Cir.) *cert. denied*, 434 U.S. 837 (1977); *United States v. Brennan*, 538 F.2d 711 (5th Cir.) *cert. denied*, 429 U.S. 1092 (1976); *United States v. Anderson*, 500 F.2d 1311 (5th Cir., 1974). *See United States v. One 1967 Cessna Aircraft*, 454 F. Supp. 1352 (C.D. Cal., 1978).

9. *United States v. Alexander*, 559 F.2d 1339, 1342 (5th Cir., 1977). *See also United States v. Luck*, 560 F. Supp. 258 (N.D. Ga., 1983).

10. 559 F.2, 1343.

11. 559 F.2, 1344. *See McCray v. Illinois*, 386 U.S. 300 (1967); *Bourbois v. United States*, 530 F.2d 3 (5th Cir., 1976).

12. Willing, R., Surveillance gets a satellite assist, *USA Today*, June 10, 2004, 3A .

13. 39 C.F.R. § 233.3 Mail Covers.

14. U.S. Customs Service, Office of Enforcement, *Criminal Investigators Handbook*, 1203.07.

15. U.S. Constitution, Amendment IV.

16. *Katz v. United Stales*, 389 U.S. 347 (1967).

17. *Boyd v. United States*, 116 U.S. 616 (1886).

18. 18 USC § 2703(c).

19. BATF Manual: *Investigative Priorities, Procedures, and Techniques,* Ch. N, 162(b).

20. 12 USC §§ 3401 et seq.

21. *United States v. Bernal-Obeso,* 989 F.2d 331 (9th Cir., 1993).

22. *United States v. Bernal-Obeso,* 989 F.2d 332 (9th Cir., 1993).

23. *Brady v. Maryland,* 373 U.S. 83 (1963).

24. *Giglio v. United States,* 405 U.S. 150 (1972).

25. 989 F.2d, 333.

26. Use and Management of Criminal History Record Information: A Comprehensive Report, U.S. Department of Justice, Bureau of Justice Statistics, Office of Justice Programs, 1.

27. Use and Management of Criminal History Record Information: A Comprehensive Report, U.S. Department of Justice, Bureau of Justice Statistics, Office of Justice Programs, 2.

28. U.S. Department of Justice, Office of Justice Programs, Bureau of Justice Statistics, Criminal History Record Information: Compendium of State Privacy and Security Legislation.

29. Compendium of State Privacy and Security Legislation: 1994 Overview, Access to Criminal History Records for Non-criminal Justice Purposes; U.S. Department of Justice, Bureau of Justice Statistics (Jan. 1995), at 7.

30. Birbiglia, J.M., The use of informants in drug cases, *NARC Officer Magazine,* International Narcotics Enforcement Officers Association, Jan./Feb. 1996, 20; Informant Interaction, DEA Office of Training Lesson Plan, Quantico, VA; Fitzgerald, D.G., Snitches, narcs and making cases, *Champion Magazine,* National Association of Criminal Defense Lawyers, Sept. 1995.

31. International Association of Chiefs of Police, Confidential Informants: Concepts and Issues Paper, June 1990, pp. 2, 3.

32. Polygraph Policy Model for Law Enforcement, FBI Law Enforcement Bulletin, June 1987, p. 12.

33. Polygraph Policy Model for Law Enforcement, FBI Law Enforcement Bulletin, pp. 10, 11, June 1987. *See also* § 11.4, *infra.*

Informants and Electronic Surveillance

9

9.1 Generally

Criminal cases involving undercover agents and informants routinely involve the recording or listening to warrantless consensual interceptions of wire, oral, and electronic communications.[1] The two most common examples of this investigative technique are:

1. Consensual telephone conversation intercepts.[2]
2. Concealed transmitters or tape recorders worn or carried on the person of the consenting party.[2]

The consensual interception of an oral, wire, or electronic communication occurs when a conversation between two or more people is monitored or recorded either by or under the direction of a law enforcement officer with the knowledge and prior consent of one or more of the participants to the conversation. 18 USC § 2511(2)(c) provides that "it shall not be unlawful under this chapter for a person acting under color of law to intercept a wire, oral, or electronic communication, where such person is a party to the communication or one of the parties to the communication has given prior consent to such interception."[2] Thus, Title III Wiretap[3] procedures are not applicable to consensual interceptions,[4] and interception orders[5] are not necessary.[4,6]

9.2   Consensual Telephone Conversation Intercepts

Consensual telephone intercepts are routinely used as a method of documenting a conversation between a criminal target and either an informant or undercover agent. Several U.S. Supreme Court cases have held that consensual interceptions or recordings do not violate the Fourth Amendment.[7]

Consensually monitored telephone conversations initiated by an informant to a criminal target should occur at the direction and supervision of his control agent. A good rule to follow is that all conversations between the confidential informant (CI) and potential defendants during the conduct of an investigation should be recorded. Such a policy prevents the defense from charging that the government selectively taped only favorable evidence and ignored evidence showing the defendant's innocence.

The equipment used to consensually tape record a telephone conversation is not complex. The most common technique is the application of a suction cup microphone to the ear portion of the telephone receiver. The microphone has a wire approximately three feet long that plugs into a standard cassette or digital tape recorder. The cassette tape-records the voice of both parties to the conversation.

Informants are often provided equipment to record unsupervised incoming telephone calls from the target. They should be instructed by their control agent to record all calls received that pertain to the investigation.[7]

CIs should not initiate telephone calls to the target unless directed to do so by the control agent. This practice avoids the selectively taped argument[8] by the defense and allows the agent to maintain control over the investigation.

Most state courts[9] and legislatures[10] adhere to the one-party consent provisions of Title III.[11] Many states require a warrant or have imposed statutory[12] or constitutional[13] restrictions.

Police agencies complying with their individual state's regulations are often required to complete formal requests for permission to consensually tape record conversations. Police agencies often enforce internal regulations regardless of state regulations. The practice is designed to maintain internal control over the use of electronic surveillance equipment.

9.2.1   Concealed Transmitters and Recording Devices

Consensual undercover recordings of face-to-face conversations between an informant (or undercover agent) and a target of investigation are obtained by either of two methods:

1.   Placing a concealed transmitter on or about the person consenting[14] to the electronic surveillance.

2. Providing a concealable tape-recording device that can be activated by the consenting[14] party.

Concealed transmitters allow the conversation to be both overheard and recorded at a remote location. A tape-recording device does what its name implies, providing a tape recording of the conversation.

Caveat: Concealed transmitters and concealed tape recording devices can be turned on or off at the discretion of the consenting party. Informants have been known to deactivate both devices to facilitate their own agendas during meetings with a criminal target.[14]

9.3   Concealed Transmitters

Police and prosecutors often refer to concealed transmitters as "body bugs," "body wires," or simply as a "wire."[15] Manufacturers of electronic surveillance devices refer to the equipment as a body transmitter.[16] Concealed transmitters are utilized primarily for agent or informant safety. Surveillance agents monitoring transmissions can react to events as they occur.

The most commonly used body transmitter is housed in a lightweight, flat metal container approximately the same size as a rectangular lighter. It is equipped with a flexible wire antenna and a condenser microphone attached to a wire approximately 18 inches in length. The container also has an on/off switch.[17] Transmitters are powered by batteries. Performance failure in the field is often traced to old batteries. Operating time with a fresh power source can range from three to six hours.

Most transmitters have from 250-mW to 1-W radio frequency (RF) power output. They are crystal-controlled, narrow-band FM. Their frequency range varies but is usually 150 to 174 MHz.

The most widely used RF transmitter case is attached to the wearer's body by elastic bandage or surgical tape. It is usually placed around the consenting person's waist. The antenna is fully extended vertically to maximize output and is usually secured to the wearer's chest with adhesive tape.

The microphone is attached in the same manner as the antenna. Failure to follow the manufacturer's instruction for either antenna installation or microphone placement can result in complete transmission failure or a poor tape recording.

The consenting party's conversation is transmitted to a frequency-synthesized VHF-FM high-performance receiver. Housed in a briefcase, the receiver is extremely portable, only weighing several pounds.[18] In addition to the VHF-FM receiver, most units contain a built-in tape recorder, an AC power cable, a vehicular power cable, an internal rechargeable battery power pack, earphones, a built-in receiver antenna, and an external antenna for use in a motor vehicle.

A surveillance agent trained in the operation of the receiver monitors the transmitted conversation.[19] His duties include activating the internal tape recorder and advising surveillance agents about what is occurring during the monitored meeting. It is his responsibility to alert agents to assist the informant or undercover agent if he is in danger. Communication with surveillance agents is via radio or cellular telephone. Additional portable receivers are also available, allowing surveillance agents to simultaneously monitor the transmitter. There are no communication capabilities in the equipment allowing contact with the person wearing the transmitter.

Informants and undercover agents have often complained that "wearing a wire" is uncomfortable and makes them more apprehensive while meeting with a target. Many law enforcement instructors warn that the mere fact that an individual is wearing a "wire" puts them in a life-threatening situation if a criminal target discovers the device.

New technology enables conversations to be monitored by transmitters that are not concealed on the consenting party.[20] There is no requirement[21] that the monitoring equipment be on the person of the informant or undercover agent.

If the transmitter or recorder is not on the consenting party's person, he is not to leave the device activated while he is not present. It must be turned off to avoid the possibility of intercepting nonconsensual private conversations occurring between other people in his absence.[22]

Some examples of transmitters that do not have to be concealed on the person of the consenting party include:

- Briefcase transmitter
- Cigarette pack transmitter
- Baseball cap transmitter
- Eyeglass case transmitter
- Pager transmitter
- Cellular telephone transmitter

Larger containers for the transmitter usually provide more room to conceal batteries. Generally, they are capable of longer usable operating time.

Concealed transmitters should not be used when the only desired result is to obtain a tape recording for evidentiary purposes. The equipment is employed as a safety measure for the undercover agent or informant wearing the device. Transmitters frequently malfunction for a variety of reasons including lack of training for the operator[23] in the equipment's use, interference by steel buildings, and radio frequency interference (RFI) caused by power lines, other radios, and electronic equipment in use in the area.

9.4   Tape Recorders

Concealed tape recorders produce a superior recording when compared to those recordings produced by a recorder connected to a VHF-FM receiver. Commercially manufactured microcassette and digital recorders are frequently used by law enforcement agencies. There are also extremely expensive tape recorders manufactured exclusively for law enforcement purposes.[24] Some are more complex than a commercial recorder and require training of the operator prior to being used in the field.

9.5   Establishing Consent

The consent to record a conversation utilizing a concealed transmitter or tape recorder must be given voluntarily by the individual wearing or carrying the device.[25] At trial, the burden is on the government to prove that one of the parties to the conversation had given prior consent.[26]

Consent should not be an issue when the device is worn by an undercover agent, victim,[27] or a volunteer.[28] It has been suggested that the prosecution's burden is met when it simply shows that the conversation was recorded or transmitted by the consenting person. If the defendant alleges that the consent was coerced, then the prosecution must show that there were no undue threats, pressure, or improper inducements.[29]

Many agencies require their informants to sign a consent form prior to any monitoring or recording occurring. The forms usually contain the following language:

Consent for Use of Electronic Surveillance

Case Number: _____   Date: _____-____-____

I, _____, do hereby consent to the use of electronic surveillance devices, installed by, or operated by officers of the [Agency], or any other law enforcement agencies working in conjunction with the [Agency], to monitor and record any and all conversations and activities which I may engage in, in conjunction with the matter under investigation.

> I acknowledge that I have been advised that I am not required by law to consent to the interception, monitoring, and recordings of my communications or activities. Furthermore, I acknowledge that I have given consent to the monitoring and recording of my communications and activities without threat or duress, and without promise of any special considerations, remuneration, or compensation by officers of the [Agency].[30]

The informant is requested to sign the consent form before participating in the consensual recording. At least two agents should witness his signature.

All nontelephone consensual electronic surveillance conducted by federal agencies is supposed to be reported to the U.S. Department of Justice.[31] To comply with Department reporting requirements, the following information is recorded on a Report of Electronic Surveillance Form:

1. *Reasons for the Monitoring.* The request must contain a reasonably detailed statement of the background and need for the monitoring.
2. *Offense(s).* If an interception is for investigative purposes, the request must include a citation to the principal criminal statute(s) involved.
3. *Danger.* If an interception is for protection purposes, the request must explain the danger to the consenting party or other persons.
4. *Location of Devices.* The request must state where the interception device will be hidden, i.e., on the person, in personal effects, or in a fixed location.
5. *Location of Interception.* The request must specify the location and primary judicial district where the interception will take place. An interception authorization is not restricted to the original district. However, if the location of an interception changes, notice should be promptly given to the approving official. The record maintained on the request should reflect the location change.
6. *Time.* The request must state the length of time needed for the interception. Initially, an authorization may be granted for up to 90 days from the day the interception is scheduled to begin. If there is need for continued interception, extensions for periods of up to 90 days may be granted. In special cases (e.g., "fencing" and money laundering operations run by law enforcement agents or long-term investigations that are closely supervised by the Department's Criminal Division), authorization for up to 180 days may be granted with similar extensions.
7. *Names.* The request must give the names of persons, if known, whose communications the department or agency expects to intercept and

the relation of such persons to the matter under investigation or to the need for the interception.

8. *Trial Attorney Approval.* The request must state that the facts of the surveillance have been discussed with the U.S. Attorney, an Assistant U.S. Attorney, or the previously designated Department of Justice attorney responsible for a particular investigation, and that such attorney advises that the use of consensual monitoring is appropriate under this Memorandum (including the date of such advice). The attorney must also advise that the use of consensual monitoring on the facts of the investigation does not raise the issue of entrapment. Such statements may be made orally. If the attorneys described above cannot provide the advice for reasons unrelated to the legality of or propriety of the consensual monitoring, the advice must be sought and obtained from an attorney of the Criminal Division of the Department of Justice designated by the Assistant Attorney General in charge of that Division. Before providing such advice, a designated Criminal Division attorney shall notify the appropriate U.S. Attorney or other attorney who would otherwise be authorized to provide the required advice under this paragraph.

9. *Renewals.* A request for renewal authority to intercept verbal communications must contain all the information required for an initial request. The renewal request must also refer to all previous authorizations and explain why an additional authorization is needed as well as provide an updated statement that the attorney advice required under paragraph (8) has been obtained in connection with the proposed renewal.[31]

The Supreme Court has held that failure to follow internal agency guidelines regulating consensual electronic surveillance does not require suppression.[32]

There are six instances where prior Department of Justice approval is required for a consensual intercept of verbal communication:

1. The monitoring relates to an investigation of a member of Congress, a federal judge, a member of the Executive Branch at Executive Level IV or above, or a person who has served in such capacity within the previous two years.

2. The monitoring relates to an investigation of the Governor, or Lieutenant Governor, of any State or Territory, and the offense investigated is one involving bribery, conflict of interest, or extortion relating to the performance of his or her official duties.

3. Any party to the communication is or has been a member of the diplomatic corps of a foreign country.
4. Any party to the communication is or has been a member of the Witness Security Program, and that fact is known to the agency involved or its officers.
5. The consenting or nonconsenting person is in the custody of the Bureau of Prisons or the U.S. Marshals Service.
6. The Attorney General, Deputy Attorney General, Associate Attorney General, any Assistant Attorney General, or the U.S. Attorney in the district where an investigation is being conducted has requested the investigating agency to obtain prior written consent for making a consensual interception in a specific investigation.[31]

It is not unlawful under federal law[33] for a private party to record his own conversations with others. An exception would be when the recording is being conducted for the purpose of committing any criminal or tortious act in violation of federal or state law.[34] The consenting party's motive in taping must be to only preserve an accurate record of the conversation.[35]

Privately recorded tapes have provided law enforcement investigators with valuable evidence.[36] The tapes generally surface when a suspect is arrested in a conspiracy and decides to cooperate and testify for the government.[37] Privately recorded tape recordings have also been admitted as evidence where the consenting party's motives in taping were questionable.[38]

9.6   Video Surveillance

Informants are also equipped with video recording devices to record either photographic evidence or both conversation and photographic evidence. The use of surreptitious video tape recordings has increased with advances in technology. Examples of covert video cameras on the law enforcement market today include:

- Concealed miniature video recorders in coats or vests
- Video jacket
- Briefcase camera
- Video glasses
- Video briefcase
- Watch camera
- Cellular telephone camera
- Video lamp
- Video radar detector

Subminiature pinhole television cameras, both black and white and color, have nearly made the imagination the limit on where video equipment can be installed; from a hole as small as 2.5 mm some equipment is adaptable to a closed circuit television camera or an eyepiece for visual observation. The lens employed uses an offset view to allow full sight of a room's activities.[39]

Federal law regulates only the interception or recording of wire and oral communications.[40] As a result, if only a video recording is produced[41] and the subject has no reasonable expectation of privacy, the statute does not apply.[42] If the informant consents to the videotaping[43] and the criminal target has no reasonable or justifiable expectation of privacy,[44] the audio portion of the tape is admissible as a consent surveillance exception in § 2511(2)(c) and (d).

Video surveillance is frequently used in hotel rooms rented by the control agent to conduct narcotics transactions between an informant and a trafficker. Provided there is a consenting party with authority over the video surveilled area, the video recording is allowed.[45] Fourth Amendment principles only apply to a surreptitious video taping of an individual with an expectation of privacy.[46] As with consensual tape recording with a device not worn by the informant, no videotaping can occur if the informant leaves the room and others are still present.

Although consent surveillance by a private party is lawful, sale of a device whose design is primarily useful for the surreptitious interception of oral, wire, or electronic communication is unlawful.[47] Under 18 USC § 2512 it is unlawful to make, assemble, possess, or sell such a device or advertise the equipment for sale. Exceptions to the statute are common carriers such as telephone service providers, law enforcement officers, or companies under contract with either of the two listed exceptions that manufacture the devices.[54]

Section 2512 also prohibits the possession of a device whose design is primarily useful for the surreptitious interception of oral, wire, or electronic communication. Some of the devices Congress intended to outlaw, at the time the law was passed, included spike microphones, microphones disguised as wristwatches, picture frames, cufflinks, tie clips, fountain pens, staplers, and cigarette packages. Advances in technology have added to the list as microphones and lenses become miniaturized.

9.7 Use of Informants in Telephone Wiretaps

Informants and undercover agents are also used to develop probable cause to support an application for a telephone wiretap[48] under Title III of the Omnibus Crime Control and Safe Streets Act of 1968.[49] It is the inability of the informant or undercover agent to adequately penetrate an organization that must be mentioned in the wiretap affidavit as an investigative method that is either too dangerous,[50] has failed, or is reasonably likely to fail.[51]

That is not to say that undercover operatives do not play a vital role while an intercept is being conducted. While agents are prohibited from advising an informant that a wiretap is in place, they routinely direct informants to place calls to the targeted telephone number. For example, in a drug-related wiretap an informant may be directed by his control agent to place an order for a quantity of drugs. Agents assigned to surveil the target will observe the activity that follows the informant's call in an attempt to identify sources of supply and other coconspirators. In effect, the informant plays an unwitting role in the success of the wiretap.

The language found in many wiretap applications follows:

Reliable confidential informants/cooperating sources have been developed and used, and will continue to be developed and used[52] in regard to this investigation, but these sources:

- Exist on the fringe of this organization and, therefore, have no direct contact with mid- or high-level members of the organization; or such contact is virtually impossible because the sources have no need to communicate with such individuals.
- Refuse to testify before the Grand Jury or at trial because of a fear for personal or family safety; or their testimony would be uncorroborated[53] or otherwise subject to impeachment (due to prior record, criminal involvement, etc.).
- Are no longer associated with the targets of this investigation, and their information is included for historical purposes only.

None of the confidential informants described in this affidavit are able to furnish information that would identify fully all members of this ongoing criminal conspiracy or define the roles of those conspirators sufficiently for prosecution or that would identify sufficiently the source(s) of supply or all details of delivery, quantities, financial arrangements, and the like.[54]

Affiant believes that information provided by the confidential sources, even if all sources agreed to testify, would not, without the evidence available through the requested electronic surveillance, result in a successful prosecution of all of the participants.[55]

9.7.1 "Nonhuman" Informants[56]

Wiretaps are often referred to as informants in investigative reports and affidavits for search warrants.[57] The purpose is not to mislead the magistrate but to conceal the existence of the wiretap. The wiretap is literally given an informant code number for reference purposes while the interception is occurring. If information concerning a crime is learned from the interception that must be acted upon immediately, the source of the "tip"[57] is reported as coming from an informant, not a wiretap.[58]

Appendix 9A: Customs Service Request for Authorization to Intercept Nontelephone Communications

Memorandum

FILE:_____

CASE FILE:_____

TO: Director, Special Investigations Division Office of Enforcement
FROM: Special Agent in Charge, Resident Agent in Charge
SUBJECT: Request for Authorization to Intercept Nontelephone Communications with
    Consent of a Party (Exigent Circumstances)

This is to confirm authorization granted by me under exigent circumstances on _____. In the continuing investigation your authorization is requested to intercept nontelephone communications with the consent of a party from _____ to _____ for a period of _____ days under the following conditions:

1. REASON FOR INTERCEPTION
2. <u>TYPE OF EQUIPMENT TO BE USED:</u> (List all equipment)
3. <u>OFFENSE:</u> (Cite Titles and Sections of violations)
4. <u>METHOD OF INSTALLATION/LOCATION OF EQUIPMENT</u>
5. PARTICIPANTS:
   Consenting Party: ( ) Customs Officer
             ( ) Cooperating Individual
   Name of Suspect(s):
6. EXPLANATION OF EXIGENT CIRCUMSTAMCES UNDER WHICH AUTHORIZATION WAS CONDUCTED

7. VERBAL AUTHORIZATION FROM LOCAL ASSISTANT UNITED STATES ATTORNEY
   Verbal authorization has been obtained from _____an AUSA
       in the _____ Judicial District of _____at _____ am/pm,
       on _____, 20____.

IT IS MY CONSIDERED JUDGMENT THAT THIS INTERCEPTION IS WARRANTED AND IN THE INTEREST OF EFFECTIVE LAW ENFORCEMENT.

_____
Director, Special Investigations Division, Office of Enforcement

Appendix 9B: Monitoring/Interception of Consensual Communications Report of Use

MONITORING/INTERCEPTION OF CONSENSUAL COMMUNICATIONS REPORT OF USE*

DATE OF AUTHORIZATION: _____/_____/_____
PERIOD OF INTERCEPTION: ___/___/___ – ___/___/___
    TYPE OF INTERCEPTION: ( ) Telephone ( ) Nontelephone
HQS APPROVING OFFICIAL: _____
    (Nontelephone Only)
REPORTING FIELD OFFICE:_____
CASE NUMBER: _____
OFFENSES (U.S. CODES): 18 USC _____ 21 USC _____
                22 USC _____ 31 USC _____
                OTHER _____
TYPE OF EQUIPMENT USED: ( ) NAGRA ( ) AID KIT ( ) KEL KIT
      ( ) MICROCASSETTE ( ) TRANSMITTER
      ( ) RECEIVER/RECORDER ( ) PEARLCORDER
      ( ) SME 700 ( ) INDUCTION COIL
      OTHER _____

Did the electronic surveillance corroborate the offenses?
( ) YES ( ) NO ( ) NOT USED

SUBJECTS INTERCEPTED:

_____

(Include addresses

_____

and/or telephone

_____

numbers monitored below)

_____

CALL NO.	TELEPHONE NO. CALLED	DATE/TIME CALLED	ADDRESSES OF NO. CALLED

* FORM UTILIZED BY U.S. CUSTOMS

Appendix 9C: U.S. Customs Service Confirmation of Approval for Interception of Nontelephone Communications

Memorandum

DATE: _____
FILE: _____

TO: _____

FROM: Director, Special Investigations, Division Office of Enforcement

SUBJECT: Confirmation of Approval for Interception of Nontelephone Communications with the Consent of a Party

This memorandum is to confirm the approval for the interception of nontelephone communications with the consent of one party as requested by your office. Outlined below are the pertinent data:

PERIOD OF INTERCEPT: _____ – _____
                                      Begin   End
DATE OF HQS APPROVAL: _____/_____/_____
HQS APPROVING OFFICIAL: _____
CASE NUMBER: _____
CASE AGENT: _____

As per instructions in Chapter 40 of the *Special Agent Handbook*, pages 37–40, a report of results should be submitted to Headquarters immediately upon termination of the interception.

Director
Special Investigations Division

Appendix 9D: Certification of Consent

I, _____, hereby certify that I am about to participate in a discussion concerning the manufacture, delivery, or possession with the intent to manufacture or deliver a controlled substance, legend drug, or imitation controlled substance. I willingly and freely provide my consent for officers of the _____ to intercept, transmit, and/or record conversations and communications that I will be involved in during the time necessary to complete this investigation. No threats or promises have been made to me to force this consent and I have had an opportunity to ask and resolve any questions I have concerning this consent to my satisfaction.

_____ _____
Signature   Date   Witness # 1

                                 _____
                                 Witness #2

FORM UTILIZED BY U.S. CUSTOMS

References

1. *United States v. White*, 401 U.S. 745 (1971); *United States v. Caceres*, 440 U.S. 741 (1979).

2. 18 USC § 2511(2(c).

3. Title III of the Omnibus Crime Control and Safe Streets Act of 1968, as amended by the Electronic Communications Privacy Act of 1986 (ECPA).

4. 18 USC § 2511(2)(c).

5. 18 USC § 2518.

6. *Electronic Surveillance Manual 36* (1991).

7. *On Lee v. United States*, 343 U.S. 747, *reh'g denied*, 344 U.S. 848 (1952); *Lopez v. United States*, 373 U.S. 427, *reh'g denied*, 375 U.S. 870 (1963); *United States v. White*, 401 U.S. 745, *reh'g denied*, 402 U.S. 99, *on remand*, 454 F.2d 435 (7th Cir., 1971), *cert. denied*, 406 U.S. 962 (1972); *United States v. Caceres*, 440 U.S. 741, 79-1 U.S. Tax Cas. (CCH) 9294, 43 A.F.T.R. 2d (P-H) H 79-872 (1979) (*endorsing White* plurality).

8 Waldman, As Sheik Omar case nears end, neither side looks like a winner, *Wall Street Journal*.

9. *Smithey v. State*, 269 Ark. 538, 602 S.W.2d 676, 679 (1980); *State v. Del Vecchio*, 191 Conn. 412, 464 A.2d 813, 823 (1983); *State v. Grullon*, 212 Conn. 195, 562 A.2d 481, 486–488 (1989); *State v. Tomasko*, 238 Conn. 253, 681 A.2d 922 (1996); *Humphrey v. State*, 231 Ga. 855, 204 S.E.2d 603, *cert. denied*, 419 U.S. 839 (1974); *Mitchell v. State*, 239 Ga. 3, 235 S.E.2d 509, *appeal after remand*, 142 Ga. App. 802, 237 S.E.2d 243 (1977); *Green v. State*, 250 Ga. 610, 299 S.E.2d 544 (1983); *State v. Lee*, 67 Haw. 307, 686 P.2d 816, *reconsideration denied*, 744 P.2d 780 (Haw., 1984); *State v. Jennings*, 101 Idaho 265, 611 P.2d 1050 (1980); *State v. Couch*, 103 Idaho 205, 646 P.2d 447, 449 (App., 1982); *Lawhorn v. State*, 452 N.E.2d 915 (Ind., 1983), *habeas corpus proceeding*, 620 F. Supp. 98 (N.D. Ind., 1984); *State v. Reid*, 394 N.W.2d 399, 405 (Iowa 1986); *State v. Johnson*, 229 Kan. 42, 621 P.2d 992, 994 (1981); *State v. Roudybush*, 235 Kan. 834, 686 P.2d 100, 107–109 (1984); *State v. Petta*, 359 So. 2d 143, 145 (La., 1978); *State v. Bellfield*, 275 N.W.2d 577 (Minn., 1978); *Lee v. State*, 489 So. 2d 1382 (Miss., 1986); *State v. Engleman*, 634 S.W.2d 466, 477 (Mo., 1982); *State v. Brown*, 232 Mont. 1, 755 P.2d 1364, 1368–1369 (1988); *State v. Manchester*, 200 Neb. 41, 367 N.W.2d 733, 735 (1985); *State v. Kilgus*, 128 N.H. 577, 519 A.2d 231, 238–241 (1986); *People v. Lasher*, 58 N.Y.2d 962, 447 N.E.2d 70, 460 N.Y.S.2d 522 (1983); *State v. Levan*, 326 N.C. 155, 388 S.E.2d 429, 437–438 (1990); *Ferguson v. State*, 644 P.2d 121, 123 (Okla. App., 1982); *State v. Ahmadjian*, 438 A.2d 1070, 1079–1082 (R.I., 1981); *State v. Woods*, 361 S.W.2d 620 (S.D., 1985); *State v. Braddock*, 452 N.W.2d 785, 788 (S.D., 1990); *Stroup v. State*, 552 S.W.2d 418 (Tenn. App.), *cert. denied*, 434 U.S. 955 (1977); *State v. Erickson*, 36 Utah Adv. Rep. 3, 722 P.2d 756 (1986); *Cogdill v. Commonwealth*, 219 Va. 272, 247 S.E.2d 392, 12 A.L.R.4th 406 (1978); *Blackburn*

v. State, 290 S.E.2d 22, 32 (W. Va., 1982); *Auclair v. State*, 660 P.2d 1156, 1158 (Wyo.), *cert. denied and app. dism'd*, 464 U.S. 909 (1983).

10. 18 USC § 2511(C)(2). *See also* Ariz. Rev. Stat. Ann. § 13-3005; Cal. Penal Code. § 633; 11 Del. Code. Ann. § 1336(c)(2); Haw. Rev. Stat. § 803-42(b)(3); Idaho Code § 18-6702(2)(C); Iowa Code § 727.8; Minn. Code § 626A(2)(2); Neb. Rev. Stat. § 86-701(2); N.H. Rev. Stat. Ann. § 570-A:2, II(d); Ohio Rev. Stat. § 2933.52(B)(3) & (F)(2); 13 Okla. Code § 176.4(4); S.D. Codified Laws Ann. § 23A-35A-20; Texas Code Crim. Proc. art. 18.20 § 17(3); Utah Code Ann. § 77-23a-4(2)(b); Va. Code Ann. §§ 19.2-61 et seq.; Wyo. Code § 7-3-602(b)(iv).

11. 18 USC § 2511(c)(2).

12. Nev. Rev. Stat. §§ 179.410 et seq.; N.J. Stat. Ann. § 2A:156A-4(c); N.M. Stat. Ann. §§ 30-12-11; *Arnold v. State*, 94 N.M. 381, 610 P.2d 1210 (1980); 1980-2 CCH Trade Cases H 63318; Or. Rev. Stat. § 165.540(l)(a); *State v. Underwood*, 293 Or. 389, 648 P.2d 847 (1982); 18 Pa. Cons. Stat. Ann. § 5704; Wash. Rev. Code § 9.73.090(2); *State v. Fjermestad*, \ 14 Wash. 2d 828,791 P.2d 897, 902 (1990).

13. *State v. Glass*, 583 P.2d 872 (Alaska, 1978), *on rehearing*, 596 P.2d 10 (Alaska, 1979), *overruled on other grounds by Juneau v. Quinto*, 684 P.2d 127 (Alaska, 1984); *Thiel v. State*, 762 P.2d 478, 483–484 (Alaska App., 1988); Fla. Stat. Ann. § 934.03(2)(C); *State v. Tsavaris*, 394 So.2d 418 (Fla., 1981), *appeal after remand*, 414 So. 2d 1087 (Fla. App., 1982), *petition denied*, 424 So. 2d 763 (Fla., 1983); *Hoberman v. State*, 400 So. 2d 758 (Fla., 1981); Mass. Gen. Laws. Ann. Ch. 272 § 99B4; *Commonwealth v. Blood*, 400 Mass. 61, 507 N.E.2d 1029, 1044 (1987); *Commonwealth v. Penta*, 423 Mass. 546, 669 N.E.2d 767 (1996); *Commonwealth v. Thorpe*, 384 Mass. 271, 424 N.E.2d 250, 258–259, 27 A.L.R.4th 430, *cert. denied*, 454 U.S. 1147 (1981).

14. 18 USC § 2511(2)(c)

15. *United States v. Zuber*, 899 F. Supp. 188 (D. Utah, 1995).

16. National Institute of Justice, Technology Assessment Program, Surveillance Receivers and Recorders, NIJ Standard 0222.00.

17. National Institute of Justice, Technology Assessment Program, NIJ Standard 0214.01, Body Worn FM Transmitters.

18. National Institute of Justice, Technology Assessment Program, NBSIR 86-3501, Evaluation of Electronic Monitoring Devices.

19. *United Stales v. Biggins*, 551 F.2d 64 (5th Cir., 1977). *See also United States v. McKeever*, 169 F. Supp. 426 (D.N.Y., 1958), *rev'd on other grounds, 111* F.2d 669 (2nd Cir., 1959); *United States v. McMillan*, 508 F.2d 101, 104 (8th Cir., 1974), *cert. denied*, 421 U.S. 916 (1975); *United States v. Britton*, 68 F.3d 262 (8th Cir., 1995) and *United States v. Webster*, 84 F.3d 1056 (8th Cir., 1996).

20. *United States v. Yonn*, 702F.2d 1341 (11th Or., 1983); *United States v. Bennett*, 538 F. Supp. 1045 (D.P.R., 1982).

21. 18 USC § 2511(2)(c).

22. Title III of the Omnibus Crime Control and Safe Streets Act of 1968, as amended by the Electronic Communications Privacy Act of 1986 (ECPA). *See United States v. Padilla,* 520 K2d 526 (1st Cir., 1975); *U.S. Attorneys Manual,* 9.

23. *United States v. Shabazz,* 724 F.2d 1536 (11th Cir., 1984); *United States v. Hughes,* 658 F.2d 317 (5th Cir., 1981), *cert. denied,* 455 U.S. 922 (1982); *United States v. Greenfield,* 574 F.2d 305 (5th Cir.) *cert. denied,* 439 U.S. 860 (1978); *United States v. Corel,* 622 F.2d 100 (5th Cir., 1979), *cert. denied,* 455 U.S. 943 (1980).

24. National Institute of Justice, Miniature Surveillance Recorders 0226.00, Jan. 1990.

25. 18 USC § 2511(2)(c).

26. *United States v. Napier,* 451 F.2d 552, 553 (5th Cir., 1971); *Whack v. State,* 94 Md. App. 107, 615 A.2d 1226, 1233 (1992).

27. *People v. Fredrics,* 76 111. App. 3d 1043, 395 N.E.2d 723 (1979).

28. *United States v. Hodge,* 539 F.2d 898, 904 (6th Cir., 1976), *cert. denied,* 429 U.S. 1091 (1977); *United States v. Hall,* 424 F. Supp. 508, 520 (W.D. Okla., 1975), *aff'd,* 536 F.2d 313 (10th Cir.), *cert. denied,* 429 U.S. 919 (1976).

29. *State v. Whitt,* 184 W. Va. 340, 400 S.E.2d 584, 588 (1990).

30. *United States v. Juarez,* 573 F.2d 267 (5th Cir., 1978); *United States v. Frank,* 511 F.2d 25 (6th Cir., 1975); *United States v. Dewdy,* 479 F.2d 213 (4th Cir., 1973). *See also State v. Jones,* 562 So. 2d 740, 741 (Fla. App., 1990).

31. *U.S. Attorneys Manual,* Ch. 9-7.013.

32. *United States v. Caceres,* 440 U.S. 741, 99 S. Ct 1465, 59 L. Ed. 2d 733 (1979).

33. 18 USC § 2511(2)(d).

34. *United States v. Baiter,* 91 F.3d 427 (3rd Cir., 1996).

35. *United States v. Cassiere,* 4 F.3d 1006, 1021 (1st Cir., 1993); *United States v. Dale,* 991 F.2d 819, 841 (D.C. Cir., 1993).

36. *United States v. Vest,* 813 F.2d 477, 481 (1st Cir., 1987).

37. *United States v. Nietupski,* 731 F. Supp. 881, 883 (C.D. III., 1990).

38. *United States v. Underhill,* 813 F.2d 105, 111 (6th Cir., 1987); *Traficant v. Commissioner,* 884 F.2d 258, 261 (6th Cir., 1989).

39. Surveillance Show, *Law Enforcement Technology Magazine,* April 1996.

40. *United States v. Torres,* 751 F.2d 875, 880 (7th Cir., 1984), *cert. denied,* 470 U.S. 1087 (1985); *United States v. Williams,* 124 F.3d 411 (3rd Cir., 1997).

41. *Technologically-Assisted Physical Surveillance Standards,* American Bar Association.

42. *United States v. Biasucci,* 786 F.2d 504, 508 (2nd Cir., 1986); *United States v. Koyomejian,* 970 F.2d 536 (9th Cir., 1992), *cert. denied,* 117 S. Ct. 617 (1993); *United States v. Falls,* 34 F.3d 674, 680 (8th Cir., 1994). *See United States v. Chen,* 979 F.2d 714, 717 (9th Cir., 1992).

43. *United States v. Allen,* 513 F. Supp. 547 (W.D. Okla., 1981); *Hoback v. State,* 286 Ark. 153, 689 S.W.2d 569, 571 (1985); *People v. Knight,* 288 111. App. 3d 232, 327 N.E.2d 518, 521–522 (1975).

44. *United States v. Myers,* 692 F.2d 823, 859 (2nd Cir., 1982), *cert. denied,* 461 U.S. 961 (1983); *United States v. Felder,* 572 F. Supp. 17 (E.D. Pa.), *aff'd,* 722 F.2d 735 (3rd Cir., 1983).

45. *United States v. Laetividal-Gonzalez.,* 939 F.2d 1455, 1461 (11th Cir., 1991); *United States v. Cox,* 836 F. Supp. 1189, 1198 (D. Md., 1993).

46. *State v. Casconi,* 766 P.2d 397 (Or. App., 1988).

47. 18 USC § 2512.

48. Robinson, P., Challenging the wiretap, *Champion Magazine,* April 1996. *See also* Suro, R. and Corceran, E., The keys to high-tech cover, *Washington Post,* March 30, 1998.

49. 18 USC §§ 2510–2520.

50. *United States v. Plescia,* 773 F. Supp. 1068, 1072 (N.D. 111. 1991).

51. *United States v. Kalustian,* 529 F.2d 585, 589–590 (9th Cir., 1975).

52. *United States v. Maxwell,* 25 F.3d 1389, 1394 (8th Or., 1994).

53. *United States v. Petti,* 973 F.2d 1441, 1446 n.7 (9th Cir., 1992), *cert. denied,* 113 S. Ct. 1859 (1993).

54. *United States v. Butz,* 982 F.2d 1378, 1383 (9th Cir., 1993), *cert. denied,* 114S, Ct. 250(1994).

55. *United States v. Stevens,* 800 F. Supp. 892, 906 (D. Haw., 1992); *United States v. Focarile,* 340 F. Supp. 1033, 1042 (4th Cir., 1972); *United States v. Giordano,* 469 F.2d 522 (4th Cir., 1972), *aff'd,* 416 U.S. 505 (1974).

56. Title III of the Omnibus Crime Control and Safe Streets Act of 1968.

57. *United States v. Cruz,* 594 F.2d 268 (1st Or., 1979).

58. Brown, T.J., Capt., International task force aids DEA in maritime cases, *DEA World,* June 1997.

Controlling the Informant

10

10.1 Generally

Failure to control informants has undermined costly long-term investigations,[1] destroyed the careers of prosecutors[2] and law enforcement officers,[3] and caused death[4] and serious injuries[5] to innocent citizens and police.[6] In many cases, the sequence of events leading to disaster began during the selection or recruitment of the informant.[7]

The Court in *United States v. Bernal-Obeso* made this observation about the character of informants:

> By definition, criminal informants are cut from untrustworthy cloth and must be managed and carefully watched by the government and the courts to prevent them from falsely accusing the innocent, from manufacturing evidence against those under suspicion of crime, and from lying under oath in the courtroom.[8]

The plethora of rules and regulations in place in federal and local law enforcement agencies governing the control of informants (see appendices at the end of this chapter). ("Informant Guidelines and Instructions") dramatically illustrates official recognition of the dangers informants pose to agents and the public.[9]

According to the Federal Bureau of Investigation (FBI): "Successful operation of informants demands more of an Agent than almost any other investigative activity.[10] An Agent's judgment, skill, resourcefulness, and patience are tested constantly."[11] "Every effort should be made to control the informant's activities ... to ensure that the informant's conduct will be consistent with legal and administrative restrictions."[12]

Common sense would suggest that useful informants do not come free of criminal history[13] and that the quality of usefulness may depend to a degree on the depth of a person's prior criminal experience.[14] If repeated criminal behavior is an indicator of a limited likelihood of successful rehabilitation,[15] a criminal informant's resistance to official control should be anticipated.[16]

Federal Judge and former prosecutor Stephen Trott noted that:

> Criminals are likely to say and do almost anything to get what they want, especially when what they want is to get out of trouble with the law. ... [T]his willingness to do anything includes not only truthfully spilling the beans on friends and relatives, but also lying, committing perjury, manufacturing evidence, soliciting others to corroborate their lies with more lies, and double-crossing anyone with whom they come into contact, including — and especially — the prosecutor. A drug addict can sell out his mother to get a deal; and burglars, robbers, murderers and thieves are not far behind. They are remarkably manipulative and skillfully devious. Many are outright conscienceless sociopaths to whom "truth" is a wholly meaningless concept. To some, conning people is a way of life. Others are just basically unstable people. A "reliable informant" one day may turn into a consummate prevaricator the next.[17]

The American Psychiatric Association's criteria for antisocial personality disorder diagnosis are remarkably similar to much of Judge Trott's description of a reliable informant:

1. Current age at least 18.
2. Evidence of conduct disorder with onset before age 15.
3. A pervasive pattern of disregard for and violation of the rights of others occurring since age 15, as indicated by three of the following:
   A. Failure to conform to social norms with respect to lawful behaviors as indicated by repeatedly performing acts that are grounds for arrest.
   B. Irritability and aggressiveness, as indicated by repeated physical fights or assaults.
   C. Consistent irresponsibility, as indicated by repeated failure to sustain consistent work behavior or honor financial obligations.
   D. Impulsivity or failure to plan ahead.

E. Deceitfulness, as indicated by repeated lying, use of aliases, or conning others for personal profit or pleasure.

F. Reckless disregard for the safety of self or others.

G. Lack of remorse, as indicated by being indifferent to or rationalizing having hurt, mistreated, or stolen from another.[18]

10.2 Agents and Prosecutors

Agents bring to their careers a personal background of character and experience pristine enough to withstand the intense scrutiny of a rigorous preemployment background investigation. Their lives, placed in juxtaposition to their informants, usually expose striking contrasts in life experience.

Many informants have risen to the top of their criminal organizations utilizing the survival skills acquired by a life on the street. The *New York Times* described a long-time FBI informant:

Inside the Mafia, Gregory Scarpa, Sr. could have served as a role model for ambitious gangsters. His underworld persona was that of a steadfastly loyal capo, or captain, in the Colombo crime family who for three decades ran rackets in New York City that enriched himself and his mob partners … . Guile and ruthlessness earned him the underworld nickname of "Hannibal" for his tactics and the "grim reaper" for his violence.[19]

The concept that an informant with such extensive criminal skills could manipulate his control agent is not difficult to envision.[20] Following Scarpa's death in 1994, an FBI internal investigation of the control agent, R. Lindley DeVecchio, began when a former associate of the confidential informant (CI) and member of his "crew" became a prosecution witness in Colombo family cases.[20,21] According to the *New York Times*, an FBI report turned over to defense lawyers said that Mr. Scarpa had boasted to the witness that during the Colombo wars, a law enforcement agent gave Scarpa the locations of hideouts of members of the opposing Orena gang faction. The witness said that Mr. Scarpa frequently referred to the law enforcement confidant who slipped him information as "the girlfriend."[20,21] Mr. Scarpa pled guilty to three murders and attempts to murder nine other supporters of Mr. Orena's faction. He died in federal prison in 1994.

The accused agent denied any wrongdoing. On March 30, 2006, DeVecchio was indicted on murder charges for allegedly taking bribes from Scarpa to supply him with inside information that led to four underworld slayings in Brooklyn.

At the time, the FBI reacted to the Scarpa revelations as an isolated incident. That was until 1995, when an informant operated by the FBI's Boston Office was arrested on charges of racketeering and extortion. Stephen "The Rifleman" Flemmi would fight the charges on grounds that the FBI had granted him and fellow gangster/informant James "Whitey" Bulger permission to commit crimes short of murder in exchange for information.

The FBI does allow its informants to commit crimes, but denied Flemmi's claims. The "Attorney General's Guidelines Regarding the Use of Confidential Informants" (§ I.B.10) permit the FBI to authorize confidential informants to engage in activities that would otherwise constitute crimes under state or federal law if engaged in by someone without such authorization. Such conduct is termed "otherwise illegal activity" or OIA.

There are two types, or levels, of OIA: "Tier 1 OIA" and "Tier 2 OIA." Tier 1 OIA, the most serious, is defined as any activity that would constitute a misdemeanor or felony under federal, state, or local law if engaged in by a person acting without authorization and that involves a commission or the significant risk of the commission of certain offenses, including acts of violence; corrupt conduct by senior federal, state, or local public officials; or the manufacture, importing, exporting, possession, or trafficking in controlled substances of certain quantities. "Tier 2 OIA" is defined as any other activity that would constitute a misdemeanor or felony under federal, state, or local law if engaged in by a person acting without authorization. Both Tier 1 and Tier 2 OIA must be authorized in advance, in writing, and for a specified period not to exceed 90 days.

The court hearings that followed dredged up some of the Boston FBI's darkest secrets, including revelations of agents accepting payoffs and leaking information to shield Flemmi and Bulger from arrest by other law enforcement agencies. The investigation that followed revealed that the two informants were linked to 21 murders.

Bulger fled Boston just 10 days before a warrant was issued for his arrest. He remains second on the FBI's Ten Most Wanted List with a $1 million reward for his arrest. He was number one on the list until Osama bin Laden was added in 2001.

Bulger and Flemmi's FBI Agent handler since 1975, John Connolly, Jr., is serving a 10-year prison sentence for alerting his informant of the pending arrest warrant. Former Boston FBI Agent H. Paul Rico, 78, died in custody in 2004 before he could be tried on charges that he conspired with Bulger and Flemmi to commit murder. That would not be the last heard on the case.

In November 2003, a congressional committee issued a report entitled *Everything Secret Degenerates: The FBI's Use of Murderers as Informants* (H.R. Report 108-414). The report concluded that the Boston FBI scandal "must be considered one of the greatest failures in the history of federal law enforcement."

The investigation continued, and on May 4, 2005, Connolly was indicted in Florida. He was charged with first-degree murder and conspiring with Bulger and Flemmi to kill John Callahan, a Florida businessman who was a financial adviser to the South Boston Winter Hill Gang. The scandal has resulted in nearly $2 billion in lawsuits.[22]

It was not until September 2005, when the U.S. Department of Justice (DOJ), Office of the Inspector General's 297-page report was released, that the full extent of the lapses in informant handling in both cases would be revealed. Entitled *"The Federal Bureau of Investigation's Compliance with the Attorney General's Investigative Guidelines,"* the report includes the most complete examination of the Sarpa, Bulger, and Flemmi cases available to the public. The report's case studies follow:

Confidential Informant Case Study 1

FBI Informants James J. "Whitey" Bulger and Stephen J. "The Rifleman" Flemmi

FBI agent John Connolly, Jr. was sentenced in September 2002 to 10 years in prison for racketeering, obstruction of justice, and making false statements to investigators — all stemming from his handling of two FBI informants, James J. "Whitey" Bulger and Stephen J. "The Rifleman" Flemmi, leaders of South Boston's Winter Hill Gang.

Bulger, Flemmi, and other defendants were indicted in January 1995 and charged with multiple counts of racketeering, extortion, and other crimes. Four days after Flemmi's arrest and the day before his indictment, the Special Agent in Charge (SAC) of the FBI's Boston field office notified the U.S. Attorney in the District of Massachusetts for the first time that Bulger and Flemmi had been informants for the FBI for much of the period covered by the indictment. In August 1995, the government disclosed to the presiding magistrate that Flemmi had been a confidential informant for the FBI and that Flemmi's informant file was being reviewed by senior DOJ officials to determine whether it contained any exculpatory material discoverable under *Brady v. Maryland,* 373 U.S. 83 (1963), and its progeny.

In a 10-month evidentiary hearing that concluded in October 1998, after which the Court denied Flemmi's motion to dismiss the indictment, a federal judge heard evidence produced in response to Flemmi's claim that the indictment against him should be dismissed based on "outrageous government misconduct," including a claim that the government promised that he and Bulger would be protected from prosecution as long as they continued to cooperate with the FBI about La Cosa Nostra. The judge heard evidence that Connolly and FBI Supervisory Special Agent John Morris became increasingly close to their informants and had filed false reports of information purportedly provided to them by the informants, ignored evidence that the informants were extorting others, caused the submission of false and misleading applications for electronic surveillance, and disclosed other confidential law enforcement information to them. Among the district court's findings of fact in its 661-page opinion was a condemnation of the FBI's failure to follow the Informant Guidelines. The Court found that:

- The informants' handler and supervisors failed to fully inform the FBI Director as to why Bulger and Flemmi had been closed as FBI informants.
- Flemmi's FBI handler failed to tell Flemmi that he was no longer an active FBI informant; during the 3-year period when he was administratively closed, the handler had over 40 contacts with him.
- Contrary to FBI policy requiring the SAC to consult personally with the U.S. Attorney as to whether to authorize extraordinary criminal activity involving a "serious risk of violence" and to review all such criminal activity at least every 90 days, the SAC delegated this responsibility to the informant's handler and his immediate supervisor.
- The FBI "ignored the essential point of the Attorney General's Guidelines, which required consultation with the Assistant Attorney General for the Criminal Division when the FBI learns that an informant has engaged in criminal activity but wishes to continue to utilize the informant rather than share the pertinent information concerning the illegal activity with another law enforcement agency."
- An Assistant Special Agent in Charge (ASAC) in the Boston field office only considered the informant's productivity and failed to weigh critical factors in considering the informant's suitability, including the nature of the matter under investigation and the importance of the information being furnished as compared to the seriousness of past and contemporaneous criminal activity of which the informant may

be suspected, or how closely the FBI would be able to monitor his activities acting on behalf of the FBI. 91 F. Supp. 2d at 201, 211, 216, 233, 249

The government took an interlocutory appeal of the district court's ruling that the FBI had made an enforceable promise of immunity with respect to the electronic surveillance evidence. The First Circuit reversed, holding that: (1) FBI agents lack authority to promise immunity to informants, and absent such authority, any promise made to Flemmi was unenforceable; (2) no prosecutor ratified the agents' promise of immunity to Flemmi; (3) Flemmi's reliance on a promise of immunity did not warrant suppression of evidence; and (4) any promise of immunity did not render Flemmi's statements in connection with the surveillance involuntary. *United States v. Flemmi,* 225 F.3d 78 (1st Cir. 2000).

In December 1999, a grand jury convened by a special DOJ Task Force returned a RICO indictment against Connolly charging him with protecting Bulger and Flemmi through a pattern of obstruction of justice, including leaking to Bulger and Flemmi the names of several cooperating individuals who were later killed. Flemmi was also charged with racketeering, obstruction of justice, and conspiracy in the same indictment along with Bulger, against whom charges were dropped due to RICO Double Jeopardy concerns. In September 2001, Bulger and Flemmi were charged in a new indictment with committing 19 and 10 murders, respectively, and with conspiratorial liability for a total of 21 murders, all committed while they were providing information to the FBI. Flemmi pled guilty to the charges in the Connolly indictment at the same time he pled guilty in the new case. Connolly was tried and convicted in April 2002, the jury finding him guilty of multiple acts of obstruction of justice, including tipping Bulger to the 1995 indictment so he could flee. However, the jury acquitted Connolly on several of the racketeering acts, including those relating to the leaks of the identities of cooperating individuals leading to their deaths. Connolly received a 10-year sentence, which he is currently serving and which was upheld on appeal. On May 4, 2005, Connolly was indicted in Florida for first-degree murder and conspiring with Bulger and Flemmi to kill John Callahan, a Florida businessman who was a financial adviser to the Winter Hill Gang.

In addition, the Tulsa District Attorney's Office charged another retired FBI agent, H. Paul Rico, who had been Flemmi's original handler, with aiding and abetting murder. Rico died of natural causes at age 78 while awaiting trial.

Bulger remains a fugitive and is on the FBI's Ten Most Wanted List.

Confidential Informant Case Study 2

FBI Informant Gregory Scarpa, Sr. and his FBI Handler, R. Lindley DeVecchio

Gregory Scarpa, Sr., who was involved in organized crime for most of his life, served as an FBI confidential informant at various times from 1980 until the early 1990s. His relationship with the FBI and, in particular, with his sole handler, R. Lindley DeVecchio, factored in a number of major prosecutions against New York members of La Cosa Nostra (LCN) in the 1990s. In some cases, Scarpa's status as an FBI informant was known during trial; in another, it was not revealed until postconviction motions were filed and Scarpa had died.

Victor Orena and Pasquale Amato. In two separate federal trials in 1992 and 1993, juries found Victor J. Orena, the "acting boss" of the Colombo Family, and Pasquale Amato guilty of racketeering, conspiracy, and firearms charges. The events leading to the convictions of Orena and Amato stemmed from the "Colombo Wars," a power struggle between two Colombo factions, the Persicos and the Orenas, that lasted from the fall of 1991 through the spring of 1992. At Orena's trial, DeVecchio, who headed the Colombo LCN squad in the FBI's New York Field Office, testified as an expert witness about the nature and structure of organized crime. Both defendants were sentenced to life in prison, and the Second Circuit affirmed both convictions and sentences.

Years after their convictions and following exhaustion of all appeals, Orena and Amato filed motions for dismissal of their indictments or for new trials alleging a violation of the government's disclosure obligations under *Brady v. Maryland,* 373 U.S. 83 (1963). Their motions were based upon DeVecchio's "questionable ethics and judgments" as revealed in proceedings in another case. After learning that Scarpa was a long-time FBI informant, Orena and Amato contended that it was not they, but DeVecchio, who conspired with Scarpa to instigate the Mafia war and caused the killing of their partner and loan shark, Thomas Ocera, one of the murders for which Orena and Amato were convicted.

The trial court denied the posttrial motions, *Orena v. United States*, 956 F. Supp. 1071 (E.D.N.Y. 1997). However, the court closely examined the relationship between DeVecchio and Scarpa, who rose to the position of a "capo" or captain in the Colombo family. According to the trial court, in the 1970s and perhaps as early as the 1960s, Scarpa had been regularly in touch with an FBI agent. The relationship was broken off until DeVecchio succeeded in renewing Scarpa's informant status in December 1980. DeVecchio acted as Scarpa's sole FBI handler from that time until Scarpa was finally terminated as an FBI informant after the Colombo Wars were over in 1992, despite an FBI protocol which required informants to be handled by two agents at a time.

As a "top echelon" informant, Scarpa initially provided the FBI with information pertaining to organizational activity and personnel movements within the Colombo Family. After the Colombo Wars commenced in late 1991, he provided detailed reports of perpetrators and strategic planning of the opposing factions.

The court found that DeVecchio reciprocated by passing along unauthorized information to Scarpa. For example, evidence was presented indicating that DeVecchio warned Scarpa of his pending arrest on federal credit card fraud charges and may have intervened with the sentencing judge to request lenient treatment. There also was suspicion that in 1987 DeVecchio leaked to Scarpa information that the Wimpy Boys Social Club, a favorite Colombo gathering place, was subject to court-ordered electronic surveillance; that he tipped off Scarpa to the planned Drug Enforcement Administration (DEA) arrest of his son, Gregory Scarpa, Jr., and others in connection with the criminal activity at the social club; and that, as a result of the warning, Gregory Scarpa, Jr. became a fugitive. With respect to the Confidential Informant Guidelines, the court also found that:

- On March 3, 1992, Scarpa was closed as an informant after the ASAC of the Criminal Division of the New York FBI Division, Donald North, "found credible allegations that Scarpa was involved in planning violent criminal activity." In informal conversations with North, DeVecchio was allegedly "adamant" that Scarpa was not involved in violent activity. In early April 1992, DeVecchio initiated the process of having Scarpa reopened, and the FBI granted authority to reopen Scarpa on April 8, 1992, pending completion of a suitability inquiry. On April 22, 1992, DeVecchio notified FBI Headquarters that such an inquiry had been conducted and that Scarpa was deemed suitable.

- During the summer of 1992, Special Agent Christopher Favo, who was working with DeVecchio during the investigation, became strongly suspicious of DeVecchio. Believing that DeVecchio was engaged in misconduct and fearing that he might disrupt current investigations, Favo began to withhold information from DeVecchio pertaining to Scarpa. Other subordinates of DeVecchio's suspected that Scarpa was a murderer, but none of them reported their suspicions about Scarpa or DeVecchio to superiors or to the U.S. Attorney despite the fact that the Informant Guidelines required agents to report any knowledge of an informant committing violent crimes.

- Scarpa was arrested by the New York City Police in August 1992 on a firearms charge. Shortly thereafter, a federal indictment charging Scarpa with the commission of the three murders, among other crimes, was handed down. Scarpa was released on bail under strict house confinement as one of the conditions of release because of failing health. In late December 1992, his bail was revoked because of his involvement in a shooting. Scarpa was sentenced to 10 years in prison in December 1993 after pleading guilty to two counts of murder.

- In January 1994, Favo and other agents approached ASAC North to report their concerns about DeVecchio's relationship with Scarpa. Consistent with FBI policy, North immediately submitted a report to the FBI's Office of Professional Responsibility (OPR). OPR determined that DeVecchio was appropriately a subject of investigation. In September 1996, the Public Integrity Section determined that prosecution of DeVecchio was not warranted, and the OPR investigation was closed. DeVecchio retired from the FBI in October 1996. Scarpa died in a federal prison in June 1994.

In its ruling on Orena's and Amato's motions for dismissal of their indictments or new trials, the district court held that (1) the defendants either knew or should have known that a member of the organized crime family to which they belonged had acted as an informant, so the government's failure to disclose that fact did not warrant a new trial; (2) evidence that a government agent had leaked information to an informant and that a second government agent had concerns regarding the relationship between the first agent and the informant was not material to the Government's charges, so the Government's failure to disclose did not warrant relief under *Brady;* and (3) newly discovered evidence did not warrant a new trial.

On the issue of leaking information to an informant and the relationship between DeVecchio and Scarpa, the district court observed that, while the CI Guidelines provide guidance on "sanctioning criminal conduct on the part of informants where necessary 'to establish and maintain credibility or cover with persons associated with criminal activity under investigation,'" the "line between the value of an informer and the unreasonable risks of encouraging serious criminal activity requires judgment of senior supervisors with sound ethical compasses; people in the field are often not in a position to provide the necessary direction." *Orena v. United States,* 956 F. Supp. 1071, 1102 (E.D.N.Y. 1997). The court noted that, according to the Attorney General Guidelines, the FBI does exercise control at the supervisory level in Washington and locally. In the case of Scarpa, however, "these administrative controls failed to work because DeVecchio was not properly supervised locally and because ... he failed to inform his supervisors in Washington of the probability that Scarpa was engaged in violence." *Orena v. United States,* 956 F. Supp. 1071, 1103 (E.D.N.Y. 1997).

Victor Orena, Jr., John Orena, Thomas Petrizzo, et al. In June 1995, a jury acquitted seven reputed associates of the Orena wing of the Colombo family of conspiring to murder members of the rival Persico faction of the family. Scarpa's status as an FBI informant became a pivotal issue during the trial. Fellow FBI agents testified that they had become suspicious of DeVecchio and were particularly concerned that he had fed confidential information to Scarpa which helped him to evade arrest.

Anthony Russo, Joseph Russo, and Joseph Monteleone. Scarpa's relationship with the FBI generated posttrial motions in another case following the conviction of LCN defendants on murder and conspiracy to murder charges. In that case, in March 1997, the trial judge granted a motion for a new trial to Anthony Russo, Joseph Russo, and Joseph Monteleone, finding that the Government had improperly failed to disclose evidence bearing on Scarpa's credibility. The Court of Appeals reversed that portion of the district court's order that granted a new trial, rejecting the trial court's conclusion that evidence that Scarpa lied to the FBI about his involvement in certain other murders gave rise to an inference that he lied to his coconspirators about the murders in question.

10.2.1   Pressure to Recruit Informants

Immediately after graduation from training, FBI agents are expected to recruit and control informants.

> Each Agent involved in investigative activity is obligated to develop and operate productive informants. Those Agents who cannot develop productive informants must overcome the lack of informants through some other substantial contribution, such as the continued development during investigative assignments of Cooperative Witnesses. The proper operation of informants is a basic skill that requires dedication and ingenuity. The success each Agent enjoys normally depends on the strength of the Agent's personality and resourcefulness exercised in obtaining information.[23]

Pressure to develop informants,[24] coupled with lack of training and inexperience, resulted in the indictment by a state grand jury of an FBI agent for burglary.[25] The charges were the result of the utilization of an untested informant who committed burglaries and auto theft[26] with the permission of an FBI agent (see Appendix 10E, "FBI Authorization for Informant to Participate in Ordinary Criminal Activity") who was unable to control his informant.[20] During one of the burglaries, the informant went so far as to ask the agent to act as a "look out" during the commission of the crime.[20] Demonstrating the impact that the lack of control over an informant and pressure to develop informants can have, the agent testified:

> Colvin was the first informant in my career who began giving information of criminal activity after just appearing at the office.[27] His information and his conversations with me over a period of time indicated that he had the information concerning the activities of several individuals in the Kentucky/Indiana area. His information to me was always that *someone else was the moving force in the criminal activity*. As an informant, he told me that his relationships with people would allow him to get close to and report on these individuals. Since I had been in the division for

18 months and had not developed a quality informant, *I suppose I was overwhelmed by what it appeared he could do.* He started providing me with information and it was in the context of "so and so is going to do this and we will be able to make a case."[27]

Failure in the management of cooperating individuals constitutes, perhaps, the most obvious single cause of serious integrity problems in the DEA and other law enforcement agencies.[28] The DEA, presumably a leading "consumer" of informant services, investigated those integrity problems involving CIs. Their Office of Professional Responsibility investigators concluded that "many, if not most, such integrity problems could not have occurred without some lapse in supervisory or management oversight procedures." The study concluded that "in order to remedy these shortcomings, strong, consistent management needs to enforce all current requirements contained in the DEA manuals.[28]

Professional Responsibility investigators listed several of the most common violations committed by agents in their supervision and handling of informants; seven involved money or gifts and gratuities:

- Socializing with informants and/or their families.[29]
- Becoming romantically involved with CIs.
- Purchasing items from CIs.[30]
- CIs purchasing items from DEA employees.
- Borrowing money from CIs.
- Receiving gifts or gratuities from CIs.
- Entering into business relationships with CIs.
- Contacting CIs alone.
- Paying CIs without benefit of witnesses.
- Encouraging CIs to sign blank DEA-103 forms [receipts for payments to informants].

Commenting on the listed deficiencies in professional conduct, the investigation reported "many instances" of lapses in following rules governing informant payment activity.[31] Special Agents had been making unwitnessed payments to cooperating individuals, clearly a reckless practice and outside of required operating procedures.[32] Without a witness to a payment, the agent exposes himself to allegations being made by the informant that the payment was not made or the agent received a "kick-back." Special Agents had also been encouraging Cooperating Individuals to sign blank copies of DEA Form 103, Voucher for Payment for Information and Purchase of Evidence.[33] An agent with a presigned DEA-103 could easily fill in a payment amount, withdraw the funds from the DEA cashier and keep the money for himself.

The newsletter[34] conspicuously states:

Remember

Nothing leaves a Special Agent more vulnerable to allegations of wrongdoing than meeting with and paying Cooperating Individuals alone.

DO NOT DO IT! A CI will be your friend only as long as it suits his or her agenda.[34]

DEA trains its new agents that:

The use of informants in drug enforcement is so fundamental as to be considered the single most elemental technique available to the Special Agent. As such, it is essential that the successful drug enforcement agent develop and continuously expand the skills required to develop, maintain and utilize these vital human resources. The annals of drug law enforcement are replete with examples of successful investigations resulting from the professional management of good informants. Likewise, these same annals are littered with unfortunate reminders of what happens when Agents fail to calculate the liability of mismanagement of these same informants. The skill level of the DEA employee serves as a catalyst for success or failure in this crucial equation.[35]

The admonition is equally applicable to all agencies that employ informants.[36] Once the breakdown in control of an informant occurs, it is difficult for the agent to regain the upper hand in the relationship.[37] Often the informant will attempt to control the course of an investigation without the agent's knowledge.[38] When motivated by money[39] or sentencing consideration,[40] he controls his income or his freedom. The expertise of the control agent is the only obstacle between the informant and his goal.[40]

10.2.2   The Prosecutor

New prosecutors are at an even greater disadvantage than a new agent is during their first encounter with an informant-witness. Unlike agent training academies where informant handling is taught, nothing in law school prepares the new prosecutor for the challenges presented by an informant. According to Judge Trott:

In this perilous world, "character" and "credibility" aren't just interesting issues in a book about evidence — they become the pivotal win or lose elements in the prosecution's case, from start to finish. How these witnesses are managed and how these issues are approached and handled may determine the success or failure of the case. In this vein, the prosecutor on occasion will surprisingly discover that his or her own personal integrity is on the line, and this is not a laughing matter. It is neither helpful to a prosecutor's case nor very comforting personally to have the defense arguing to the court and jury, for example, that you, as a colossal idiot, have given immunity to the real killer in order to prosecute an innocent man.[17]

No other case illustrates the devastating effect that failing to control defendant informants can have on prosecutors than *United States v. Boyd*,[41] better known as the "El Rukns" prosecutions.[42] The RICO prosecution alleged racketeering acts including as many as 20 murders, 12 attempted murders, 11 conspiracies to murder, large-scale drug distribution, kidnapping, and witness intimidation and retaliation. Following four years of litigation and trials, the cases resulted in 37 convictions and 16 guilty pleas. Five defendants were sentenced to life and two other defendants to 50-year sentences.[42]

The government's case depended heavily upon the testimony of six former gang leaders who had become defendant informants. Following the testimony of 29 witnesses at a posttrial hearing, the district court granted defendants a new trial on the grounds that the government had knowingly allowed the two primary informants to perjure themselves at trial. The court also found that prosecutors withheld from the defense evidence that during the trial, all six witnesses who were being held at the Metropolitan Correctional Center (MCC) had used illegal drugs and received unlawful favors from prosecutors and their staff.[43]

The court found that the following informant misconduct occurred:

The prosecutors allowed the defendant informants (prisoner witnesses) to have "contact visits" with visitors both at the U.S. Attorneys office in the Federal Courthouse and in the Bureau of Alcohol, Tobacco, and Firearms (BATF) Office adjacent to the Courthouse. Most of the visitors were women and there was seldom supervision by agents or attorneys. These visits were permitted even though officers at MCC had revoked visitation privileges after finding one of the witnesses having sex with his visitor on the floor of the visiting room.[44] Another incarcerated informant testified that he had sex with his wife on several occasions while being guarded by BATF agents.[45]

Prisoner informants were observed snorting cocaine and heroin while in MCC. One fellow inmate reported that one of the informants was "high on drugs from almost the time he arrived."[46] The drugs were alleged to have been passed during the unsupervised contact visits at the government's offices.

Prosecutors were also alleged to have given their prisoner informants unlimited and unsupervised telephone privileges while they were in government offices. Prosecutors, paralegals, and secretaries also accepted "hundreds" of collect telephone calls from the informants and forwarded the calls to other parties.[47] One of the forwarded informant telephone calls was to his drug supplier complaining about the poor quality of the drugs brought to him during a "contact visit."[48]

Illustrating the pervasiveness of the effects that loss of control over an informant can have was the involvement of the Assistant U.S. Attorney's (AUSA's) paralegal. She allegedly developed a personal relationship with the witnesses, engaging in "phone sex" with one of the lead defendant informants.[49] The paralegal, testifying under immunity at the motion for a new trial, also admitted to giving presents to the informants, supplying beer to the informants during a party at the U.S. Attorney's Office while celebrating a conviction, and smuggling contraband for them into the MCC.[50]

The inmate informants were also allowed to move about freely within the U.S. Attorney's Office while participating in debriefings and pre-indictment preparation. Lack of supervision allowed them to steal preindictment prosecution memorandum and other materials relating to the "El Rukns" cases. Those materials were transported back to the MCC, where they were provided to other witnesses in the case.[51]

One of the lead AUSAs in the prosecution of the "El Rukns" trials allegedly allowed himself to be named as one of the inmate witnesses' beneficiaries of his property, second only to the informant's mother.[52] Another AUSA approached one of the inmate informants about co-authoring a book about the "El Rukns." The business discussions occurred during the prosecution of one of the cases calling for the testimony of the informant witness.[53]

Three federal district judges reversed 13 of the "El Rukn" convictions in 1993, accusing the lead AUSA of misconduct.[54] The U.S. Attorneys Office also agreed to sharply reduced sentences for 23 defendants, and charges were dropped against four others.

In April 1996, the lead AUSA was fired from his $98,500-per-year position. The Justice Department said in its letter of termination that he knew or should have known about two government witnesses who tested positive for drugs while in custody.[55] In 1998, however, an administrative judge supported the AUSA's contentions that he had never seen the drug test results and that a conversation with a fellow prosecutor about the drug use never took place. He was awarded back pay with interest and reinstated.[43]

10.3   Investigations

The majority of informants are criminals skilled in capitalizing on any weakness regardless of the activity they are engaged in. The dynamics involved in the agent–informant relationship constantly present opportunities for a skilled informant to resist efforts to control his activities. If successful, the informant is able to guide an investigation in the direction he wishes it to take, contrary to the instructions given him by the control agent.

The Drug Enforcement Administration identifies control as the most important aspect in successful CI management.[56] Agents are instructed that the informant must never be allowed to run the investigation regardless of how insistent or argumentative they may become. He or she must know that the ultimate decision maker during the case is the Special Agent.[56] The Bureau of Alcohol, Tobacco, and Firearms cautions that Special Agents must make certain that it is the Special Agent, not the informant, who directs the investigation.[57]

The motivation for an informant to dominate an investigation may be twofold. The defendant informant who is "working off some charges"[58] may be attempting to fulfill his substantial assistance commitment without actually producing the results desired by his control agent. Either he may be attempting to produce an alternative target and not "burn any bridges," or he may never have been able to deliver the target he promised.

Informants faced with a specific time frame in which to produce a case may become desperate and view attempts to control their activity as contrary to their own best interests. In *United States v. Medina-Reyes*,[59] the informant was given specific individuals as targets. His cooperation and plea agreement conspicuously stated that if his obligations were "not completed within 30 days of the signing of this agreement, for whatever reason, the defendant [informant] will not be entitled to any recommendations of leniency by the State."[60]

Throughout the period of the informant's "cooperation" he repeatedly violated the terms of his cooperation and plea agreement. Two of the major contacts he claimed to have had with targeted individuals were initiated by the CI "on his own without the direction of law enforcement officers."[61] The informant also continued to engage in drug trafficking while operating as a

CI. During the period that he was assisting agents, officers at the Des Moines Airport detained him, and $20,000 in drug money was seized from him.

In granting a motion to suppress evidence obtained during the execution of a search warrant, the *Medina-Reyes* court was extremely critical of the control agents' management and control of the informant.

> [S]uch a dark shadow is cast on the reliability of the confidential informant, that probable cause cannot be found. He had no past track record as an informant demonstrating reliability; he was seriously flawed by his own drug dealing, drug usage, lies to [his control agent] and violations of the *control provision* of his cooperation agreement; and he was *under heavy pressure to make* a prosecutable case against [the targets]. One cannot reasonably conclude that information from such a person rose to the level of probable cause.[61,62]

The use of informants and the methods used to control them is a clandestine activity. It does not routinely expose itself to close examination by those outside of law enforcement circles.[63] It is not until a case spins seriously out of the control of the case agent or the prosecutor that even a partial analysis is permitted.

The court in *United States v. Brumel-Alvarez*[64] provided an opportunity for such an analysis. The court held that the government violated both *Brady*[65] and the Jencks Act by failing to disclose an internal government memorandum questioning the reliability of an informant and his general influence and control over an investigation.[66] The case provided a rare opportunity for the court to examine an investigation driven by a manipulative defendant informant who was successful in both determining the course of an investigation and pitting the U.S. Customs Service against the Drug Enforcement Administration.

The informant had been involved in illegal drug operations for 25 years,[67] far longer than his Customs agent handlers had been employed. The path to becoming an informant in the case was a typical one. Following his arrest for possessing one kilogram of cocaine and a plea of guilty, the informant was able to convince a Customs agent that he could lead the U.S. Customs Service to high-level Mexican government officials involved in drug trafficking.[68]

The agent arranged for the informant's release from jail, and a government "sting operation" was initiated, targeting individuals in Mexico and Bolivia. The primary target named by the CI was a Mexican General he claimed provided protection for shipments of cocaine smuggled into the U.S. by aircraft. Throughout the course of the investigation, the informant was successful in preventing agents from either meeting with or tape recording conversations with the General, and he thwarted other opportunities to gather crucial evidence.[69]

A 42 page memorandum by DEA supervisor Michael Levine[70] chronicled the control problems he observed and the influence the CI had over Customs agents and the government's investigation.[71] The memorandum was an indirect result of the informant's allegations of agent misconduct, including claims by the informant that he had bribed DEA agents. Originally withheld from the defense at trial, *de novo* review by the appellate court concluded that there was "a reasonable probability that had the [Levine Memorandum and attachments] been disclosed, the result of the proceeding would have been different such that [our] confidence in the outcome is undermined."[72]

Excerpts from the Levine Memorandum describing the lack of control over the informant when compared to prescribed handling techniques[73] follow:

> I noticed that when Customs officers were talking about [the informant] it was almost as if they were in awe of him. They were ecstatic [sic] at the results of his cooperation to that point ...[71]

> The [Customs Undercover agent] later confided in me [DEA Group Supervisor Levine] that he often found himself pitted between his "bosses" (who preferred to follow [the informant's] suggestions) and me. He also stated that ... he was very "uncomfortable" with the latitude and freedom the informant had been given, but being a new agent in Customs ... he had felt often "trapped" in his role.[71]

> There was much uncontrolled [sic] telephone contact between [the informant] and the violators [some of the defendants]. He often, without consulting or coordinating with the DEA control agent ... or myself, would speak to the violators telling them "Luis said ..." This utilizing my undercover identity to manipulate the case the way he [the informant] saw fit. Weeks later I had to overcome many statements he attributed to "Luis" (my undercover identity). He was constantly allowed to operate in this fashion *throughout the investigation,* unless I was present. I made it clear, when I was present, that it was a drug case and that I was a DEA Agent, and that it would be done my way — which [the informant] never ceased to fight against.[71,74]

The points of the various arguments [with the informant] were usually not as important as the control they signified. The issue was that the CI [the confidential informant] was out of control, in that he believed himself on an equal par with the investigating agents. Being an outsider in a case, I still did not think it my place to "rein him in."[71,75]

As a further demonstration of [the informant's] influence during the investigation, Levine observed: In the San Diego Customs office [the informant] seemed to have full run of the place, using telephones and desks at his will and was on a first name "kidding" basis with many of the agents and secretaries. He was extremely familiar with those "controlling" him, often joking about matters private and personal to each. He, in fact, — while no violators were present — not only had the full run of the undercover house, but the keys to all the leased undercover cars, which he utilized at his whim.[76,77]

Commenting exclusively on the behavior of his own agents Levine described the operation as "a nightmarish, failed, buy/bust operation in Panama during which DEA functioned at its absolute worst." According to Levine, government agents involved in the undercover operation "were too drunk to deal with on a logical basis," thereby jeopardizing not just the investigation, but perhaps the lives of agents involved in the investigation.[78]

The defense capitalized on the government's lack of control over the informant. Some of their arguments were described by the court as "insightful." They further illustrate the impact of lack of control.

[Millions of dollars are talked about but not one speck of cocaine shows up at any time and not one sample is gathered by the government and nothing really is seen except, surprise, surprise, surprise, that which [the informant] says he saw ...[79]

The Government, the individuals involved in this case, through their trust and through their misguided confidence in [the informant], ignored by choice or by lack of wisdom points throughout this whole investigation that if they had been reviewed under even the most glancing of considerations would have revealed that this was all a scam.[79]

What is incredible is that this man was essentially placed in charge of the investigation. We have 10, 15 agents milling around in the background, but the person who led this investigation throughout it was a convicted criminal who had not [had] verified any of the truths that supposedly he had told the government.[79]

We have [the informant] and unfortunately in this screenplay of a case, Mr. Wheeler (the informant) was producer, director, screenwriter and actor. Not one of the agents involved in this case really supervised what this man did.[79]

The court agreed with the defendants that [the informant's] deliberate thwarting of Levine's attempt to tape-record a telephone conversation with the General [was] critically important.[79] The informant's actions in deliberately acting contrary to instructions by Levine to bring the defendants to an undercover meeting so that a telephone call to the General could be made gave rise to the suspicion the informant knew or suspected that there was no General to call.[80]

10.4   Governmental Liability for Torts Committed by Informants

Generally, the federal government has been successful in avoiding liability for torts committed by its informants. A major part of this success has been predicated on the Federal Tort Claims Act (FTCA), 28 USC § 1346. By relying upon the "discretionary function" of the FTCA, the government has successfully argued that because the use of informants is discretionary (i.e., left up to the decisions of the individual law enforcement agency) rather than ministerial, there should be no liability upon the government for torts committed by an informant because the government, under the FTCA, did not waive immunity for discretionary acts.

10.5   Applicable Federal Tort Claims Act (FTCA)

The FTCA constitutes a broad waiver of the United States' sovereign immunity from tort liability.[81] The Act gives federal courts jurisdiction to hear actions for injury or loss of property, or personal injury or death caused by the negligent or wrongful act or omission of any employee of the government. The employee must be acting within the scope of his office or employment, under circumstances where the United States, if a private person, would be liable to the claimant in accordance with the law of the place where the act or omission occurred.[82]

Prior to the passage of the FTCA, victims of torts committed by federal employees had to seek relief by seeking a private relief bill from Congress.[83] The FTCA's basic purpose was to relieve Congress of the burden of considering these bills and to entrust their consideration to the courts.[84] Enacted as part of the Legislative Reorganization Act of 1946, the FTCA was meant "to provide for increased efficiency in the legislative branch of government."[85]

However, certain exceptions were provided which limited this "broad" waiver of sovereign immunity. Of greatest importance is the "discretionary function" exception to the waiver of immunity.[86] The text of the discretionary exception reads as follows:

> The provisions of this chapter and Section 1346(b) of this title shall not apply to:
>
> (a) Any claim based upon an act or omission of an employee of the Government, exercising due care, in the execution of a statute or regulation, whether or not such statute or regulation be valid, or *based upon the exercise or performance or the failure to exercise or perform a discretionary function or duty on the part of a federal agency or an employee of the Government, whether or not the discretion involved be abused.*[86]

At least one court has recognized that it is not the mere exercise of judgment that immunizes the United States from liability for the torts of its employees.[87] Instead, the discretionary function immunizes government employees while they are formulating policy.[88] Another exception to the FTCA is the "intentional torts" exception under 28 USC § 2680(h).

10.6   Intentional Torts Exception

If a plaintiff who has been injured by the tortious actions of an informant sues the government, one argument that the government may assert is that it has not waived liability for such actions evidenced by the Intentional Torts exception to the FTCA. In addition to the discretionary function exception to the federal government's waiver of immunity for suit, the FTCA also employs an "intentional torts exception" to the general waiver of immunity.[89] The intentional torts exception states that the waiver of immunity (28 USC § 1346(b)) shall not apply to:

Any claim arising out of assault, battery, false imprisonment, false arrest, malicious prosecution, abuse of process, libel slander, misrepresentation, deceit, or interference with contract rights: *Provided,* that with regard to acts or omissions of investigative or law enforcement officers of the U.S. Government, the provisions of this title shall apply to any claim arising, on or after the date of imprisonment, false arrest, abuse of process, or malicious prosecution. For the purposes of this subsection, "investigative or law enforcement officer" means any officer of the United States who is empowered by law to execute searches, or to seize evidence, or to make arrests for violations of Federal Law.[89]

Although the exception looks as though it could easily be construed broadly, the U.S. Supreme Court interpreted it narrowly in 1988.[90] In *Sheridan,* an off-duty and "obviously intoxicated" serviceman fired several shots into an automobile, injuring the plaintiff and causing damage to his car. The plaintiff sued the government under the Federal Tort Claims Act, alleging negligence on the part of the Navy corpsmen because they did not prevent the serviceman's use of the rifle. The serviceman was a naval medical aide at the Bethesda Naval Hospital in Maryland. The corpsmen had found the drunken serviceman in a hospital building and attempted to take him to the emergency room. After they noticed that the drunk serviceman had a rifle, the corpsmen fled, took no further action to subdue the serviceman, and did not alert the proper authorities that the serviceman was intoxicated and brandishing a weapon.[91]

The district court held that the action was barred and the plaintiff subsequently appealed. After the Fourth Circuit affirmed the district court's holding,[92] the U.S. Supreme Court granted *certiorari* and found that the intentional torts exception to the FTCA did not apply to torts that fell outside the scope of the FTCA's general waiver, and therefore, the claim was not barred because of the intoxicated serviceman's conduct.[93] "The negligence of other Government employees who allowed a foreseeable assault and battery to occur may furnish a basis for Government liability that is entirely independent of Carr's [the drunken serviceman] employment status."[94]

The claim asserted by a plaintiff for an informant-committed tort would be that the government was negligent in its supervision and control of the informant's actions and that the government could reasonably foresee that the tortious acts could have been committed by the informant. The government, however, will assert the intentional torts bar to recovery applied under the arising out of language in 28 USC § 2680(h), arguing that the plaintiff's negligence claim should be barred, for in the absence of the informant's tort, there would be no claim.

One critical inquiry is whether the informant is considered a government employee, particularly if the informant is a paid informant. For instance, the Tenth Circuit has found that when the government has a duty to prevent a nonemployee from committing an assault and fails to fulfill that duty, Section 2680(h) does not bar a negligence claim based on that resulting injury.[95] Additionally, in cases involving federal negligence combined with a nongovernment employee's intentional tort, courts "do not consider the plaintiff's injuries to have arisen out of the intentional tort."[96] Most courts have found that informants are not considered employees, however, which would thus strengthen the argument that the intentional torts exception should not apply.[97]

10.7　The Entrapment Defense

The defense of entrapment is often raised in criminal cases that were developed through the use of undercover agents and/or informants. Although entrapment is a complete defense to a crime, it is extremely difficult for the defense to prove.

While undercover agents and agents controlling informants should use caution as they develop a criminal case to avoid entrapment issues, that is not always the case. Agent training on the issue varies from agency to agency.[98]

The FBI addressed entrapment in their "Legal Handbook for Special Agents–Informants and Entrapment." The following is taken directly from their Handbook:

> **Section 8-3.5 Entrapment**
>
> Entrapment is a defense asserted frequently by defendants in cases in which informants have played an active role. Entrapment is established if the evidence shows the idea or plan for the criminal act originated with the Government, and the Government implanted that idea by various forms of inducement in the mind of an otherwise innocent (not predisposed) person who then commits the alleged crime.
>
> In enacting Federal criminal statutes, Congress intended that otherwise innocent people should not be convicted where they were enticed by the Government into violating the law. If the evidence in the case establishes that the defendant was predisposed to

commit the offense, however, the defense of entrapment will be defeated.

Predisposition in Federal cases can be established by many different types of evidence. Federal courts generally permit the government to introduce at trial the following types of predisposition evidence as long as it is similar to the crime for which the defendant is currently charged:

- Prior convictions.

- Prior arrests.

- Preoffense criminal activity. For example, the defendant is charged with selling a controlled substance. Prior to the offense charged, he/she sold a similar substance to undercover agents.

- Postoffense criminal activity. For example, the defendant is charged with selling cocaine. A few months later he/she attempts to sell another controlled substance to undercover agents.

A defendant's response to a Government inducement can also be considered as evidence of predisposition. A defendant's ready and unhesitating acceptance of the Government's offer to commit a crime is substantial evidence that he/she was predisposed to do so.

Section 8-3.6 Governmental Participation

It should be noted that under the entrapment test used in Federal courts, governmental involvement in the criminal activity does not constitute entrapment if the defendant was predisposed to commit the crime. For example, the Supreme Court has held there was no entrapment in the prosecution for manufacturing narcotics, even though an undercover agent supplied a predisposed defendant with an ingredient essential to the manufacturing process. Merely furnishing the opportunity to violate the law does not constitute entrapment. Entrapment lies only when the Government induces a suspect to commit a crime he/she is indisposed to commit.

Section 8-3.6.1 The Due Process Defense

It is clear from the foregoing discussion that proof of predisposition to commit a crime will bar application of the entrapment defense, notwithstanding some governmental involvement in the criminal activity. However, the courts have held that fundamental fairness will not permit a defendant to be convicted when the conduct of informants or agents was outrageous. This differs from the entrapment defense in that the conduct of the government, rather than the predisposition of the defendant, determines if the defense is available.

As stated in the preceding paragraph, some Government involvement in criminal activity is permissible. But when the involvement is outrageous, and offends common concepts of decency, the courts are prepared to dismiss the charges on Due Process grounds.

Whether an informant's conduct offends fundamental fairness is a question which is resolved on a case-by-case basis. It is, therefore, difficult to predict with certainty if a given factual situation will offend the Due Process standard. Nevertheless, certain activity, by its very nature, lends itself to a Due Process claim.

Some of the factors the courts have considered in deciding whether an informant's conduct violates Due Process are whether the informant, by himself/herself or with Government assistance, instigated crime or simply infiltrated an ongoing criminal enterprise; whether the informant directed or controlled the criminal activities of the criminal enterprise or merely took orders from the criminals involved; and whether the informant supplied the criminal enterprise with a substantial amount of essential resources and technical expertise to enable them to commit the offense. The existence of any of the above factors in a case would not necessarily result in a court finding that a Due Process violation has occurred. A violation of Due Process is more likely, however, where more of such circumstances are present.

Appendix 10A: Confidential Informant Agreement*

AGENCY: _____ UNIT: _____

THIS DOCUMENT IS TO BE READ TO THE INFORMANT WITH EACH QUESTION EXPLAINED, ANSWERED, AND RECORDED BY THE OFFICER. THE TAPE RECORDING WILL BE MAINTAINED WITH THIS DOCUMENT

NAME: _____

AGE: _____ DOB: _____

1. Do you understand that you are not to break any laws during your association with this law enforcement agency?
2. Do you understand that you are not an employee of this agency?
3. Do you understand that you are not to disclose your association with this agency to anyone except as directed by your control agent or in response to a subpoena issued by a court of law?
4. Do you understand that you are not to release any funds entrusted to you until you have first received the drugs for which you are negotiating?
5. Do you understand that you are not to purchase drugs from anyone you cannot identify?
6. Do you understand that you are not a police officer and you are not to carry any documents or equipment that indicates your association with law enforcement?
7. Do you understand that you are not to effect an arrest of any type?
8. Do you understand that you are not to use your association with the unit to resolve personal matters?
9. Do you understand that you are to confine your activity to seeking out drug violations unless prior authorization is obtained from your control agent?
10. Do you understand that you are not to begin negotiations for any drugs without first notifying this agency and receiving permission to proceed?
11. Do you understand that you are not to enter a foreign country without the approval of your control officer?
12. Do you understand that at all times that you are associated with this law enforcement unit, you must keep your control agent informed of your whereabouts and how you can be contacted?
13. Do you understand that you must contact your control agent at least ____ times a week?
14. Do you understand that contact must be maintained with this agency until all investigations and prosecutions are completed and your control agent tells you that you do not need to maintain contact?
15. Do you understand that you are not to provide or offer to provide any quantity of marijuana, narcotics, dangerous drugs, or prescription-only drugs to any investigative target?
16. Do you understand that *under no circumstances* will you carry any type of a weapon while working as an informant with this agency?
17. Do you understand that you are *not* to unlawfully entrap any person while working as an informant for this agency? A person is unlawfully entrapped if the intent to commit the crime did not arise in their mind because they are an innocent person who is not predisposed to commit that crime. The innocent person is unlawfully entrapped where they are unduly persuaded and induced to commit a crime that

they would not otherwise commit. Merely affording opportunities for the commission of the crime is not unlawful entrapment.

18. A reasonable effort will be taken to make sure that your role and association with this unit remains confidential and that you do not become a material witness on a case. In the prosecutor's opinion, if there are sufficient legal grounds to oppose a motion to reveal your identity, the State will oppose the motion. If you do not follow the instructions of your control officer, you will probably become a material witness in a case, and the court will order that your identity be disclosed to the defense attorney. If this happens, the case will not be dismissed and your identity and association with this agency will not remain confidential.

19. Do you understand that if you become a material witness and are required to testify or give an interview, that you must tell the truth, the whole truth and nothing but the truth regardless of whether it is embarrassing to you, is favorable or unfavorable to you or to anybody else, including the State?

I have reviewed the terms of this agreement with the control agency listed below. I understand each and every term and agree to abide by each.

_____   _____
Dated   Signature

I have reviewed the terms of this agreement and discussed them with the above-named person. I have answered all questions asked and believe that he/she understands the agreement.

_____   _____
Dated   Control Officer

I have reviewed the terms of this agreement and discussed the facts of the case with the control agent. I approve the use of this informant and believe that his/her use is consistent with the currently applicable County Attorney policy and good law enforcement practice.

_____ Supervisor (date)

*Developed by the National Institute for Drug Enforcement Training

Appendix 10B: Bureau of Alcohol, Tobacco, and Firearms Informant Agreement

This confirms the agreement entered into between the Bureau of Alcohol, Tobacco, and Firearms (BATF) and_____

1. BATF has asked me to assist in an official investigation. In furtherance of this investigation, I agree to:

    _____

    (Describe above the activity that the informant or cooperating witness or subject will be doing for BATF.)

2. BATF has assigned Special Agent _____ to serve as my supervisor in this investigation. It is imperative that I maintain contact with Special Agent _____ and advise him of my activities and abide by his instructions.

3. I will not participate in any unlawful activities except insofar as BATF determines that such participation is necessary to this investigation and BATF expressly authorizes such acts in advance. I understand that any violation of the law not expressly authorized by BATF may result in my prosecution.

4. Under no circumstances will I participate or be permitted to participate in acts of violence. If I am asked to participate in any act of violence or learn of such plans, I will attempt to discourage those plans or acts and will promptly notify BATF.

5. I will not initiate any plans to commit criminal acts. Further, I understand that I will not induce an individual to commit a crime that he or she has no predisposition to commit.

6. I will not attempt to be present during conversations between individuals under criminal indictment and their attorney. If I am inadvertently present and learn of defense plans or strategy, I am *not* permitted to report such conversations without prior approval from the U.S. Attorneys Office.

7. While I will be working closely with BATF for purposes of this investigation, I understand that I am not a law enforcement officer, an employee, or an agent of BATF and that I will not hold myself out to be such.

8. I understand that information that I provide to BATF may be used in a criminal proceeding. All legal means available will be used to maintain the confidentiality of my identity, but I may be required to testify before a grand jury and at any subsequent hearing and trial. I understand that I have an obligation to provide truthful information and testimony, and that any deliberate false statement or testimony will subject me to criminal prosecution.

9. If, as a result of being a cooperating witness, it is determined by BATF that my life (or that of any member of my immediate family) may be in danger, BATF will, with my permission, apply to the Department of Justice to admit me to the Witness Protection Program. I understand that the final decision is made solely by, and in the discretion of, the Department of Justice and not BATF.

10. I will in no way reveal the confidential and sensitive nature of this investigation. Further, I will not undertake any publication or dissemination of any information or material that results from this investigation without the prior express authorization of BATF.

11. BATF will reimburse me for expenses incurred which are deemed by BATF to be reasonable and in furtherance of this investigation.

I have read this AGREEMENT in its entirety and hereby acknowledge that I understand the terms and will abide by this AGREEMENT.

_____   x _____
Date   Signature

_____   x _____
Date   Witness

_____   x _____
Date   Special Agent, Bureau of Alcohol, Tobacco, and Firearms

Appendix 10C: DOJ/DEA Cooperating Individual Agreement

DEA SENSITIVE

U.S. Department of Justice/Drug Enforcement Administration Confidential Source Agreement

The undersigned confidential source agrees to the following:

1. I will not violate criminal laws in furtherance of gathering information or providing services to DEA, and any evidence of such a violation will be reported by DEA to the appropriate law enforcement agency.
2. I have no official status, implied or otherwise, as Agent or employee of DEA.
3. That the information I provide may be used in a criminal proceeding and I may be called upon to testify to such information in a court of law, and although DEA will use all lawful means to protect my confidentiality, this cannot be guaranteed.
4. I am advised that it is a Federal offense to threaten, harass, or mislead anyone who provides information about a Federal crime to a Federal law enforcement agency. If I experience anything of this nature, as a result of my cooperation with DEA, I will contact my controlling agent immediately.

I have read and understand the above regarding my conduct as a DEA Confidential Source.

CS was advised by Agents _____ and _____ that CS is responsible to report any financial payment received by CS for cooperation to the IRS.*

_____
Signature/Date

WITNESSED BY:

_____

_____

CS File Number:_____

DEA FORM 473

Appendix 10D: Confidential Source Acknowledgment

Confidential Source Number _____

I do hereby acknowledge being advised of and fully understand the following statements:

- I am not an employee of FDLE* and I will not identify myself as an employee of FDLE.
- I will not furnish information concerning any FDLE investigation to anyone, including other police agencies, without approval of FDLE.
- I will not reveal my association with FDLE to anyone, including other police agencies, without the approval of FDLE.
- My association with FDLE does not grant me police arrest powers.
- My association with FDLE does not authorize me to carry firearms.
- Any payment received from FDLE is to be considered as income.
- I have been advised of FDLE's jurisdiction.
- All my activities are voluntary.
- I have advised FDLE of all my past criminal history information.
- I will not operate any motor vehicle, motorcycle, water vessel, aircraft or other conveyance without valid, lawful operator license(s) and mandated certification and/or appropriate documents as may be required by law.
- I understand that I will be required to sign a receipt for any payment received from FDLE. If I desire to use an alias to sign FDLE receipts, that alias will be

_____.

                                                    (Print Alias)
I understand that no other alias signature will be allowed.

_____ _____   _____ _____
Signature   Date   Alias Signature   Date

_____ _____   _____ _____
FDLE Agent Signature   Date   Witness Signature   Date

* Florida Department of Law Enforcement.

Appendix 10E: FBI Authorization for Informant to Participate in Ordinary Criminal Activity

Memorandum

To: SPECIAL AGENT IN CHARGE Date:
From: SUPERVISOR JAMES SMITH
Subject: AUTHORIZATION TO PARTICIPATE IN <u>ORDINARY</u> CRIMINAL ACTIVITY

The purpose of this memo is to document SAC/ASAC/SUPERVISOR approval for captioned informant to engage in ordinary criminal activity in the following investigation:

CASE TITLE/FILE NUMBER:
SQUAD NUMBER:
CASE AGENT:
AGENT ASSIGNED INFORMANT:
AUTHORIZED CRIMINAL ACTIVITY:
FROM:
TO: _____
(This period is not to exceed 90 days)
SUMMARY OF FACTS SUPPORTING THIS AUTHORIZATION:

_____
(SUPERVISORY SPECIAL AGENT)

_____
(ASSISTANT SPECIAL AGENT IN CHARGE)

_____
SPECIAL AGENT IN CHARGE

Appendix 10F: FBI Informant Guidelines and Instructions

Memorandum

(FBI)

To: SPECIAL AGENT IN CHARGE   Date:
From: SA
Subject:

GUIDELINES AND INSTRUCTIONS — INFORMANTS

All criminal informants, except CS type, must be made aware of the items listed no later than the second contact after suitability certification and at least annually thereafter. Upon receipt of this memo into the file, the writer acknowledges that he/she had advised captioned informant of the following:

Voluntary Relationship
FBI Jurisdiction
Confidential Relationship
Not Employee of Bureau or Undercover Agent
Promptly Furnish and Report Information when obtained
only to the bureau
Payments are income
Policy regarding Defense Plans and Strategy

The writer further acknowledges, pursuant to AG guidelines in the use of informants, he/she has advised captioned informant of the following:

Informant shall not
    Participate in acts of violence;
    Use an unlawful technique (e.g., breaking and entering, unauthorized electronic surveillance, opening or otherwise tampering with the mail to obtain information for the FBI);
    Initiate a plan to commit criminal acts; participate in criminal activities of persons under investigation, except insofar as determined by the FBI that such participation is necessary to obtain information needed for purposes of Federal prosecution.

_____
Agent Signature

References

1. *United States v. Boyd,* 55 F.3d 239 (7th Cir., 1995).

2. *United States v. Burnside,* 824 F. Supp. 1215 (N.D. Ill., 1993).

3. *Commonwealth v. Lewin,* 405 Mass. 566, 542 N.E.2d 275 (1989).

4. *Vaughn v. United States,* Eastern District of Kentucky, Case #93-9.

5. *Ostera v. United States,* 769 F.2d 716, 85 A.L.R. Fed. 843 (11th Cir.), *reh'g denied, en banc,* 715 F.2d 304 (11th Cir., 1985).

6. *Commonwealth v. Lewin,* 405 Mass. 566, 542 N.E.2d 2275 (1989).

7. *United States v. Bernal-Obeso,* 989 F.2d 331, 333 (9th Cir., 1993). *See also* Hight, J.E., M.P.A., Avoiding the informant trap, a blueprint for control, *F.B.I. Law Enforcement Bull.,* Nov. 1998, pp. 1–5.

8. *United States v. Bernal-Obeso,* 989 F.2d 331, 333 (9th Cir., 1993).

9. Emshwiller, J.R., Deal with informants raises questions, *Wall Street Journal,* Aug. 28, 1997.

10. Murphy, S., Sidekick's double-dealing career worthy of master spy, *Boston Globe,* July 20, 1998. *See also* Toobin, J., Killer instincts, did a famous prosecutor put the wrong man on death row? *The New Yorker,* Jan. 17, 2005.

11. *FBI Manual of Investigative Operations and Guidelines (MIOG),* Vol. II, Part I, § 137-5(1).

12. *FBI Manual of Investigative Operations and Guidelines (MIOG),* Vol. II, Part I, § 137-5(3).

13. Lorant, R., Informants claim FBI was cozy with Boston mob, *Associated Press,* Jan. 12, 1998.

14. *Ostera v. United States,* 769 F.2d 716, 85 A.L.R. Fed. 843 (11th Cir.), *reh'g denied, en banc,* 775 F.2d 304 (11th Cir., 1985).

15. *Federal Sentencing Guidelines Manual.*

16. Sandlin, S., "Star" witness demoted; pedophile may not testify at trial, *Albuquerque Journal,* Jan. 22, 1996.

17. Trott, S.F., The Successful Use of Snitches, Informants, Coconspirators, and Accomplices as Witnesses for the Prosecution in a Criminal Case (Jan. 1984). Assistant Attorney General Criminal Division, Public Integrity Section, U.S. Department of Justice.

18. American Psychiatric Association Anti-Social Personality Disorder (301.7) (1987).

19. Raab, S., Court disclosures expose mobster who died of AIDS as FBI mole, *New York Times,* Nov. 20, 1994, p. 19.

20. Butterfield, F., Use of informers may taint FBI cases, *New York Times,* June 17, 1997.

21. *Associated Press,* FBI blamed for Tulsa probe snag: mob quest thwarts Roger Wheeler murder investigation, report says, Nov. 10, 1997.

22. *United States v. Salemme,* 91 F. Supp. 2d 141 D. Mass. 1999, *rev'd sub nom; United States v. Flemmi,* 225, F 3d 78 (1st Cir., 2000). *See also* Finer, J., Notorious fugitive as elusive as a ghost. Boston mobster Whitey Bulger still on the loose after 10 years, *Washington Post,* Jan. 30, 2005; *Associated Press,* Ex-agent charged in 1981 mob hit, Oct. 12, 2003.

23. *FBI Manual of Investigative Operations and Guidelines (MIOG),* § 137-2(3).

24. Lehr, D., Agents gave Bulger starring role in mafia case — but was it real? *Boston Globe,* July 20, 1998.

25. *Kentucky v. Long,* 837 F.2d 727, 731 (6th Cir., 1988). *See also* Raab, S., Charges against FBI agent threaten a major mob case, *New York Times,* June 14, 1997.

26. Freedberg, S.P., FBI allegedly shielded suspects in Miami murder, *Miami Herald,* Aug. 2, 1998.

27. *Motivations to Cooperate as an Informant,* Ch. 2 § 2.6, Walk-In Informants.

28. Integrity Assurance Notes, Drug Enforcement Administration, Planning and Inspection Division, Vol. 1, No. 1 (Aug. 1991). *See DEA Agents Manual,* 6612.61, Management and Review of Informants. *See also United States v. Gardner,* 658 F. Supp. 1573, 1575 (W.D. Pa., 1987).

29. Lehr, D., Agent, mobster forge pact on Southie ties, *Boston Globe,* July, 1998.

30. Attorney Generals Guidelines Regarding the Use of Confidential Informants, III, A, 2, a.

31. Kidwell, D., Report chastises chief of South Florida Customs, *Miami Herald,* Sept. 14, 1998.

32. *DEA Agents Manual,* 6612.41(c).

33. *DEA Agents Manual,* 6612.45(B).

34. Integrity Assurance Notes, Drug Enforcement Administration, Planning and Inspection Division, Vol. 1, No. 1, (Aug. 1991). *See DEA Agents Manual,* 6612.61, Management and Review of Informants. *See also United States v. Gardner,* 658 F. Supp. 1573, 1575 (W.D. Pa., 1987).

35. Cooperating Individual Management, p. 1, U.S. Department of Justice, Drug Enforcement Administration Office of Training, Quantico, VA.

36. Lehr, D., The official Bulger FBI file: some tall tales, *The Boston Globe,* July 21, 1998.

37. Kelley, M., Associated Press, Men in fatal break-in not bounty hunters, *Seattle Times,* Sept. 7, 1997.

38. *United States v. Brumel Alvarez,* 976 F.2d 1235 (9th Cir., 1992).

39. *United States v. Grimes,* 438 F.2d 391, 395–396 (6th Cir., 1971).

40. *United States v. Hernandez-Escarsega,* 886 F.2d 1560 (9th Cir., 1989), *cert. denied,* 497 U.S. 1003, 110 S. Ct. 3237, 111 L. Ed. 2d 748 (1990).

41. *United States v. Boyd,* 55 F.3d 239 (7th Cir., 1995).

42. *United States v. Burnside,* 824 F. Supp. 1215 (N.D. 111., 1993); *United States v. Andrews,* 824 F. Supp. 1273 (N.D. 111., 1993).

43. Stern, A., U.S. prosecutor, fired over gang trials, exonerated, Reuters, July 24, 1998.

44. *United States v. Andrews*, 824 F. Supp. 1273, 1286–1287 (N.D. 111., 1993).

45. *United States v. Burnside*, 824 F. Supp. at 1242.

46. *United States v. Burnside*, 824 F. Supp. at 1228.

47. *United States v. Andrews*, 824 F. Supp. at 1286.

48. *United States v. Burnside*, 824 F. Supp. at 1246.

49. *United States v. Burnside*, 824 F. Supp. at 1248.

50. *United States v. Boyd*, 55 F.3d 239, 244 (7th Cir., 1995).

51. *United States v. Burnside*, 824 F. Supp. at 1244.

52. *United States v. Andrews*, 824 F. Supp. at 1285.

53. *United States v. Boyd*, 874 F. Supp. 179, 181 (N.D. 111., 1994).

54. *United States v. Burnside*, 824 F. Supp. 1215 (N.D. 111., 1993); *United States v. Andrews*, 824 F. Supp. 1273 (N.D. 111., 1993); *United States v. Boyd*, 833 F. Supp. 1277 (N.D. 111., 1993). *See also United States v. Boyd*, 55 F.3d 239 (7th Cir., 1995).

55. United States fires Chicago gang prosecutor, *Miami Herald* (*Associated Press* Chicago), May 3, 1996, p. A6.

56. Seven Steps to Successful Informant Management, DEA Informant Interaction, U.S. Drug Enforcement Administration, Office of Training, Quantico, VA (July 1992).

57. *BATF Manual*, p. 23 (BATF 03210.7b) Subsection (f).

58. *United States v. Medina-Reyes*, 877 F. Supp. 468, 472 (S.D. Iowa 1995).

59. *United States v. Medina-Reyes*, 877 F. Supp. 468, 470, 471 (S.D. Iowa 1995).

60. *United States v. Medina-Reyes*, 877 F. Supp. 468, 471 (S.D. Iowa 1995).

61. *Medina-Reyes*, 877 F. Supp. at 475.

62. Lichtblau, E., FBI spy case highlights problem with informants, *New York Times*, April 20, 2003.

63. Intelligence, Surveillance and Informants: Integrated Approaches, Police Research Group, Crime Detection and Prevention Series: Paper No. 64, London Home Office, Crown Copyright 1995.

64. *United States v. Brumel-Alvarez*, 976 F.2d 1235 (9th Cir., 1992).

65. *Brady v. Maryland*, 373 U.S. 83, 87, 83 S. Ct. 1194, 1196, 10 L. Ed. 2d 215 (1963).

66. *United States v. Brumel-Alvarez*, 976 F.2d 1235, 1236 (9th Cir., 1992).

67. *United States v. Brumel-Alvarez*, 976 F.2d 1239, 1239 (9th Cir., 1992).

68. *United States v. Brumel-Alvarez*, 976 F.2d 1235, 1238 (9th Cir., 1992).

69. *United States v. Brumel-Alvarez*, 976 F.2d 1235, 1244 (9th Cir., 1992).

70. Levine Memorandum, written by then DEA Group Supervisor, Michael Levine, now retired [hereinafter Levine Memorandum].

71. *Brumel-Alvarez*, 976 F.2d at 1241.

72. *Brumel-Alvarez*, 976 F.2d at 1246, *citing United States v. Lai*, 944 F.2d 1434, 1440 (9th Cir., 1991), *cert. denied*, 502 U.S. 1062, 112 S. Ct. 947, 117 L. Ed. 2d 116 (1992).

73. *DEA Agents Manual*, Appendix IV.

74. Levine Memorandum at 5 (emphasis added).

75. Levine Memorandum at 8.

76. *Brumel-Alvarez*, 976 F.2d at 1241 n.5

77. Levine Memorandum at 4.

78. *Brumel-Alvarez*, 976 F.2d at 1247.

79. *Brumel-Alvarez*, 976 F.2d at 1242.

80. *Brumel-Alvarez*, 976 F.2d at 1244.

81. *Downs v. United States*, 522 F.2d 990 (6th Cir., 1975).

82. *Downs v. United States*, 522 F.2d 995. *See also* 28 USC § 1346(b).

83. *Downs v. United States*, 522 F.2d 990, 995 (6th Cir., 1975).

84. *United States v. Muniz*, 374 U.S. 150, 153–154, 83 S. Ct. 1850, 10 L. Ed. 2d 805 (1963). *See also Dalehite v. United States*, 346 U.S. 15, 24–25, 73 S. Ct. 956, 97 L. Ed. 1427 (1953); *Larson v. Domestic & Foreign Commerce Corp.*, 337 U.S. 682, 703–704, 69 S. Ct. 1457, 93 L. Ed. 1628 (1949).

85. Chapter 753, 60 Stat. 812 (1946).

86. 28 USC § 2680(a).

87. *Downs v. United States*, 522 F.2d 990, 995 (6th Cir., 1975), *citing* F. Harper & F. James, *The Law of Torts* 1658 (1956).

88. *Downs* at 995. *See also Ostera v. United States*, 169 F.2d 716, 718 (11th Cir., 1985).

89. 28 USC § 2680(h), Pub. L. No. 93-253, § 2, 88 Stat. 50.

90. *Sheridan v. United States*, 487 U.S. 392, 108 S. Ct. 2449, 101 L.Ed.2d 352 (1988). *See also United States v. Muniz*, 374 U.S. 150, 83 S. Ct. 1850, 10 L. Ed. 2d 805 (1963). *See also County of Sacramento v. Lewis*, 118 S. Ct. 1708 (1998).

91. 487 U.S. at 392.

92. *Sheridan v. United States*, 823 F.2d 820 (4th Cir., 1987).

93. *Sheridan v. United States*, at note 12 (4th Cir., 1987).

94. 487 U.S. at 394.

95. *Naisbitt v. United States*, 611 F.2d 1350, 1352–1353 (10th Cir.), *cert. denied*, 449 U.S. 885 (1980).

96. Section 2680(h) of the Federal Tort Claims Act; Government Liability for the Negligent Failure to Prevent an Assault and Battery by a Federal Employee, 69 Geo. L.J. 803, 822–825 (1981), *citing Brown v. United States*, 486 F.2d 284, 288 (8th Cir., 1973); *Rogers v. United States*, 397 F.2d 12, 15 (4th Cir., 1968); *Panella v. United States*, 216 F.2d 622, 624 (2nd Cir., 1954).

97. *Slagle v. United States*, 612 F.2d 1157 (9th Cir., 1980).

98. *See Sorrells v. United States*, 287 U.S. 435 (1932); *Sherman v. United States*, 356 U.S. 369 (1958); *United States v. Russell*, 411 U.S. 423 (1973); *Hampton v. United States*, 425 U.S. 484 (1976); *Jacobson v. United States*, 503 U.S. 540, 112 S.Ct. 1535 (1982); *Matthews v. United States*, 485 U.S. 58 (1988).

The Witness Security Program

<big>**11**</big>

11.1 Historical Overview of the U.S. Witness Security Program (WITSEC)

11.1.1 Truthful Testimony = Lifetime Protection

Organized crime's oldest and most effective protection against criminal prosecution is to either murder the witness the government plans to use or to frighten the witness from testifying. In the United States prior to 1970, neither course presented significant difficulty in accomplishing. It was not unusual for individuals who did take the witness stand to be brutally tortured and murdered.[1]

Prior to the creation of the Witness Security Program, the protection of witnesses was the responsibility of the law enforcement agency bringing a case for prosecution. From 1961 to 1965 the Department of Justice Organized Crime Program "lost" more than 25 informants. Hundreds of prosecutions reportedly did not go forward because the witnesses feared being murdered.[2]

In 1966, President Lyndon Johnson's Crime Commission responded to the problem of safeguarding witnesses by delegating the responsibility to the U.S. Marshals Service. This was not a simple task for an agency whose primary responsibility at the time was to provide for the security of the courts and the judiciary.

In its early stages, the task of protecting a witness was accomplished by establishing a series of "safe houses"[2] strategically located throughout the United States. The program was short on staff and severely underfunded. Marshals were assigned to protect the witness 24 hours a day at the safe house until the witness testified. That method proved to be a shortsighted approach to a problem that could literally last the lifetime of the witness. The resulting murders of informants long after trial illustrated that organized crime had a long memory. To succeed, the program needed drastic changes.

In 1970, Congress passed the Organized Crime Control Act of 1970.[3] Title V of the Act granted the Attorney General authority to expend funds for the protection of endangered witnesses.[4] However, only witnesses involved in organized crime prosecutions could be protected under the Act. The U.S. Marshals Service was formally named as the agency with the sole responsibility for developing an effective witness protection program.[1]

The Comprehensive Crime Control Act of 1984[5] repealed Title V of the Organized Crime Control Act of 1970 that had provided only for the protection of organized crime witnesses. Dramatically expanding the original law, the new act replaced it with the following:

> *Witness Security Reform Act of 1984 Part F.* Authorizes the Attorney General to relocate and protect a witness or a potential witness for the Federal government or a state government and his immediate family in a proceeding involving organized criminal activity or ***other serious offense*** (relocation may include new housing, provision of documents to establish a new identity, payments to cover basic living expenses and/or assistance in obtaining employment); requires the Attorney General to enter into a memorandum of understanding with any person to whom relocation assistance is to be provided; establishes a procedure to enable the plaintiff in a civil action against a person later granted protection under this Act to obtain compliance with the judgment; establishes a Victim Compensation Fund to pay restitution to, or compensation for, the victim of a violent crime committed by a person provided protection under this Act; and repeals Title V of the Organized Crime Control Act of 1970, 18 USC § 3481.[6]

The most significant impact of the repeal of Title V was expanding protection to those testifying in cases involving ***other serious offenses***. Today a witness may be considered for the Witness Security Program if the person is an essential witness in a specific case of the following types:

1. Any offense defined in Title 18 USC § 1961(1) (organized crime and racketeering).
2. Any drug trafficking offenses described in Title 21 USC § 841.

3. Any other serious federal felony for which a witness may provide testimony that may subject the witness to retaliation by violence or threats of violence.

4. Any state offense that is similar in nature to those set forth above.

5. Certain civil and administrative proceedings in which testimony given by a witness may place the safety of that witness in jeopardy.[7]

The authority to use appropriations of the Department of Justice for the payment of "compensation and expenses of witnesses and informants" is provided by 28 USC § 524.

Since its inception in 1971 until 1988, the Witness Security Program (WITSEC) had protected, relocated, and provided new identities to more than 5,000 principal witnesses[8] (those individuals targeted for retaliation). By 2003, more than 7,500 primary witnesses and more than 9,600 family members or associates had entered the Witness Security Program. The U.S. Marshals Service (USMS) devoted $59.7 million and 173 staff positions to the WITSEC Program in 2003.[9,10]

The Witness Security Program appears to be achieving its stated goals. No witness who has followed the security rules of the program has been killed.[10] The USMS claims an 89% conviction rate in cases where protected witnesses have testified.[11] Not only do witnesses feel safe to speak out against their confederates, but in the majority of cases they go on to live normal law-abiding lives.[12]

11.1.2   A Two-Tiered Program

There are two tiers to the traditional Federal Witness Security Program. The first tier involves the relocation of nonincarcerated witnesses from one area of the United States to another and is administered by the U.S. Marshals Service. The second tier provides for the hiding of prisoner witnesses within the nation's federal prison system. These are individuals who have testified, or agreed to testify, but who must serve prison sentences themselves. That tier of the program is administered by the Bureau of Prisons (BOP).

Today, approximately 50% of new witnesses authorized into the Program go into each of these components. To meet the unique security needs of incarcerated Witness Security Program participants, the Federal Bureau of Prisons has built several special Protective Custody Units, which are basically prisons within prisons, so that witnesses can be housed with other witnesses.[10,13] The BOP reports that, as of 2000, they protected 475 prisoner witnesses.

11.2   Administration and Eligibility for the Witness Security Program

The U.S. Department of Justice, Office of Enforcement Operations (OEO), Criminal Division, is charged with overseeing the Witness Security Program (WITSEC). The internal guidelines for prosecutors are contained in the *U.S. Attorneys Manual*[14] and the Criminal Resource Manual.[15]

Investigative agents and government trial attorneys are *not* authorized to make representations to witnesses regarding funding, protection, or other Witness Security Program services, including admission into the Program.[16] Representations or agreements, including those contained in plea agreements concerning the Program are not authorized and will not be honored without specific authorization from OEO.[17]

11.2.1   Eligibility Requirements for the Witness Security Program

In order to facilitate the processing of a request by a government attorney for a witness' acceptance into the Witness Security Program, the OEO's Witness Security Unit designed an application form that requests the specific information needed to support the request. The form requires a summarization of the testimony to be provided by the witness and other information evidencing the witness's cooperation, the threat to the witness, and any risk the witness may pose if relocated to a new community.

To avoid any unnecessary delay in processing a Program application, government attorneys are required to note the following:

1. In order to make certain that each application for entry of a witness into the Program is both appropriate and timely, the witness should, prior to his or her acceptance into the Program, either appear and testify before the grand jury or in some other manner have committed himself or herself to providing testimony at trial. This requirement relates to the commitment of the witness to testify and is intended to ensure that the witness's testimony is available at the time of trial. It is equally as important a requirement that the prosecutor intend to have the witness testify, and that the witness's testimony be significant and essential to the success of the prosecution.

2. The protection and relocation of witnesses and family members are expensive and complicated. In addition, the DOJ is obligated to provide for the safety and welfare of a protected witness and family members long after the witness has testified. It is imperative, therefore, that the request for entry of a witness into the Program be made only after the sponsoring attorney has determined that the witness's

testimony is significant and essential to the success of the prosecution, as well as credible and certain in coming.[18]

11.2.2 Threat Assessment

While providing testimony in a criminal trial may expose a witness to potential danger, the level of exposure to harm must be evaluated before admittance to the program can be considered. A witness does not have to be threatened to reach this stage of the admittance procedure. If the criminal or the criminal organization the witness is testifying against has the record or reputation for violence, or intelligence information indicates the capability to launch an attack against a witness, it is enough to recommend the witness for WITSEC. The investigative agency managing the threatened witness must prepare both a Threat Assessment Report and a Risk Assessment Report. The reports must include the following information:

- A statement that the appropriate U.S. Attorney has recommended the person for participation in the program.
- The facts of the specific case or cases in progress, including the role of the person recommended, the record and reputation of the defendants, the criminal organization, and the illegal activities.
- The criminal record and reputation of the person recommended.
- Detailed information on the threat, whether direct or potential, to the witness and his or her family as a result of his or her cooperation with the government.
- The involvement of any other agencies in the investigation.
- The names of any relatives or members of the household of the principal witness, their criminal background, and the information documenting the threat against their safety.
- Names and identifying data for all individuals who may pose a danger to the witness.

11.2.3 Risk Assessment

A large percent of those considered for witness protection have criminal records, many for serious violent crimes. The risk assessment is meant to evaluate the risk the protected witness might pose to his relocation community. The report must include the following information:

- Significance of the investigation or case in which the witness is cooperating.

- The possible danger from the witness to other persons or property in the relocation area if the witness is placed in the program (applies to the witness and his or her family members).
- The alternatives to program use which were considered and why they will not work.
- Whether the prosecutor can secure similar testimony from other sources.
- The relative importance of the witness's testimony.
- Whether the need for the witness's testimony outweighs the risk of danger he or she may pose to the public (applies to the witness and his or her family members).[19]

11.3 Informants, Aliens, and Nonfederal Witnesses

The safety and security of an informant assisting in an investigation is the responsibility of the investigative agency utilizing the informant. An informant is only eligible for participation in the Witness Security Program if he or she is also a bona fide witness as defined in 18 USC § 3521.

Prosecutors are reminded that merely requiring an informant to testify with the intent that he or she might become eligible for the Program is not a sufficient qualification. He or she must still meet the requirements of being a significant and essential witness.[20]

11.3.1 Illegal Aliens

Upon the submission of a Witness Security Program application for an illegal alien, the sponsoring attorney and/or investigative agency must obtain from the Immigration and Naturalization Service (INS) the appropriate documents that authorize the prospective witness and family members to remain in the United States and facilitate relocation by the USMS out of the state in which they registered. Program candidates who are illegal aliens cannot be relocated by the USMS until all INS requirements are satisfied and necessary documents have been provided to the OEO or the USMS. *(Author's Note: Latest available USAM continues to refer to INS. Their function is now performed by Immigration and Customs Enforcement (ICE), an agency of the Department of Homeland Security.)* In cases where the INS procedure to legalize the alien's status may require a lengthy time period, the sponsor or agent should secure from INS a letter of intent to change the witness's status as part of the requirements for relocation under the Program. Excludable alien witnesses who do not need the protective services of the USMS, but who need to remain in the United States, should have their sponsoring government attorney apply for S-visa classification instead of seeking assistance from the Witness Security Program.[21]

The S-visa, sometimes referred to as the "Snitch Visa," includes two categories, the S-5 and the S-6. The S-5 is for an alien who has important information on a criminal organization or whose presence is needed by the law enforcement authorities investigating or prosecuting the matter. An example of a criminal organization would be a drug trafficking cartel.

The S-6 is for an alien supplying key and reliable information to law enforcement regarding a terrorist organization, and in doing so, is placing him- or herself in danger. Thus, S-6 is a type of witness protection provision. The element of danger is not required for the S-5, but it is likely that many S-5s are also in vulnerable positions and also may be able to obtain some type of appropriate protection.

11.3.2 State and Local Witnesses

The introduction of joint federal, state, and local law enforcement task forces in the late 1970s and their successes in organized crime and drug prosecutions created a need for the protection of nonfederal witnesses. Prior to the joint task forces, little protection was available. The Witness Security Reform Act of 1984 filled that gap and authorized the Attorney General to provide protection to state and local witnesses. If a request for witness protection is received, the state is asked to reimburse the United States for expenses incurred in providing protection. The requesting agency is required to enter into an agreement in which the State agrees to cooperate with the Attorney General in carrying out the provisions of the Witness Security Reform Act. The terms of the reimbursement agreements are determined by the USMS. If the state or local witness is under state or local supervision, either probation or parole, the supervising agency must agree to transfer jurisdiction and supervision to federal supervising authorities, prior to the witness's acceptance into the Witness Security Program.[22]

11.4 Program Participants' Financial Obligations

Prior to Program authorization, witnesses are required to make payment of any known debt for which there is a valid judgment, or make satisfactory arrangements to pay the debt[23]; to satisfy all outstanding criminal and civil obligations (e.g., fines, community service, restitution); to provide appropriate child custody documents; and to provide appropriate immigration documents as necessary. In addition, as a condition of authorization into the Program, the Department may, at its discretion, mandate random drug or alcohol testing and/or substance abuse counseling and set other conditions believed to be in the best interests of the Program.[24]

11.5   Psychological Testing and Evaluation

Before authorizing any witness to enter the Witness Security Program, the OEO will arrange for psychological testing and evaluation for each prospective witness and all adults (18 years of age and older) and members of the witness's household that are also to be protected. The testing, to the extent possible, determines whether the individuals may present a danger to their relocation communities. Because the reports of the psychologists may contain information that is discoverable as potentially exculpatory *Brady*[25] material in the criminal prosecution in which the witness is to testify, all materials submitted by the psychologists are forwarded by the OEO to the appropriate U.S. Attorneys Office (USAO) for review.

Before undergoing psychological evaluation, the witness must sign a release form authorizing the Department to use the results of the psychological evaluation to the extent necessary in connection with the witness' application for acceptance into the Program or for other lawful uses. It is the responsibility of the sponsoring prosecutor or agent to have the witness sign the form prior to the evaluation.[26]

11.6   Memorandum of Understanding

The newly accepted participant must enter into a finalized "Memorandum of Understanding" setting forth the following[27]:

1. The agreement of the person, if a witness or potential witness, to testify in and provide information to all appropriate law enforcement officials concerning all appropriate proceedings.
2. The agreement of the person not to commit any crime.
3. The agreement of the person to take all necessary steps to avoid detection by others.
4. The agreement of the person to comply with legal obligations and civil judgments against that person.
5. The agreement of the person to cooperate with all reasonable requests of officers and employees of the government who are providing protection.
6. The agreement of the person to designate another person to act as agent for the service of process.

7. The agreement of the person to make a sworn statement of all out-standing legal obligations, including obligations concerning child custody and visitation.
8. The agreement of the person to disclose any probation or parole responsibilities, and if the person is on probation or parole under State law, to consent to Federal supervision.

Each such memorandum of understanding also describes the protection which the Attorney General has determined will be provided to the person and the procedures to be followed in the case of a breach of the memorandum of understanding. It includes a procedure for filing and resolution of griev-ances. This procedure shall include the opportunity for resolution of a griev-ance by a person who was not involved in the case.[28]

11.7 Denying Admission to the Witness Security Program

Not every candidate for admission to the Witness Security Program is granted protection. The decision to place someone in WITSEC is a policy decision shielded by the discretionary function exception of the Federal Tort Claims Act.[29]

Admission to the program is tightly controlled. Applications received and admissions approved by the Office of Enforcement Operations reveals the following[30]:

Year	Applications	Accepted
1987	260	173
1988	305	205
1989	338	183
1990	310	173
1991	282	162
1992	352	219
1993	480	231
1994	392	200
1995	356	132
1996	177	88

Note: 1997–2004 have not been released by the USMS.

The Victim and Witness Protection Act of 1982 provides no private right of action against the federal government by witnesses refused admission to the Program. Under 18 USC § 3521(a)(3) the United States and its officers and employees shall not be subject to any civil liability due to a decision to provide or not to provide protection.[27]

A witness refused admission to the Program might attempt to seek relief under the Federal Tort Claim Act (FTCA).[31] Actions under the FTCA are limited to those in which the U.S. Government has consented to being sued.[32]

A federal witness may try to bring a suit under the FTCA § 1346(b) alleging that the government negligently failed to provide adequate protection. It would only apply if the government had undertaken to protect the individual and has done so negligently or if a duty to protect exists under state law.[33]

11.8   Entering the Program

There is little in the life experience of any family, perhaps even the most hardened criminal's,[34] to prepare them for entry into the Witness Security Program.[35] "There is a unique trauma involved when a family is uprooted and moved to an entirely new community," said Witness Security Inspector Larry Holland. "Remember your own feelings — if you have ever moved to a new city where you know no one — the adjustment was somewhat difficult, particularly hard on your spouse and your children. Now, think of that same situation, but imagine giving up the name you have known since birth and not being able to tell anyone back home — even your relatives and closest friends — where you are."

"Imagine trying to make friends in your new community without saying anything about your background, always being on guard that you might accidentally blurt out a reference to your past. Once simple and automatic actions like signing your name must initially be done with great concentration so that you do not lapse and sign your old, familiar name."[36]

That trauma begins in a variety of ways for the prospective participants in WITSEC. For emergency participants, some are quickly moved from their residences and evacuated by their case agent to a remote location, usually a hotel in a remote city. There the witness and his family are guarded around the clock by a least two armed special agents and debriefed.

The more fortunate are moved to one of seven so-called "safe sites" located throughout the United States in large metropolitan areas. The locations are also used to house witnesses when they return to their "danger area" to testify.[37]

Safe sites are described by the Marshals Service as self-contained secure units designed to provide witnesses and their families ultimate protection in a hotel setting at a significant savings to the government. The units are complete with dining, exercise, and entertainment facilities and the latest in closed-circuit television networks, intruder alarm systems, and radio and telephone communication systems. Deputy U.S. Marshals are assigned at safe sites to protect the witnesses from harm.[37]

11.8.1   Safe-Site and Orientation Center

Since 1988, protected witnesses are formally processed through the Safe-site and Orientation Center, a secret location in the metropolitan Washington, D.C. area. The facility contains six fully equipped apartments for nonprisoner witnesses and their families. It also has four holding cells for incarcerated witnesses. A polygraph room, interview rooms, and full medical and dental examination facilities are on site.[37]

The witness is usually flown to the Washington, D.C. area, arriving at either Dulles, National, or any of the smaller regional airports.[38] Extremely high-risk arrivals and departures use any one of the surrounding military air bases.

The Marshals Service operates its own air fleet including three Boeing 727s, two DC-9s, and several smaller jet aircraft, many obtained through the Asset Forfeiture Program.[39] The protected witness is accompanied by a least two armed and fully trained special agents of the agency utilizing the witness. One agent must be of the same sex as the witness and one agent should be conversant in the witness's native language. Those agents must be prepared to stay with the witness until relieved of the responsibility both by their agency and the Marshals Service.

The protected witness is driven to the center in an armored vehicle with darkened windows.[40] The extreme security measures are designed to not only protect the individual in transit from harm but are also intended to thwart efforts to monitor the movement of witnesses to and from the center.[40]

The physical complex itself is described by the USMS as "a secure area within a secure area." The outer perimeter is patrolled, while the actual grounds of the center, which are enclosed by a physical barrier, are under constant surveillance. The security network is managed by a cadre of witness security inspectors who direct the movement of all personnel within the center's grounds.[41]

The witness is met by a U.S. Marshal whose title is Witness Security Inspector. The position is unique to federal law enforcement. The inspector is not only the participant's link to WITSEC but he also becomes the witness's "protector, support system, and confidant"[42] as he moves through the system. There are approximately 160 Witness Security Inspectors stationed throughout the United States whose only responsibility is to protect and assist the program participant.

Organizationally, the program is operated from three levels: Marshals Service Headquarters; eight regional offices; and Metro units which have a

Witness Security Inspector assigned to provide assistance to witnesses and to serve as an advisor to the local Marshal on witness security matters. The Witness Security Inspectors are supported by 150 Deputy U.S. Marshals who share their regular assignment with WITSEC.[42]

Shortly after the witness's arrival, a special team of security specialists from Marshals Service Headquarters begins the task of determining where to relocate the witness. That decision follows a detailed interview where extensive background information is collected and assessed.

The participant's ultimate destination, referred to by Marshals as the "relocation area," is predicated on the witness's ethnic background, where he has lived and visited in the past, any special medical or educational requirements for him or his family, the availability of employment, and where the Marshals Service can best service him.[43]

While at the Orientation Center, participants receive a thorough physical and dental examination. They also receive counseling to prepare them for the move and the challenges it will present.[37]

The Center gives the participants the opportunity to begin the redocumentation of identity procedure starting with the selection of a new name. Before leaving, they will be provided with new driver's licenses, social security cards and records, birth certificates, and school and medical records all designed to correspond to their identity.[37]

All records are designed to be verifiable and able to stand even the closest scrutiny. No participant receives educational documentation or work history that puts them in either a better or worse position professionally, i.e., no one is certificated above a level they legitimately attained in a field or profession. However, many do reap benefits from the program. Some are removed from lifestyles that inhibited personal growth and find the program an opportunity for a new start.[37]

Once the witness is relocated, a WITSEC field inspector assists the family in finding permanent housing, enrolling the children in school, locating doctors and dentists, and with the multitude of other tasks attendant to moving into a new community. In the past, arrangements were made to securely move the family furniture and personal belongings from the danger area to their new home without detection. The practice of moving furniture has been abolished in favor of purchasing new furniture. The previous practice apparently proved to be inefficient and needlessly exposed one more stage of the resettlement process to compromise.

The resettlement must be accomplished in a seemingly normal fashion without drawing attention to the family, but all the while maintaining absolute security with no connection to the danger area or the past. Once the family is settled in, the inspector continues to stay in touch with the family.[37]

"Some witnesses experience a big change in lifestyle after they enter the program," according to an inspector who has been with the Program since its inception. "They may have had a very affluent lifestyle, driving new cars and living in a big house with maids. But their lives are drastically different once they enter the WITSEC Program. The witness may now have to rent an apartment and drive a used car. The transition into the Program can take some time."[37]

Relocating presents many unexpected sacrifices for the protected family. All ties to the family's previous community must be severed. Witnesses can continue to stay in contact with friends and relatives but only by mail forwarded through secure channels of the Marshals Service.

Many participants are divorced and custodial parents. Nonparticipant parents are still entitled to visitation of children, presenting costly logistical hurtles for the USMS to overcome.[44] Inspectors reportedly average arranging between 15 and 18 visits per child per year.[45] Obviously, the visits must take place away from the participants "danger zone" and the city of relocation to ensure the integrity of the program.[45]

Protected witnesses receive a monthly maintenance allowance in their new city until they are gainfully employed or become self-sufficient through other means. Monthly payments are based upon the Department of Labor (DOL) cost of living indices. (The U.S. is currently divided into eight DOL Regions each with different costs of living indexes.) No additional consideration is given to restore a participant to an opulent lifestyle he once may have enjoyed. Subsistence terminates six months after the first payment is made. There are provisions for a 90-day extension of benefits for circumstances outside the control of the participant.[46] Lengthy trials and multitrial appearances often delay the employment process and require an extension of the subsistence allowance.

The Marshals Service is only responsible for providing one job opportunity to the witness after relocation. If the participant has a valid reason for not accepting the position, one more job opportunity is offered.[47] The USMS has a network of over 300 employers in the U.S. that accept WITSEC participants.[48] The employment offer should be in a field compatible to the participant's work history. For those without transferable skills, there are provisions for job training. Participants are also free to fulfill their own career goals. Failure to seek employment or continued opposition to employment opportunities can cause the discontinuance of subsistence payments.

The participant is expected to become self-sufficient as soon as possible after admission to the Program. Under no circumstances will the witness be considered "entitled" to subsistence payments until they have testified. The prosecutor will be advised of the scheduled termination of a witness's funding and is invited to comment.[46]

Participants in the program are still entitled to reward monies from the agency that had control over their activities. The agency headquarters must coordinate the payment through the OEO and the U.S. Marshals Service for the disbursement of the funds. Reflecting the USMS commitment to secrecy and the witness's safety, "neutral site" meetings solely for the purpose of paying a reward to the witness is prohibited. Funds are disbursed through U.S. Marshals Headquarters.[49]

11.8.2   Hiding in Plain Sight

Once the witness is relocated to a safe location, he is no longer provided physical protection by members of the Marshals Service. It is the responsibility of the witness to preserve the secrecy of his new identity and place of residence. Disclosing either is grounds for expulsion from the program.

11.9   Requests for Witness to Return to Danger Area for Court Appearances, Pretrial Conferences, and Interviews

Requests for the appearance of a relocated witness for trial or pretrial conferences and interviews are made by the prosecutor to the Witness Security Inspector in the prosecutor's area. The request must be made at least 10 working days in advance of the appearance date. Requests include the following: purpose of appearance, date/time, place, and estimated duration of appearance.

Investigative agents make requests for interviews of a relocated witness for cases other than the Program case through authorized agency channels for approval by the OEO. Requests include purpose, date, and estimated duration of the appearance, and if applicable, any other persons to be present in addition to the requestor. The OEO forwards approved requests to the USMS or to the BOP (whichever is appropriate).

Prosecutors and investigative agents are required to conduct conferences or interviews of relocated witnesses at neutral sites, or, of prisoner-witnesses, at the prisoner's assigned BOP Facility. The practice substantially reduces the personnel requirements of the USMS. The USMS determines the location of all "neutral sites" for relocated witness interviews and advises the requestor directly.

It is the responsibility of the prosecutor and the investigative agents to ensure that maximum use is made of the witness's appearance in the danger area. In the interests of security and limiting the expenses involved, the witness must be returned to the relocation area or designated facility as soon as practicable.[50]

11.10   WITSEC Participants as Informants

Informants who enter the Witness Security Program and begin a new life do occasionally resurface as cooperating individuals.[51] They can also reenter the WITSEC Program if necessary.[52]

That practice was evidenced in the high-profile FBI arrest of Malcolm X's daughter in a murder-for-hire case in 1994.[53] The informant used in the case had previously participated in the investigation of a militant group who had planned to bomb an Egyptian government tourist office in New York in 1978. Following that case he was placed in the WITSEC Program.[53]

The Reuters News Service quoted him as saying that he expected to receive $45,000 from the FBI for his latest services. He said he was paid $34,000 and expected to receive the balance plus expenses as "compensation for having to relocate and adjust to a new life in the witness protection program. He reentered the program after the indictment of the target of the investigation."[53]

In an interview with *Newsweek* the informant was asked a series of questions about his involvement in the case. Concerning his motive to once again become involved as an informant, he was also asked questions concerning the Program.[54] His answers provide a commentary on the realities of the Program.

Q.   Maybe you just wanted an easy life in the federal witness-protection program?

A.   I'd been in the program before [after the 1978 case]. I knew what a horrible life it was. I did not leave my friends and loved ones willingly. The $45,000 the government paid me was calculated to equal six months of my salary at the job I'd have to leave. Would you take six month's salary to leave everyone and everything you know?

Q.   What is it like?

A.   Short of a jail cell, this is the hardest existence I can fathom. Imagine sitting in a Sleepy 8 motel room for months when your only social contact is the Domino's delivery man. Since January, I think I've lived in six cities, give or take. Last week, after the settlement, I saw my girlfriend for the first time in almost four months. We were allowed to embrace for 15 minutes, with six federal marshals standing nearby.[54]

The Drug Enforcement Administration views admission into WITSEC as permanent, and once admitted the informant will not be utilized again. The prohibition extends to any family member who is relocated as a result of the informant's cooperation. The DEA Manual acknowledges that the Department of Justice may waive the prohibition.[55]

The Office of Enforcement Operations does not foreclose utilizing a protected witness as an informant. Instead they acknowledge an "ongoing relationship" between the witness and Department.[56]

The consent of the OEO is required before any of the following persons may be used as an informant: a currently protected witness, anyone relocated because of a witness's cooperation, or a former protected witness.

The following information must be supplied to the OEO for its use in evaluating requests to use anyone as an informant who has received protective services through the Program.

1. Name of the person to be used as an informant.
2. Alias(es) used by the proposed informant.
3. Approval of appropriate headquarters official of concerned agency.
4. If the informant is not the witness, what is the relationship of the informant to the witness, and name the witness.
5. Identifying data on the informant, including date of birth, place of birth, sex, social security number, FBI number, and BOP registration number.
6. Informant's employment; if unemployed, how informant is subsisting; and extent the proposed activity may jeopardize the informant's livelihood.
7. Name(s) of target(s) of investigation and role in the activities under investigation.
8. Significance and/or scope of the criminal activity and target(s).
9. Informant's relationship or association with the target(s) under investigation.
10. Necessity of utilizing the informant in the investigation, including details about the nature of the use being requested.
11. Consideration of alternatives to informant's use and indication of why they will not work.
12. Detailed account of informant's involvement in criminal activity subsequent to being approved for the Witness Security Program.
13. Appraisal of whether proposed use centers on informant's new criminal involvement, and how informant is aware of new criminal activity.
14. The benefit that the informant expects in return for his/her cooperation.
15. Statement about whether informant's activity is expected to require the informant to testify.

16. Indication about whether witness completed testimony in case in which he/she was placed into the Program.

17. Details about other agencies' use of informant since relocation.

18. Supervision status of informant — if on probation, supervised release, or pretrial supervision, the prior approval of the Court — through the U.S. Probation or Pretrial Services Officer — must be obtained. If the witness is on parole, approval of the U.S. Parole Commission must be obtained through the U.S. Probation Officer.

19. Security measures to be taken to ensure informant's safety and to minimize risk to the public.

20. Use of electronic devices, body wires, video, etc.

21. Length of time the informant is to be needed.

22. Whether the informant is incarcerated; and if so, whether prosecutor and/or judge should be advised.

23. If the witness is a prisoner, where incarcerated.

24. Whether the prisoner/informant will remain in custody of the investigative agency, be housed in jails or similar facilities at certain times, or be unguarded.

25. Whether a prison redesignation will be necessary upon completion of informant activity.

26. If applicable, whether activity has been endorsed by appropriate Federal/State prosecutor; if so, name, telephone number, and location of prosecutor.

27. Whether informant activity will require submission of new Program request and subsequent relocation.

28. Whether the informant is expected to be charged/indicted in this investigation.[57]

11.11 Ejection from the WITSEC Program

The USMS reported in a January 1996 memorandum that a high percentage of WITSEC participants (less than 50%) are ejected from the program for failure to follow the established rules of conduct. The memorandum reports that program participants are generally given a second chance. Difficulty in following the strict rules of the Program is probably understandable, since more than 97% of the protected witnesses have extensive criminal records.[11] According to another memorandum prepared in 1996, approximately 80% of the WITSEC principal witnesses are from drug prosecutions.

The Marshals Service acknowledges that some witnesses do return to crime,[58] but only between 17 and 23%.[11] The rate of recidivism among program participants is less than half the rate of those released from the

nation's prisons. Consequently, the program does appear to have a rehabili-
tative effect.[11]

11.12   Short-Term Protection Program

Many threats made against witnesses and informants do not rise to the level
required for admission to the federal Witness Security Program. To fill that
gap, several states and cities have initiated their own witness protection
programs. They include:

- The California Victim/Witness Assistance Program, Office of Criminal Justice Planning, Los Angeles County District Attorney's Office.
  Witness Protection efforts under Penal Code Section 1054 reported
  to have received $100,000 in federal grant money for witness protec-
  tion in 1996.
- Colorado Witness Protection Program, established in 1996 under
  Section 24.33.5-106 C.R.S.
- Connecticut Witness Protection Program, established January 1999
  under Substitute Bill No. 916, Public Act No. 99-240, also classifying
  intimidating a witness as a class C felony.
- Maryland Witness Protection Program, administered through Maryland State's Attorney Office.
- Wisconsin Victim/Witness Program, created in 1982.

Conversely, many individuals who otherwise would qualify for the full level
of protection refuse the option due to the drastic changes it will create for
themselves and their family. Instead, they elect short-term protection.

In January 1991, the U.S. Marshals Service realized that many witnesses
needed some measure of protection but did not merit entrance into the
Witness Security Program. To fill that void the Short-Term Protection
Program (dubbed "WITSEC Lite" in the Miami, Florida, U.S. Attorneys
Office) was developed. The program has proven to be successful and in
recent Department of Justice budgets has received additional funding and
personnel.

The Short-Term Protection Program was designed to provide temporary
relocation away from the danger area for those witnesses whom it was anticipated could safely return home after their testimony was completed. The
Program does not provide the full complement of services, such as legal name
changes and assistance in finding long-term employment, as does the Federal
Witness Security Program. Witnesses who enter this Short-Term Protection

Program are not required to break all ties with family and friends, as are those witnesses who enter the regular Program.

Gerald Shur of the Office of Enforcement Operations described the evolution of the Short-Term Protection Program and its function to the Subcommittee on Crime and Criminal Justice prior to his retirement:

> In the late 1980s and early 1990s, as more localized violent criminal and street-gang-type organizations came into prominence and began to pose a different kind of threat to different kinds of witnesses, the Department recognized the need for a more limited services protection program, to serve as an alternative to the full services of the regular Witness Security Program. For example, members of so-called "traditional" organized crime groups such as La Cosa Nostra almost never threatened to kill persons outside their own criminal group who testified against them, or to kill law enforcement officers. Many of today's criminals come from a different criminal traditional and social setting. They will kill anyone, no matter whom, that they perceive as a threat to them and to their continued ability to operate on the fringes of society, and on their freedom.

The identification of this changing type of criminal, and the need for new types of witness protection led to the creation of a Short-Term Protection Program,[59] which was a joint effort of several agencies including: the Justice Department Criminal Division, Office of Enforcement Operations; the U.S. Attorneys Office, District of Columbia; the U.S. Marshals Service; and the Washington, D.C. Metropolitan Police Department."[10]

11.13   The Emergency Witness Assistance Program

Another tool at the disposal of the U.S. Attorney in the prosecution of cases involving witnesses who have a perceived threat of danger is the Emergency Witness Assistance Program (EWAP). The program became operational in 1997 and is available to witnesses who are going to testify in cases, but have a reservation about testifying, not an actual threat.

The purpose of EWAP is to provide the U.S. Attorneys offices with the flexibility to address a critical need: assistance to witnesses on an emergency basis to ensure their well-being so that those witnesses will be available for trial, other court proceedings, or activities on an ongoing case. The program also addresses a witness's or prospective witness's physical, mental, or emotional reservations about participating in a specific matter before or after he or she has agreed to cooperate with, testify, or be available for, the government. The *U.S. Attorneys Manual* recommends that the program should be used as a last resort in support of witnesses.

Each district has an implementation plan which further describes the uses of the funds. Funding is limited to $4,000 per witness, not to exceed one month. However, additional funding can be requested.[60]

11.14 Witness Protection Alternatives Offered by Investigative Agencies

Some agencies offer an alternative measure of protection through a less formal relocation of the witness. The Drug Enforcement Administration offers financial assistance for their informant's relocation from the agency's internal expense budget, known as PE/PI funds (purchase of evidence/payment for information).[61] Those monies can be used to pay for moving household goods, apartment leases, and transportation. Such expenditures require receipts and documentation.

An alternate method compensates for the cost of relocation when determining the amount of reward to be paid to the cooperating witness.[62] The informant is given a "lump sum" payment, which includes the cost of his relocation. Experience would dictate that the alternate method is a risky course, as the additional money given to the informant may not necessarily go toward relocation. Most informants generally have limited success in governing their personal affairs and need the direction of the case agent to properly relocate.[63]

The Bureau of Alcohol, Tobacco, and Firearms maintains a "source of highly confidential funds which are available for use in exigent circumstances. The account . . . enables the Bureau to meet its responsibilities to those informants and witnesses whose cooperation with BATF results in an immediate threat to their lives."[64] Known as the Emergency Expense Fund (EEF),[64] the monies allow BATF the flexibility of providing short-term protection and immediate relocation of a witness. It is a remedial measure compared to the Witness Security Program, but effective in the short term.

11.15 Criminalizing Acts Taken against Witnesses

Witness protection occurs either after a witness is threatened or when the likelihood of violent actions taken against a witness appears likely. As a deterrent, legislation was enacted to further protect citizens who provide evidence. Of greatest importance in safeguarding informants and witnesses **before** testifying is 18 USC § 512. Section 1513 is intended to protect the individual **after** providing testimony or having given information to law enforcement officials.

11.16   Crimes Committed by WITSEC Participants[51]

As noted earlier, many protected witnesses do return to crime. One WITSEC participant with an extensive criminal history went on an interstate crime spree murdering four people and robbing six banks. Shortly after the first murder, he was held for questioning by a local sheriff. When the suspect's fingerprints were sent to the FBI for a record check, the response was "no known criminal record" due to the secrecy imposed by the WITSEC Program. He was released and went on to commit the next three murders and robberies.

The dilemma that faced the Justice Department and the USMS as the Program became more sophisticated and the number of participants increased was how to respond to legitimate law enforcement inquiries about Program participants. High-profile and violent crimes committed by protected witnesses and the inability of local law enforcement officers to obtain a criminal history of a suspect who was a program participant was the catalyst for change. Provisions within 18 USC § 3521 appear to solve the problem.

The Attorney General can take such action determined necessary to protect the participants in the Program from bodily injury and to assure the health, safety, and welfare of that person. That action can include a decision to:

> … disclose or refuse to disclose the identity or location of the person relocated or protected, or any other matter concerning the person or the program after weighing the danger such a disclosure would pose to the person, the detriment it would cause to the general effectiveness of the program, and the benefit it would afford to the public or to the person seeking the disclosure, except that the Attorney General shall, upon the request of State or local law enforcement officials or pursuant to a court order, without undue delay, disclose to such officials the identity, location, criminal records and fingerprints relating to the person relocated or protected when the Attorney General knows or the request indicates that the person is under investigation for or has been arrested for or charged with an offense that is punishable by more than one year in prison or that is a crime of violence.[65]

The FBI, the U.S. Marshals Service,[65] and the Office of Enforcement Operations have worked out a mechanism to, when warranted, securely disseminate protected witness's arrest records and information in response to legitimate law enforcement requests.[66] That process begins at the Safe-site and Orientation Center, where witnesses are provided with new identities and are fingerprinted. The names and fingerprints are maintained in the FBI's Witness Protection Program Index.[67]

Law enforcement requests to the FBI for information concerning a protected witness is immediately "red flagged" and labeled as a "special handling case." Following a law enforcement inquiry, a designated FBI official contacts the USMS and relays the nature of the inquiry and the agency and the name of the officer making the request. The Witness Security Inspector assigned to the WITSEC participant is then contacted, and a decision is made to either honor the law enforcement agency's request and give the witness' true criminal history or to maintain the secrecy of the witness' criminal history.

If a witness is sentenced to a period of incarceration as a result of a state conviction for a crime committed after relocation, the sponsoring federal investigative agency will be asked to advise the state authorities of the details of his or her cooperation to ensure the state's appropriate action in maintaining the witness' security. State authorities should also be advised that, if they believe that they will not be able to protect the witness, either in their own system or through transfer to another state system, they can so advise the OEO, which will review the case for the witness' reinstatement in the Witness Security Program as a prisoner. If reinstated, the prisoner will be transferred to the custody of the BOP, but will not ordinarily be placed in a Protective Custody Unit, because he or she has engaged in criminal activity after having participated in the Program.[68]

In the case of a crime of violence committed by a Program participant,[69] a fund was established to compensate the victim.

> The Attorney General shall establish guidelines and procedures for making payments under this section. The payments to victims under this section shall be made for the types of expenses provided for in section 3579(b)[70] of this title, except that in the case of the death of the victim, an amount not to exceed $50,000 may be paid to the victim's estate. No payment may be made under this section to a victim unless the victim has sought restitution and compensation provided under Federal or State law by civil action. Such payments may be made only to the extent the victim, or the victim's estate, has not otherwise received restitution and compensation, including insurance payments for the crime involved. Payments may be made under this section to victims of crimes occurring on or after the date of the enactment of this chapter. In the case of a crime occurring before the date of the enactment of

this chapter, a payment may be made under this section only in an amount not exceeding $25,000, and such a payment may be made notwithstanding the requirements of the third sentence of this subsection.[71]

There is a total of $1 million budgeted each year under this section. The funds also cover funeral expenses for victims of WITSEC participants.[72]

11.17   Liability Issues at the State and Local Levels

The excerpt below is from the National Institute of Justice's *Preventing Gang and Drug Related Witness Intimidation, Issues and Practices*.[73] It addresses liability issues associated with state and local witness security programs:

> Many witness security programs are just beginning to address the complex issues of liability associated with caring for intimidated witnesses. Only a handful of witnesses or their families have sued municipalities, the police, or prosecutors in relation to witness security.[74]

There is no consensus among courts concerning the liability of government entities for failure by law enforcement agencies to provide adequate protection to the public as a group. Many courts have held that, where there is no statute to the contrary, government entities are not liable for injuries caused by the negligence of its law enforcement agencies.[75] However, exceptions to this general standard of governmental immunity exist when courts have found, by an examination of the facts of individual cases, that a "special relationship" had been created between the injured individual — often a threatened victim or witness — and the government entity. A special relationship may arise from:

- A report to the police agency by a third party of a specific threat to the witness.
- A promise by the prosecutor or a police officer to provide added security to a threatened victim or witness.
- A promise by the police department to alert the victim to the release from jail of a known intimidator.
- In some cases, a request for protection directly from the intimidated victim or witness.[76]

Requests from frightened individuals are sometimes not considered sufficient by the courts to create a special relationship between the government entity and the potential victim.[77] Given these criteria, it seems likely that participation in a witness security program, whether it is managed by a law enforcement agency or by a prosecutor's office, is likely to create the very sort of special relationship between the threatened victim or witness and the government entity that may make the agency or office liable if the program does not handle the case conscientiously.

In Los Angeles, witness protection lawsuits have reached the courts. *Carpenter v. City of Los Angeles*[78] concerned a robbery in which a police officer was aware that a defendant had contracted to have Carpenter, a prosecution witness, killed but did not inform the witness of the potential danger or provide security. Carpenter was subsequently wounded by the defendant, and the police officer who had failed to warn Carpenter was fatally shot by the defendant following his own testimony in the case. The court awarded Carpenter $1.2 million in damages.

Wallace v. City of Los Angeles[79] concerned a young woman who had been enlisted to testify in a homicide case that the district attorney subsequently declined to prosecute. The woman received no warning and no security services despite death threats from the defendant, the defendant's known history of witness intimidation, and his suspected involvement in two other homicides. The witness was killed before she could testify. The court awarded the plaintiff, the murdered witness' mother, $750,000 in damages, ruling that a special relationship had been created between the detective and the witness by her cooperation and that a duty to warn her of danger arising from that special relationship had been breached. The court established a duty to protect a witness once the person has been enlisted to testify even if the case is later declined.

Early experience suggests that, if police investigators and prosecutors are conscientious about the protection they are offering and promising to victims and witnesses, they can avoid liability even where a special relationship has been established. For example, in a case in Washington State, the City of Seattle was held not to be liable for the death of a female victim with whom the police investigator had established a special relationship but who had refused an offer to be taken to a safe location. The court ruled that, although a special relationship had existed between the police department and the woman, it had been terminated when she refused its offer to take her to a place of safety.[80]

Police investigators and prosecutors in smaller jurisdictions often observed that intimidation attempts rarely escalate into actual physical violence. In such jurisdictions, prosecutors and police were advised to exercise special care in their risk assessments and subsequent discussions with witnesses, so they could identify cases in which the threat was genuine, rather than simply assuming that all claims were exaggerated. It is also important to note that these early liability cases did not involve witnesses who were receiving protection from police investigators or prosecutors but were nevertheless harmed; rather, they concerned decisions by investigators or prosecutors not to inform witnesses of a threat or not to provide security to a threatened witness who had been promised protection.

11.18   Prisoner–Witnesses

Prisoners in a state or federal institution are eligible for participation in the Witness Security Program provided all other criteria are met. The program is administered by the Bureau of Prisons. If the prisoner is in state custody, the state must agree to the prisoner serving his or her sentence in the custody of the Bureau of Prisons. The application should be made as prescribed for other witnesses; however, because there is no assessment of the risk to the public unless a witness is to be relocated in the community, there is also no need for a psychological evaluation nor an assessment of the risk to the public (normally submitted by the sponsoring attorney or investigative agency).

No preliminary interview is conducted by the USMS until the prisoner is between six to nine months from release and is being considered for the full services of the Program — including relocation. If application is being made for the prisoner's family to be relocated while the prisoner is incarcerated, psychological evaluations and risk assessments are needed for all adult family members, and it must be demonstrated that there is no alternative to placement of the family in the Program at that time.

11.18.1   Polygraph Examinations for Prisoner–Witness Candidates

A polygraph examination is required of all Witness Security Program candidates who are incarcerated in order to maintain the security of those individuals who are housed in a BOP Protective Custody Unit. Authorization for the Program may be rescinded or denied if the results of the polygraph examination reflect that the candidate intends to harm or disclose the location of other protected witnesses or disclose information obtained from such witnesses.

As soon as the prisoner begins cooperating, if the prisoner is in BOP custody, the prosecutor or investigative agency will be responsible for notifying officials at the institution in which the witness is incarcerated of his or her security needs, to ensure that appropriate security precautions are taken prior to possible acceptance in the Program. This information should include the names of individuals and groups from which the prisoner should be separated and the level of danger to the witness. Any special requirements, such as being transported alone, should also be communicated.

11.18.2   Utilization of Prisoners for Investigative Purposes

Requests to use, for investigative purposes, persons who are in the custody of the USMS or BOP, or who are under BOP supervision, or to target such individuals in covert investigations, must be submitted to the OEO for review and prior approval. Requests must first be approved by the designated official(s) at the agency's headquarters.[81]

References

1. The Witness Security Program: Truthful Testimony = Lifetime Protection, *The Pentacle*, official publication of the U.S. Marshals Service, Feb. 1988, p. 3 [hereinafter *The Pentacle*].

2. Commentary on WITSEC by Shur, G., former Senior Associate Director, Office of Enforcement Operations, U.S. Department of Justice.

3. Pub. L. No. 91-452.

4. Pub. L. No. 91-452, Title V.

5. Pub. L. No. 98-473.

6. Witness Security Reform Act of 1984, Part F.

7. *U.S. Attorneys Manual*, 9-21.100, Eligibility.

8. Morris, S.E., USMS Director, The Witness Security Program.

9. USMS Administration of the Witness Security Program, Office of the Inspector General, March 2005. *See* USMS Pub. 4/29/99 supplementing USMS, Financial Management Branch Witness Security Division, Jan. 1996.

10. Shur, G., Senior Associate Director, Office of Enforcement Operations, Criminal Division, statement before the Subcommittee on Crime and Criminal Justice, Committee on the Judiciary, U.S. House of Representatives Concerning Witness Intimidation, Aug. 4, 1994.

11. *The Pentacle*, p. 7.

12. McShane, L., Witness protection is an offer that more can refuse; informants find less to fear from today's Mafia, *Seattle Times/Associated Press*, Jan. 2, 2000.

13. Fried, J.P., Guards let mobsters turn jail into "social club," U.S. claims, *Miami Herald*, May 23, 1997; Operation Badfellas, *Corrections Journal*, Pace Publications, NY, June 9, 1997.

14. USAM Criminal Resource Manual, 9.21.00.

15. USAM Criminal Resource Manual, 701 USDOJ, 1998.

16. *Doe v. Civiletti*, 635 F.2d 88, 96 (2nd Cir., 1980).

17. USAM Criminal Resource Manual, 9.21.310.

18. USAM Criminal Resource Manual, 9.21.100.

19. BATF Manual: *Investigative Priorities, Procedures, and Techniques*, Ch. D, 46(a)(b); *DEA Agents Manual* at 6612.73G.

20. USAM Criminal Resource Manual, 9-21.110.

21. USAM Criminal Resource Manual, 9-21.410.

22. USAM Criminal Resource Manual, 9-21.140

23. *Boda v. United States*, 698 F.2d 1174, 1175 (11th Cir., 1983); *Melo-Tone Vending, Inc. v. United States*, 666 F.2d, 689.

24. USAM Criminal Resource Manual, 9-21.100.

25. *Brady v. Maryland*, 373 U.S. 83, 87, 83 S. Ct. 1194, 10 L. Ed.2d 215 (1963).

26. USAM Criminal Resource Manual, 9-21.330

27. 18 USC §§ 3521 *et seq.*

28. 18 USC § 3521.

29. 28 USC § 2680(a). *See also Bergmann v. United States*, 689 F.2d 789 (8th Cir., 1982).

30. U.S. Department of Justice, data are as of June 1, 1996 and does not include short-term witnesses.

31. FTCA, 28 USC §§ 2671–2680.

32. FTCA, 28 USC § 2674. *See also* § 2680(a).

33. *Leonard v. United States*, 633 F.2d 599, 623 n.35 (2nd Cir.), *cert. denied*, 451 U.S. 908 (1982). *See also Barbera v. Smith*, 836 F.2d 96 (2nd Cir., 1987); *Swanner v. United States*, 309 F. Supp. 1183 (M.D. Ala., 1970). *See also* Rosen, P.M., The Bivens constitutional tort: an unfulfilled promise, 67 N.C. L. Rev. 337, 338 (1989).

34. Mass, P., My secret talks with Sammy the Bull, *Parade Magazine*, April 1997. *See also* McShane, L., Witness protection is an offer that more can refuse, *Seattle Times*/Associated Press, Jan. 2, 2000.

35. Mass, P., *Underboss, Sammy the Bull Gravano's Story of Life in the Mafia*, Harper Collins, NY, 1997; Sabbag, R., Disappearing, the invisible family, *New York Magazine*, Feb. 11, 1996.

36. *The Pentacle*, p. 10.

37. *The Pentacle*, p. 9.

38. *The Pentacle*, p. 8.

39. U.S. Marshals Service Pub. No. 17, 4/27/99.

40. Earley, P. and Shur, G., *WITSEC: Inside the Federal Witness Protection Program*, Bantam Books, Feb. 2002.

41. Earley, P. and Shur, G., *WITSEC: Inside the Federal Witness Protection Program*, Bantam Books, Feb. 2002, p. 9.

42. Earley, P. and Shur, G., *WITSEC: Inside the Federal Witness Protection Program,* Bantam Books, Feb. 2002, p. 10.

43. Earley, P. and Shur, G., *WITSEC: Inside the Federal Witness Protection Program,* Bantam Books, Feb. 2002, p. 11.

44. *Prisco v. United States Department of Justice,* 851 F.2d 93 (1988), *cert. denied,* 490 U.S. 1089 (1989).

45. *The Pentacle,* p. 12.

46. USAM Criminal Resource Manual, 706.

47. USAM Criminal Resource Manual, 707.

48. *The Pentacle,* p. 5.

49. USAM Criminal Resource Manual, 9-21.920.

50. USAM Criminal Resource Manual, 9-21.700.

51. Bill Moushey, Deals with the Devil, Protected Witnesses, *Pittsburgh Post Gazette,* May 26–31, 1996. "The Federal Witness Protection Program often gives freedom and riches to heinous criminals . . . . once in the program, some can't resist the temptation of returning to the criminal life."

52. USAM Criminal Resource Manual, 9-21.800.

53. Shabazz informant says he was paid, *Miami Herald,* March 24, 1995.

54. Cormick, J.M., I was in it to save lives, *Newsweek,* May 15, 1995.

55. *DEA Agents Manual,* 6612.73(k).

56. USAM Criminal Resource Manual, 9-21.800.

57. USAM Criminal Resource Manual, 702.

58. Lawson, R.J., Lying, cheating and stealing at government expense: striking a balance between the public interest and the interests of the public in the Witness Protection Program, 24 *Ariz. St. L. J.* 1429 (1992).

59. USMS, Financial Management Branch, Witness Security Division.

60. *U.S. Attorneys Manual,* 3.7.340, Emergency Victim/Witness Programs, [rev. 02/20/98].

61. *DEA Agents Manual,* Ch. 61.

62. *DEA Agents Manual,* 6612.43.

63. U.S. Department of Housing and Urban Development. Notice PIH 96-16, One Strike and You're Out, Screening and Eviction Guidelines for Public Housing Authorities (PHAs).

64. BATF Manual: *Investigative Priorities, Procedures, and Techniques,* Ch. 45.

65. 18 USC § 5321(b)(1)(G).

66. Bohning, D., St. Kitts case may hold key to drug war, island's future, *Miami Herald,* July 1, 1998.

67. 28 USC § 534.

68. USAM Criminal Resource Manual § 709.

69. *Bergmann v. United States,* 689 F.2d 789 (8th Cir., 1982).

70. 18 USC § 3579(b).

71. 18 USC § 3525(d).

72. USAM Criminal Resource Manual, 9-21.1020.

73. *Preventing Gang and Drug Related Witness Intimidation,* Series: NIJ Issues and Practices.

74. *Carpenter v. City of Los Angeles,* 230 Cal. App. 3d 923 1991; *Parrotina v. Jacksonville,* 628 So.2d 1097 (Fla. Dec. 2, 1993). *See also Greene v. New York,* 152 Misc. 2d 786, 583 N.Y.S.2d 766 (1992).

75. 57 Am. Jur. 2d, Municipal, School, and State Tort Liability, Section 27, cited in 46 A.L.R. 4th 948, Section 2 (Police Protection — Crime Victim).

76. 46 A.L.R. 4th 948, Section 3.

77. *Feise v. Cherokee County,* 434 S.E.2d 551 (1993); *cert. denied,* (Ga.) Slip op. (1993); *Jane Doe v. Calumet City,* 641 N.E.2d 498 (Ill., 1994); *Morgan v. District of Columbia,* 468 A.2d 1306 (Dist. Col. App., 1983); and *Hartzler v. San Jose,* 46 Cal. App. 3d 6 (1 Dist., 1975).

78. *Carpenter v. City of Los Angeles,* 230 Cal. App. 3d 923 (1991).

79. *Wallace v. City of Los Angeles,* 12 Cal. App. 4th 1385 (2 Dist., 1993) (No. BO45271), *opinion modified* (Feb. 4, 1993), *rehearing denied* (March 1, 1993), *review denied* (May 27, 1993).

80. *Donaldson v. Seattle,* 831 P.2d 1098 (1992), *op. corrected* (July 1, 1992) *review dismissed,* 847 P.2d 481 (1993).

81. USAM Criminal Resource Manual, 9-21.600.

Appendix I

The Attorney General Guidelines Regarding the Use of Confidential Informants

Preamble

The following Guidelines regarding the use of confidential informants are issued under the authority of the Attorney General as provided in sections 509, 510, and 533 of title 28, United States Code. They apply to the use of confidential informants in criminal investigations and prosecutions by Department of Justice Law Enforcement Agencies and Federal Prosecuting Offices as specified in paragraph (I)(A) below.

I.   General Provisions

A.   Purpose and Scope

1. The purpose of these Guidelines is to set policy regarding the use of Confidential Informants, as defined below, in criminal investigations and prosecutions by all Department of Justice Law Enforcement Agencies and Federal Prosecuting Offices, as defined below.
2. These Guidelines do not apply to the use of Cooperating Defendants/Witnesses or Sources of Information, as defined below, unless a Department of Justice Law Enforcement Agency, in its discretion, chooses to apply these Guidelines to such persons.

3. These Guidelines are mandatory and supersede the Attorney Generals Guidelines on the Use of Informants in Domestic Security, Organized Crime, and Other Criminal Investigations (December 15, 1976); the Attorney Generals Guidelines on FBI Use of Informants and Confidential Sources (December 2, 1980); Resolution 18 of the Office of Investigative Agency Policies (August 15, 1996); and any other guidelines or policies that are inconsistent with these Guidelines. These Guidelines do not supersede otherwise applicable ethical obligations of Department of Justice attorneys, which can, in certain circumstances (for example, with respect to contacts with represented persons), have an impact on law enforcement agents' conduct.

4. These Guidelines do not limit the ability of a Department of Justice Law Enforcement Agency to impose additional restrictions on the use of Confidential Informants.

5. These Guidelines apply to the use of a Confidential Informant in a foreign country only to the extent that the Confidential Informant is reasonably likely to be called to testify in a domestic case.

6. These Guidelines do not apply to the use of Confidential Informants in foreign intelligence or foreign counterintelligence investigations.

B.   Definitions

1. "Department of Justice Law Enforcement Agency" or "JLEA"
   a. The Drug Enforcement Administration;
   b. The Federal Bureau of Investigation;
   c. The Immigration and Naturalization Service (INS);
   d. The United States Marshals Service; and
   e. The Department of Justice Office of the Inspector General.

2. "Field Manager" — a JLEA's first-line supervisor, as defined by the JLEA (typically, GS-14 rank or higher).

3. "Senior Field Manager" — a JLEA's second-line supervisor, as defined by the JLEA (typically, GS-15 rank or higher).

4. "Federal Prosecuting Office" or "FPO"
   a. The U.S. Attorneys Offices;
   b. The Criminal Division, Tax Division, Civil Rights Division, Antitrust Division, and Environmental and Natural Resources Division of the Department of Justice; and
   c. Any other litigating component of the Department of Justice with authority to prosecute federal criminal offenses.

5. "Chief Federal Prosecutor" — the head of a FPO.
6. "Confidential Informant" or "CI" — any individual who provides useful and credible information to a JLEA regarding felonious criminal activities, and from whom the JLEA expects or intends to obtain additional useful and credible information regarding such activities in the future.
7. "Cooperating Defendant/Witness" — any individual who:
   a. meets the definition of a CI;
   b. has agreed to testify in a proceeding as a result of having provided information to the JLEA; and
   c. (i) is a defendant or potential witness who has a written agreement with a FPO, pursuant to which the individual has an expectation of future judicial or prosecutive consideration or assistance as a result of having provided information to the JLEA, or
   (ii) is a potential witness who has had a FPO concur in all material aspects of his or her use by the JLEA.
8. "Source of Information" — any individual who:
   a. meets the definition of a CI;
   b. provides information to a JLEA solely as a result of legitimate routine access to information or records, such as an employee of the military, a law enforcement agency, or a legitimate business (e.g., phone company, banks, airlines), and not as a result of criminal association with persons of investigative interest to the JLEA; and
   c. provides such information in a manner consistent with applicable law.
9. "High Level Confidential Informant" — a CI who is part of the senior leadership of an enterprise that
   a. has: (i) a national or international sphere of activities, or (ii) high significance to the JLEA's national objectives, even if the enterprise's sphere of activities is local or regional; and
   b. engages in, or uses others to commit, any of the conduct described below in paragraph (I) (B) (10) (b) (i)–(iv).
10. "Tier 1 Otherwise Illegal Activity" — any activity that:
   a. would constitute a misdemeanor or felony under federal, state, or local law if engaged in by a person acting without authorization; and

    b. that involves

      (i) the commission, or the significant risk of the commission, of any act of violence by a person or persons other than the Confidential Informant;*

      (ii) corrupt conduct, or the significant risk of corrupt conduct, by senior federal, state, or local public officials;

      (iii) the manufacturing, importing, exporting, possession, or trafficking of controlled substances in a quantity equal to or exceeding those quantities specified in U.S. Sentencing Guidelines § 2D1.1(c)(1);

      (iv) financial loss, or the significant risk of financial loss, in an amount equal to or exceeding those amounts specified in U.S. Sentencing Guidelines § 2B1.1(b)(1)(I);**

      (v) a Confidential Informant providing to any person (other than a JLEA agent) any item, service, or expertise that is necessary for the commission of a federal, state, or local offense, which the person otherwise would have difficulty obtaining; or

      (vi) a Confidential Informant providing to any person (other than a JLEA agent) any quantity of a controlled substance, with little or no expectation of its recovery by the JLEA.

11. "Tier 2 Otherwise Illegal Activity" — any other activity that would constitute a misdemeanor or felony under federal, state, or local law if engaged in by a person acting without authorization.

12. "Fugitive" — an individual:

    a. for whom a federal, state, or local law enforcement agency has placed a wanted record in the NCIC (other than for a traffic or petty offense);

---

* Bookmaking that is significantly associated with, or substantially controlled by, organized crime ordinarily will be within the scope of paragraph (I)(B)(10)(b)(i). Thus, for example, where bookmakers have a financial relationship with members or associates of organized crime, or use members or associates of organized crime to collect their debts, the conduct of those bookmakers would create a significant risk of violence, and would therefore fall within the definition of Tier 1 Otherwise Illegal Activity.

** The citations to the U.S. Sentencing Guidelines (U.S.S.G.) Manual are to the 2001 Edition. The references herein to particular U.S.S.G. Sections are intended to remain applicable to the most closely corresponding U.S.S.G. level in subsequent editions of the U.S.S.G. Manual in the event that the cited U.S.S.G. provisions are amended. Thus, it is intended that subsection (iii) of this paragraph will remain applicable to the highest offense level in the Drug Quantity Table in future editions of the U.S.S.G. Manual, and that subsection (iv) of the paragraph will remain applicable to dollar amounts that, in future editions of the U.S.S.G. Manual, trigger sentencing enhancements similar to those set forth in the current section 2B1.1(b)(1)(I). Any ambiguities in this regard should be resolved by the Assistant Attorney General for the Criminal Division.

       b. who is located either within the United States or in a country with which the United States has an extradition treaty; and

       c. whom the law enforcement agency that has placed the wanted record in the NCIC is willing to take into custody upon his or her arrest and, if necessary, seek his or her extradition to its jurisdiction.

13. "Confidential Informant Review Committee" or "CIRC" — a committee, created by a JLEA for purposes of reviewing certain decisions relating to the registration and utilization of CIs, the chair of which is a JLEA official at or above the level of Deputy Assistant Director (or its equivalent) and the membership of which includes the following two representatives designated by the Assistant Attorney General for the Criminal Division of the Department of Justice (each of whom shall be considered a "Criminal Division representative"): (i) a Deputy Assistant Attorney General for the Criminal Division; and (ii) an Assistant U.S. Attorney.

C.   Prohibition on Commitments of Immunity by Federal Law Enforcement Agencies

A JLEA agent does not have any authority to make any promise or commitment that would prevent the government from prosecuting an individual for criminal activity that is not authorized pursuant to paragraph (III)(C) below, or that would limit the use of any evidence by the government, without the prior written approval of the FPO that has primary jurisdiction to prosecute the CI for such criminal activity. A JLEA agent must take the utmost care to avoid giving any person the erroneous impression that he or she has any such authority.

D.   Revealing a Confidential Informant's True Identity

Except in the case of approvals and reviews described below in paragraphs (II)(A)(3) (review of long-term CIs), (III)(B)(8) (coordination concerning payments to CIs), (IV)(D)(1) (notification that CI has obtained privileged information), and (V)(D) (coordination concerning deactivation of CI, but only with respect to a CI whose identity was not previously disclosed), whenever a JLEA is required to make contact of any kind with a FPO pursuant to these Guidelines regarding a CI, the JLEA may not withhold the true identity of the CI from the FPO.

E.   Duty of Candor

Employees of the entities to which these Guidelines apply have a duty of candor in the discharge of their responsibilities pursuant to these Guidelines.

F.   Maintaining Confidentiality

1. A JLEA agent must take the utmost care to avoid conveying any confidential investigative information to a CI (e.g., information relating to electronic surveillance, search warrants, or the identity of other actual or potential informants), other than what is necessary and appropriate for operational reasons.

2. The Chief Federal Prosecutor and his or her designee are required to maintain as confidential the identity of any CI and the information the CI has provided, unless obligated to disclose it by law or Court order. If a JLEA provides the Chief Federal Prosecutor or his or her designee with written material containing such information:

   a. Such individual is obligated to keep it confidential by placing it into a locked file cabinet when not in his or her direct care and custody;

   b. Access to the information shall be restricted to the Chief Federal Prosecutor or his or her designee and personnel deemed necessary to carry out the official duties related to the case;

   c. The Chief Federal Prosecutor or his or her designee is responsible for assuring that each person permitted access to the information is made aware of the need to preserve the security and confidentiality of the information, as provided in this policy;

   d. Prior to disclosure of the information to defense counsel or in open Court, the Chief Federal Prosecutor or his or her designee must give the JLEA an opportunity to discuss such disclosure and must comply with any other applicable provision of 28 C.F.R. §§ 16.21–16.29; and

   e. At the conclusion of a case or investigation, all written materials containing the information that have not been disclosed shall be forwarded to the JLEA that provided them.*

3. Employees of a JLEA and employees of a FPO have a continuing obligation after leaving employment with the Department of Justice and its constituent components to maintain as confidential the identity of any CI and the information he or she provided, unless the employee is obligated to disclose it by law or Court order. See 28 C.F.R. §§ 16.21–16.29.

---

* This requirement shall not prevent the Chief Federal Prosecutor or his or her designee from keeping in the relevant case file materials such as motions, responses, legal memoranda, Court orders, and internal office memoranda and correspondence. If any such materials contain information revealing a CI's true identity, the Chief Federal Prosecutor or his or her designee shall maintain the materials in accordance with the provisions of paragraph I(F)(2)(a)–(d), above.

G.   Exceptions and Dispute Resolution

1. Whenever any of the entities to which these Guidelines apply believes that an exception to any provision of these Guidelines is justified, or whenever there is a dispute between or among any such entities (other than a dispute with the Criminal Division of the Department of Justice) regarding these Guidelines, an exception must be sought from, or the dispute shall be resolved by, the Assistant Attorney General (AAG) for the Criminal Division or his or her designee. The Deputy Attorney General or his or her designee shall hear appeals, if any, from decisions of the AAG.

2. Whenever there is a dispute between the Criminal Division and any of the other entities to which these Guidelines apply, such dispute shall be resolved by the Deputy Attorney General or his or her designee.

3. Any exception granted or dispute resolved pursuant to this paragraph shall be documented in the JLEA's files.

H.   Rights of Third Parties

Nothing in these Guidelines is intended to create or does create an enforceable legal right or private right of action by a CI or any other person.

I.   Compliance

1. Within 120 days of the approval of these Guidelines by the Attorney General, each JLEA shall develop agency-specific guidelines that comply with these Guidelines, and submit such agency-specific guidelines to the AAG for the Criminal Division for review. The agency-specific guidelines must ensure, at a minimum, that the JLEA's agents receive sufficient initial and in-service training in the use of CIs consistent with these Guidelines, and that compliance with these Guidelines is considered in the annual performance appraisal of its agents. As part of such compliance the JLEA shall designate a senior official to oversee all aspects of its CI program, including the training of agents; registration, review and termination of CIs; and notifications to outside entities.

2. Within 30 days of the approval of these Guidelines, each JLEA shall establish a Confidential Informant Review Committee (CIRC) for the purpose of conducting the review procedures specified in paragraphs (II)(A)(3), (II)(D)(1), and (II)(D)(2).

II.   Registering a Confidential Informant

A.   Suitability Determination

1.   *Initial Suitability Determination*

Prior to utilizing a person as a CI, a case agent of a JLEA shall complete and sign a written Initial Suitability Report and Recommendation, which shall be forwarded to a Field Manager for his or her written approval. In completing the Initial Suitability Report and Recommendation, the case agent must address the following factors (or indicate that a particular factor is not applicable):

   a. the person's age;
   b. the person's alien status;
   c. whether the person is a public official, law enforcement officer, union official, employee of a financial institution or school, member of the military services, a representative or affiliate of the media, or a party to, or in a position to be a party to, privileged communications (e.g., a member of the clergy, a physician, or a lawyer);
   d. the extent to which the person would make use of his or her affiliations with legitimate organizations in order to provide information or assistance to the JLEA, and the ability of the JLEA to ensure that the person's information or assistance is limited to criminal matters;
   e. the extent to which the person's information or assistance would be relevant to a present or potential investigation or prosecution and the importance of such investigation or prosecution;
   f. the nature of any relationship between the CI and the subject or target of an existing or potential investigation or prosecution, including but not limited to a current or former spousal relationship or other family tie, and any current or former employment or financial relationship;
   g. the person's motivation in providing information or assistance, including any consideration sought from the government for this assistance;
   h. the risk that the person might adversely affect a present or potential investigation or prosecution;
   i. the extent to which the person's information or assistance can be corroborated;
   j. the person's reliability and truthfulness;
   k. the person's prior record as a witness in any proceeding;

l. whether the person has a criminal history, is reasonably believed to be the subject or target of a pending criminal investigation, is under arrest, or has been charged in a pending prosecution;

m. whether the person is reasonably believed to pose a danger to the public or other criminal threat, or is reasonably believed to pose a risk of flight;

n. whether the person is a substance abuser or has a history of substance abuse;

o. whether the person is a relative of an employee of any law enforcement agency;

p. the risk of physical harm that may occur to the person or his or her immediate family or close associates as a result of providing information or assistance to the JLEA; and

q. the record of the JLEA and the record of any other law enforcement agency (if available to the JLEA) regarding the person's prior or current service as a CI, Cooperating Defendant/Witness, or Source of Information, including, but not limited to, any information regarding whether the person was at any time terminated for cause.

2. *Continuing Suitability Review*

a. Each CI's file shall be reviewed by the case agent at least annually. The case agent shall complete and sign a written Continuing Suitability Report and Recommendation, which shall be forwarded to a Field Manager for his or her written approval. In completing the Continuing Suitability Report and Recommendation, the case agent must address the factors set forth above in paragraph (II)(A)(1) (or indicate that a particular factor is not applicable) and, in addition, the length of time that the individual has been registered as a CI and the length of time that the individual has been handled by the same agent or agents.

b. Each JLEA shall establish systems to ensure that all available information that might materially alter a prior suitability determination, including, but not limited to, information pertaining to unauthorized illegal activity by the CI, is promptly reported to a Field Manager and then recorded and maintained in the CI's file. See (IV)(B)(2) below. Upon receipt of any such information, the Field Manager shall ensure that a new Continuing Suitability Report and Recommendation is promptly prepared in light of such new information.

3. *Review of Long-Term Confidential Informants**

    a. When a CI has been registered for more than six consecutive years, and, to the extent such a CI remains open, every six years thereafter, the CIRC shall review the CI's completed Initial and Continuing Suitability Reports and Recommendations and decide whether, and under what conditions, the individual should continue to be utilized as a CI. A Criminal Division representative on the CIRC who disagrees with the decision to approve the continued use of such an individual as a Confidential Informant may seek review of that decision pursuant to paragraph (I)(G).

    b. Every three years after a CI's file is reviewed pursuant to the provisions of paragraph (II)(A)(3)(a), if the CI remains registered, the JLEA shall conduct an internal review, including review by a designated senior headquarters official, of the CI's completed Initial and Continuing Suitability Reports and Recommendations. If the designated senior headquarters official decides that there are any apparent or potential problems that may warrant any change in the use of the CI, the official shall (i) consult the appropriate Senior Field Manager and (ii) provide the Initial and Continuing Suitability Reports and Recommendations to the CIRC for review in accord with paragraph (II)(A)(3)(a).

B.   Registration

After a Field Manager has approved an individual as suitable to be a CI, the individual shall be registered with that JLEA as a CI. In registering a CI, the JLEA shall, at a minimum, document or include the following in the CI's files:

    1. a photograph of the CI;
    2. the JLEA's efforts to establish the CI's true identity;
    3. the results of a criminal history check for the CI;
    4. the Initial Suitability Report and Recommendation;
    5. any promises or benefits, and the terms of such promises or benefits, that are given a CI by a JLEA or any other law enforcement agency (if available to the JLEA);

---

* This provision did not apply until one year after these Guidelines' original effective date of January 8, 2001, when the first set of Continuing Suitability Reports and Recommendations was completed. Further, during the first three years that this provision is in effect, each CIRC may stagger the review of some long-term CIs in order to even out the number of files that must initially be reviewed. However, no later than four years after the original effective date of these Guidelines, all of the CIs who were registered for more than six consecutive years as of the original effective date of these Guidelines must be reviewed pursuant to this provision.

6. any promises or benefits, and the terms of such promises or benefits, that are given a CI by any FPO or any state or local prosecuting office (if available to the JLEA); and
7. all information that is required to be documented in the CI's files pursuant to these Guidelines (e.g., the provision of the instructions set forth in the next paragraph).

C.   Instructions

1. In registering a CI, at least one agent of the JLEA, along with one additional agent or other law enforcement official present as a witness, shall review with the CI written instructions that state that:
    a. information provided by the CI to the JLEA must be truthful;
    b. the CI's assistance and the information provided are entirely voluntary;
    c. the U.S. Government will strive to protect the CI's identity but cannot guarantee that it will not be divulged;
    d. [if applicable:] the JLEA on its own cannot promise or agree to any immunity from prosecution or other consideration by a Federal Prosecutor's Office or a Court in exchange for the CI's cooperation, since the decision to confer any such benefit lies within the exclusive discretion of the Federal Prosecutor's Office and the Court. However, the JLEA will consider (but not necessarily act upon) a request by the CI to advise the appropriate Federal Prosecutor's Office or Court of the nature and extent of his or her assistance to the JLEA;*
    e. [if applicable:] the CI has not been authorized to engage in any criminal activity and has no immunity from prosecution for any unauthorized criminal activity;**
    f. the CI must abide by the instructions of the JLEA and must not take or seek to take any independent action on behalf of the U.S. Government;
    g. the CI is not an employee of the U.S. Government and may not represent himself or herself as such;

---

*   This instruction should be provided if there is any apparent issue of criminal liability or penalties that relates to the CI. Whether or not this instruction is given to a CI, the JLEA does not have any authority to make any promise or commitment that would prevent the government from prosecuting an individual, except as provided in paragraphs (I)(C) above and (III)(C) below, and a JLEA agent must avoid giving any person the erroneous impression that he or she has any such authority.
**   This instruction should be provided to any CI who is not authorized to engage in otherwise illegal activity. See paragraph (III)(C)(4) for instructions that must be provided to a CI who is, in fact, authorized to engage in otherwise illegal conduct.

       h. the CI may not enter into any contract or incur any obligation on behalf of the U.S. Government, except as specifically instructed and approved by the JLEA;

       i. the JLEA cannot guarantee any rewards, payments, or other compensation to the CI;

       j. in the event that the CI receives any rewards, payments, or other compensation from the JLEA, the CI is liable for any taxes that may be owed; and

       k. [if applicable:] no promises or commitments can be made, except by the Immigration and Naturalization Service, regarding the alien status of any person or the right of any person to enter or remain in the United States.*

2. The content and meaning of each of the foregoing instructional points must be clearly conveyed to the CI. Immediately after these instructions have been given, the agent shall require the CI to acknowledge his or her receipt and understanding of the instructions. The agent and the other law enforcement official shall document that the instructions were reviewed with the CI and that the CI acknowledged the instructions and his or her understanding of them. As soon as practicable thereafter, a Field Manager shall review and, if warranted, approve the documentation.

3. The instruction and documentation procedures shall be repeated whenever it appears necessary or prudent to do so, and in any event at least every 12 months.

D.   Special Approval Requirements

1.   *High Level Confidential Informants*

    a. Prior to utilizing an individual as a High Level Confidential Informant, a case agent of a JLEA shall first obtain the written approval of the CIRC. A Criminal Division representative on the CIRC who disagrees with a decision to approve the use of an individual as a High Level Confidential Informant may seek review of that decision pursuant to paragraph (I)(G).

    b. In deciding whether to approve the use of a High Level Confidential Informant, the CIRC shall have access to any Initial or Completed Suitability Reports and Recommendations for the individual in question.

---

* This instruction should be provided if there is any apparent issue of immigration status that relates to the CI and the JLEA is not the Immigration and Naturalization Service.

c. After a final decision has been made to approve the use of a High Level Confidential Informant, the CIRC shall consider whether to notify the Chief Federal Prosecutor of any FPO that is participating in the conduct of an investigation that is, or would be, utilizing the High Level Confidential Informant, or any FPO that has been, or would be, working with that individual in connection with a prosecution, of the decision to approve that individual as a High Level Confidential Informant. If the CIRC determines that no such notification shall be made, the reason or reasons for the determination shall be provided to the Criminal Division representatives on the CIRC. A Criminal Division representative on the CIRC who disagrees with a decision not to provide such notification may seek review of that decision pursuant to paragraph (I)(G).

2. *Individuals under the Obligation of a Legal Privilege of Confidentiality or Affiliated with the Media*

a. Prior to utilizing as a Confidential Informant an individual who is under the obligation of a legal privilege of confidentiality or affiliated with the media, a case agent of a JLEA shall first obtain the written approval of the CIRC. A Criminal Division representative on the CIRC who disagrees with a decision to approve the use of such an individual as a Confidential Informant may seek review of that decision pursuant to paragraph (I)(G).

b. In deciding whether to approve the use as a Confidential Informant of an individual who is under the obligation of a legal privilege of confidentiality or affiliated with the media, the CIRC shall have access to any Initial or Completed Suitability Reports and Recommendations for the individual in question.

c. After a final decision has been made to approve the use of an individual who is under the obligation of a legal privilege of confidentiality or affiliated with the media as a Confidential Informant, the CIRC shall consider whether to notify the Chief Federal Prosecutor of any FPO that is participating in the conduct of an investigation that is, or would be, utilizing the individual, or any FPO that has been, or would be, working with that individual in connection with a prosecution, of the decision to approve that individual as a Confidential Informant. If the CIRC determines that no such notification shall be made, the reason or reasons for the determination shall be provided to the Criminal Division representatives on the CIRC. A Criminal Division representative on the CIRC who disagrees with a decision not to provide such notification may seek review of that decision pursuant to paragraph (I)(G).

3. *Federal Prisoners, Probationers, Parolees, Detainees, and Supervised Releasees*

a. Consistent with extant Department of Justice requirements, a JLEA must receive the approval of the Criminal Division's Office of Enforcement Operations (OEO) prior to utilizing as a CI an individual who is in the custody of the U.S. Marshals Service or the Bureau of Prisons, or who is under Bureau of Prisons supervision. See U.S.A.M. § 9-21.050.

b. Prior to utilizing a federal probationer, parolee, or supervised releasee as a CI, a Field Manager of a JLEA shall determine if the use of that person in such a capacity would violate the terms and conditions of the person's probation, parole, or supervised release. If the Field Manger has reason to believe that it would violate such terms and conditions, prior to using the person as a CI, the Field Manager or his or her designee must obtain the permission of a federal probation, parole, or supervised release official with authority to grant such permission, which permission shall be documented in the CI's files. If such permission is denied or it is inappropriate for operational reasons to contact the appropriate federal official, the JLEA may seek to obtain authorization for the use of such individual as a CI from the Court then responsible for the individual's probation, parole, or supervised release, provided that the JLEA first consults with the FPO for that District.

c. In situations where a FPO is either participating in the conduct of an investigation by a JLEA in which a federal probationer, parolee, or supervised releasee would be utilized as a CI, or where a FPO would be working with a federal probationer, parolee, or supervised releasee in connection with a prosecution, the JLEA shall notify the attorney assigned to the matter prior to using the person as a CI.

4. *Current or Former Participants in the Witness Security Program*

a. Consistent with extant Department of Justice requirements, a JLEA must receive the approval of OEO and the sponsoring prosecutor (or his or her successor) prior to utilizing as a CI a current or former participant in the Federal Witness Security Program, provided further that the OEO will coordinate such matters with the U.S. Marshals Service. See USAM § 9-21.800.

b. In situations where a FPO is either participating in the conduct of an investigation by a JLEA in which a current or former participant in the Witness Security Program would be utilized as a CI, or where a FPO would be working with a current or former participant in the Witness Security Program in connection with a prosecution, the JLEA shall notify the attorney assigned to the matter prior to using the person as a CI.

5. *State or Local Prisoners, Probationers, Parolees, or Supervised Releasees*

a. Prior to utilizing a state or local prisoner, probationer, parolee, or supervised releasee as a CI, a Field Manager of a JLEA shall determine if the use of that person in such a capacity would violate the terms and conditions of the person's incarceration, probation, parole, or supervised release. If the Field Manger has reason to believe that it would violate such terms and conditions, prior to using the person as a CI, the Field Manager or his or her designee must obtain the permission of a state or local prison, probation, parole, or supervised release official with authority to grant such permission, which permission shall be documented in the CI's files. If such permission is denied or it is inappropriate for operational reasons to contact the appropriate state or local official, the JLEA may seek to obtain authorization for the use of such individual as a CI from the state or local Court then responsible for the individual's incarceration, probation, parole, or supervised release.

b. In situations where a FPO is either participating in the conduct of an investigation by a JLEA in which a state or local prisoner, probationer, parolee, or supervised releasee would be utilized as a CI, or where a FPO would be working with a state or local prisoner, probationer, parolee, or supervised releasee in connection with a prosecution, the JLEA shall notify the attorney assigned to the matter prior to using the person as a CI.

6. *Fugitives*

a. Except as provided below, a JLEA shall have no communication with a current or former CI who is a fugitive.

b. A JLEA is permitted to have communication with a current or former CI who is a fugitive:

(i) if the communication is part of a legitimate effort by that JLEA to arrest the fugitive; or

(ii) if approved, in advance whenever possible, by a Senior Field Manager of any federal, state, or local law enforcement agency that has a wanted record for the individual in the NCIC and, in the case of a federal warrant, by the FPO for the issuing District.

c. A JLEA that has communication with a fugitive must promptly report such communication to all federal, state, and local law enforcement agencies and other law enforcement agencies having a wanted record for the individual in the NCIC, and document those communications in the CI's files.

III. Responsibilities Regarding Registered Confidential Informants

A. General Provisions

1. *No Interference with an Investigation of a Confidential Informant*

A JLEA agent must take the utmost care to avoid interfering with or impeding any criminal investigation or arrest of a CI. No agent shall reveal to a CI any information relating to an investigation of the CI. An agent shall not confirm or deny the existence of any investigation of the CI, unless authorized to do so by the Chief Federal Prosecutor; nor shall an agent agree to a request from a CI to determine whether the CI is the subject of any investigation.

2. *Prohibited Transactions and Relationships*

a. A JLEA agent shall not: (i) exchange gifts with a CI; (ii) provide the CI with any thing of more than nominal value; (iii) receive any thing of more than nominal value from a CI; or (iv) engage in any business or financial transactions with a CI. Except as authorized pursuant to paragraph (III)(B) below, any exception to this provision requires the written approval of a Field Manager, in advance whenever possible, based on a written finding by the Field Manager that the event or transaction in question is necessary and appropriate for operational reasons. This written finding shall be maintained in the CI's files.

b. A Federal Law Enforcement agent shall not socialize with a CI except to the extent necessary and appropriate for operational reasons.

c. In situations where a FPO is either participating in the conduct of an investigation by a JLEA that is utilizing a CI, or working with a CI in connection with a prosecution, the JLEA shall notify the attorney assigned to the matter, in advance whenever possible, if the JLEA approves an exception under paragraph (III)(A)(2)(a) or if a Federal Law Enforcement agent socializes with a CI in a manner not permitted under paragraph (III)(A)(2)(b).

B.   Monetary Payments

1.   General
Monies that a JLEA pays to a CI in the form of fees and rewards shall be commensurate with the value, as determined by the JLEA, of the information he or she provided or the assistance he or she rendered to that JLEA. A JLEA's reimbursement of expenses incurred by a CI shall be based upon actual expenses incurred.

2.   Prohibition against Contingent Payments
Under no circumstances shall any payments to a CI be contingent upon the conviction or punishment of any individual.

3.   Approval for a Single Payment
A single payment of between $2,500 and $25,000 per case to a CI must be authorized, at a minimum, by a JLEA's Senior Field Manager. A single payment in excess of $25,000 per case shall be made only with the authorization of the Senior Field Manager and the express approval of a designated senior headquarters official.

4.   Approval for Annual Payments
Consistent with paragraph (III)(B)(3) above, payments by a JLEA to a CI that exceed an aggregate of $100,000 within a one-year period, as that period is defined by the JLEA, shall be made only with the authorization of the Senior Field Manager and the express approval of a designated senior headquarters official. The headquarters official may authorize additional aggregate annual payments in increments of $50,000 or less.

5.   Approval for Aggregate Payments
Consistent with paragraphs (III)(B)(3)–(4), and regardless of the time frame, any payments by a JLEA to a CI that exceed an aggregate of $200,000 shall be made only with the authorization of the Senior Field Manager and the express approval of a designated senior headquarters official. After the headquarters official has approved payments to a CI that exceed an aggregate of $200,000, the headquarters official may authorize, subject to paragraph (III)(B)(4) above, additional aggregate payments in increments of $100,000 or less.

6.   Documentation of Payment

The payment of any monies to a CI shall be witnessed by at least two law enforcement representatives. Immediately after receiving a payment, the CI shall be required to sign or initial, and date, a written receipt.* At the time of the payment, the representatives shall advise the CI that the monies may be taxable income that must be reported to appropriate tax authorities. Thereafter, those representatives shall document the payment and the advice of taxability in the JLEA's files. The documentation of payment shall specify whether the payment is for information, services, or expenses.

7.   Accounting and Reconciliation Procedures

Each JLEA shall establish accounting and reconciliation procedures to comply with these Guidelines. Among other things, these procedures shall reflect all monies paid to a CI subsequent to the issuance of these Guidelines.

8.   Coordination with Prosecution

In situations where a FPO is either participating in the conduct of an investigation by a JLEA that is utilizing a CI, or working with a CI in connection with a prosecution, the JLEA shall coordinate with the attorney assigned to the matter, in advance whenever possible, the payment of monies to the CI pursuant to paragraphs (III)(B)(3)–(5) above.

C.   Authorization of Otherwise Illegal Activity

1.   General Provisions

a.   A JLEA shall not authorize a CI to engage in any activity that otherwise would constitute a misdemeanor or felony under federal, state, or local law if engaged in by a person acting without authorization, except as provided in the authorization provisions in paragraph (III)(C)(2) below.

b.   A JLEA is never permitted to authorize a CI to:
   (i)   participate in an act of violence;
   (ii)   participate in an act that constitutes obstruction of justice (e.g., perjury, witness tampering, witness intimidation, entrapment, or the fabrication, alteration, or destruction of evidence);
   (iii) participate in an act designed to obtain information for the JLEA that would be unlawful if conducted by a law enforcement agent (e.g., breaking and entering, illegal wiretapping, illegal opening

---

* The CI may sign or initial the written receipt by using a pseudonym which has been previously approved and documented in the CI's files and designated for use by only one CI.

or tampering with the mail, or trespass amounting to an illegal search); or

(iv) initiate or instigate a plan or strategy to commit a federal, state, or local offense.

2. *Authorization*

a. Tier 1 Otherwise Illegal Activity must be authorized in advance and in writing for a specified period, not to exceed 90 days, by:
   (i) a JLEA's Special Agent in Charge (or the equivalent); and
   (ii) the appropriate Chief Federal Prosecutor.*

b. Tier 2 Otherwise Illegal Activity must be authorized in advance and in writing for a specified period, not to exceed 90 days, by a JLEA's Senior Field Manager.

c. For purposes of this paragraph, the "appropriate Chief Federal Prosecutor" is the Chief Federal Prosecutor that: (i) is participating in the conduct of an investigation by a JLEA that is utilizing that active CI, or is working with that active CI in connection with a prosecution; (ii) with respect to Otherwise Illegal Activity that would constitute a violation of federal law, would have primary jurisdiction to prosecute the Otherwise Illegal Activity; or (iii) with respect to Otherwise Illegal Activity that would constitute a violation only of state or local law, is located where the otherwise criminal activity is to occur.

3. *Findings*

a. The JLEA official who authorizes Tier 1 or 2 Otherwise Illegal Activity must make a finding, which shall be documented in the CI's files, that authorization for the CI to engage in the Tier 1 or 2 Otherwise Illegal Activity is
   (i) necessary either to:
      (A) obtain information or evidence essential for the success of an investigation that is not reasonably available without such authorization, or
      (B) prevent death, serious bodily injury, or significant damage to property; and

---

* Even without an express act of Congress authorizing the conduct at issue, it is within the power and the duty of federal prosecutors, as executive branch officers, to take reasonable measures to discharge the duties imposed on them as executive branch officers, and they will be immune from state action if they take such measures under color of federal law and in good faith.

(ii) that in either case the benefits to be obtained from the CI's participation in the Tier 1 or 2 Otherwise Illegal Activity outweigh the risks.

b. In making these findings, the JLEA shall consider, among other things:
   (i)   the importance of the investigation;
   (ii) the likelihood that the information or evidence sought will be obtained;
   (iii) the risk that the CI might misunderstand or exceed the scope of his authorization;
   (iv) the extent of the CI's participation in the Otherwise Illegal Activity;
   (v)   the risk that the JLEA will not be able to supervise closely the CI's participation in the Otherwise Illegal Activity;
   (vi) the risk of violence, physical injury, property damage, and financial loss to the CI or others; and
   (vii) the risk that the JLEA will not be able to ensure that the CI does not profit from his or her participation in the authorized Otherwise Illegal Activity.

4.   *Instructions*

a. After a CI is authorized to engage in Tier 1 or 2 Otherwise Illegal Activity, at least one agent of the JLEA, along with one additional agent or other law enforcement official present as a witness, shall review with the CI written instructions that state, at a minimum, that:
   (i)   the CI is authorized only to engage in the specific conduct set forth in the written authorization described above and not in any other illegal activity;
   (ii) the CI's authorization is limited to the time period specified in the written authorization;
   (iii) under no circumstance may the CI:
         (A) participate in an act of violence;
         (B) participate in an act that constitutes obstruction of justice (e.g., perjury, witness tampering, witness intimidation, entrapment, or the fabrication, alteration, or destruction of evidence);
         (C) participate in an act designed to obtain information for the JLEA that would be unlawful if conducted by a law enforcement agent (e.g., breaking and entering, illegal wiretapping, illegal opening or tampering with the mail, or trespass amounting to an illegal search); or

(D) initiate or instigate a plan or strategy to commit a federal, state, or local offense;

(iv) if the CI is asked by any person to participate in any such prohibited conduct, or if he or she learns of plans to engage in such conduct, he or she must immediately report the matter to his or her contact agent; and

(v) participation in any prohibited conduct could subject the CI to full criminal prosecution.

b. Immediately after these instructions have been given, the CI shall be required to sign or initial, and date, a written acknowledgment of the instructions.*[0] As soon as practicable thereafter, a Field Manager shall review and, if warranted, approve the written acknowledgment.

5.   *Precautionary Measures*

Whenever a JLEA has authorized a CI to engage in Tier 1 or 2 Otherwise Illegal Activity, it must take all reasonable steps to: (a) supervise closely the illegal activities of the CI; (b) minimize the adverse effect of the authorized Otherwise Illegal Activity on innocent individuals; and (c) ensure that the CI does not profit from his or her participation in the authorized Otherwise Illegal Activity.

6.   *Suspension of Authorization*

Whenever a JLEA cannot, for legitimate reasons unrelated to the CI's conduct (e.g., unavailability of the case agent), comply with the precautionary measures described above, it shall immediately: (a) suspend the CI's authorization to engage in Otherwise Illegal Activity until such time as the precautionary measures can be complied with; (b) inform the CI that his or her authorization to engage in any Otherwise Illegal Activity has been suspended until that time; and (c) document these actions in the CI's files.

7.   *Revocation of Authorization*

a. If a JLEA has reason to believe that a CI has failed to comply with the specific terms of the authorization of Tier 1 or 2 Otherwise Illegal Activity, it shall immediately: (i) revoke the CI's authorization to engage in Otherwise Illegal Activity; (ii) inform the CI that he or she is no longer authorized to engage in any Otherwise Illegal Activity;

---

* [0] Even without an express act of Congress authorizing the conduct at issue, it is within the power and the duty of federal prosecutors, as executive branch officers, to take reasonable measures to discharge the duties imposed on them as executive branch officers, and they will be immune from state action if they take such measures under color of federal law and in good faith.

(iii) comply with the notification requirement of paragraph (IV)(B) below; (iv) make a determination whether the CI should be deactivated pursuant to paragraph (V); and (v) document these actions in the CI's files.

b. Immediately after the CI has been informed that he or she is no longer authorized to engage in any Otherwise Illegal Activity, the CI shall be required to sign or initial, and date, a written acknowledgment that he or she has been informed of this fact.[*1] As soon as practicable thereafter, a Field Manager shall review and, if warranted, approve the written acknowledgment.

8. *Renewal and Expansion of Authorization*

a. A JLEA that seeks to reauthorize any CI to engage in Tier 1 or 2 Otherwise Illegal Activity after the expiration of the authorized time period, or after revocation of authorization, must first comply with the procedures set forth above in paragraphs (III)(C)(2)–(5).

b. A JLEA that seeks to expand in any material way a CI's authorization to engage in Tier 1 or 2 Otherwise Illegal Activity by the JLEA must first comply with the procedures set forth above in paragraphs (III)(C)(2)–(5).

9. *Emergency Authorization*

a. In exceptional circumstances, a JLEA's Special Agent in Charge (or the equivalent) and the appropriate Chief Federal Prosecutor may orally authorize a CI to engage in Tier 1 Otherwise Illegal Activity without complying with the documentation requirements of paragraphs (III)(C)(2)–(4) above when they each determine that a highly significant and unanticipated investigative opportunity would be lost were the time taken to comply with these requirements. In such an event, the documentation requirements, as well as a written justification for the oral authorization, shall be completed within 48 hours of the oral approval and maintained in the CI's files.

[*1] The CI may sign or initial the written acknowledgment by using a pseudonym which has been previously approved and documented in the CI's files and designated for use by only one CI. If the CI refuses to sign or initial the written acknowledgment, the JLEA agent who informed the CI of the revocation of authorization shall document that the CI has orally acknowledged being so informed and the Field Manager shall, as soon as practicable thereafter, review and, if warranted, approve the written documentation.

b. In exceptional circumstances, a JLEA's Senior Field Manager may orally authorize a CI to engage in Tier 2 Otherwise Illegal Activity without complying with the documentation requirements of paragraphs (III)(C)(2)–(4) above when he or she determines that a highly significant and unanticipated investigative opportunity would be lost were the time taken to comply with these requirements. In such an event, the documentation requirements, as well as a written justification for the oral authorization, shall be completed within 48 hours of the oral approval and maintained in the CI's files.

10. Designees

A JLEA's Special Agent in Charge (or the equivalent) and the appropriate Chief Federal Prosecutor may, with the concurrence of each other, agree to designate particular individuals in their respective offices to carry out the approval functions assigned to them above in paragraphs (III)(C)(2)–(9).

D. Listing a Confidential Informant in an Electronic Surveillance Application

1. A JLEA shall not name a CI as a named interceptee or a violator in an affidavit in support of an application made pursuant to 18 USC § 2516 for an electronic surveillance order unless the JLEA believes that: (a) omitting the name of the CI from the affidavit would endanger that person's life or otherwise jeopardize an ongoing investigation; or (b) the CI is a bona fide subject of the investigation based on his or her suspected involvement in unauthorized criminal activity.
2. In the event that a CI is named in an electronic surveillance affidavit under paragraph (III)(D)(1) above, the JLEA must inform the Federal prosecutor making the application and the Court to which the application is made of the actual status of the CI.

IV. Special Notification Requirements

A. Notification of Investigation or Prosecution

1. When a JLEA has reasonable grounds to believe that a current or former CI is being prosecuted by, is the target of an investigation by, or is expected to become a target of an investigation by a FPO for engaging in alleged felonious criminal activity, a Special Agent in Charge (or the equivalent) of the JLEA must immediately notify the

Chief Federal Prosecutor of that individual's status as a current or former CI.*²

2. Whenever such a notification is provided, the Chief Federal Prosecutor and Special Agent in Charge (or the equivalent), with the concurrence of each other, shall notify any other federal, state or local prosecutor's offices or law enforcement agencies that are participating in the investigation or prosecution of the CI.

B.   Notification of Unauthorized Illegal Activity

1. Whenever a JLEA has reasonable grounds to believe that a CI who is currently authorized to engage in specific Tier 1 or 2 Otherwise Illegal Activity has engaged in unauthorized criminal activity, or whenever a JLEA knows that a CI who has no current authorization to engage in any Tier 1 or 2 Otherwise Illegal Activity has engaged in any criminal activity, a Special Agent in Charge of the JLEA (or the equivalent) shall immediately notify the following Chief Federal Prosecutors of the CI's criminal activity and his or her status as a CI:

   a. the Chief Federal Prosecutor whose District is located where the criminal activity primarily occurred, unless a state or local prosecuting office in that District has filed charges against the CI for the criminal activity and there clearly is no basis for federal prosecution in that District by the Chief Federal Prosecutor;

   b. the Chief Federal Prosecutor, if any, whose District is participating in the conduct of an investigation that is utilizing that active CI, or is working with that active CI in connection with a prosecution; and

   c. the Chief Federal Prosecutor, if any, who authorized the CI to engage in Tier 1 Otherwise Illegal Activity pursuant to paragraph (III)(C)(2)(a) above.**³

2. Whenever such notifications are provided, the Chief Federal Prosecutor(s) of the FPOs and the Special Agent in Charge (or the equivalent), with the concurrence of each other, shall notify any state or local prosecutor's office that has jurisdiction over the CI's criminal activity, and that has not already filed charges against the CI for the criminal activity, of the fact that the CI has engaged in such criminal activity. The Chief Federal Prosecutor(s) and the Special Agent in

---

* ² A target is "a person as to whom the prosecutor or the grand jury has substantial evidence linking him or her to the commission of a crime and who, in the judgment of the prosecutor, is a putative defendant." U.S.A.M. § 9-11.151.

** ³ Whenever such notifications to FPOs are provided, the JLEA must also comply with the Continuing Suitability requirements described above in paragraph (II)(A)(2).

Charge (or the equivalent) are not required, but may with the con-currence of each other, also notify the state and local prosecutor's office of the person's status as a CI.

C. Notification Regarding Certain Federal Judicial Proceedings

Whenever a JLEA has reasonable grounds to believe that: (1) a current or former CI has been called to testify by the prosecution in any federal grand jury or judicial proceeding; (2) the statements of a current or former CI have been, or will be, utilized by the prosecution in any federal judicial proceeding; or (3) a federal prosecutor intends to represent to a Court or jury that a current or former CI is or was a coconspirator or other criminally culpable participant in any criminal activity, a Special Agent in Charge (or the equiv-alent) of the JLEA shall immediately notify the Chief Federal Prosecutor for that proceeding of the individual's status as a current or former CI.

D. Privileged or Exculpatory Information

1. In situations where a FPO is either participating in the conduct of an investigation by a JLEA that is utilizing a CI, or working with a CI in connection with a prosecution, the JLEA shall notify the attorney assigned to the matter, in advance whenever possible, if the JLEA has reasonable grounds to believe that a CI will obtain or provide infor-mation that is subject to, or arguably subject to, a legal privilege of confidentiality belonging to someone other than the CI.

2. If the JLEA has reasonable grounds to believe that a current or former CI has information that is exculpatory as to a person who is expected to become a target of an investigation, or as to a target of an investi-gation, or as to a defendant (including a convicted defendant), the JLEA shall notify the Chief Federal Prosecutor responsible for the investigation or prosecution of such exculpatory information.

E. Responding to Requests from Chief Federal Prosecutors Regarding a Confidential Informant

If a Chief Federal Prosecutor seeks information from a Special Agent in Charge (or the equivalent) as to whether a particular individual is a current or former CI, and states the specific basis for his or her request, the Special Agent in Charge (or the equivalent) shall provide such information promptly. If the Special Agent in Charge (or the equivalent) has an objection to pro-viding such information based on specific circumstances of the case, he or she shall explain the objection to the Chief Federal Prosecutor making the request and any remaining disagreement as to whether the information should be provided shall be resolved pursuant to paragraph (I)(G).

F.   File Reviews

Whenever a JLEA discloses any information about a CI to a FPO pursuant to paragraphs (IV)(A)–(E), the Special Agent in Charge (or the equivalent) and the Chief Federal Prosecutor shall consult to facilitate any review and copying of the CI's files by the Chief Federal Prosecutor that might be necessary for the Chief Federal Prosecutor to fulfill his or her office's disclosure obligations.

G.   Designees

A Special Agent in Charge (or the equivalent) and a Chief Federal Prosecutor may, with the concurrence of each other, agree to designate particular individuals in their respective offices to carry out the functions assigned to them in paragraphs (IV)(A)–(F).

V.   Deactivation of Confidential Informants

A.   General Provisions

A JLEA that determines that a CI should be deactivated for cause or for any other reason shall immediately:

1. deactivate the individual;
2. document the reasons for the decision to deactivate the individual as a CI in the CI's files;
3. if the CI can be located, notify the CI that he or she has been deactivated as a CI and obtain documentation that such notification was provided in the same manner as set forth in paragraph (II)(C)(2); and
4. if the CI was authorized to engage in Tier 1 or Tier 2 Otherwise Illegal Activity pursuant to paragraph (Ill)(CX2)(a)–(b), revoke that authorization under the provisions of paragraph (III)(CX7).

B.   Delayed Notification to a Confidential Informant

A JLEA may delay providing the notification to the CI described above in paragraph (V)(Λ)(3) during the time such notification might jeopardize an ongoing investigation or prosecution or might cause the flight from prosecution of any person. Whenever a decision is made to delay providing a notification, that decision, and the reasons supporting it, must be documented in the CI's files.

C.   Contacts with Former Confidential Informants Deactivated for Cause

Absent exceptional circumstances that are approved by a Senior Field Manager, in advance whenever possible, an agent of a JLEA shall not initiate contacts with, or respond to contacts from, a former CI who has been deactivated for cause. When granted, such approval shall be documented in the CI's files.

D.   Coordination with Prosecutors

In situations where a FPO is either participating in the conduct of an investigation by a JLEA that is utilizing a CI, or working with a CI in connection with a prosecution, the JLEA shall coordinate with the attorney assigned to the matter, in advance whenever possible, regarding any of the decisions described in paragraphs (V)(A)–(C).

Date: May 30, 2002
John Ashcroft
Attorney General

Appendix II

The Attorney General Guidelines on Federal Bureau of Investigation Undercover Operations

Preamble

The following Guidelines on the use of undercover activities and operations by the Federal Bureau of Investigation (FBI) are issued under the authority of the Attorney General as provided in sections 509, 510, and 533 of title 28, United States Code. They apply to investigations conducted by the FBI pursuant to the Attorney General Guidelines on General Crimes, Racketeering Enterprise and Terrorism Enterprise Investigations.

I.   Introduction

The use of undercover techniques, including proprietary business entities, is essential to the detection, prevention, and prosecution of white collar crimes, public corruption, terrorism, organized crime, offenses involving controlled substances, and other priority areas of investigation. However, these techniques inherently involve an element of deception and may require cooperation with persons whose motivation and conduct are open to question, and so should be carefully considered and monitored.

II. Definitions

A. **"Undercover Activities"** means any investigative activity involving the use of an assumed name or cover identity by an employee of the FBI or another federal, state, or local law enforcement organization working with the FBI.

B. **"Undercover Operation"** means an investigation involving a series of related undercover activities over a period of time by an undercover employee. For purposes of these Guidelines, a "series of related undercover activities" generally consists of more than three separate substantive contacts by an undercover employee with the individual(s) under investigation. However, undercover activity involving sensitive or fiscal circumstances constitutes an undercover operation regardless of the number of contacts involved. A contact is "substantive" if it is a communication with another person, whether by oral, written, wire, or electronic means, which includes information of investigative interest. Mere incidental contact, e.g., a conversation that establishes an agreed time and location for another meeting, is not a substantive contact within the meaning of these Guidelines.

Note: In the context of online communications, such as e-mail and Internet Relay Chat (IRC), multiple transmissions or e-mail messages can constitute one contact, much like a series of verbal exchanges can comprise a single conversation. Factors to be considered in determining whether multiple online transmissions constitute a single contact or multiple contacts include the time between transmissions, the number of transmissions, the number of interruptions, topical transitions, and the media by which the communications are exchanged (i.e., e-mail vs. IRC). For more detailed discussion, see the Online Investigative Principles for Federal Law Enforcement Agents, Principle 6, Section C.

C. **"Undercover Employee"** means any employee of the FBI, or employee of a federal, state, or local law enforcement agency working under the direction and control of the FBI in a particular investigation, whose relationship with the FBI is concealed from third parties in the course of an investigative operation by the maintenance of a cover or alias identity.

D. **"Proprietary"** means a sole proprietorship, partnership, corporation, or other business entity operated on a commercial basis, which is owned, controlled, or operated wholly or in part on behalf of the FBI, and whose relationship with the FBI is concealed from third parties.

E. **"Appropriate Federal Prosecutor"** means a U.S. Attorney or Section Chief in the Criminal Division of the Department of Justice (DOJ).

F. **"Joint Undercover Operation"** means an undercover operation conducted jointly by the FBI and another law enforcement agency, except that an operation in which FBI participation is confined to contribution of limited financial or equipment resources or technical advice does not constitute a joint undercover operation.

III. General Authority and Purpose

The FBI may engage in undercover activities and undercover operations pursuant to these Guidelines that are appropriate to carry out its law enforcement responsibilities, including the conduct of preliminary inquiries, general crimes investigations, and criminal intelligence investigations. In preliminary inquiries, these methods may be used to further the objective of inquiry into possible criminal activities by individuals or groups to determine whether a full investigation is warranted. In general crimes investigations, these methods may be used to further the investigative objectives of preventing, solving, and prosecuting crimes. In criminal intelligence investigations — i.e., racketeering enterprise investigations and terrorism enterprise investigations — these methods may be used to further the investigative objective of ascertaining such matters as the membership, finances, geographical dimensions, past and future activities, and goals of the enterprise under investigation, with a view to the longer range objectives of detection, prevention, and prosecution of the criminal activities of the enterprise.

These guidelines do not apply to investigations utilizing confidential informants, cooperating witnesses, or cooperating subjects, unless the investigation also utilizes an undercover employee. However, the FBI, through the development of internal policy, may choose to apply these Guidelines to certain confidential informant, cooperating witness, and cooperating subject operations by referring such matters to the Undercover Review Committee pursuant to Section IV.D(6).

The FBI may participate in joint undercover activities with other law enforcement agencies and may operate a proprietary to the extent necessary to maintain an operation's cover or effectiveness. Joint undercover operations are to be conducted pursuant to these Guidelines. However, if a joint undercover operation is under the direction and control of another federal law enforcement agency and is approved through a sensitive operations review process substantially comparable to the process under these Guidelines, the other agency's process may be relied on in lieu of the process under these Guidelines. In any undercover activity or operation in which an FBI undercover employee participates, Sections IV.H and

VI.A–B of these Guidelines shall apply, regardless of which agency directs and controls the operation.

IV. Authorization of Undercover Operations

A.   General Approval Standards

Any official considering approval or authorization of a proposed undercover application shall weigh the risks and benefits of the operation, giving careful consideration to the following factors:

(1) The risk of personal injury to individuals, property damage, financial loss to persons or businesses, damage to reputation, or other harm to persons;

(2) The risk of civil liability or other loss to the Government;

(3) The risk of invasion of privacy or interference with privileged or confidential relationships and any potential constitutional concerns or other legal concerns;

(4) The risk that individuals engaged in undercover operations may become involved in illegal conduct restricted in Section IV.H below; and

(5) The suitability of Government participation in the type of activity that is expected to occur during the operation.

B.   Undercover Operations Which May Be Authorized by the Special Agent in Charge (SAC)

(1) The establishment, extension, or renewal of all undercover operations to be supervised by a given field office must be approved by the SAC. If the undercover operation does not involve any of the factors listed in Section IV.C below, this approval shall constitute authorization for the operation. Approval requires a written determination, stating supporting facts and circumstances, that:

(a) Initiation of investigative activity regarding the alleged criminal conduct or criminal enterprise is warranted under any applicable departmental guidelines;

(b) The proposed undercover operation appears to be an effective means of obtaining evidence or necessary information. This finding should include a statement of what prior investigation has been conducted and what chance the operation has of obtaining evidence or necessary information concerning the alleged criminal conduct or criminal enterprise;

Note: The gathering of evidence and information through undercover operations furthers the investigative objectives of detecting,
preventing, and prosecuting crimes. See Sections I and III above. In
furthering these objectives, the Attorney General's Guidelines on
General Crimes, Racketeering Enterprise, and Terrorism Enterprise
Investigations (Part I) state that "[t]he FBI shall not hesitate to use
any lawful techniques consistent with these Guidelines, even if intrusive, where the intrusiveness is warranted in light of the seriousness of a crime or the strength of the information indicating its
commission or potential future commission. This point is to be
particularly observed in the investigation of terrorist crimes and in
the investigation of enterprises that engage in terrorism." As with
other investigative techniques, Special Agents in Charge should be
guided by this principle in considering and approving undercover
operations. The principle, as noted, applies with particular force
where the undercover operation is directed to gathering information
that will help to solve and prosecute terrorist offenses or prevent the
future commission of acts of terrorism.

(c) The undercover operation will be conducted with minimal intrusion consistent with the need to collect the evidence or information in a timely and effective manner;

(d) Approval for the use of any confidential informant has been obtained as required by the Attorney General's Guidelines Regarding
the Use of Confidential Informants;

(e) Any foreseeable participation by an undercover employee in illegal
activity that can be approved by the SAC on his or her own
authority is justified by the factors noted in paragraph H; and

(f) If there is no present expectation of the occurrence of any of the
sensitive or fiscal circumstances listed in paragraph C, a statement
to that effect.

(2) Undercover operations may be authorized pursuant to this subsection
for up to six months and continued upon renewal for an additional
six-month period, for a total of no more than one year. Undercover
operations initiated pursuant to this subsection may not involve the
expenditure of more than $50,000 ($100,000 in drug cases of which
a maximum of $50,000 is for operational expenses), or such other
amount that is set from time to time by the Director, without approval
from FBI Headquarters (FBIHQ).

(3) The SAC may delegate the responsibility to authorize the establishment, extension, or renewal of undercover operations to designated
Assistant Special Agents in Charge. The delegation of this responsibility
by the SAC should be in writing and maintained in the appropriate

field office. However, all undercover operations which must be authorized at FBIHQ must be approved by the SAC.

(4) A copy of all written approvals described in (1) above shall be forwarded promptly to FBIHQ.

C.   Operations Which Must Be Approved at FBIHQ

(1)   Fiscal Circumstances

In all undercover operations involving the fiscal circumstances set out below, the SAC shall submit an application to FBIHQ in accordance with Section IV.F below. A recommendation for authorization may be forwarded directly to the Director or designated Assistant Director or, in operations involving only fiscal circumstances (a)–(c), to the designated Deputy Assistant Director for final review and authorization, provided that the approval levels conform to all applicable laws.

Applications for approval of undercover operations referred to FBIHQ only because of fiscal circumstances need not be considered or approved by the Undercover Review Committee. For purpose of these Guidelines, an undercover operation involves fiscal circumstances if there is a reasonable expectation that the undercover operation will

(a) Require the purchase or lease of property, equipment, buildings, or facilities; the alteration of buildings or facilities; a contract for construction or alteration of buildings or facilities; or prepayment of more than one month's rent;
Note: The purchase, rental, or lease of property using an assumed name or cover identity to facilitate a physical or technical surveillance is not an undercover operation for purposes of these Guidelines. However, since the expenditure of appropriated funds is involved, approval must be obtained from FBIHQ in conformance with applicable laws.

(b) Require the deposit of appropriated funds or proceeds generated by the undercover operation into banks or other financial institutions;

(c) Use the proceeds generated by the undercover operation to offset necessary and reasonable expenses of the operation;

(d) Require a reimbursement, compensation, or indemnification agreement with cooperating individuals or entities for services or losses incurred by them in aid of the operation (any such agreement entered into with third parties must be reviewed by the FBI's Office of the General Counsel and Office of the Chief Contracting Officer); or

(e) Exceed the limitations on duration or commitment of resources established by the Director for operations initiated at the field office level.

(2)   *Sensitive Circumstances*

In all undercover operations involving any sensitive circumstances listed below, the SAC shall submit an application to FBIHQ in accordance with paragraph F below. The application shall be reviewed by appropriate supervisory personnel at FBIHQ and, if favorably recommended, sent to the Undercover Review Committee for consideration. The application shall then be forwarded to the Director or a designated Assistant Director, who may approve or disapprove the application.

For purposes of these Guidelines, sensitive circumstances are involved if there is a reasonable expectation that the undercover operation will involve —

(a) An investigation of possible criminal conduct by any elected or appointed official, or political candidate, for a judicial, legislative, management, or executive-level position of trust in a federal, state, or local governmental entity or political subdivision thereof;

(b) An investigation of any public official at the federal, state, or local level in any matter involving systemic corruption of any governmental function;

(c) An investigation of possible criminal conduct by any foreign official or government, religious organization, political organization, or the news media;

Note: There are some circumstances involving officials in judicial, legislative, management, or executive-level positions which may logically be considered nonsensitive. In such instances, the Section Chief, Integrity in Government/Civil Rights Section, Criminal Investigative Division, FBIHQ, who is a member of the Criminal Undercover Operations Review Committee and has a national perspective on matters involving public officials, must be consulted for a determination as to whether the undercover operation should be presented to the Undercover Review Committee.

(d) Engaging in activity having a significant effect on or constituting a significant intrusion into the legitimate operation of a federal, state, or local governmental entity;

(e) Establishing, acquiring, or operating a proprietary;

(f) Providing goods or services which are essential to the commission of a crime, which goods and services are reasonably unavailable to a subject of the investigation except from the Government;

(g) Activity by an undercover employee that is proscribed by federal, state, or local law as a felony or that is otherwise a serious crime — but not including the purchase of stolen or contraband goods; the delivery or sale by the Government of stolen property whose ownership cannot be determined; the controlled delivery of drugs which will not enter commerce; the conduct of no more than five money laundering transactions, not to exceed a maximum aggregate amount of $1 million; the payment of bribes which are not included in the other sensitive circumstances; or the making of false representations to third parties in concealment of personal identity or the true ownership of a proprietary (this exemption does not include any statement under oath or the penalties of perjury — see paragraph H below);

Note: Some of the above activities — for example, the controlled delivery of drugs, bribe payments, and certain transactions that involve depositing funds into banks or other financial institutions — are subject to specific review and approval procedures. These matters must be coordinated with FBIHQ.

(h) A significant risk that a person participating in an undercover operation will be arrested or will supply falsely sworn testimony or false documentation in any legal or administrative proceeding (see paragraph H below);

(i) Attendance at a meeting or participation in communications between any individual and his or her lawyer;

(j) A significant risk that a third party will enter into a professional or confidential relationship with a person participating in an undercover operation who is acting as an attorney, physician, clergyman, or member of the news media;

(k) A request to an attorney, physician, member of the clergy, or other person for information that would ordinarily be privileged or to a member of the news media concerning an individual with whom the newsperson is known to have a professional or confidential relationship;

(l) Participation in the activities of a group under investigation as part of a terrorism enterprise investigation or recruiting a person from within such a group as an informant;

(m) A significant risk of violence or physical injury to individuals or a significant risk of financial loss;

(n) Activities which create a realistic potential for significant claims against the United States arising in tort, contract, or for compensation for the "taking" of property, or a realistic potential for significant claims against individual government employees alleging constitutional torts; or

(o) Untrue representations by a person participating in the undercover operation concerning the activities or involvement of any third person without that individual's knowledge or consent.

D. Criminal Undercover Operations Review Committee (Undercover Review Committee)

(1) The Undercover Review Committee shall consist of appropriate employees of the FBI designated by the Director and Criminal Division attorneys designated by the Assistant Attorney General in charge of the Criminal Division, DOJ, to be chaired by a designee of the Director.

(2) When an application from a SAC for approval of an undercover operation involving sensitive circumstances specified in paragraph C(2) is received by FBIHQ, upon recommendation by the FBIHQ substantive section, the Committee members will meet to review the application. Criminal Division members of the Committee may consult with appropriate FBI personnel, senior DOJ officials, and the U.S. Attorney as deemed appropriate. The Committee shall submit the application to the Director or designated Assistant Director with a recommendation for approval or disapproval of the request and any recommended changes or amendments to the proposal.

(3) In addition to the considerations contained in Section IV.A above, the Committee shall also examine the application to determine whether adequate measures have been taken to minimize the incidence of sensitive circumstances and reduce the risks of harm and intrusion that are created by such circumstances. If the Committee recommends approval of an undercover operation, the recommendation shall include a brief written statement explaining why the operation merits approval in light of the anticipated occurrence of sensitive circumstances.

(4) The Committee shall recommend approval of an undercover operation only upon reaching a consensus, provided that:

(a) If one or more of the designees of the Assistant Attorney General in charge of the Criminal Division does not join in a recommendation for approval of a proposed operation because of legal, ethical, prosecutive, or departmental policy considerations, the designee shall promptly advise the Assistant Attorney General and no further action shall be taken on the proposal until the designated Assistant Director has had an opportunity to consult with the Assistant Attorney General; and

(b) If, upon consultation, the Assistant Attorney General disagrees with a decision by the designated Assistant Director to approve the proposed operation, no further action shall be taken on the proposal without the approval of the Deputy Attorney General or the Attorney General.

(5) The Committee should consult the Office of the General Counsel of the FBI and the Office of Legal Counsel or other appropriate division or office at the DOJ about significant unsettled legal questions concerning authority for, or the conduct of, a proposed undercover operation.

(6) The Director, Assistant Attorney General, or other official designated by them may refer any sensitive investigative matter, including informant, cooperating witness, and cooperating subject operations, to the Undercover Review Committee for advice, recommendation or comment, regardless of whether an undercover operation is involved. A SAC may, consistent with FBI policy, submit an undercover operation for review by FBIHQ and the Undercover Review Committee, regardless of whether the sensitive circumstances listed in these Guidelines are present.

(7) The U.S. Attorney, SAC, or any member of their staffs may attend the Undercover Review Committee in order to advocate for the approval of an undercover operation.

(8) If the SAC and the U.S. Attorney jointly disagree with any stipulation set by the Undercover Review Committee regarding the approval of an undercover operation, they may consult with the chairman of the Committee who may schedule a meeting of the committee to reconsider the issue in question.

(9) At any time during the undercover operation the SAC can appeal any FBIHQ decision directly to the Assistant Director. Likewise, the U.S. Attorney can appeal directly to the Assistant Attorney General, Criminal Division, or the Deputy Attorney General as appropriate.

E. Approval by the Director, Deputy Director, Designated Executive Assistant Director, or Designated Assistant Director

A designated Assistant Director may approve an undercover operation considered by the Undercover Review Committee, unless the investigation involves sensitive circumstance (l) or (m). Except in the limited circumstances described in paragraph I below, only the Director, the Deputy Director, or a designated Executive Assistant Director may approve a proposed operation if a reasonable expectation exists that:

(1) The undercover operation will be used to participate in the activities of a group under investigation as part of a terrorism enterprise investigation or to recruit a person from within such a group as an informant (sensitive circumstance [l]); or

(2) There may be a significant risk of violence or personal injury to individuals or a significant risk of financial loss (sensitive circumstance [m]).

F.   Application/Notification to FBIHQ

(1) Application to FBIHQ must be made for any undercover operation requiring FBIHQ approval. Each application shall include:

(a) The written SAC approval described in paragraph B(1) above;

(b) A description of the proposed operation and the particular cover to be employed; any informants or other cooperating persons who will assist in the operation, including background information, arrest record, and plea agreements; the particular offense or criminal enterprise under investigation; and any individuals known to be involved;

(c) A statement of the period of time for which the operation would be maintained;

(d) A description of how the requirements concerning any inducements to be offered as discussed in Section V.B. below have been met; and

(e) A statement of proposed expenses.

(2) Applications for approval of undercover operations involving sensitive circumstances listed in paragraph C(2) shall also include the following information:

(a) A statement of which circumstances are reasonably expected to occur, what the facts are likely to be, and why the undercover operation merits approval in light of the circumstances, including:

(i) For undercover operations involving sensitive circumstance (g), a statement why the participation in otherwise illegal activity is justified under the requirements of paragraph H below; and

(ii) For undercover operations involving sensitive circumstance (l), a statement why the infiltration or recruitment is necessary, a description of procedures to minimize any acquisition, retention, and dissemination of information that does not relate to the matter under investigation or to other authorized investigative activity, and an explanation of how any potential constitutional concerns and any other legal concerns have been addressed.

(b) A letter from the appropriate federal prosecutor indicating that he or she has reviewed the proposed operation, including the sensitive circumstances reasonably expected to occur, agrees with the proposal and its legality, and will prosecute any meritorious case that has developed. The letter should include a finding that the proposed investigation would be an appropriate use of the undercover technique and that the potential benefits in detecting, preventing, or prosecuting criminal activity outweigh any direct costs or risks of other harm.

(3)　An application for the extension or renewal of an undercover operation should describe the results obtained from the operation or explain any failure to obtain significant results and, where sensitive circumstances are involved, should include a letter from the appropriate federal prosecutor favoring the extension or renewal of authority.

(4)　The FBI shall immediately notify the Deputy Attorney General whenever FBIHQ disapproves an application for approval of an undercover operation and whenever the Undercover Review Committee is unable to reach consensus concerning an application.

G.　Duration of Authorization

(1)　An undercover operation approved by FBIHQ may not continue longer than is necessary to achieve the objectives specified in the authorization, nor in any event longer than six months, without new authorization to proceed, except pursuant to subparagraph (3) below.

(2)　If there is significant change in either the direction or objectives of an undercover operation approved by FBIHQ, the operation must be reviewed by the Undercover Review Committee to determine whether a new authorization is necessary.

(3)　An undercover operation which requires review by the Undercover Review Committee may be initiated or extended on an interim basis by the designated Assistant Director in the event of exigent circumstances, for a period not to exceed 30 days. In the case of an initial authorization, budget enhancement, or change in focus, the interim authority must be ratified by the Undercover Review Committee at its next scheduled meeting.

(4)　An undercover operation initially authorized by the SAC must be reauthorized by a designated Assistant Director, pursuant to Section IV.C–F, if it lasts longer than 12 months or involves the expenditure of more than $50,000 ($100,000 in drug cases of which a maximum of $50,000 is for operational expenses), or such other amount that is set from time to time by the Director. No undercover operation approved at the field office level may continue for more than one year without obtaining approval at FBIHQ.

(5) An undercover operation approved by a SAC is deemed to commence on the date approved, not on the date covert activity is begun.

(6) Among the factors to be considered in a determination by any approving official of whether an undercover operation should be renewed or extended are:
(a) The extent to which the operation has produced the results anticipated when it was established;
(b) The potential for future success beyond that initially targeted;
(c) The extent to which the investigation can continue without exposing the undercover operation; and
(d) The extent to which continuation of the investigation may cause injury, financial or otherwise, to innocent parties.

H. Participation in Otherwise Illegal Activity by Undercover Employees

Except when authorized pursuant to these Guidelines, no undercover employee shall engage in any activity that would constitute a violation of federal, state, or local law if engaged in by a private person acting without authorization. For purposes of these Guidelines, such activity is referred to as Otherwise Illegal Activity.

(1) Justification: No official shall recommend or approve participation by an undercover employee in otherwise illegal activity unless the participation is justified:
(a) to obtain information or evidence necessary for the success of the investigation and not reasonably available without participation in the otherwise illegal activity;
(b) to establish or maintain credibility of a cover identity; or
(c) to prevent death or serious bodily injury.

(2) Minimization: The FBI shall take reasonable steps to minimize the participation of an undercover employee in any otherwise illegal activity.

(3) Prohibitions: An undercover employee shall not:
(a) participate in any act of violence except in self-defense;
(b) initiate or instigate any plan to commit criminal acts except in accordance with Section V (concerning avoidance of entrapment) below; or
(c) participate in conduct which would constitute unlawful investigative techniques (e.g., illegal wiretapping, illegal mail openings, breaking and entering, or trespass amounting to an illegal search).

(4) Self-Defense: Nothing in these Guidelines prohibits an undercover employee from taking reasonable measures of self-defense in an emergency to protect his or her own life or the lives of others against

wrongful force. Such measures shall be reported to the appropriate federal prosecutor and FBIHQ, who shall inform the Assistant Attorney General for the Criminal Division as soon as possible.

(5) Authorization:

(a) The SAC must approve all undercover operations and activities, including those which contemplate participation in otherwise illegal activity. This approval shall constitute authorization of:

    (i)   otherwise illegal activity which is a misdemeanor or similar minor crime under federal, state, or local law;

    (ii) consensual monitoring, even if a crime under local law;

    (iii) the purchase of stolen or contraband goods;

    (iv) the delivery or sale of stolen property which cannot be traced to the rightful owner;

    (v) the controlled delivery of drugs which will not enter commerce;

    (vi) the payment of bribes which is not included in the sensitive circumstances;

    (vii) the making of false representations to third parties in concealment of personal identity or the true ownership of a proprietary (but not any statement under oath or the penalties of perjury, which must be authorized pursuant to subparagraph [b] below); and

    (viii) conducting no more than five money laundering transactions, not to exceed a maximum aggregate amount of $1 million.

(b) Participation in otherwise illegal activity which is a felony or its equivalent under federal, state, or local law and which is not otherwise excepted under Section IV.C(2)(g) above, requires additional authorization by the Assistant Director after review by the Undercover Review Committee. See Section IV.E.

(c) Participation in otherwise illegal activity which involves a significant risk of violence or physical injury requires authorization by the Director, Deputy Director, or designated Executive Assistant Director after review by the Undercover Review Committee. See Section IV.E.

(d) If an undercover employee believes it to be necessary and appropriate under the standards set out in paragraph H(1) above, to participate in otherwise illegal activity that was not foreseen or anticipated, every effort should be made to consult with the SAC, who shall seek emergency interim authority from the designated Assistant Director, and review by the Undercover Review Committee if possible, or, if necessary, may provide emergency authorization under paragraph I below. If consultation is impossible, and the undercover employee concludes that there is an immediate and grave threat to life, physical safety, or property, the undercover employee may participate in the otherwise illegal activity, so long as he does not take part in and makes every effort to prevent any act of violence. A report to the SAC shall be made as soon as possible, who shall submit a written report to FBIHQ, which shall promptly inform the Undercover Review Committee. A decision by an undercover employee to participate in otherwise illegal activity under this subsection may be retroactively authorized if appropriate.

(e) If an undercover operation results in violence in the course of criminal activity, and an undercover employee, informant, or co-operating witness has participated in any manner in the criminal activity, the SAC shall immediately inform the appropriate federal prosecutor and FBIHQ, which shall inform the Assistant Attorney General in charge of the Criminal Division as soon as possible.

I.   Interim/Emergency Authorization

(1) In situations which require the prior written authorization of the SAC, the SAC may orally approve an undercover operation when he or she determines that a significant investigative opportunity would be lost were the time taken to prepare a written authorization. The required written authorization, with the justification for the oral approval included, shall be prepared promptly and forwarded to FBI-HQ.

(2) Emergency interim authorization procedures are in place within FBI-HQ that provide for expeditious review and authorization of a proposed undercover operation. See paragraph G(3). If the SAC concludes that a situation exists which makes even this expedited procedure too lengthy, in any of the following situations, the SAC may authorize the undercover operation:

(a) In situations which would otherwise require approval by the designated Assistant Director, the SAC may approve an undercover operation when he or she determines that without immediate initiation, extension, or renewal of an operation, life, property, or personal safety of individuals would be placed in serious danger.

(b) In situations which involve sensitive circumstance (l) or (m), the SAC may approve an undercover operation when he or she determines that the initiation, extension, or renewal of an operation is imperative to protect life or prevent serious injury.

(c) In situations which involve sensitive circumstance (l), or other investigative activity relating to terrorism, the SAC may approve an undercover operation when he or she determines that the initiation, extension, or renewal of an operation is necessary to avoid the loss of a significant investigative opportunity. Before providing authorization in these situations, the SAC shall attempt to consult with the appropriate federal prosecutor and with a designated Assistant Director.

(3) The power to provide emergency authorizations under subparagraph (2) may not be delegated pursuant to Section IV.B(3).

(4) In situations arising under subparagraph (2), a written application for approval must be submitted to FBIHQ within 48 hours after the operation has been initiated, extended, or renewed, together with the initial finding and a written description of the emergency situation. As soon as it is notified of an emergency authorization, FBIHQ shall notify the DOJ members of the Undercover Review Committee. If the subsequent written application for approval is denied, a full report of all activity undertaken during the course of the operation must be submitted to the Director, who shall inform the Deputy Attorney General.

(5) In online undercover operations, a SAC or his or her designee may authorize, in writing, continued online undercover contact for a period not to exceed 30 days if it is essential to continue online contact with a subject in order to either maintain credibility or avoid permanent loss of contact with a subject during the period of time in which an application for an online undercover operation is being prepared and submitted for approval. If the proposed undercover operation is one that must be approved by an Assistant Director under Section IV.C(2), the appropriate offices at FBIHQ must be notified promptly of the decision to grant this interim authority. Furthermore, a full report of all online activity occurring during this period must be submitted to the approving authority as soon as practicable. If approved, the undercover employee maintaining online contact during this period must:

(a) Maintain an accurate recording of all online communication;

(b) Avoid otherwise illegal activity;

(c) Maintain as limited an online profile as possible consistent with the need to accomplish the objectives stated above;

(d) Avoid physical contact with subjects;

(e) Take all necessary and reasonable actions during the interim period to protect potential victims and prevent serious criminal activity if online contact reveals a significant and imminent threat to third party individuals, commercial establishments, or government entities; and

(f) Cease undercover activities if, during the 30-day period, a determination is made to disapprove the undercover operation.

V.   Protecting Innocent Parties against Entrapment

A.   Entrapment

Entrapment must be scrupulously avoided. Entrapment occurs when the Government implants in the mind of a person who is not otherwise disposed to commit the offense the disposition to commit the offense and then induces the commission of that offense in order to prosecute.

B.   Authorization Requirements

In addition to the legal prohibition on entrapment, additional restrictions limit FBI undercover activity to ensure, insofar as it is possible, that entrapment issues do not adversely affect criminal prosecutions. As a result, no undercover activity involving an inducement to an individual to engage in crime shall be authorized unless the approving official is satisfied that —

(1)   The illegal nature of the activity is reasonably clear to potential subjects; and

(2)   The nature of any inducement offered is justifiable in view of the character of the illegal transaction in which the individual is invited to engage; and

(3)   There is a reasonable expectation that offering the inducement will reveal illegal activity; and

(4)   One of the two following limitations is met:
  (i) There is reasonable indication that the subject is engaging, has engaged, or is likely to engage in the illegal activity proposed or in similar illegal conduct; or
  (ii) The opportunity for illegal activity has been structured so that there is reason to believe that any persons drawn to the opportunity, or brought to it, are predisposed to engage in the contemplated illegal conduct.

C.   Exception

The alternative requirements of paragraph B (4), while not required by law, are imposed to ensure the Government does not offer inducements to crime to persons who are not predisposed to do so. These standards can be waived only by the Director upon a written finding that the activities are necessary to protect life or prevent other serious harm.

VI. Monitoring and Control of Undercover Operations

A.   Preparation of Undercover Employees, Informants, and Cooperating Witnesses

(1) Prior to the investigation, the SAC or a designated Supervisory Special Agent shall review with each undercover employee the conduct that the undercover employee is expected to undertake and conduct that may be necessary during the investigation. The SAC or Agent shall discuss with each undercover employee any of the sensitive or fiscal circumstances specified in Section IV.C (1) or (2) that are reasonably likely to occur.

(2) Each undercover employee shall be instructed that he or she shall not participate in any act of violence; initiate or instigate any plan to commit criminal acts; use unlawful investigative techniques to obtain information or evidence; or engage in any conduct that would violate restrictions on investigative techniques or FBI conduct contained in the Attorney General's Guidelines or departmental policy; and that, except in an emergency situation as set out in Section IV.H(5)(d), he or she shall not participate in any illegal activity for which authorization has not been obtained under these Guidelines. The undercover employee shall be instructed in the law of entrapment. When an undercover employee learns that persons under investigation intend to commit a violent crime, he or she shall try to discourage the violence.

B.   Review of Conduct

From time to time, during the course of the undercover operation, the SAC shall review the conduct of the undercover employee(s) and others participating in the undercover operation, including any proposed or reasonably foreseeable conduct for the remainder of the investigation. Any findings of impermissible conduct shall be discussed with the individual and promptly reported to the designated Assistant Director and the members of the Undercover Review Committee, and a determination shall be made as to whether the individual should continue his or her participation in the investigation.

C. Continuing Consultation with the Appropriate Federal Prosecutor

Upon initiating and throughout the course of any undercover operation, the SAC or a designated Supervisory Special Agent shall consult on a continuing basis with the appropriate Federal prosecutor, particularly with respect to the propriety of the operation and the legal sufficiency and quality of evidence that is being produced by the activity.

D. Serious Legal, Ethical, Prosecutive, or Departmental Policy Questions, and Previously Unforeseen Sensitive Circumstances

(1) The SAC shall consult with the chairman of the Criminal Undercover Operations Review Committee, FBIHQ whenever a serious legal, ethical, prosecutive, or departmental policy question arises in any undercover operation or if sensitive circumstances occur that were not anticipated. The FBI shall consult with the U.S. Attorney, or Assistant Attorney General, or their representative, and with DOJ members of the Undercover Review Committee on whether to modify, suspend, or terminate the investigation related to such issues.

(2) When unforeseen sensitive circumstances arise, the SAC shall submit a written application to FBIHQ for authorization of an undercover operation previously approved at the field office level, or amend the existing application to FBIHQ pursuant to Section IV.F.

E. Annual Report of the Undercover Review Committee

(1) The Undercover Review Committee shall retain a file of all applications for approval of undercover operations submitted to it, together with a written record of the Committee's action on the application and any ultimate disposition by the approving official. The FBI shall also prepare a short summary of each undercover operation recommended for approval by the Committee. These records and summaries shall be available for inspection by a designee of the Deputy Attorney General and of the Assistant Attorney General in charge of the Criminal Division.

(2) On an annual basis, the Committee shall submit to the Director, the Attorney General, the Deputy Attorney General, and the Assistant Attorney General in charge of the Criminal Division a written report summarizing:

(a) the types of undercover operations approved and disapproved together with the reasons for disapproval;

(b) the major issues addressed by the Committee in reviewing applications and how they were resolved; and

(c) any significant modifications to the operations recommended by the Committee.

F.   Deposit of Proceeds; Liquidation of Proprietaries

As soon as the proceeds from any undercover operation are no longer necessary for the conduct of the activity, the remaining proceeds shall be deposited in the Treasury of the United States as miscellaneous receipts.

Whenever a proprietary with a net value over the amount specified by the Department of Justice Appropriation Authorization Act or other applicable laws is to be liquidated, sold, or otherwise disposed of, the FBI shall report the circumstances to the Attorney General and the Comptroller General. The proceeds of the liquidation, sale, or the disposition, after obligations are met, shall be deposited in the Treasury of the United States as miscellaneous receipts.

VII. Reservation

These Guidelines are set forth solely for the purpose of internal DOJ guidance. They are not intended to, do not, and may not be relied upon to create any rights, substantive or procedural, enforceable by law by any party in any matter, civil or criminal, nor do they place any limitations on otherwise lawful investigative or litigative prerogatives of the Department of Justice.

Date: May 30, 2002 (signature)_____
John Ashcroft
Attorney General

Appendix III

Internal Revenue Services Manual: 9.4.2.5 Informants

9.4.2.5 (08-10-2004) Informants

1. Some criminal investigations undertaken by special agents cannot be successfully completed except through the use of an informant and the direct purchase of information.
2. In addition to purchasing specific information from an informant, special agents occasionally encounter situations where an expenditure of funds is required to lay the groundwork for the procurement of information related to undercover operations, and for other activities involving the expenditures of funds to obtain testimony and evidence essential to an investigation of such a nature that their disclosure might jeopardize the investigating special agent.
3. The decision to use a confidential informant (CI) is sensitive and requires the agency to perform due diligence concerning the background of the individual who will be providing information or receiving direction from the Internal Revenue Service (IRS).
4. Informants and the subclasses of informants have characteristics that distinguish them from typical witnesses who provide information and testimony to the government. These characteristics create a sensitive relationship between the individual and the IRS based on the amount of direction provided to the individual, payments made to the individual, and the underlying motivation of the individual.

9.4.2.5.1 (08-10-2004) Informant Information — Generally

1. Payment, without the filing of a claim for reward, may be made for information related to violations of federal statutes arising from the administration and enforcement of the Internal Revenue laws and related offenses. Such payments should occur only in those circumstances where the information sought is vital to the investigation or project and cannot be obtained through any other means.
2. When practical, such payments should be made only after the information has been obtained, evaluated, and determined worthy of compensation.
3. Limitations on the dollar amounts which may be approved by authorized management officials for the purchase of such information will be imposed by the Commissioner, IRS. See subsection 9.4.2.5.3.1 paragraph 3.

9.4.2.5.2 (12-20-2001) Definition and Classification of an Informant

1. The following factors distinguish an informant from a typical witness. These characteristics also determine the subclass of informant and the level of approval necessary:
   A. unwillingness to testify
   B. amount of direction the individual receives from the IRS
   C. compensation for the information; can include monetary payment as well as the individual's expectation of receiving a reduced sentence for assisting the government
   D. expectation of the individual that the government will not divulge his/her identity
2. Informants are classified as:
   A. anonymous informants
   B. confidential sources of information
   C. confidential informants (CI)
   D. cooperating witnesses (CW)
   E. cooperating defendants (CD)
3. Federal, state, and local law enforcement officials and other governmental officials, acting within the scope of their authority, who provide information to the IRS are not considered informants. However, if such officials provide information with regard to corruption within their own agency, such as the acceptance of bribes by police officers, the officials shall be considered informants.

9.4.2.5.2.1 (12-20-2001) Anonymous Informant

1. An anonymous informant is an individual who either refuses to identify himself/herself or uses a fictitious or code name, and whose true identity is unknown to the IRS. An anonymous informant can neither be paid nor work at the direction of the IRS.

9.4.2.5.2.2 (12-20-2001) Confidential Source of Information

1. A confidential source of information is an individual who:
   A. provides information without seeking payment (other than a claim for reward),
   B. does not gather information at the direction of the IRS, and
   C. is not expected to testify

9.4.2.5.2.3 (08-10-2004) Confidential Informant

1. A confidential informant (CI) is an individual who:
   A. is not expected to testify, but
      • may be paid for the information provided, and/or
      • gathers information and evidence at the direction of the IRS

9.4.2.5.2.4 (08-10-2004) Cooperating Witness

1. A cooperating witness (CW) is an individual who:
   A. is expected to testify and
   B. is a consenting party in a consensually monitored conversation
      • may be paid for the information provided, and/or
      • gathers information and evidence at the direction of the IRS.

9.4.2.5.2.5 (08-10-2004) Cooperating Defendant

1. A cooperating defendant (CD) is an individual who has committed criminal violations and does more to assist the government than testify based on past activity. He/she may be charged or not charged with the criminal violations.
2. A CD is typically not paid as his/her motivation for cooperation is based upon charging or sentencing considerations rather than money. Further, each CD is expected to testify and:
   A. gather information and evidence at the direction of the IRS or
   B. is a consenting party in a consensually monitored conversation (see subsection 9.4.2.5.3.1, paragraph 2 for an exception)

9.4.2.5.3 (08-10-2004) Authorization for Use of Confidential Informants/Cooperating Witnesses/Cooperating Defendants

1. When special agents believe that an individual is in a position to obtain relevant information under the direction of the IRS, is motivated by financial reward for providing the information, or is a consenting party to a monitored conversation, the special agents must obtain authorization for use of the individual.
2. The approval process applies when the IRS enters into a relationship with the individual providing the information. If any of the following situations exist, approval of the CI/CW/CD is required:
    A. payment is required to be made to the individual
    B. the individual receives direction from the IRS
    C. the individual consents to a monitored conversation (an exception exists for a cooperating defendant who consents to monitored conversations with alleged coconspirators to corroborate the CD's information; see IRM 9.4.7, Consensual Monitoring, for consensual monitoring requirements)
3. Delegation Order No. 16, Authorization to Approve Confidential Expenditures, authorizes payments for information, as well as other expenses necessary for gathering information in an investigation. The required authorization levels are as follows:
    A. Special Agent in Charge: $10,000 or less
    B. Director, Field Operations: $20,000 or less
    C. Chief/Deputy Chief: amounts greater than $20,000
4. The approving official will provide the Director, Special Investigative Techniques with the following information concerning the CI/CW/CD's identity:
    A. full name
    B. any known aliases
    C. DOB
    D. SSN
    E. activation date

    Note: The approving official will also provide the names and phone numbers of the special agents controlling the CI/CW/CD. Form 13316, Request for Control Number for Approved Confidential Informant/Cooperating Witness/Cooperating Defendant, should be used for this purpose. The Director, Special Investigative Techniques will add the CI/CW/CD information to the master database and assign a control number for field office use.

9.4.2.5.3.1 (08-10-2004) Approval Level — Special Agent in Charge or Director, Field Operations

1. The SAC may authorize the use of most CI/CW/CDs except when the following sensitive suitability factors are present, in which case the Director, Field Operation is the approving official:
   A. risk of physical harm that may occur to the CI/CW/CD and/or the CI/CW/CD's immediate family or close associates as a result of assisting the IRS
   B. risk that the CI/CW/CD's activities may adversely affect another investigation or potential prosecution
   C. whether the CI/CW/CD is a public official, law enforcement officer, member of the military services, a representative of the news media, or potentially a party to privileged communications (e.g., a member of the clergy, a physician, a lawyer, or certain experts retained by a lawyer)
   D. whether it is believed that the individual is the subject of a pending criminal investigation, poses a danger to the public or other criminal threat, or poses a risk of flight

9.4.2.5.3.2 (08-10-2004) Approval Level — Director, Operations Policy and Support

1. Approval by the Director, Operations Policy and Support is required in the following situations:
   A. When the CI/CW/CD is a foreign national. A foreign national is defined as not being a United States citizen.
   B. When the CI/CW/CD will obtain information from a foreign country.
   C. When foreign travel by any CI/CW/CD is anticipated.

9.4.2.5.3.3 (08-10-2004) Approval Level — Director, Operations Policy and Support and Department of Justice, Office of Enforcement Operations

1. The use of any current or former participant in the federal Witness Security Program, or the use of a federal prisoner or other individual under the control of the U.S. Marshals Service, as a CI/CW/CD requires the approval of the Director, Operations Policy and Support and the Department of Justice, Office of Enforcement Operations (OEO).

9.4.2.5.3.4 (08-10-2004) Approval Procedures for Foreign Nationals, Information Obtained from a Foreign Country, or Foreign Travel Is Anticipated by a CI/CW/CD

1. The field office will conduct the normal background and suitability checks for any CI/CW/CD as discussed in subsection 9.4.2.5.4. The field office will prepare a registration file, index file, control file, and the requisite Forms 9831, 9835, 9836, and 13316. The Office of Special Investigative Techniques will issue the CI/CW/CD an identifying number.

2. The SAC of the field office will submit a memorandum through the Director, Field Operations to the Director, Operations Policy and Support, requesting approval to use the CI/CW/CD. The memorandum should be routed to the Office of Special Investigative Techniques for processing. The memorandum should address the following factors:

   A. CI/CW/CD's number or code name.
   B. Country of citizenship and current US immigration status, i.e., tourist visa, business visa, or resident alien, if applicable.
   C. Position currently held by the CI/CW/CD (e.g., foreign government official or bank official).
   D. Pertinent background information such as criminal record, associates, and employment history.
   E. Reliability of the CI/CW/CD.
   F. Criminal violations the CI/CW/CD is providing information about, approximate dollar amounts of the violations, and years under investigation.
   G. Detailed statement explaining the background of the investigation, what information the CI/CW/CD's participation can provide, how the CI/CW/CD will obtain the information, why the information is needed, and any other pertinent facts.
   H. If the CI/CW/CD is obtaining information from a foreign country, identify the country, the nature of the information, and how the CI/CW/CD is obtaining the information.
   I. If foreign travel is involved, detail the country or countries to be visited, a complete itinerary, and a description of the circumstances that require the CI/CW/CD to travel.

   Note: If items (h) and (i) are applicable, the concurrence of the Director, International (CI:OPS:I) is also required.

9.4.2.5.3.5 (08-10-2004) Department of Justice Approval Required

1. The use of protected witnesses, prisoners, probationers, or parolees requires special approval.
2. Consistent with DOJ requirements, approval by the Office of Enforcement Operations (OEO) is required for:
   A. use of federal prisoners or individuals under the control of the U.S. Marshals Service as informants, (see subsection 9.4.2.5.10, Witnesses)
   B. use of current or former participants in the federal Witness Security Program as informants (see subsection 9.4.2.5.10, Witnesses)
   C. use of informants to engage in the warrantless interception of certain sensitive categories of verbal communications as specified by the Attorney General (see IRM 9.4.7, Consensual Monitoring)

9.4.2.5.3.6 (08-10-2004) Before Using Federal or State Probationers, Parolees, or Supervised Releasees

1. Prior to using federal or state probationers, parolees, or supervised releasees as informants, the SAC shall make a determination if the use of the individual in the anticipated capacity would violate the terms and conditions of their probation, parole, or supervised release.
2. This determination shall be documented in the informant's control file.
3. If it is determined that there would be a violation of probation, parole, or supervised release prior to using the informant, the SAC must obtain the permission of the relevant probation, parole, or supervised release official. This approval shall be documented in the informant's control file.
4. The IRS shall comply with any applicable state or local laws, rules, and regulations pertaining to the use of state or local prisoners as informants.

9.4.2.5.4 (08-10-2004) Evaluation of a Confidential Informant/Cooperating Witness/Cooperating Defendant

1. When evaluating the potential use of a CI/CW/CD, the approving official should consider, at a minimum, the following suitability factors to determine whether or not to authorize the use of the CI/CW/CD and, if so, whether certain precautions must be taken. Form 9836, Request for Approval to Use CI/CW/CD, will be used to

evaluate the informant's suitability and should contain the following information:

A. the individual's age
B. criminal history
C. tax filing and payment history, particularly any delinquencies (problems in this area do not necessarily preclude use of the informant; however, steps should be taken to correct any problems prior to the individual's working with the IRS)
D. reliability and truthfulness, including the person's motivation
   Note: People provide information for various reasons. In evaluating an informant's reliability and credibility, his/her motives need to be considered. Possible motives may include seeking monetary gain, gaining revenge, altruism, self-aggrandizement, law enforcement buff, or eccentric thrill seeking.
E. source and means of securing information
F. extent to which the information provided is relevant to a present or potential investigation and can be corroborated
G. whether the individual is presently serving as a cooperating witness or a confidential informant for another agency
H. any record of past performance as a CI/CW/CD (provided by CI:OPS:SIT, when the control number is provided to the field office)
I. if it is believed the individual previously served as a cooperating witness or confidential informant for another law enforcement agency, determination whether that law enforcement agency terminated that relationship for cause
J. nature and importance of the information to a present or future investigation
K. alien or residency status, if applicable
L. whether the individual is a substance abuser or has a history of substance abuse
M. whether the individual is related to an employee of any law enforcement agency
N. risk of physical harm that may occur to the individual, his/her immediate family, and/or his/her close associates as a result of assisting the IRS
O. potential effect upon an investigation being conducted in another field office or by another agency
P. whether the CI/CW/CD is the subject of an investigation being conducted by another field office or by another agency that does not know or consent to the individual becoming a CI/CW/CD

Q. whether the individual is a public official, law enforcement officer, member of the military services, a representative of the news media, or a party to privileged communications (e.g., a member of the clergy, a physician, a lawyer, or certain experts retained by a lawyer)

R. whether it is believed that the individual is the subject of a current or pending criminal investigation, poses a danger to the public or other criminal threat, or poses a risk of flight

S. whether the individual is a tax professional, including an attorney, accountant, return preparer, or enrolled agent; if so, a CT Counsel must be contacted for advice on using this person, and the following factors should be considered:
  - whether the tax professional has a Power of Attorney (POA) from the potential subject
  - whether the tax professional currently has an agreement to work as an attorney for the potential subject
  - whether the tax professional is owed money by the potential subject
  - whether the potential subject is aware that he/she is being investigated
  - whether the subject has invoked the Fifth Amendment relative to the IRS investigation

T. whether the individual has a present or past relationship with the subject of the provided information

2. Although not required, the use of a polygraph to test the individual's credibility should be considered by the approving official.

9.4.2.5.5 (12-20-2001) Control of Confidential Informant/Cooperating Witness/Cooperating Defendant

1. To protect the integrity of the relationship with the CI/CW/CD and to enhance security, two special agents will be assigned to control the CI/CW/CD.

9.4.2.5.5.1 (08-10-2004) Instructions to the Confidential Informant/Cooperating Witness/Cooperating Defendant

1. After the approving official authorizes use of the individual, a registration file must be established for each CI/CW/CD (see subsection 9.4.2.5.6.4.1.)

2. After the CI/CW/CD has been registered, the special agents will review with the CI/CW/CD written instructions regarding his/her responsibilities and relationship with the IRS. This review will be documented using Form 9831, Approved CI/CW/CD Advice, and placed in the CI/CW/CD registration file. At a minimum, the instructions shall state that:

   A. The CI/CW/CD must not engage in unlawful acts, except as specifically authorized by the special agents, and is subject to prosecution for any unauthorized, unlawful act.

   B. The CI/CW/CD must provide truthful information at all times.

   C. The CI/CW/CD must abide by the instructions of the special agents and must not seek to take any independent action on behalf of the U.S. Government.

   D. The CI/CW/CD is not an employee of the U.S. Government and may not represent himself/herself as such.

   E. The CI/CW/CD must not engage in witness tampering, witness intimidation, or fabrication, alteration, or destruction of evidence.

   F. The CI/CW/CD is liable for any taxes on any moneys paid to him/her for information or services.

   G. The informant is not guaranteed any rewards, payments, or other compensation by the IRS, nor can the individual's tax liability be abated or compromised.

   H. When a CD is cooperating with the IRS in exchange for consideration by a prosecuting office, and upon request of the CD, the IRS will advise the prosecuting office of the nature and extent of the CD's assistance to the IRS but cannot make any recommendations regarding prosecution or sentencing. The terms and conditions for cooperation, including any plea agreements and/or proffers, should be discussed with the cooperating defendant, his/her defense attorney, and the attorney for the government assigned to the investigation.

   I. In investigations involving foreign nationals, no promises or representations can be made regarding the CI/CW/CD's alien or residency status or his/her right to enter or remain in the United States.

   J. The IRS will strive to protect the CI/CW/CD's identity, but cannot guarantee that it will not be divulged.

   K. The CI/CW/CD may not enter into any contracts or incur any obligations on behalf of the U.S. Government, except as specifically instructed by the IRS.

9.4.2.5.5.2 (08-10-2004) Responsibility of Special Agents When Dealing with a Confidential Informant/Cooperating Witness/Cooperating Defendant

1. Special agents need to be fair and truthful with a CI/CW/CD, and should make no promises that cannot be fulfilled.
2. Special agents should never let a CI/CW/CD determine the procedure to be used in the investigation or otherwise control the investigation.
3. Special agents must not condone any violation of law in order for a CI/CW/CD to obtain information. If a defendant can show that the CI/CW/CD was acting under some arrangement with federal agents, he/she will have a viable defense. Whenever there appears to be a possibility of entrapment or some other unlawful act by a CI/CW/CD, he/she should be guided in a manner that will prevent the occurrence of such acts.
4. Special agents must maintain a professional relationship with the CI/CW/CD based upon mutual respect. Special agents should guard against the relationship becoming personal instead of professional. A special agent's ability to be objective is jeopardized if a personal relationship develops with the CI/CW/CD.
5. The special agents will not make any commitments for payment or protection to a CI/CW/CD without proper authorization from the approving official as set forth in IRM 9.11.1, Fiscal and Budgetary Matters. Agreements made without authorization may become the personal responsibility of the maker.
6. Special agents will not intervene on behalf of a CI/CW/CD with the IRS or with any other federal, state, or local agencies. Special agents shall not offer to have the tax liability of a CI/CW/CD compromised in exchange for information about another taxpayer. This prohibition includes, but is not limited to, agreeing to a reduction or elimination of the tax liability of an attorney, accountant, enrolled agent, or other return preparer in exchange for information about the client or such person. Questions in this area should be addressed to CT Counsel assigned to the field office.
   Note: Taxpayers may bring civil suit for damages against the government where determination or collection of tax is intentionally compromised by a federal officer or employee.
7. As long as the CI/CW/CD is active, a log (Form 9834, Approved CI/CW/CD Quarterly Log) will be prepared and filed each quarter with the SAC's office. Any substantive contact with the CI/CW/CD will require an entry in the log and a backup document (either a Memorandum of Contact, Form 9833 or a Receipt for Cash, Form

9832). If no contacts occurred during the month, a Form 9834 will be prepared reflecting no contacts and forwarded to the SAC's office. A copy of this log will be maintained in a control file by the SAC.

8. When a CI/CW/CD is no longer providing information or assistance to IRS, the individual should be deactivated. The IRS may also terminate the relationship for cause if the CI/CW/CD engages in conduct that violates the individual's agreement with the IRS. In either case, appropriate notification documented in writing and witnessed by two special agents shall be made if the CI/CW/CD can reasonably be located. If the CI/CW/CD cannot be located, efforts to locate the informant shall be documented.

9. Whenever a CI/CW/CD is deactivated, the Director, Special Investigative Techniques, will be notified in writing. The notification should include the control number, date of deactivation, and reason for deactivation.

9.4.2.5.5.3 (12-20-2001) Debriefing the Confidential Informant/Cooperating Witness/Cooperating Defendant

1. After registration of the CI/CW/CD and documentation that the appropriate instructions have been given, the special agents will fully debrief the CI/CW/CD concerning his/her knowledge of criminal or unlawful activities.

2. Special agents should always make every effort to elicit all facts known by the CI/CW/CD at the initial contact. CI/CW/CDs frequently supply only the information they think is important rather than relating all relevant facts.

3. The special agents will advise the CI/CW/CD that any information submitted by him/her concerning violations not under the IRS' jurisdiction will be furnished to the appropriate enforcement agency in accordance with IRS procedures (see IRM 11.3, Disclosure of Official Information).

4. If the CI/CW/CD appears knowledgeable concerning potential narcotics violations, the special agents will encourage the CI/CW/CD to meet directly with Drug Enforcement Administration (DEA) or Federal Bureau of Investigation (FBI) personnel. If the CI/CW/CD declines, the special agents will debrief the CI/CW/CD of the information relating to potential narcotics violations and will transmit such information either directly to the DEA, FBI, or to the Assistant Attorney General, Criminal Division, Department of Justice, in

accordance with the disclosure laws and regulations (see IRM 9.3.1, Disclosure).

5. In the event that the CI/CW/CD provides information that is subject to a legal claim of privilege, the special agents should contact the appropriate CT Counsel assigned to the field office and/or attorney for the government.

9.4.2.5.5.4 (12-20-2001) Payments to Confidential Informants/Cooperating Witnesses/Cooperating Defendants

1. Criminal Investigation employees must adhere to the following guidelines when involved in paying a CI/CW/CD:
   A. When a CI/CW/CD will not furnish information without payment, the special agents should first advise the individual of IRS reward procedures and the use of Form 211, Application for Reward for Original Information. If the individual does not wish to use these procedures, the special agents may find it necessary to purchase specific information. In these situations, the special agents should negotiate the value of the information and advise the individual that tentative agreement for payment is subject to approval by higher authorities.
   B. Direct payment to a CI/CW/CD should be made only after the information has been obtained and determined to be worthy of compensation, unless the payment is needed in order for the CI/CW/CD to pay expenses to obtain the information. Any expense payment will not be outstanding for more than 30 calendar days and should be determined using a reasonable evaluation of its potential value compared to the estimated expenses required for the CI/CW/CD to obtain it. When making such an evaluation, consideration should be given to whether the information would have been brought to IRS' attention from other sources, the information has significant tax administration implications, the information has any potential probative value, and the investigative time that was saved by obtaining the information in this manner.
   C. Each payment to a CI/CW/CD should be made by the paying special agent in the presence of another special agent acting as a witness. In appropriate situations, and with approval of the SAC, the witness can be a revenue agent or other federal or local law enforcement agent who is involved in the same investigation. In extraordinary situations, a special agent may pay a CI/CW/CD without a witness if, in advance of the payment, the SAC approves

of the arrangement. The approval must be documented in the CI/CW/CD file and, if possible, the payment should be made by a cashier's check.

D. At the time of payment, the special agent should obtain a signed receipt from the CI/CW/CD showing the date the information was received, the date of payment, and the amount of payment, preferably using Form 9832, Informant Receipt for Cash Payment. The CI/CW/CD should sign his/her fictitious name or code on the receipt. Both special agents should then sign the receipt and include the CI/CW/CDs designated number. If it is impossible to obtain a signed receipt at the time of payment, a special agent should properly document the activity and obtain a receipt from the CI/CW/CD as soon as possible. The SAC must approve waivers and ensure they were justified and properly documented. The special agent should not request a CI/CW/CD to sign a blank Form 9832, Informant Receipt for Cash Payment.

E. If a special agent reimburses a CI/CW/CD for expenses or other nontaxable items (lodging expenses, M & IE, photocopies, etc.), he/she should obtain a Form 9832 and note that the payment was made to reimburse expenses.

F. The special agent should request and obtain, if possible, major receipts and other documentation from the CI/CW/CD such as airline tickets, hotel bills, etc. At a minimum, a special agent should document the expenditures by having the CI/CW/CD list the date, description, and amount of expense separately rather than reporting a lump-sum figure.

G. In accounting for payments to a CI/CW/CD, a special agent should submit to the SAC, through channels, a memorandum detailing the information for which the payment was made, Form 9832, Informant Receipt for Cash Payment and SF 10411, Reimbursement Claim for Confidential Expenditures.

H. To avoid making duplicate payments, coordination with other affected field offices may be necessary when information relates to more than one investigation. The SAC will notify the Director, Field Operations who is responsible for this coordination. In addition, the Informant Claims Examiner (ICE) will be contacted to determine if the CI/CW/CD filed a Form 211, Application for Reward for Original Information. The specific procedures for contacting the ICE are outlined in IRM 25.2, Information and Informants' Rewards.

I. Payments to a CI/CW/CD who provides information to the IRS may be made as a confidential expenditure from the imprest fund, the asset sharing fund, or by the CI/CW/CD filing a Claim for Reward, Form 211.

J. Under no circumstances are IRS employees authorized to assure that a reward will be paid in any amount, to indicate the amount of probable recovery, or to confirm that a recovery was based upon the information submitted by the CI/CW/CD.

K. If an inquiry is made as to the amount which may be received, the inquirer should be furnished Publication 733, Rewards for Information Given to the Internal Revenue Service.

L. All CI/CW/CD payments are charged to subobject code (SOC) 9101.

M. Income Tax Regulations, Section 1.6041-3(L) provides that Returns of Information, which include Forms 1099, Miscellaneous Income, are not required when payments are made to informers related to criminal activity and payment is made by the United States, a state, or a political subdivision thereof.

Appendix IV

U.S. Drug Enforcement Administration: Chapter 66, Subsection Chapter 661, § 6612 — Confidential Sources

6612.1 General Policies

A. This section contains policies and procedures to be followed in the establishment, use, and handling of confidential sources by the Drug Enforcement Administration (DEA). To a considerable extent, it is based upon the requirements prescribed by the Domestic Operations Guidelines.

The title "Confidential Source" covers the following:

1. Confidential Source: A person who, under the direction of a specific DEA agent, and with or without expectation of compensation, furnishes information on drug trafficking or performs a lawful service for the DEA in its investigation of drug trafficking.

2. Defendant/Confidential Source: As above, but subject to arrest and prosecution for a federal offense; or a defendant in a pending federal or state case who expects compensation for his assistance in either the form of judicial or prosecutive consideration, or compensation of another form.

3. Restricted-Use Confidential Source: Any confidential source who meets any of the following criteria shall be considered a "restricted-use confidential source," subject to use as authorized below:

   a. Persons less than 18 years of age: Only with written consent of parent or legal guardian.

b. Persons on probation or parole (federal or state): Special Agents in Charge (SACs) will establish procedures to obtain permission to use persons on probation (federal or state) and parole (state) within the SAC's area of responsibility.

For persons on federal parole, SACs will contact the Regional Parole Commissioner of the region in which the releasee is under supervision at least (except when emergency circumstances dictate otherwise) 30 days prior to the proposed use of the person (releasee). See exhibit 1 for locations of Regional Parole Commissioners. SACs will furnish in writing an overview of the proposed utilization of the person's services to include:

(1) Confidential sources instructions (6612.31 F.1, 2, 3, 4).

(2) Administrative controls (Domestic Guidelines).

(3) Potential risk to the person.

(4) Measures to be taken to ensure the person's safety.

(5) Why the potential benefit to the Government outweighs the risk of the person's reinvolvement.

(6) Length of time the person is needed (up to 90 days).

If the Commission approves the SAC's request, the conditions of the person's cooperation will be set forth in a memorandum from the Regional Commissioner to the SAC.

Note: Where the person is currently a federal prisoner, and the intended utilization will require temporary furlough or transfer from his detention site, or the use of consensual monitoring devices, it is necessary to obtain prior Departmental approval. This approval will be requested by teletype to Headquarters Investigative Support Section (OS) for action and to the appropriate Drug Section for information. The teletype must contain the following information:

1. Name and identifying data of the prisoner.

2. Present location of the prisoner.

3   Type of sentence the prisoner is serving, including date of incarceration.

4. Charges for which the prisoner is incarcerated.

5. Necessity of using the prisoner. What, if any, other techniques have been tried; why they have failed or are unworkable.

6. Name(s) of target(s) of the investigation; their role in the crimes or organization under investigation.

7. Nature and circumstances of the intended use.

8. Security measures to be taken to ensure the prisoner's safety and to prevent the prisoner's escape.

9. Length of time the prisoner is needed.

10. Whether the prisoner is to remain in DEA custody, be housed in jails or similar facilities at certain times, or be unguarded except for his/her own protection.
11. Whether the prisoner will be needed as a witness.
12. Whether it will be necessary to relocate the prisoner to another prison upon completion of the activity.
13. The name of the concurring Assistant U.S. Attorney (AUSA).
14. Citizenship of the prisoner. If the prisoner is a foreign national, has an Immigration and Naturalization Service (INS) detainer been lodged?

B. The title "confidential source," as well as the informant requirements of the Domestic Operations Guidelines, does not apply to "sources of information." A source of information is a person or organization, not under the direction of a specific agent, who provides information without becoming a party to the investigation itself (e.g., a business firm furnishing information from its records; an employee of an organization who, through the routine courses of his activities, obtains information of value to the DEA; or a concerned citizen who witnesses an event of interest to the DEA).

Should a person who would otherwise be considered a source of information become a continuing active part of the investigation, then his status should be shifted to that of a confidential source. Should a source of information seek financial compensation or become a recipient of an award from the Asset Forfeiture Fund, then he must be established and assigned a code number for purpose of payment. The source of information is not to be considered a confidential source in this type of situation.

Generally, a person or organization fitting this definition can be identified by name in investigative reports. However, if there is cause to preserve anonymity, yet the circumstances do not warrant establishing the source as a confidential source, the term "source of information" may be used. Sources of information will be identified in an administrative memorandum (see 6211.7) attached to the report.

C. There are three criteria that must be met to establish a person as a DEA confidential source:
1. The person is in a position to measurably assist the DEA in a present or future investigation.
2. To the extent a prudent judgment can be made, the person will not compromise DEA interests and activities.
3. The person will accept the measure of direction necessary to effectively utilize his services.

D. If there is reason to believe that a confidential source or defendant/confidential source has committed a serious criminal offense (i.e., a felony), the appropriate U.S. Attorneys Office will be notified. The U.S. Attorneys Office, after consultation with the Department of Justice (DOJ), will determine whether the DEA may continue to use the individual as a confidential source.

E. In the situation described in D above, the law enforcement agency having jurisdiction over the crime will also be notified. If it is felt that immediate and full notification would jeopardize an ongoing investigation or endanger the life of an agent or other person, then this notification may be limited to just apprising the agency that the crime was committed. In this instance, all evidence of the crime will be preserved for subsequent transfer to the agency at a point in time when full disclosure is possible.

F. Confidential sources under the control of another agency are not subject to the requirements of the Domestic Operations Guidelines. Frequently, however, situations occur in which control of the confidential source is shared between the DEA and the other agency, or the control by the other agency is nominal, or the DEA provides direction to the confidential source through the other agency. The nature of the relationship between the three parties will be continuously reviewed by the agent involved and his immediate supervisor. Should control shift to where more rests with the DEA than the other agency, the confidential source will be established as a DEA confidential source.

G. The following additional requirements shall apply to the DEA's development of the defendant/confidential source.

1. The approval of the appropriate prosecutor (i.e., federal, state, or local) will be obtained *prior* to seeking the cooperation of a defendant.

2. A defendant may be advised that his cooperation will be brought to the attention of the appropriate prosecutor. No further representations or assurances may be given without approval by the SAC. The prosecuting attorney shall have sole authority to decide whether or not to prosecute a case against a defendant/confidential source.

3. The appropriate prosecutor shall be advised of the nature and scope of the defendant's cooperation throughout the period of his use. The procedures and frequency of this reporting shall be set by the prosecutor.

4. Prior to formally seeking the dismissal of any criminal charge against a defendant/confidential source the SAC must obtain the

written approval of the Headquarters (DO). Requests under this requirement will be made via teletype. The teletype will include the confidential source's code number, the specific charge, the informal views of the appropriate prosecutor, and a terse justification in terms of advantage to the DEA. Written approval or disapproval will be via return teletype.

H. The Domestic Operations Guidelines do not apply to confidential source development and handling by the DEA's foreign offices. Nevertheless, to the extent that the policies contained in this section can be applied, they should. Any deviation from these policies must be specifically approved by Headquarters (DO), based upon factors specific to the foreign country involved.

6612.2 Establishing Confidential Sources

6612.21 General

All persons who will be utilized as DEA confidential sources will be formally established as such. The specific procedures required in establishing a person as a confidential source vary somewhat, depending upon the characteristics of the person involved.

In instances of either extreme sensitivity or where a "source of information" is being established for payment purposes, certain establishment procedures may be waived by the SAC or Country Attaché. Such exemptions from the norm will be used judiciously. Those procedures that may be exempted under these criteria are so indicated below. Any such exemption must be specifically documented in item 58 of the DEA Form 512 Confidential Source Establishment Report.

6612.22 Confidential Source Code Number

A. Each DEA confidential source will be assigned a code number.
B. [REDACTED]
    Note: DEA state and local task forces will use a sequential numbering system separate from the DEA field office.
C. [REDACTED]
D. Confidential sources under the control of another agency will not usually be assigned DEA code numbers. This will be necessary, however, if the confidential source is to be paid with DEA funds.

6612.23 Confidential Source Code Book

Each office will maintain a confidential source code book.
   [REDACTED]

6612.24 Confidential Source Files

A. For each confidential source a separate DEA-5 File Jacket will be established by the establishing office, the managing Division Office (if appropriate), and Headquarters (AMRI). These files will be kept in a separate and secure storage facility, segregated from any other files, and under the exclusive control of the office head or an employee designated by him. The facility will be locked at all times when unattended. Access to these files will be limited to those employees who have a necessary, legitimate need. A confidential source file may not leave the immediate area except for review by a management official or the handling agent, and will be returned prior to the close of business hours. Sign-out logs will be kept indicating the date, confidential source number, time in and out, and the signature of the person reviewing the file. (Also see 8615 of the Planning and Inspection Manual).
   Note: Country Attachés, at their discretion, may adjust the foregoing insofar as which offices will maintain sets of confidential source files.

B. In certain instances of extreme sensitivity, files of those confidential sources for whom a waiver of establishment procedures was granted per 6612.21 may be stored separately from other confidential source files, accessible only to the SAC (or Country Attaché) and those DEA personnel designated by him to control the confidential source's utilization. Upon deactivating any such confidential source, the SAC (or Country Attaché) will determine whether his file should be integrated into the regular confidential source file storage facility.

C. Non-DEA employees, including those of other federal agencies, other law enforcement agencies, or other Department of Justice elements, will not be permitted access to these files. An exception to this is the files of those confidential sources under the control of a DEA Task Force. Conditions of access to these files will be set by the DEA Task Force management.

   On an individual file basis, a prosecuting attorney may examine a DEA confidential source file if such examination is necessary to the prosecution of a case. Unless expressly authorized by the Administrator, employees of the GAO, the Department of Justice, or others who are engaged in an evaluation of the DEA will not be permitted access to these files. Bona fide and authorized evaluators may be permitted secondary access through review of DEA-prepared summaries of or extracts from these files. In no case will the identity of a confidential source be disclosed to an external evaluator.

D. Confidential source files will be maintained in code number sequence under two headings: active confidential sources and deactivated confidential sources.

E. Confidential source files will contain the following documents:

1. DEA Form 356, Confidential Source Payment Record, kept on top of the file (except for the Headquarters confidential source file).

2. DEA Form 512, Confidential Source Establishment Report, plus any other documents connected with the confidential source's establishment.

3. DEA Form 473, Confidential Source Agreement.

4. DEA Form 103, Voucher for Payment for Information and Purchase of Evidence. The signed copy will be kept by the originating office (except for the Headquarters confidential source file).

5. Copies of all debriefing reports (except for the Headquarters confidential source file).

6. Copies of case initiation reports bearing on the utilization of the confidential source (except for the Headquarters confidential source files). See 6214.4.

7. Copies of statements signed by the source (unsigned copies will be placed in appropriate investigative files).

8. Any administrative correspondence pertaining to the confidential source including documentation of any representations made on his behalf or any other nonmonetary considerations furnished.

9. Any deactivation report or declaration of an unsatisfactory confidential source.

F. For each confidential source in an active status, the controlling agent will review the confidential source file on a quarterly basis to assure it contains all relevant and current information. Where a material fact that was earlier reported on the DEA-512 Confidential Source Establishment Report is no longer correct (e.g., a change in criminal status, means of locating him, etc.), a supplemental DEA-512 should be submitted with the corrected entry. If the new information warrants a higher level of approval than was originally necessary, this approval will be sought by this DEA-512. If the new information is routine, the approval of the immediate supervisor on the DEA-512 will suffice, regardless of the original level of approval.

G. Where a confidential source is utilized and/or paid by an office other than the establishing office, its file on that confidential source need only consist of those documents pertinent to its utilization and/or payment.

6612.25 Photographs

All confidential sources will be photographed (unless a recent photograph is already available). One print will be attached to each copy of the Establishment Report. This requirement may be waived by the SAC (or Country Attaché) pursuant to 6612.21. Confidential sources controlled by another agency who are established for payment purposes only need not be photographed.

6612.26 Fingerprinting and Criminal History

A. All confidential sources being established by a domestic field office will be checked for prior criminal records in the Narcotics and Dangerous Drugs Information System (NADDIS) and via the National Crime Information Center (NCIC). The NCIC Computerized Criminal History (CCH) and Interstate Identification Index (III) files may be checked through on-site State/Local terminals or through the DATS NCIC link. These checks are based upon the individual's Federal Bureau of Investigation (FBI) number. A copy of any positive CCH or III response should be submitted with the DEA Form 512 Establishment Report. If the potential confidential source was born prior to 1956, and the CCH and III are negative, a DEA Form 105, Request for Criminal Records, must be sent to the FBI Identification Division because a manual arrest record which has not been indexed may exist. Subjects who were born in 1956 or later who have FBI numbers have been indexed, and a DEA Form 105 is unnecessary. Results of all criminal records checks should be annotated on the Confidential Source Establishment Report.

B. Where a verified FBI number is not available, the potential confidential source should be fingerprinted. Submit a completed FD-249, Fingerprint Card, directly to the FBI. Do not enter the confidential source code number on the FD-249. Line through the space entitled "Your Number." Enter "Criminal Inquiry" in the space entitled "Charge." See 6641.34 for further information on preparing the FD-249.

C. The confidential source may be utilized on a provisional basis while awaiting a response from the FBI. Information contained in the subsequent FBI response will be reviewed from the standpoint of whether it affects the current status and utilization of the confidential source. Adjustments to procedures, status, and/or use will be made as appropriate.

D. In instances of extreme sensitivity or where a source of information is being established for payment purposes, the fingerprinting requirement may be waived per 6612.21.

E. The foregoing criminal history/fingerprint requirements do not apply to confidential sources controlled by another agency who are established for payment purposes only.

F. All confidential sources being established by a foreign field office must be fingerprinted. The only exception to this requirement is where an official of a foreign government or business entity is being established for payment purposes, or where a set of fingerprints is available from another source. In these instances, the fingerprinting requirement may be waived by the Country Attaché. Any such waiver will be specifically documented on the DEA Form 512 Establishment Report. Where a foreign confidential source is fingerprinted as per B above, the FD-249 should be sent directly to the FBI Identification Division.

G. All confidential sources being established by a foreign field office must be fingerprinted. The only exception to this requirement is where an official of a foreign government or business entity is being established for payment purposes, or where a set of fingerprint records is available from another source. In this instance, the fingerprinting requirement may be waived by the Country Attaché. Any such waiver will be specifically documented on the DEA Form 512 Confidential Source Establishment Report. Where a foreign confidential source is fingerprinted as per B above, the DEA Form 249 should be sent directly to the FBI Identification Division.

6612.27 Confidential Source Establishment Report

A. A Confidential Source Establishment Report will be prepared on DEA Form 512 for any person assigned a confidential source code.

B. The DEA Form 512 will be prepared in sufficient copies to be distributed as follows:

Original — Originating office confidential source file.

Copy — Division Office copy of source file (if applicable).

Copy — District Office copy source file (if applicable).

Copy — Headquarters (AMRI) confidential source file.

Distribution will be via registered mail, return receipt requested. It will not be sent with other reports, memoranda, etc., in the same envelope.

C. In instances of extreme sensitivity, the SAC (or Country Attaché) may waive the normal distribution of the DEA Form 282 (see 6612.21). In these instances, a single copy will be prepared and stored in the Division or Country Office confidential source file in a sealed envelope and a memorandum will be submitted to the DO detailing the waiver. Details will include the confidential source's code number (not his name), his classification (confidential source, defendant/confidential source, restricted-use confidential source), his proposed utilization, any compensation agreed upon, and the names of the DEA personnel who control his utilization. The original of this memorandum will be filed in the Headquarters confidential source file, and copies will be distributed to each field office maintaining a file on this confidential source.

D. The DEA Form 512 will be completed as fully as possible. Special instructions are as follows:
[REDACTED].

E. For confidential sources other than defendant/confidential sources and restricted use informants, the approval of the immediate supervisor is sufficient.

For defendant/confidential sources and restricted-use confidential sources, the additional approval of the SAC (or Country Attaché) is required. The SAC's (or Country Attaché's) approval is also required where any establishment procedures were waived.

The reestablishment of a confidential source previously declared unreliable requires DO approval (request and response by teletype).

F. Attach a photograph and copies of written approvals, if any, to each copy of DEA Form 512.

6612.3 Utilization of Confidential Sources

6612.31 General Policies

A. Confidential sources are assets of the DEA, not a specific agent. At its discretion, the DEA management may reassign a confidential source to the control of another agent or another office.

B. Agent confidential source contacts will be of a strictly professional nature. Extrinsic social or business contacts are expressly prohibited.

C. Contacts with confidential sources will be such that their knowledge of DEA facilities, operations, activities, and personnel is kept to the minimum necessary to their successful utilization.

D. At least two agents must be capable of contacting a confidential source. Whenever practical, two agents (or an agent and an officer of another enforcement agency) will be present at all contacts with the confidential source.

E. All significant contacts with the confidential source, and all information obtained at these contacts, will be documented in writing.

F. Confidential sources (and sources of information) shall be advised at the outset that:

1. They shall not violate criminal law in furtherance of gathering information or providing services to the DEA, and that any evidence of such a violation will be reported to the appropriate law enforcement agency.

2. They have no official status, implied or otherwise, as agents or employees of the DEA.

3. The information they provide may be used in a criminal proceeding, and that, although the DEA will use all lawful means to protect their confidentiality, this cannot be guaranteed.

4. It is a federal offense to threaten, harass, or mislead anyone who provides information about a federal crime to a federal law enforcement agency. Should they experience anything of this nature, as a result of their cooperation with the DEA, they should contact their controlling agent immediately. (See 6115.2)

5. Confidential sources will sign DEA Form 473 (Confidential Source Agreement) acknowledging that he/she has read and agrees to the above conditions. His/her signature and date will be witnessed by two agents. Should a confidential source refuse to sign the DEA Form 473, the following statement will be entered on the DEA form, and will be signed and dated by two agents: "On *date, (C.I. Number)* was advised of and agreed to the conditions set forth on this form. *(C.I. Number)* refused to sign." The DEA-473 will be filed in the appropriate C.S. file. Foreign offices will also follow this procedure.

6. The controlling Special Agent will advise all confidential sources that they must file federal income tax returns to include all payments, awards, and rewards paid to them by the DEA. In addition, the controlling Special Agent will advise the confidential source that all payments must be reported as "other income" on their federal income tax returns, and it will be their responsibility to obtain receipts and other supporting documentation to offset the legitimate expenses from income for possible audit by the Internal Revenue Service. Special Agents will advise all confidential sources that their tax liability is a matter strictly between

them and the Internal Revenue Service. A statement attesting to this policy will be documented on the back of the DEA-512. Special Agents will remind confidential sources of this policy when any payment is made.

G. See 662 for undercover purchase procedures. Where a confidential source is to participate in an undercover purchase in which he may come in contact with either official funds, controlled drugs, or anything else of potential evidentiary value, he will be thoroughly searched both before and after the undercover encounter, and where possible kept under continuous observation in between. The reason for this is to preclude questions as to the validity or integrity of the evidence. The search of the confidential source will be reported in the DEA-6 documenting the activity.

H. All interactions with the confidential source including his development, establishment, debriefing, and utilization, will be carried out with the highest regard for confidentiality. When he is to be brought to the DEA office, it will be done in a manner so as to attract minimal attention, both upon entering and exiting, and while he is in the confines of the office itself. Unnecessary disclosure of his identity in discussions will be avoided. Documents and reports concerning his confidential source status will be kept secured. Meetings outside the office will be done insofar as possible in "neutral" locations. Where the disclosure of his confidential source status to a prosecutor is necessary, the prosecutor should be reminded to handle this fact with similar regard for security.

I. Confidential sources who are injured or killed while engaged or as a result of their cooperation with the DEA are eligible for benefits under the Federal Employees Compensation Act. See Section 2810 of the Personnel Manual for details. Also see 6115 regarding threats made against confidential sources.

J. To assure proper coordination and targeting of investigative operations, any attempt to recruit as a confidential source or witness, an individual who (1) is known to be a significant target or subject in an active or pending DEA or FBI investigation; (2) is at any point in the judicial process as a result of an FBI or DEA case; or (3) is incarcerated as a result of a DEA or FBI investigation, must be thoroughly coordinated between the DEA and the FBI. This coordination must include the appropriate prosecuting attorney when the prosecutor is actively involved with the potential confidential source's prosecution. Neither the DEA nor the FBI will unilaterally attempt to recruit a confidential source or witness by utilizing the other agency's case as leverage to stimulate cooperation.

6612.32 Debriefing of Confidential Sources

A. As part of the establishment process, and prior to the supervisor granting approval to the establishment of the confidential source, a full debriefing will take place. The nature and extent of this debriefing will vary with the individual's background (e.g., whether he is a long-time associate of criminals, etc.). A line of inquiry will be developed such that all knowledge of criminals and criminal activity, both drug- and nondrug-related, will be covered.

B. The general order of priority to the criminal information sought will be as follows:

   1. Actionable drug-related criminal information.
   2. General drug-related criminal information.
   3. Nondrug-related criminal information.

   The debriefing will not be limited to, nor overly focus upon, the first priority. It could well be that a broad coverage of the second priority will lead to a better choice of targets and objectives than an oversimplified discussion of actionable information.

   In obtaining information on a drug trafficker, the financial aspects of his activities will also be included (e.g., how money is transferred, assets, proceeds, etc.). The drug-related information sought will not be limited to the traffic within the geographic boundaries of the immediate office.

C. Nondrug-related criminal information will be disseminated to the appropriate agencies unless there is a valid reason not to do so. If the information is nonspecific or of low significance, the immediate supervisor will decide whether it should be disseminated.

   If the information concerns a serious criminal offense (i.e., a felony), then the procedures described in 6612.IE shall apply. Particular attention should be paid to information that would interest the FBI (e.g., La Cosa Nostra, motorcycle gangs, etc.). Any such information will be promptly furnished to the counterpart FBI field office.

   Any information pertaining to a threat, plan, or attempt by an individual or group to physically harm, kidnap, or destroy the property of high U.S. Government officials, foreign officials, or their families will be reported to the U.S. Secret Service.

D. Information which adversely reflects upon the integrity or conduct of a DEA employee will be handled in accordance with the DEA Standards of Conduct. Information which adversely reflects upon the integrity of an FBI employee or any information concerning public corruption will be handled in accordance with the FBI/DEA Concurrent Jurisdiction Guidelines (see 6341).

E. Confidential sources will be debriefed subsequently on a periodic basis, at least every 90 days (see 6612.61).

F. All debriefings will be fully reported in a Confidential Source Debriefing Report using DEA Form 6. These reports will be written to the appropriate case or general file (and cross-filed to the confidential source file). They will be cross-filed to other case or general files, as appropriate.

If the information contained in the report is of interest to another DEA office or another agency, distribution will be indicated in the Distribution block. If only a portion of the information is of interest to another agency, it may be repeated in a letter to the agency. Such correspondence should be identified by the DEA investigative file number. Copies of this correspondence should be forwarded to all DEA offices maintaining a file on the confidential source (see 6612.24A).

G. The format of a Confidential Source Debriefing Report will be as follows:

1. No synopsis is necessary.

2. There will be three major headings: Drug-Related Information, Nondrug-Related Information, and Indexing Section. If no information is to be entered under any one of these headings, enter the word "negative."

3. Insofar as practical, the narrative sections should be formatted as follows:

    a. Information of interest to another agency should be paragraphed separately to facilitate extraction.

    b. Information that appears to exonerate a defendant or suspect should be paragraphed separately.

H. Refer to 6211.6 for instructions on the preservation of investigative notes.

6612.33 Confidential Source Statements

A. Where a confidential source has provided information or has participated in an activity (DEA directed or otherwise) to which he may be required to testify, a formal statement normally will be taken. However, where taking a statement may adversely impact an investigative outcome, this procedure may be waived if all relevant information is reported in a DEA Form 6. The immediate supervisor, in consultation with the prosecuting attorney, will decide whether or not a formal statement is necessary.

B. The original copy of the statement will be signed and filed in his confidential source file. An additional copy, identified only by confidential source code number, will be filed in the case file (copies forwarded to the other appropriate offices maintaining this case file).

C. The statement normally will be typed. This is not a mandatory requirement, provided the handwriting is legible and in ink.

D. Any mistakes, cross-throughs, etc., will be initialed by the confidential source on the original copy. Each page of the original copy will be initialed immediately at the end of the narrative on that page.

E. Two agents will take and witness the statement.

F. The format of the statement shall be as follows:

 1. Heading: The heading will contain the confidential source's code number, the date, time, and place of the statement, the agents taking the statement, and a terse explanation of the contents. For example:

 "Statement of SR1780007 at the Los Angeles District Office at 10:00 a.m. on October 2, 1978, given to DEA Agents Fred Butler and Jerry Long, regarding the introduction of Agent Long to defendant William Charles HARRISON, Rl-78-0012."

 2. Body: The body will be composed in the confidential source's words as long as the expressions are clear to the average person. The organization and sequence of material may be set by the agents. Any factual gaps, or statements which raise obvious questions, will be explained.

 3. Conclusion: The conclusion will state that the confidential source has read the foregoing statement consisting of ___ pages, that he has initialed each page and all corrections, that it is true and correct to the best of his knowledge and belief, and that he gave the statement freely and voluntarily, without threats, coercion, or promises.

 4. Signatures: The agents will sign all copies, the confidential source will sign just the original.

6612.34 Use of Polygraph Examinations

A. Information supplied by a confidential source is normally evaluated by a meld of proper debriefing techniques, prior knowledge of the facts being reported, and investigative follow-up. In certain situations, however, these approaches are not sufficient. Where this is the case, *and* where corroboration is essential to the furtherance of an important investigation or prosecution, the use of a polygraph examination should be considered.

B. Barring exigent circumstances, all polygraph examinations conducted in a DEA-controlled investigation will be done under the auspices of Headquarters (OS).

6612.35 Attendance at Meetings of Which Privileged Information May Be Disclosed. See 6621.

6612.36 Disclosure of a Confidential Source's Identity

A. As stated in 6612.3IF, confidential sources shall be advised at the outset that the information they provide may be used in a criminal proceeding, and that although the DEA will use all lawful means to protect their confidentiality, this cannot be guaranteed. In extraordinary circumstances, the SAC, with DO concurrence, may authorize that such a guarantee be given for any government-initiated proceeding (provided the prosecutor is advised of this assurance). The DEA will honor any such guarantee, regardless of the outcome of any case. Therefore, such guarantees will be issued judiciously.
B. The disclosure of a confidential source's identity, even when no prior guarantee of confidentiality was made, will be avoided whenever possible. The confidential source's confidentiality will be thoroughly discussed with the prosecutor prior to the trial or other proceedings and any alternatives will be given full consideration.
C. In situations where the disclosure of a confidential source's identity might adversely affect the outcome of a more significant investigation, the DEA may conceivably recommend dismissal of the immediate case. A decision of this nature may only be made by Headquarters (DO).
Requests for such decisions will be via teletype or telephone followed by teletype. Headquarters responses will be similarly documented.
D. If the issue of disclosure arises during an agent's testimony and he is uncertain of the legal requirement, he should request time to discuss the matter with the prosecutor.

6612.41 General Policies — Domestic

A. Any person who is to receive payments charged against PE/PI funds must be established as a confidential source. This includes persons who may otherwise be categorized as sources of information or confidential sources under the control of another agency.
B. The amount of payment must be commensurate with the value of the services and/or information provided. It will be based on the following factors:

1. The G-DEP level of the targeted individual, organization, or operation.
2. The amount of the actual or potential seizure.
3. The significance of the contribution made by the informant to the desired objectives.

C. All payments to confidential sources will be witnessed by another agent. In unusual circumstances, a nonagent DEA employee or an officer of another law enforcement agency may serve as witness.

6612.42 General Policies — Foreign

A. Payments made to foreign confidential sources will be witnessed as in 6612.41C above whenever possible. Payments may be witnessed by another embassy official. Where no other U.S. official is available and the host country authorities cannot or will not sign DEA Form 103 as witness, foreign field management may authorize payment without a witnessing signature, provided the situation is explained in the Remarks section.

B. Foreign field management may authorize payments to foreign confidential sources in the form of goods in lieu of cash, as deemed appropriate. Appropriate receipts or other documentation of value must be attached to the DEA Form 103.

C. Foreign field management may authorize payment to a foreign confidential source through an interceding third party if deemed appropriate.

D. Foreign field management will develop policies for payments to foreign confidential sources. Management of those domestic offices having foreign geographic responsibilities will likewise develop such policies. In any situation where such a payment could adversely affect host country relationships, but circumstances still warrant payment, prior approval should be obtained from Headquarters (appropriate drug section, which will coordinate with OS and OF as necessary).

6612.43 Types of Payment

There are three circumstances in which payments to confidential sources may be made:

A. Payments for Information and/or Active Participation. When a confidential source assists in developing an investigation, either through supplying information or actively participating in it, he may be paid for his services either in a lump sum or in staggered payments.

[REDACTED: **Author's Note**: In previous manuals 6612.43A.I. had directed agents to instruct confidential sources paid on a commission basis the law of entrapment.]

2. The fee arrangement should be discussed with the confidential source in detail; there should be no gaps in understanding the terms of the arrangement;

3. The usual instructions to the confidential source, the details of the fee arrangement, and the Entrapment instructions should be provided to the confidential source in writing at the beginning of the operation;

4. Every effort should be made to maximize the control and supervision of the confidential source;

5. Every effort should be made to corroborate the confidential source's statements concerning his activities;

6. Payments should be completed before the confidential source testifies; and

7. We should be prepared to give reasons why it is necessary to use confidential sources in this unusual manner.

[REDACTED: **Author's Note**: *6612.43 B in previous manuals had discussed the amounts that a Special Agent in Charge may pay a confidential source per quarter. That amount has been $25,000. Amounts beyond that need approval from DEA Headquarters.]

Payments for information leading to a seizure, with no defendants, should be held to a minimum.

C. Payment for Confidential Source Protection.

The Department of Justice has a formal witness protection program. Where circumstances are such that a confidential source needs protection, every effort should be made to have the U.S. Attorney enter the confidential source into this program (see 6612.7).

Where this cannot be done, or in the interim period until it can be done, the DEA may absorb the expenses of relocation. These expenses may include travel for the confidential source and his immediate family, movement and/or storage of household goods, and living expenses at the new location for a specific period of time (not to exceed 6 months). Payments for these expenses may be either lump sum or as they occur, and will not exceed the amounts authorized for DEA employees for these activities.

The SAC has the authority to approve payments of up to $5,000 for confidential source security expenditures from his established PE/PI funds. He should, however, coordinate the payment with the appropriate Headquarters drug section chief. Amounts exceeding

$5,000 must be precleared and approved by the Deputy Assistant Administrator for Operations (DO).

D. Payments to Confidential Sources of Another Agency.

To use or pay another agency's confidential source in a DEA-controlled investigation, he must be established as a DEA confidential source.

The DEA will not normally pay another agency's confidential source in non-DEA-controlled cases, and under no circumstance where the payment is a duplication of a payment from the other agency (sharing a payment, however, is acceptable). Such payments may not exceed $10,000 per *confidential source* per quarter, and may only be made with the approval of the SAC (or Country Attaché). Payments above this amount require approval from the Headquarters DO. (See A above.)

The confidential source must be established and coded. Item 59 of DEA Form 512, Establishment Report, must contain a statement identifying the individual as a confidential source of the other agency, the name and agency of the officer responsible for him, and a terse justification for the payment. Fingerprinting and photographing are not required. For record keeping purposes, such confidential sources will be considered deactivated once payment has been made.

6612.44 Payment of Awards from the Department of Justice Assets Forfeiture Fund

A. Types of Awards.

Two types of awards that are reimbursable from the Department of Justice Assets Forfeiture Fund, hereafter referred to as the Fund, are authorized by 28 USC 524.

1. 28 USC 524(C)(1)(B) provides for payments up to $250,000 to individuals for information or assistance directly relating to violations of the criminal drug laws of the United States. This type of award is program related and is paid in connection with one or more of a series of related criminal investigative activities, irrespective of a criminal or civil forfeiture. Eligibility for an award under 524(C)(1)(B) does not require an asset seizure in the related investigation; however, asset seizure should be a factor in consideration of the recommended amount of payment. Any award made pursuant to 524(C)(1)(B) shall preclude the recipient of such award from receiving any additional award based on a forfeiture resulting in any way from the same information or assistance.

2. 28 USC 524(C)(1)(C) provides for payment for information or assistance leading to a civil or criminal forfeiture. 524(C)(1)(C) awards are based upon and limited by amounts realized by the United States from assets forfeited in an investigation.

To qualify, an individual must provide original information to the DEA that ultimately results in the seizure and forfeiture of one or more assets. Awards paid pursuant to 524(C)(1)(C) are asset specific and payment may not exceed the lesser of $250,000 or one-fourth of the amount realized by the United States from the property forfeited.

The amount realized by the Government for purposes of 524(C)(1)(C) is defined as the gross receipt of the forfeiture (either cash or proceeds of sale), less management expenses attributable to the seizure and forfeiture of the property. Assets that are forfeited and placed into official service can be considered as a basis for an award calculation. If forfeited property is retained for official use, the amount realized by the United States from the property forfeited is the value of the property at the time of seizure less any management expenses paid from the Fund. The "net" figure is then used as the basis for calculation of the award.

3. Any award pursuant to Section 524(C)(1)(B) shall preclude the recipient of such award from receiving any additional award based on forfeiture resulting in any way from the same information or assistance. Similarly, any award pursuant to 524(C)(1)(C) shall preclude the recipient from receiving any additional award based on the same information or assistance. However, there are instances in which an individual provides very separate and distinct information which leads to several seizures under the same DEA case number. If the information is given at different times and concerns unrelated seizures, then separate requests should be very rare and the separateness and distinctness of the information must be clearly articulated in the award application.

B. Application for Awards

1. Individuals applying for either type of award must be established and assigned a code number in accordance with existing procedures. The SAC or Country Attaché may exempt an individual from certain establishment requirements such as fingerprinting and photographing as defined in Section 6612.21, as for example, where a source of information within the definition stated in 6612.1(B) is being established solely for the purpose of receiving an award from the Fund. In this case, a statement shall be set forth in the remarks section of the DEA-512 identifying the individual

as a source of information and that the assignment of a code number is for the purpose of payment and of maintaining his/her confidentiality.

2. The appropriate field office will prepare a memorandum from the SAC addressed to the Deputy Assistant Administrator for Operations providing full justification for the recommendation for the award. The award applicant will be identified only by code number except as noted below. The memorandum shall include:

   a. Type of award — 524(C)(1)(B) or 524(C)(1)(C).

   b. Amount requested by the award applicant, if such claim is made.

   c. Recommended amount or percentage basis by the SAC. The actual amount paid will be determined by the "net" proceeds, i.e., after deduction of management expenses.

   d. Identify the individual only by code number.

   e. The CAP seizure number(s) for the asset(s) involved. Include for both 524(C)(1)(B) and 524(C)(1)(C) awards.

   f. The extent to which the individual has been previously paid from other sources, i.e., PI and other agency payments in the same investigation.

   g. Whether or not there is an agreement by other federal, state, or local agencies to provide funds for an award in the same investigation and, if so, the amount.

   h. If the individual wishes the award to be paid by check, then identify by full name, address, and social security number. In this case, the memorandum must be marked "sensitive" and all applicable handling procedures must be adhered to.

   i. The extent and significance of the individual's information or assistance in the development of the investigation and the value and impact of the investigation's results, including assets seized.

   j. If the individual requests more than one award under the same case number for separate and unique sets of information and/or assistance he/she has provided giving rise to separate and distinct seizures, then these circumstances must be explicitly articulated.

3. The SAC or Country Attaché will forward the request and recommendation for award with all pertinent case documents including orders and/or judgments, transfer receipts of custodianship, and U.S. Marshal Service deposit slips and receipts directly to the Deputy Assistant Administrator for Operations (DO) for approval.

4. The Headquarters Undercover and Sensitive Operations Unit (OUS) will review the request and when circumstances dictate convene the Undercover Review Committee. Results of the review will be submitted to the Deputy Assistant Administrator for final approval of the award. If the amount of the award is $25,000 or less, a statement by the SAC or Country Attaché supporting his recommendation will ordinarily suffice for final approval.

5. In the case of 524(C)(1)(B) awards, once approval is obtained, payment may be made immediately at the direction of the SAC or Country Attaché pursuant to established guidelines.

6. In the case of approved 524(C)(1)(C) awards, the OMG will forward a copy of the award application to the Asset Forfeiture Section (CCF). Once the forfeiture actions are complete, CCF will notify in writing the Deputy Assistant Administrator for Operations of such circumstances and the award will be processed by OMGB for payment.

7. Offices having approval to make award payments from the Fund will be issued a fund cite by the OMGB in the amount of the approved award. Payments may be made from the office's imprest fund or funds for payment may be wire transferred utilizing the Federal Reserve Bank system.

8. Awards pursuant to 524(C)(1)(B) or 524(C)(1)(C) may be paid by government check at the discretion of the SAC. If the award is to be paid by check, the OMGB then will process the request through the Office of the Controller and forward the check to the SAC or Country Attaché.

9. Assets Forfeiture Fund award payments must be documented by the completion of DEA-103. The remarks section of the DEA-103 shall reflect that a payment was made pursuant either to 524(C)(1)(B) or 524(C)(1)(C). All payments must be posted to the DEA-356, Confidential Source Payment Record.

10. 524(C)(1)(C) awards may not be paid until all aspects of seizure have been successfully completed, i.e., the assets forfeited, property disposed of by sale, and management expenses paid.

C. Award Payments

1. Approval for awards from the Fund will be according to existing guidelines for paying established confidential sources from PE/PI allowances; that is, the SAC or Country Attaché may approve payments up to $25,000 per quarter; the Deputy Assistant Administrator for Operations (DO) may approve amounts beyond $25,000. (See 6612.43.) All award payments will normally be paid in cash in accordance with existing procedures governing regular

PE/PI payments. The Attorney General may delegate authority to the Administrator to approve an award in excess of $250,000. This authority may not be redelegated.

2. Offices must not promise any awards in any amount to an individual. The statutory authority provides that the payment of such awards is purely discretionary. In preparing the recommendation for award, the SAC or Country Attaché should ensure that proper discretion is exercised. Similar circumstances should warrant similar awards. Therefore, special attention should be given to the factors stated in Agents Manual Sections 6612.41(B) and 6612.44(B)(2) as a means of recommending an award consistent with the total circumstances of the involvement of the individual.

3. In cases where DEA is sharing with state and local law enforcement agencies under the equitable transfer provisions the SAC may reach an agreement with participating state or local authorities that a combination of payments by the DEA and the concerned state or local agencies to the award applicant should not exceed the monetary limits established by 524(C)(1)(B) and 524(C)(1)(C). If a state and/or local agency intends to pay the concerned individual the full amount of the award, then the DEA may use that information as the basis for denying or modifying a similar request.

6612.45 Documentation of Payments (DEA Form 103)

A. Witnessing payments to confidential sources shall be as described in 6612.41C (domestic) and 6612.42A (foreign).

B. All payments to confidential sources will be documented on the DEA-103, Voucher for Payment for Information and Purchase of Evidence. The confidential source will sign his true name on the green copy only. This copy will be detached from the completed form for filing in the informant file before distributing the remaining copies. When the paying office is different from the establishing office, a duplicate of the signed copy must be made for the paying office, and the green copy should be forwarded to the establishing office via registered mail, return receipt requested. The green copy will not be sent with other reports, memoranda, etc., in the same envelope.

C. In the case of payments of awards from the Assets Forfeiture Fund, the paying office will forward an unsigned copy of the completed DEA-103 to Headquarters OMGB within 5 days of payment. The remarks section of the DEA-103 must contain a statement that the payment is made from the Assets Forfeiture Fund either pursuant to 28 USC 524(C)(1)(B) or 524(C)(1)(C).

D. In addition to copies of all DEA Form 103's, each field office confidential source file will contain a DEA Form 356, Confidential Source Payment Record. This record will be kept on top of all the other documents in the file, and will contain a continuous record of payments made. The employee responsible for maintaining confidential source files is responsible for keeping this record current and complete.

6612.5 Deactivation of Confidential Sources

6612.51 Criteria

A. A confidential source will be deactivated when:
1. He no longer has the potential to furnish information or services which could lead to a significant prosecution or interdiction of drugs.
2. He is no longer willing to cooperate.
3. His cooperation has been determined to be unsatisfactory.
B. A confidential source will be deactivated by the decision or with the approval of that level of supervision which approved his establishment.

6612.52 Procedures

A. A DEA Form 6, entitled "Deactivation of *(code number)*," will be written to the confidential source file, containing the reason for deactivation. No cross-filing to investigative files will be made. Upon appropriate approval of the report, it will be distributed to all offices maintaining a file on the confidential source.
B. Should a confidential source be deactivated due to unsatisfactory cooperation or behavior, the SAC (or Country Attaché) will send a teletype to Headquarters (OS), followed by a DEA Form 6 (with a photograph attached). Both documents will give supporting justification and request that he be designated unsatisfactory. Both documents must be approved by a SAC (or Country Attaché). The DEA Form 6, upon approval, will be distributed to files as in A above. Upon concurrence, Headquarters will identify the confidential source as unsatisfactory in NADDIS and so notify (via teletype) all offices that have utilized his services.

C. A deactivated confidential source may be reactivated by submitting a DEA Form 6 as in A above, entitled "Reactivation of *(code number)*." In addition to containing the reason for reactivation, this report will reflect any developments during the period of deactivation which would affect the confidential source's status as a restricted-use or defendant/confidential source. Approval for reactivating a confidential source must be at least at that level of management which approved his deactivation. See also 6612.22C.

6612.6 Management Review of Confidential Sources

6612.61 Immediate Supervisor (See also 6214.21)

A. The immediate supervisor is responsible for assuring that all handling of confidential sources by employees under his supervision is in compliance with the Domestic Operations Guidelines. Factors that will be routinely considered by the immediate supervisor in carrying out this responsibility include that:
   1. Any person whose cooperation with the DEA meets the criteria for confidential source establishment is, in fact, established as such.
   2. Any factors in a confidential source's background that would warrant his being established as a restricted-use confidential source or defendant/confidential source are properly brought to light, and that the confidential source is properly classified as such.
   3. Any required external approvals for utilization are properly and fully obtained.
   4. The cautions to be given to all confidential sources at the outset (see 6612.3 IF) are in fact given and noted per DEA Form 473, Confidential Source Agreement.
   5. Each confidential source is fully and accurately debriefed on targets of immediate interest, knowledge of long-range or general interest, and knowledge of nondrug criminal activity. Further, that this information is fully and accurately reported.
   6. Each confidential source is being utilized in a manner so as to make best use of his potential.
   7. Monies paid to confidential sources are properly documented and are not excessive.
   8. Confidential sources warranting deactivation are deactivated.

9. Any appropriate requirements pertaining to review by the SAC, prosecutor, or DEA Headquarters are met insofar as it is his responsibility to do so.

There will be no separate reporting system by which the supervisor documents his adherence to the foregoing. His written approval of investigative reports signifies this adherence.

B. The immediate supervisor and/or a member of the Divisional Intelligence Unit will participate in a full debriefing of each active confidential source under his unit's control at least every 90 days. This debriefing will cover the full range of topics set forth in 6612.32, and be properly reported as with any other debriefing.

6612.62 Special Agent in Charge

(All the following requirements shall also apply to the Country Attaché.)

A. Where the nature of the confidential source is such as to require the SAC's approval for use, the SAC shall assume a responsibility paralleling that of the immediate supervisor for pertinent factors set forth in 6612.61A. This does not relieve the immediate supervisor of his responsibilities, but instead provides for a "double check."

B. On a quarterly basis, the SAC (or ASAC) shall conduct a review of all active confidential sources with the supervisors under his command. This review will cover the following points:
1. Whether these confidential sources should remain in an active status.
2. Whether these confidential sources are being appropriately targeted and utilized.
3. Whether the debriefings have been complete and fully reported.
4. Whether the appropriate initial or ongoing approval requirements are being met.
5. After completion of this review, the SAC/OA shall certify in a brief memorandum to AO entitled "Quarterly Review of Confidential Sources" that this review has been completed.

6612.7 Witness Protection Program

Note: Chapter 9-21.000 of the U.S. Attorneys Manual contains more detailed instructions on this program.

6612.71 Criteria

A. The Witness Protection Program, operated by the Department of Justice, serves to ensure the appearance of significant government witnesses at trial. Admitting an individual into this program represents a major administrative and financial burden to the government. For this reason, candidates will be carefully screened. Factors that will be considered include the following:

   1. The individual must be a *witness*. Confidential sources who are not witnesses are not eligible.

   2. Only those witnesses whose testimony is essential to the prosecution of the most significant violators will be recommended for admission. The Department of Justice uses the terminology of a nexus to organized criminal activity. Generally, the DEA will limit its selection of candidates to those witnesses who are essential to the prosecution of more than one Class I violator and/or the immobilization of a major trafficking network.

   3. There must be clear indication of a threat to the witness or a member of his immediate family. Evidence of a specific threat is not required if there is a documented pattern of violent behavior by the defendants and/or their associates.

   4. The individual must be willing to undergo a legal change of name, and to permanently relocate to a place of the *government's* choosing.

   5. The individual must not have any unresolved charges against him (federal, state, or local) involving any criminal violations.

B. Witnesses in DEA cases, DEA task force cases, and DEA state and local cooperation cases are eligible for inclusion in this program. However, the total number of witnesses that can be assimilated is limited. Therefore, a nonfederal witness will be considered only under the most extraordinary circumstances. Furthermore, the U.S. Marshals Service may make a nonfederal witness's acceptance into the program conditional upon reimbursement by the state.

6612.72 Protection Provided outside the Witness Protection Program

A. Individuals who warrant some measure of protection but do not meet the criteria for inclusion in this program may be provided financial assistance from DEA PE/PI funds. The cost of relocation may be considered in determining the amount of reward paid to a content source witness (see 6612.43).

B. The cost of temporary relocation while awaiting formal admittance to the program may be provided from DEA PE/PI funding (see 6612.43).

6612.73 Procedures

A. The Office of Enforcement Operations, Criminal Division, Department of Justice, controls the admittance to and operation of this program. The U.S. Marshals Service operates the program per se.

B. Formal requests for admittance must originate with a U.S. Attorney, not the DEA. Furthermore, these requests must be from the U.S. Attorney or the 1st Assistant U.S. Attorney, not an Assistant U.S. Attorney.

C. Requests will not be approved without DEA concurrence. This concurrence, as well as all other dialogue with the Department, will be carried out by Headquarters (OS) in cooperation with the appropriate drug section. DEA field offices will not make any direct requests of or inquiries to the Department.

D. It is important to avoid detailed discussion of the terms of the protection offered. If the witness is accepted into the program, the U.S. Marshals Service will establish all terms and provide all explanations of them to the witness. Agreements or commitments made by any other party may not be honored.

E. Where it is anticipated that a witness or potential witness will be a candidate for this program, it is important that the request for admittance be submitted as soon as possible (i.e., as soon as it is determined that the individual will be a witness and will likely need relocation).

Although a provision for emergency admittance exists, its use severely taxes the resources of the U.S. Marshals Service. This procedure will only be used in the most extraordinary circumstances.

F. Prior to making a formal request to admit a witness into this program, he will be the subject of a background investigation and a thorough debriefing.

1. The background investigation will be oriented toward his criminal history; specifically, whether he is a fugitive, illegal alien, or in any other manner is the subject of unresolved criminal or civil matters.

2. The debriefing will be oriented towards any drug- or nondrug-related criminal information he may have that would be of investigative or intelligence value.

In all probability, this will be the final opportunity for the DEA or any other agency to utilize this witness; it is therefore incumbent upon the DEA as a law enforcement agency to take maximum advantage of a resource which will shortly become unavailable.

G. The formal request shall be via memorandum from the U.S. Attorney to the Department, using the format set forth in USAM9-21.000.

In addition, both threat and risk assessment reports must be prepared.

1. The Threat Assessment Report must include a brief synopsis of the investigation including defendants, the criminal organization, the illegal activities, and detailed information on the threat, whether direct or potential, to the witness and his/her family as a result of his/her cooperation with the government. It should further include names and identifying data for all individuals who may pose a danger to the witness and information on the witness's association with defendants and/or his/her direct involvement in the illegal activity.

2. The risk assessment report, which is now required by statute, must provide a risk assessment on the witness and his/her family members/associates 18 years and older, and must include detailed information addressing the following issues:

    a. Significance of the investigation or case in which the witness is cooperating.

    b. The possible danger from the witness to other persons or property in the relocation area if the witness is placed in the program (applies to the witness and his/her family members or associates:

    c. The alternatives to program use which were considered and why they will not work.

    d. Whether or not the prosecutor can secure similar testimony from other sources.

    e. The relative importance of the witness's testimony.

    f. Whether or not the need for the witness's testimony outweighs the risk of danger he/she may pose to the public (applies to the witness and his/her family members or associates).

3. The risk assessment can be presented to the Government prosecutor for his/her endorsement to eliminate the necessity of a separate assessment. A risk assessment is not required for a prisoner witness unless family members are being considered for relocation or when a prisoner–witness is authorized additional program services upon his release from custody.

H. In practice, these reports will likely be prepared by an Assistant U.S. Attorney and the DEA case agent. It is important that these reports be prepared accurately and carefully. The DEA field office should forward a copy of these reports, with a concurring cover memorandum by the SAC, to the OS. If the DEA field office should have additional information, or a differing assessment from that contained in these reports from the U.S. Attorney, this should be included in the cover memorandum. This is particularly important with regard to the significance of the confidential source and the assessment of the threat.

I. The OS will review the submission for completeness, evaluate the significance of the confidential source and his need for protection, and make a positive or negative recommendation to Headquarters (DO). Upon review, the DO will issue the DEA's formal recommendation to the Department. Upon receipt of the report from the U.S. Attorney and written concurrence by the DEA, the Department will make the decision as to admission of the witness into the program.

J. If the individual has not been previously assigned a confidential source code number, and is being proposed for inclusion in this program as a result of testimony in a DEA case, then a code number should be assigned to him. The DEA-512 Confidential Source Establishment Report should contain an appropriate explanation in Item 58. He may be deactivated upon the Department's decision as to his inclusion in the program.

K. Admission into this program is considered to be permanent, and, once admitted, a witness will not be used as an informant again. This prohibition also extends to any family member who is relocated with the witness. In certain instances the Department may waive this prohibition and allow the reuse of a protected witness. The circumstances for such a waiver would have to be highly compelling. Any request for a Departmental waiver must be routed via memorandum through DEA Headquarters, Office of Investigative Support (OS). This memorandum must explicitly detail the confidential source's personal history data and motivational factors; the nature, duration, and location of the confidential source's anticipated service; the significance of the case; and the name of concurring Assistant U.S. Attorney. The approval process may take 5 to 10 days to complete. Under no circumstances will the confidential source be actively utilized prior to receiving the Department waiver. This policy applies even if the confidential source claims to have withdrawn from the program. The witness may, of course, be called upon to testify in the immediate case or cases for which he is being provided protection. Requests for appearances at trial or pretrial should be made by the U.S. Attorney to the Department at least 10 days in advance of any required appearance.

Appendix V

Example of Local Law Enforcement Policy Statement on Informant Handling*

I.   Purpose

The purpose of this Standard Operating Procedure (S.O.P.) is to establish guidelines for proper documentation, utilization, and compensation of Confidential Informants, Confidential Sources, and Investigative Sources.

II.   Scope

These guidelines apply to all members of the Narcotics Bureau.

III. Discussion

The Narcotics Bureau recognizes that the use of confidential informants, confidential sources, and investigative and anonymous sources are absolutely essential in many types of investigations. The motivational factors for a person becoming an informant are varied and can include: financial gain, revenge, fear, reform, expectation of a lighter sentence, and to eliminate competitors. It is for these reasons that the operational use of an informant is largely discretionary. The member must exercise the

* Prepared by the National Institute for Drug Enforcement Training.

utmost care in the controlling of the informant. The detective–informant relationship must be kept on a professional level at all times. This S.O.P. is not set forth to remove the members' discretion on informant use, but is a guideline for the administrative handling of informants. All Narcotics Bureau confidential informants and sources will be documented for purposes of reliability, accountability, and ACISS reporting.

IV. Definitions

A.   Confidential Informant

Any nonlaw enforcement person who is assisting Narcotics Bureau Detectives. This includes, but is not limited to: providing information making undercover introductions or making controlled drug purchases to a degree where it is necessary that they may be required to testify in a court proceeding regarding their information and/or actions. They may receive either monetary benefits for their assistance or consideration toward a reduced sentence. They will be documented in such a manner as to record all personal data in an informant file and assigned a confidential file number for future reference.

When a confidential informant (CI) is working off charges as a defendant, they will not be paid for their services. Any expenses they may incur while in the furtherance of investigative endeavors can be paid by Narcotics Bureau investigative funds. When a confidential informant is working for monetary compensation, they will receive no consideration toward any criminal charges.

Frequently a confidential informant begins under the status of a defendant and inevitably assists bureau members satisfactorily to work off a particular sentence. At that time, they may begin receiving monetary compensation for their assistance. Monetary compensation for their assistance will be documented as per III D. pg. 8 of this Standard Operating Procedure.

B.   Anonymous Source

An unidentified person who provides information.

C.   Confidential Source

A nonlaw enforcement person known to a member who provides information, but does not wish to be identified or take an active part in an investigation. Confidential sources are not necessarily involved in criminal activity, but due to their various occupations, are in a position to obtain pertinent information and provide it to law enforcement. They are not usually expected to become witnesses and are not monetarily compensated for their assistance.

D.   Investigative Source

Any nonlaw enforcement person who provides information to a member; however, that person is not expected to become a witness. The investigative source may be compensated with official funds for their assistance. This type of informant is not proactively seeking to make criminal cases, is not expected to make undercover introductions, and is not usually associated with criminal activities. This category of information source is created to provide a means to compensate an individual for their assistance, provide accountability for that payment, and document creditability. Also, the investigative source will be utilized on a limited basis as a nonwitness, intelligence source to members of the police department.

V.   Procedure

A.   Evaluation of Informants

An extensive initial interview is necessary to properly evaluate an informant. The members will:

1. Establish the informant's motive.
2. Evaluate the informant's capabilities and truthfulness.
3. Debrief, evaluate, and document information provided by the confidential informant. This information will be entered into ACISS under the appropriate informant debriefing report number.
4. All of the Narcotics Bureau guidelines and regulations governing the informant's behavior and working conditions will be explained in detail to the informant. This will include a section advising the informant of their responsibility to report to the Internal Revenue Service all monies paid to the confidential informant by the Narcotics Bureau of the police department. Also, the informant will be told the police department does not discriminate against race, color, religion, sex, national origin, marital status, or disability.
5. Conduct an investigation of the informant's background to include:
   a. Biographical and criminal history.
   b. Outstanding warrants.
   c. Driver's license history.
   d. Permanent and local address.
   e. Previous experience as a confidential informant.

6. The Controlling Detective will determine through checks of the existing informant files if a number exists for the prospective informant. If the search is negative, a number will be assigned by the Intelligence Division Commander or his designee.

7. All new informant files and debriefings will be checked by the detective's chain of command for accuracy and content. Supervisors will initial and date all files, indicating their approval and that all guidelines have been satisfied.

8. A master file of all confidential informants' names and numbers will be secured in the Narcotics Bureau Intelligence Division. Any component of the police department seeking to establish an informant file must procure the number from the Narcotics Bureau master file maintained by the Intelligence Division.

9. The informant's work is based upon their information concerning criminal activity. There are periods of time when an informant may not have information necessary to develop criminal cases. If this period of time exceeds one (1) year, a complete update of background information must be completed by the controlling agent and reviewed by the chain of command prior to the informant working additional cases.

10. Occasionally situations will arise when other agencies of the Criminal Justice System will have objection to the Narcotics Bureau's utilization of a specific individual as a confidential informant. Defendants of another law enforcement entity should not be utilized without that entity's notification and authorization. New nondefendant informants previously established by another entity should not be established as Narcotics Bureau informants without confirmation and evaluation from that entity.

11. The utilization of an informant on probation should be predicated on court authorization and noted in the CI's file. The utilization of a defendant pending prosecution will be coordinated through the office of the State Attorney via an SAO Assistance Request Form, which will be forwarded to the State Attorney's Office by the Intelligence Division and copy to file.

B.   Documentation of Informants

1. The following information should be detailed in the informant's file prior to submission for supervisory approval.
   a. Informant Fact Sheet — all blanks will be filled in.
   b. Photograph — current photo showing informant's face and physical build.

    c. Fingerprints — if they have not been obtained at prior arrests or bookings, obtain prints and make notation.

    d. Informant Conduct Form — this form outlines rules of conduct that informants must adhere to while working for the Narcotics Bureau. They must be signed by the informant and witnessed by a detective indicating that the detective is satisfied that the informant understands and accepts the code of conduct.

    e. Debriefing Documentation — establishment of an individual as an informant/source will necessitate a debriefing by the controlling agent and the subsequent submission of the informant's/source's debriefing documentation to the file. That documentation will address, but not be limited to, debriefing documentation in the following areas:

       (1) Sources of supply
       (2) Customers
       (3) Transporters (aircraft, vessels, vehicles)
       (4) Crewmen
       (5) Off loaders
       (6) Financiers
       (7) Money laundering
       (8) Distribution procedures (domestic, foreign)
       (9) Grow operations
       (10) Clandestine laboratories
       (11) Paraphernalia providers
       (12) Nondrug criminal intelligence (robbery, burglary, murder, etc.)

    f. The informant's/source's knowledge of the above topics will be included in an ACISS debriefing report as part of the documentation package. After final approval of the confidential informant/source, the entire package will be forwarded to the Intelligence Section where:

       (1) Intelligence supervisors will review and approve all documentation prior to filing.
       (2) The intelligence data will be subsequently disseminated to the appropriate investigative entities, both internal and external.

2. Any informant misconduct necessitating censorship or termination will be brought to the attention of the Bureau Commander through the chain of command. The incident and resolution will be fully documented in the informant file. Intelligence will make that censorship information available to appropriate law enforcement entities.

3. Significant changes to the original documentation should be made in the informant file. The areas to be updated would include, but not be limited to, address, marital status, probationary status, and additional arrests.

4. There is a category of informants which a member can choose not to identify, but will document for reporting, creditability, and accountability purposes. This type of informant will fall into an extraordinary identification exception and be known as a Confidential Source. These informants typically will be noncriminal types whose professions or acquaintanceships periodically expose them to intelligence data of value to law enforcement. This category is established to encourage receipt of data and protect the identity of the person providing the information. This category typically does not apply to: defendants working to reduce pending sentences; individuals who are being paid for their services; individuals whose testimony is reasonably anticipated; or individuals providing the service for purpose of revenge or fear.

5. When a member wishes to utilize a confidential source, the following procedure will be in effect:

   a. The member will advise their chain of command as to the nature of the confidential source and that source's information. Upon approval, the appropriate captain will direct the Intelligence Division Commander or designee to issue a number for the requesting member's confidential source. This will facilitate documentation of the informant information for ACISS reporting, reliability, and accountability.

   b. The confidential source file will contain a document which reflects supervisory authorization that the particular confidential source is controlled by a specific member of the police department. The identity of the confidential source will not be documented in that file, or any Narcotics Bureau files.

   c. If the confidential source becomes ineligible for the extraordinary identification exception, the file will either be closed or the confidential source will be documented under normal procedures as listed in paragraph B. I (Documentation of Informants) of this procedure. They will then be known as a confidential informant.

   d. It will be the controlling member's responsibility to maintain the identity of the confidential source that he wishes not to identify.

6. When a member wishes to utilize an individual who meets the criteria of an investigative source, the following procedure will be in effect. The member will fill out the basic biographical information on the investigative source form and submit it for approval via the chain of

command. Upon the approval, the Narcotics Bureau Intelligence Section will assign the investigative source an appropriate number and file. Compensation to the investigative source will be documented in the same manner as a confidential informant.

All activity by confidential informants, confidential sources, and investigative sources will be properly documented in an ACISS report. The confidential informant, confidential source, or the investigative source will be indexed by number in related subject portions of the ACISS debriefing report for retrievability.

7. The Bureau Commander, or his designee, for security purposes, may authorize changing the assigned informant number. The change will be properly documented in the original file making reference to the currently assigned number.

C.   Security of Informant Files

1. The secured filing cabinets will be kept within the Narcotics Bureau Intelligence Division. These cabinets will house all of the Narcotics Bureau informant files. The master log of all police department informants will also be kept under the same security.

2. All informants/sources will be assigned a number upon initial approval. The informant files will be maintained in numerical order.

3. Informant files maintained by the Narcotics Bureau Intelligence Division will not be removed from that section without the permission of the Intelligence Division Commander, or his designee.

   a. Should the Intelligence Division Commander or his designee approve a file removal, a file checkout card bearing the member's name and date will replace the file until such time as it is returned.

4. The informant's/source's name may appear in other documents, but his identification as an informant/source will never appear outside of the informant file. The informant will be referred to in all reports and memos by the assigned informant number, or by use of a genderless pronoun, i.e., "They" or "The CI."

   a. An exception to this requirement may be necessitated by the Office of the State Attorney when documentation of the informant's accomplishments may be required for sentence consideration, court order, or subpoena purposes.

5. The Police Chief, Deputy Chief, Commander of the Narcotics Bureau, or his designee are the only authorities authorized to release the identity of a confidential informant/source, or any information from the informant file.

D.   Compensation of Informants

Informants/sources may receive monetary compensation from the investigative expense fund. Members will adhere to the following procedure when payments are made:

1. All informant/source payments require a receipt which must be signed by the informant, the detective making the payment, and a witness. All receipts are to be placed into the informant file.
2. All payments for any single performance by the informant/source fall under these restrictions for supervisor approval:

Police Chief	5,001+up
Bureau Commander	1,001–5,000
Division Commander	501–1,000
Lieutenant	251–500
Sergeant	100–250

3. All payments must be documented properly in the Informant Activity/Expense Log contained in the informant file.
4. All payments to a confidential informant/source for services rendered relating to an open investigation will be documented in both that particular investigative case file and the informant file.

E.   Control of Informants

1. Informant control is essential to a safe and productive working relationship within the police department. All informants utilized by this agency will be available to work with any member, but will be assigned to one member at a time for control. Careful structuring should be given to the informant's visual access to other Narcotics Bureau members to minimize compromising undercover identity.
2. The Narcotics Bureau supervisor may deem it necessary to change the informant's assigned member to improve the informant's effectiveness or to equalize case load.
3. Whenever possible, the controlling member should have prior knowledge of the informant working with another member. This will curtail informants from "detective shopping" and limit duplication of targets.
4. Any time a member works with an informant, special care should be utilized to maintain control. Categories of informants that require careful scrutiny include:
   a. Juvenile Informants — should not normally be used in undercover operations. If deemed appropriate to utilize the juvenile, written parental permission must be obtained. The member is not

discouraged from eliciting information from juvenile sources. The Commander of the Narcotics Bureau or his designee may authorize an exception to this requirement for written parental permission.

b. Opposite Gender Confidential Informants/Sources — The Commander of the Narcotics Bureau will review and approve or disapprove all requests for utilization of opposite gender confidential informants, investigative sources, and confidential sources. The member's immediate supervisor or if unavailable, another detective will participate in the initial interview to evaluate the opposite gender confidential informant/sources potential. Predicated on the approval of the immediate supervisor, the member will submit a memorandum through the chain of command to the Commander of the Narcotics Bureau. The memorandum will set forth the opposite gender confidential informant's background (including criminal history), what benefits the informant expects to receive and exactly how the informant's services are to be utilized.

c. Utilizing an Opposite Gender Confidential Informant/Source — All meetings will be documented on the appropriate ACISS Report. That documentation will be required regardless of any other reports that may additionally be required. All investigative preparatory and/or Intelligence meetings with the opposite gender confidential informant will be conducted in the presence of two members of the Narcotics Bureau. All operational investigative efforts necessitating the utilization of an opposite gender confidential informant will be conducted under controlled conditions with the specific authority of the Commander of the Narcotics Bureau or his designee.

All complaints by opposite gender informants, or any known acts of impropriety, will be immediately documented and forwarded through the chain of command to the Narcotics Bureau Commander.

5. Any arrested person who is a candidate for receiving substantial assistance should be handled in a manner consistent with the current State Attorney's Office guidelines before that person is utilized by any member. Exceptions can be made with prior approval from the Narcotics Bureau Commander, or his designee.

F.   Informant Motivation

The most significant motivating factors concerning the utilization of informants are:

1. Money: Caution should be observed here as information and targets become scarce. Informants can become "creative" to maintain their income.
2. Revenge, Spite or Retaliation: includes mistreatment by associates, jealousy, and quarrels.
3. Elimination of Competition: diverting suspicion away from the informant to assist in their criminal behavior.
4. Fear: this can range from fear of law enforcement to current and past associates.
5. Self-Aggrandizement: informants seek to enhance their image or self-importance. These individuals tend to brag about their exploits and are often compromised.
6. Prosecutional or Judicial Leniency: serious difficulties can develop when a member makes promises of leniency that the agency is not authorized to fulfill.
7. Repentance: informants sometimes appear emotionally unstable or insecure.
8. Concerned Citizen: a person who may provide information out of concern for the well-being of the community.

G.   Problems with Informants

1. Lying — Informants may exaggerate or fabricate the criminal acts of targets. Some may report the truth, but not divulge the illegal means that were used to obtain the information.
2. Double-Dealing — Informants can make deals with targets and the police. They can provide criminal associates with the identity of undercover agents, cars they drive, hours they work, agency tactics, and procedures. They can be plants who confirm their criminal activities and monitor police activities.
3. Rip-Offs — Informants can position themselves to arrange rip-offs of large flash rolls. They can sell information to different agencies causing a duplication of efforts.
4. Blackmail — Informants may establish a relationship for the purpose of attempting to cause conflicts of interests for purposes of achieving an alternative advantage. Caution must be taken to maintain a professional (nonsocial) relationship with all informants.

H.   Censorship and Termination of Informants

Frequently, controlling agents must sever their relationship with confidential informants/investigative sources due to their nature and the environment in which they operate. The following are categories under which that agent will sever those relationships; they include, but are not limited to:

1. Termination — When a confidential informant/investigative source becomes unreliable, lacks productivity, relocates or is arrested.
2. Censorship — Applied to those informants that knowingly jeopardize the safety of an officer, knowingly misidentify a defendant, are charged with a violent action on a law enforcement officer or commit violent crimes.

If a confidential informant/investigative source is to be censored or terminated, the controlling member will submit a memo to the Narcotics Bureau Commander via chain of command, outlining the cause for termination/censorship.

If a member wishes to reinstate a confidential informant/investigative source, a memo to the Narcotics Bureau Commander, via chain of command, will be submitted with the reasons for reinstatement. After approval, these memos will be then contained in the appropriate informant file.

Final approval for censorship, termination, or reinstatement rests with the Narcotics Bureau Commander.

I.   Informant Testimony and Preparation

When ordered to produce a confidential informant in a hearing or trial, the law enforcement agency and the prosecutor's office must weigh the ramification of disclosure of the confidential informant's identity against the damage of terminating the charges and case. Some of the circumstances in which a court may rule that a confidential informant's identity be disclosed:

1. The sole government participation in the offense was that of the confidential informant.
2. The confidential informant witnessed a drug transaction or participated in negotiations related to the transaction.
3. The confidential informant was an active participant in events leading up to the offense.

The Narcotics Bureau members should consider using means that will not result in the disclosure of the informant's identity. Some examples are:

1. Using the confidential informant only for introductions and having undercover officers develop the relationship with the target and execute the transaction.

2. If the confidential informant must be present, instruct the confidential informant to leave as soon as possible after negotiations on transactions begin.
3. Making the confidential informant testimony cumulative. If the target can be persuaded to bring a friend, the confidential informant's testimony might be cumulative to what others present would say, and their identity may not have to be revealed.

J.   Investigator Pitfalls

The following are pitfalls which controlling agents should avoid:

1. Failure to maintain a professional relationship with the confidential informant.
2. Gullibility and a failure to fully question the confidential informant about his or her activities and seek corroboration from other sources.
3. Making promises that the agency cannot keep regarding large money payments or favorable prosecutorial or judicial outcomes.
4. Lack of accountability in handling money and property, especially controlled substances.
5. Failure to adequately document confidential informant activities.
6. Allowing unnecessary and or unsupervised contact by the confidential informant with a potential target.
7. Allowing a confidential informant to assist in planning an operation.
8. Failure to verify and investigate thoroughly, information or activities a confidential informant provides concerning a target of an investigation.

Confidential informants are an integral tool for the narcotics detective. If properly used, they can provide this agency with invaluable insight into the criminal activities of narcotic dealers.

Index